Higher Education to 2030

VOLUME 1

DEMOGRAPHY

CENTRE FOR EDUCATIONAL RESEARCH AND INNOVATION

OECD

ORGANISATION FOR ECONOMIC CO-OPERATION AND DEVELOPMENT

The OECD is a unique forum where the governments of 30 democracies work together to address the economic, social and environmental challenges of globalisation. The OECD is also at the forefront of efforts to understand and to help governments respond to new developments and concerns, such as corporate governance, the information economy and the challenges of an ageing population. The Organisation provides a setting where governments can compare policy experiences, seek answers to common problems, identify good practice and work to co-ordinate domestic and international policies.

The OECD member countries are: Australia, Austria, Belgium, Canada, the Czech Republic, Denmark, Finland, France, Germany, Greece, Hungary, Iceland, Ireland, Italy, Japan, Korea, Luxembourg, Mexico, the Netherlands, New Zealand, Norway, Poland, Portugal, the Slovak Republic, Spain, Sweden, Switzerland, Turkey, the United Kingdom and the United States. The Commission of the European Communities takes part in the work of the OECD.

OECD Publishing disseminates widely the results of the Organisation's statistics gathering and research on economic, social and environmental issues, as well as the conventions, guidelines and standards agreed by its members.

Also available in French under the title:
L'enseignement supérieur à l'horizon 2030
VOLUME 1
DÉMOGRAPHIE

Corrigenda to OECD publications may be found on line at: *www.oecd.org/publishing/corrigenda.*

Foreword

Demographic concerns are today among the major challenges facing OECD countries, whether in relation to ageing populations and their growing ethnic and cultural diversity, or to migration.

In higher education, demographic changes relate to the size and composition of the student population but also to the age structure and composition of academic teaching staff. From the standpoint of the economy and the knowledge society, countries also have to consider the proportion of tertiary graduates in their population. So what challenges of a demographic nature will public policies for higher education and higher education institutions have to address? And how do these challenges affect higher education systems and policies?

These are the questions that this book examines from several different angles as part of a project on the future of higher education, undertaken by the OECD Centre for Educational Research and Innovation (CERI).

Many countries now fear that demographic changes in their population are leading to a substantial contraction of their higher education systems, with implications for their human resources and international competitiveness. The present report shows that the expansion of higher education will most likely be sustained in the years ahead, and that most systems will continue to grow. The proportion of graduates in the general population may also be expected to increase and contribute to the well-being, innovative capacity and economic growth of countries.

Yet in higher education, demography is no less relevant in qualitative than in quantitative terms, as is clear from new access policies for students with special needs, the participation of minorities or people from immigrant backgrounds, or indeed the gradual reversal in inequalities between the sexes which seems set to continue. This book provides for a better understanding of issues and trends in higher education which are closely linked to demographic concerns, and helps to prepare more effectively for change.

In the OECD Secretariat, Stéphan Vincent-Lancrin, Senior Analyst at CERI, who has supervised the project on the future of higher education, has edited the book, with help from Kiira Kärkkäinen and Delphine Grandrieux in preparing it, and the assistance also of Ashley Allen-Sinclair and Therese Walsh. I should further like to thank all the book's authors who have provided original and complementary insights into the complex subject at issue, as well as Tom Schuller, former head of CERI, from whose own highly valuable advice the project has also benefited.

Barbara Ischinger

Director, Directorate for Education

ISBN 978-92-64-04065-6
Higher Education to 2030
Volume 1: Demography

Table of Contents

List of Figures

List of Tables

List of Boxes

ISBN 978-92-64-04065-6
Higher Education to 2030
Volume 1: Demography

Executive Summary

This volume of *Higher Education to 2030* discusses trends and prospects regarding changes in the population of students, academic teaching staff and graduates in higher education in OECD countries, from both a quantitative and qualitative standpoint. It examines in particular the link between these developments, demographic changes and higher education policy. The book is thus concerned no less with trends in the size of higher education systems than with changes affecting the academic teaching profession. It also shows how changes in policies for students with disabilities might eventually transform conventional attitudes towards access to higher education. And it examines too how the growth of migration might lead to the emergence of new issues concerning inequality. Even though demographic changes raise numerous questions for higher education policy, they do not pose major new problems as is often thought. The central future issues for many countries will be of a qualitative nature, such as inequalities in access and participation, the diversity of paths, provision and institutions in higher education, the possible social marginalisation of those persons least educated, and the need to rethink the role of the academic profession.

The following trends are apparent from the various possible scenarios for the future of higher education examined in the book:

As regards students:

- student participation will continue to expand and will in most cases be evident from growth in the size of higher education systems. Contraction will affect only a small number of countries;
- women will be in the majority in the student population;
- the mix of the student population will be more varied, with greater numbers of international students, older students and those studying part-time, etc.
- the social base in higher education will probably continue to broaden, along with uncertainty about how this will affect inequalities of educational opportunity between social groups;
- novel attitudes and assumptions regarding access to higher education will emerge and be more concerned with real student attainment, reflecting trends in access policies for students with disabilities;
- changes will occur in issues and policies relating to access and the fight to reduce inequality, as well as some broadening and changes among the groups concerned, depending on the particular country.

As regards teachers:

- the academic profession will be more internationally oriented and mobile, but still structured in accordance with national circumstances;
- the activities of the profession will be more diversified and specialised, and subject to varied employment contracts;
- the profession will move gradually away from the traditional conception of a self-regulated community of professionals, and towards a model and consensus to be based on fresh principles.

As regards society:

- the population will contain a greater proportion of graduates with positive implications for social well-being and economic growth;
- women graduates will be in the majority, while the inequalities they experience in remunerative terms will be reduced but still present;
- half or almost half of all people in the youngest age cohorts in many countries will be graduates;
- the gap between the absolute number of graduates (but not the relative number) in the OECD area and in the major emerging countries, in particular China and India, will become smaller;
- demographic trends seem likely to have little effect on higher education expenditure as a percentage of national wealth;
- challenges will arise linked to the possible social exclusion of groups not involved in higher education.

Although demographic trends appear to change little, they are often subject to unforeseeable turning points linked to political action or technological developments

Chapter 1 (Le Bras) explains how demographic trends that remain stable over a long period may undergo sudden turning points, or how apparently rapid changes are in reality brief deviations from a basic underlying trend. Political action or technological changes may suddenly transform well-established trends or patterns of conduct, and suggest that care should be taken when drawing up projections. Indeed, the chapter serves as a word of warning for the entire book: extrapolation of past trends is not necessarily foolproof, and good sense dictates the need to speculate about the future solely in terms of possible scenarios, which political action in particular may influence.

In a steady trend scenario, demographic changes can be expected to have a moderate impact on size, expenditure and policies in higher education

Chapter 2 (Vincent-Lancrin) thus considers various scenarios for projections of student enrolments, expenditure, student-teacher ratios and graduates in the population for the period up to 2025. Even though the situation varies markedly across OECD countries, growth in the size of higher education systems should remain the norm within the OECD area, allowing for just a few exceptions. It should not lead to any radical changes in expenditure as a percentage of national assets. Neither should the replacement of academic staff constitute a major problem: in fact, existing tensions are more related to particular academic subject areas than to demographic changes. The proportion of graduates in the population should have substantially increased by 2025, but in a very varied manner across countries. Continued growth should also alter the qualitative composition of the student population: while participation in higher education should become increasingly broadly based, the impact of expansion on inequalities of opportunity among different social groups appears far less certain. As in the past, the various policy responses to changes in the size of higher education systems may involve diversification of the student population, institutions and courses, or new cost-sharing arrangements. Yet far from being determined by demography alone, these policies will be part of a broader debate on subjects such as globalisation, excellence or an appropriate match between higher education and the labour market.

Ageing in the academic teaching profession is not a function of ageing among the general population; it is a consequence of the growth or shrinkage in student enrolments in an employment system typified by permanence

Following an introductory review of major demographic trends in OECD countries, *Chapter 3* (Willekens) examines key factors shaping the age pyramid of academic teaching staff, and considers the impact of population size differences between the OECD area and two countries with massive populations, China and India, on their future highly educated workforces. While it might be thought that the ageing of academics broadly reflects ageing among the population as a whole, this chapter demonstrates how the age pyramid of these staff depends above all on an employment system whose hallmark is permanence and on efforts to maintain a fixed student-teacher ratio. Rising student enrolments are conducive to a relatively stable age structure, whereas staff are collectively subject to rapid ageing or rejuvenation if student numbers fall or level out. A second demographic consideration is the size of the age cohorts: because of the differences in size of the younger age cohorts in India and China, only a slight increase in higher education participation rates in these countries would be needed to inject into their economies the same amount of work performed by graduates in OECD countries.

Despite the process of ageing, major changes in the academic teaching profession have less to do with demographic factors – as exemplified by changes in the proportion of foreign or women teachers – than with the way the profession itself develops

Chapter 4 (Enders and Musselin) examines trends and transformations in the academic teaching profession, with the growth in staff, their differing status, and the emergence of an international market for academics increasing the importance of mobility, even though the profession remains conditioned by national circumstances. While the profession is ageing in some countries and contains only a modest proportion of women, the chapter shows that changes in the profession and the main challenges facing it are not so much the outcome of demographic trends, as symptoms of a more fundamental ongoing transformation: the diversification of the profession, the restructuring of the relations between academics and their institutions, along with the fact that the employment relations of academic staff are increasingly coming to resemble those of an employee/employer relationship, mean that the search for a consensus regarding the essential nature of the profession will be the top priority for the future.

The past expansion of higher education systems puts the significance of demographic expansion in perspective

Chapter 5 (Teichler and Bürger) highlights the fact that demography has only recently become a concern in debate on higher education policy, and that the past growth of systems in OECD countries has had little to do with demographic changes. The increase in rates of admission to higher education has been of greater importance than the size of age cohorts. Furthermore it has been fuelled by changes in the coverage of the sector and more differentiated forms of provision, especially with the introduction of short courses. The growth in numbers of foreign or international students does not appear to have been a decisive factor in the growth of systems. The chapter also examines changes in the subsequent careers of graduates and demonstrates that expansion has not weakened the advantages they enjoy in terms of pay, even though they appear slightly more vulnerable to unemployment. One of the major issues arising from the expansion of systems may in fact concern the possible exclusion of those who have not benefited from higher education.

Contraction in the size of higher education systems has begun in Japan and Korea, and demographic changes in the United States point to changes in policies for equity vis-à-vis *new minorities*

Chapter 6 (Anderson and Cook) shows once more how there is little connection between demography and the size of higher education systems, while stressing the significance that changes in the qualitative composition of the general population may have for the student population. In the United States, the system grew when the size of the younger age cohorts was decreasing, and was also noteworthy for a big proportion of older "less typical" students. With renewed expansion of the young age cohorts, the size of the system should continue to increase. But changes in the composition of the population, with a lower proportion of whites and an increase in minorities – and especially Hispanic minorities – among young people, seem to present the main demographic challenge for the system. In some States, the majority of students are from a minority background. Given that the Hispanic minority is going to overtake the African-American minority, one may well speculate as to how this change will affect the "affirmative action" policy for equity in higher education, whose main past developments are reviewed in the chapter, and on its cultural and linguistic implications in particular. As relatively few Hispanics indeed enter higher education, an effective drive against inequalities appears essential to raise once more the percentage of tertiary graduates in the population, which recently has altered very little.

Chapter 7 (Yonezawa and Kim) examines the reaction of two OECD countries, Korea and Japan, in which the size of systems has started to decrease and in which this trend is very likely to continue. It explains in detail how the higher education policies adopted in these countries may be interpreted in the light of the trend, with rationalisation of the system encouraging lifelong learning, the internationalisation of higher education and balanced regional development in the broader context of globalisation and a "neo-liberal" reform model. While the hierarchical stratification of the two systems does not seem to be destined to change subsequent to their contraction, both countries are only just beginning to develop long-term policies, with a fresh emphasis on the issues of social cohesion and equality.

The issues of inequality or the composition of the student and graduate population seem likely to remain major challenges in decades ahead, whether in relation to social inequalities or those associated with disability, immigration or gender

Chapter 8 (Ebersold) deals with the access of students with disabilities to higher education, which has sharply increased in recent years. It reveals in particular how two distinct sets of attitudes and perceptions regarding disability lead to different policies, one of which concentrates on minimising barriers to access and the other on supervising students and ultimately ensuring that they do well. Recent decades have witnessed something of a shift from the first to the second approach in many countries. The chapter suggests that the greater responsiveness to diversity, which the approach to disability exemplifies, should become more widespread in the interests of all students, such as mobile students in the Bologna process. This outlook is already apparent to some extent in the United States community colleges. By examining several models for inclusiveness, with their own particular tensions, the chapter demonstrates how greater openness towards diversity presupposes that, in practice, higher education institutions regard themselves as learning organisations which attach importance to diversification in their search for excellence, efficiency and fairness.

Chapter 9 (Marmolejo, Manley-Casimir and Vincent-Lancrin) shows how the growth of migratory flows may pose new problems of inequity in access to higher education. The situation in the United States and France shows how these population flows have both foreseeable and unexpected consequences for the public authorities and societies. A variety of factors restrict and in some cases prevent migrants or their children from gaining access to higher education in their host country, including language and cultural barriers, lack of information, limited financial means, their previous education, their migrant status and the negative prejudices and stereotyping that often accompany it. Restricted access to higher education hinders the social integration of immigrants in their new environment. It also limits the possibility of them improving their economic and social well-being, thus aggravating their socio-economic marginalisation. Providing access to higher education for certain immigrant groups thus appears to be a significant issue for the future.

Chapter 10 (Vincent-Lancrin) considers the reasons for the reversal of gender inequality in higher education and its possible implications. While men were numerically superior by far among students and graduates in higher education two decades ago, women are now in the majority in nearly all OECD countries. Yet there is still significant discrimination between the sexes in some academic subjects, which partly accounts for the labour market income inequalities experienced by women. The reversal of inequalities between the sexes can be attributed to educational, social, economic and demographic factors that are not expected to disappear in the years ahead. Women should thus remain in the lead in terms of participation and graduation in higher education. While it remains hard to fully appreciate the implications of this social change, policies designed to revive the participation of young men might be justified in the interests of ensuring a more satisfactory (or varied) mix of students and preventing poorly educated men from being marginalised, and also because such policies might help to lessen the labour market income differentials that penalise women, if sexual discrimination within academic disciplines were reduced.

ISBN 978-92-64-04065-6
Higher Education to 2030
Volume 1: Demography

Chapter 1

Are Long-term Demographic Forecasts Possible? Turning Points and Trends

by

Hervé Le Bras*

This chapter serves as a methodological warning for the entire book: we demonstrate that it is the turning points that in fact play the most important role in demographic trends. We first discuss external migration, where the contrast between past and future is most glaring, and then show that the same holds true for the fertility trend, but with latencies and lags that are often lengthy. We close with a remarkable example of a turning point in the trend in age-specific mortality, to conclude that demographic trends cannot be extrapolated directly, but only explored through forward-looking scenarios incorporating political and economic factors.

* French National Institute for Demographic Studies (INED) and School for Advanced Studies in the Social Sciences (EHESS).

There is a great contrast between descriptions of the demographic past and future. While the latter is generally projected as being regular and as behaving in ways that tend to be self-perpetuating, the former is marked by numerous turning points. This difference is usually justified by treating the irregularities of the past as random fluctuations around a more stable trend. It is argued that only the trend is extrapolated into the future, for it alone is relevant. In this paper we shall propose a diametrically opposed vision by showing that, on the contrary, it is the turning points that in fact play the most important role in trends. This approach has its equivalent in the physical sciences with the catastrophe theory developed by René Thom who argued that, to describe a form, one need only know its points of discontinuity or catastrophes, which Thom categorised into seven distinct types (such as the fold, cusp, swallowtail, etc.). The entire form is deduced from these points alone through a generalised interpolation.

We shall begin by discussing external migration, where the contrast between past and future is most glaring. We shall show that the turning points can only appear as random to observers on a distant planet revolving around the star Sirius, but that for Earthlings they quite accurately mirror political and economic events. We shall then show that the same holds true for the fertility trend, but with latencies and lags that are often lengthy. We shall close with a remarkable example of a turning point in the trend in age-specific mortality, using a mathematical analysis to isolate this point amidst the complex mass of observations. This will enable us to conclude that demographic trends cannot be extrapolated directly, but only explored through forward-looking scenarios incorporating political and economic factors.

1.1. External migration: frequent turning points linked to political events

Figure 1.1 shows external migration trends for nine developed countries between 1950 and 2050. Until 2000, the data are drawn from two sources, the annual OECD reports of SOPEMI and the United Nations Population Division. For the period after 2000, only the latter organisation has ventured a general forecast of migration up until 2050. The contrast between before and after 2000 is striking. The point corresponding to the years 2000-04 is generally known, but beyond that date it is a forecast. We see that this forecast is doubly cautious: firstly, by 2015 at the latest, net migration levels off in all countries and remains constant year after year until 2050, independently of the total population trend in the country considered. Secondly, these net migration numbers are quite low, standing at 60 000 people annually in France and Spain, 200 000 in Germany and 120 000 in Italy. Yet the net migration shown for most developed countries in this figure seems to be in a phase of rising rather than levelling off.

Symmetrically, as we see in Figure 1.2 showing net migration trends in four major developing countries (China, India, Indonesia and Mexico), the trend is towards a rapidly growing migration deficit between 1950 and 2000, while the United Nations predicts that net migration will subsequently stabilise at a relatively low level.

We shall not dwell any longer on these regular forecasts the ideological content of which is clear, but shall instead focus on the irregularities during the known period

Figure 1.1. **Migration observed between 1950 and 2005 and projected until 2050 in selected developed countries**

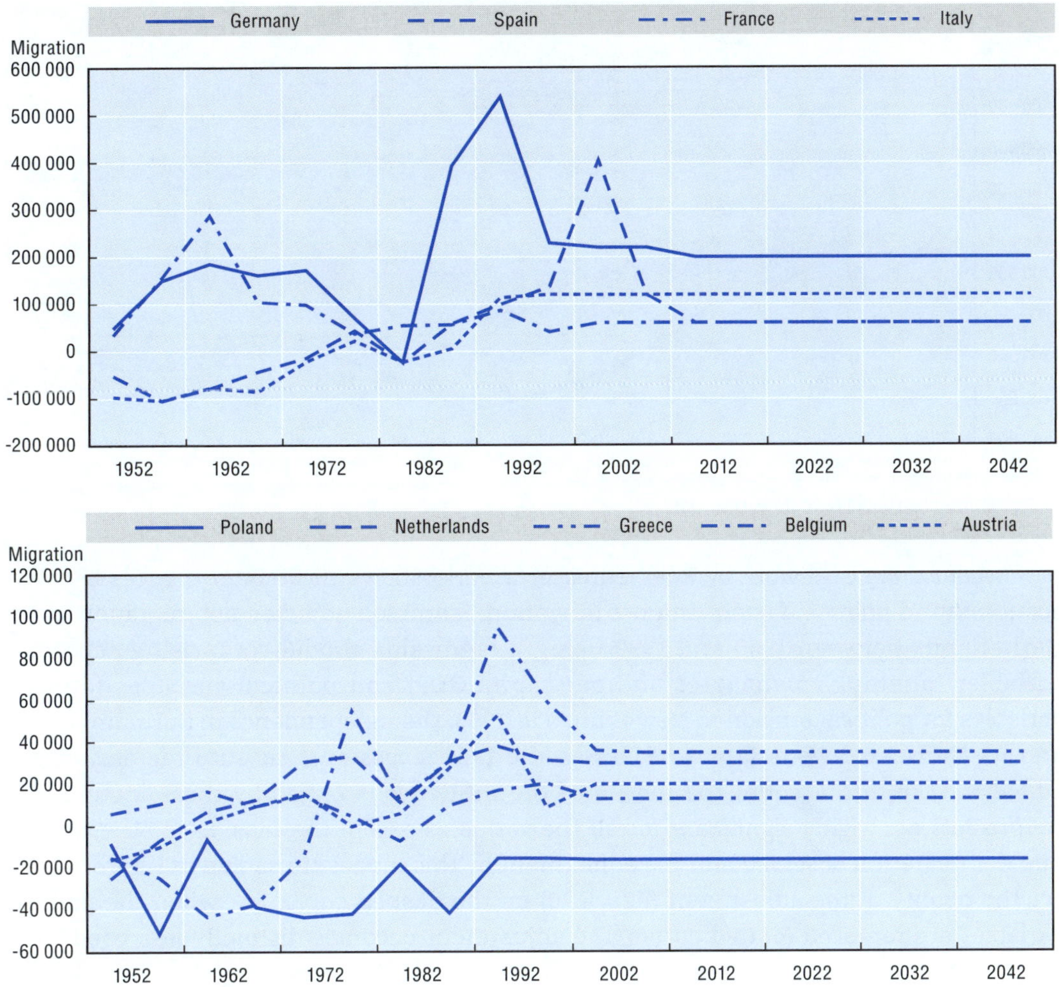

Source: OECD, SOPEMI (for migration observed only) and the United Nations Population Division (for migration observed and projected).

(1950-2005). Can these be considered random? First of all, the most rapid random fluctuations have been eliminated for we have already smoothed them by consolidating the net migration over five year periods (the figures show annual averages). Next, we clearly see a trough appear at the same time in nearly all the developed countries during the 1980-85 period. Next, country by country, the peaks of net migration coincide with major political events. For France, the peak in 1960-65 coincides with the return of repatriates from Algeria and other colonies that had gained their independence. For Germany, the peak between 1985 and 1995 reflects the return of "ethnic" Germans after the Berlin Wall came down. In Spain, Italy and Greece, entry into the European Union led to a reversal of the previous negative migration trend. It is not reasonable to consider these to be random factors that distorted a regular trend of the type forecasted by the United Nations. The idea underlying the projection of migration up until 2050 is that certain countries are structurally either receiving or sending countries. Yet there is, on the contrary, reason to believe that political and economic events are key factors in determining whether countries export or import labour.

Figure 1.2. **Migration observed between 1950 and 2005 and projected until 2050 for selected major developing countries**

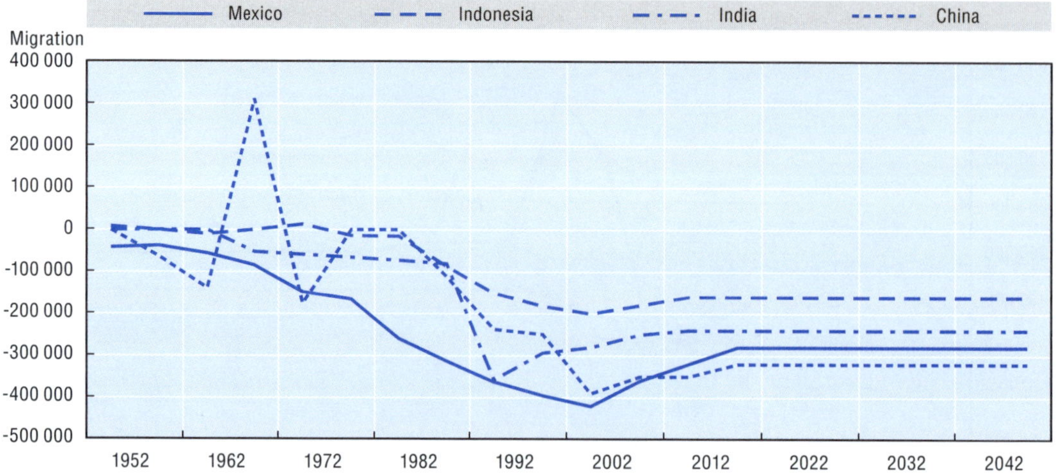

Source: United Nations Population Division.

Recent statistical work by Roel Jennissen clearly shows these interferences between economic and political factors and net migration. Jennissen adjusted net migration in the Netherlands between 1960 and 1999 using a regression model comprising economic variables (unemployment rates and per capita GDP) and political variables (dummy variables for political tension in New Guinea in 1963, the independence of Surinam in 1975 and its backlash 5 years later and, lastly, the 1967 recession). An auto-regression was added to take into account the inertia of the influences exerted by these factors. The coefficients are highly significant for all the variables except the tension in New Guinea. The net migration observed and the adjustment by this model are shown in Figure 1.3. We see the quality of the adjustment (R2 = 0.76) on the dashed curve. But when the political variables are removed (dotted curve), the adjustment becomes distinctly less good. Only

Figure 1.3. **Reconstruction of net migration in the Netherlands on the basis of multiple regressions using exogenous economic and political variables**

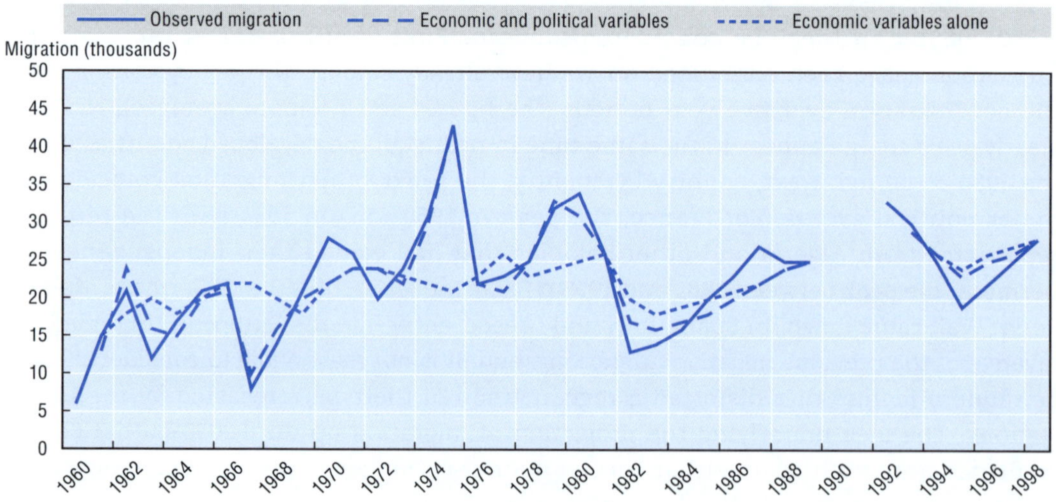

Source: Jennissen (2004).

per capita GDP and the autocorrelation are significant and the resulting curve follows the medium-term trend with the high and low fluctuations shaved off.

The conclusion to be drawn from these initial examples is that net migration does not follow an independent demographic rationale (for example, as a consequence of fertility and mortality levels). It is therefore impossible to forecast its future trend without also forecasting future economic and political trends. To project migration in 2020 or 2050 as the United Nations Population Division does, it would first be necessary to project economic and political trends for this time frame, which is clearly impossible.

1.2. Fertility: infrequent turning points with lasting effects

Thus far, we have shown that political events (dummy variables) and economic events (continuous variables corrected by their autocorrelation) have an influence on net migration in a given year. In the case of fertility, two stronger factors emerge. The events that change fertility behaviour are infrequent and exert a lasting influence. We shall show this by studying the example of France and then extending the study to other European countries.

The case of France

The trend in France's total fertility rate over the past century is a good example (Figure 1.4). This trend is summarised by just three major events. The first is a fertility dip caused by the war of 1914, which separated young men from their families or delayed their marriage. As soon as the war was over, the men came home, married and had children. Demographers speak of "recovery". Then the long-term trend resumed. The other two events are quite different, *i.e.* the beginning of the baby-boom in 1945 and then its end, which was marked by a decline in fertility spread over the 1965-75 period. The characteristics of these two shifts are well known: as the prevalence of childless or single-child families diminished after the Second World War, the prevalence of families with more than one child increased and fertility therefore rose (families with more than one child replacing families with no children or with a single child). Starting in 1965, modern

Figure 1.4. **Total fertility rate and mean age at childbearing of mothers under 30 (proxy of the age of first maternity) between 1900 and 2000 in France**

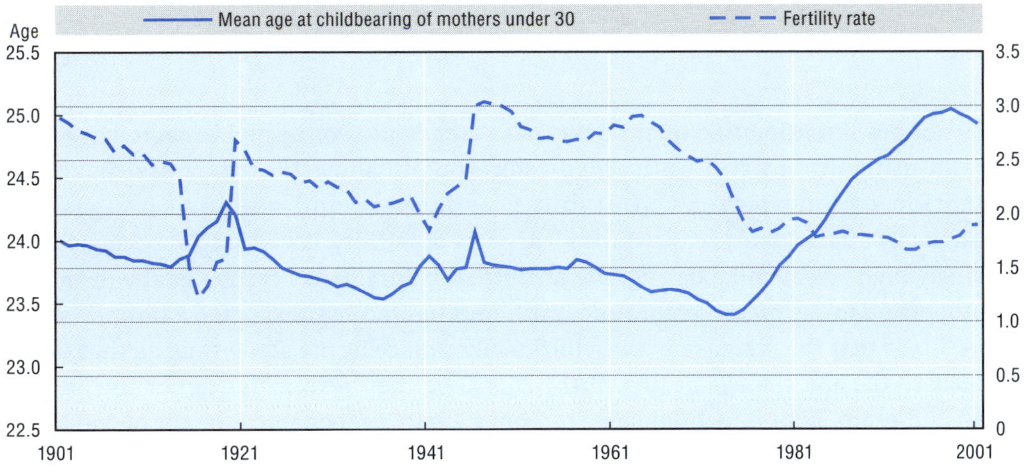

means of contraception enabled couples to avoid "unwanted" births which, according to surveys, accounted for 30% of total births, and this therefore lowered the birth rate proportionately. However, no one had foreseen these two developments.

Analysing fertility more closely, it can be seen that birth control is accompanied by two even clearer shifts. The age of mothers when their first child is born (we approximated this in Figure 1.4 with the mean age of childbearing before the age of 30), which had been declining since the 19th century, suddenly began to rise in 1974. The influence of the oil crisis is obvious, but what is less obvious is that this age then continued to rise very regularly until 2000, when it seemed to level off. At the same time, the proportion of births out of wedlock, which had been stable at around 8% for over a century, also began to increase rapidly and steadily (Figure 1.5). Its fluctuations closely parallel those of the age of mothers when their first child is born. During the two wars, both indices grew and then returned to their initial values when hostilities were over. These simultaneous reactions can even be observed during the 1939-45 war, with in both cases a surge in 1940 and then in 1944-45. It is as if a change that had been germinating was released during the war and then brought under control once it ended. But in 1974, control could no longer be regained and a different form of family came into being in which women had children late, families averaged around two children and there was, so to speak, a decoupling of marriage and fertility.

Figure 1.5. **Proportion of out-of-wedlock births between 1900 and 2000 in France**

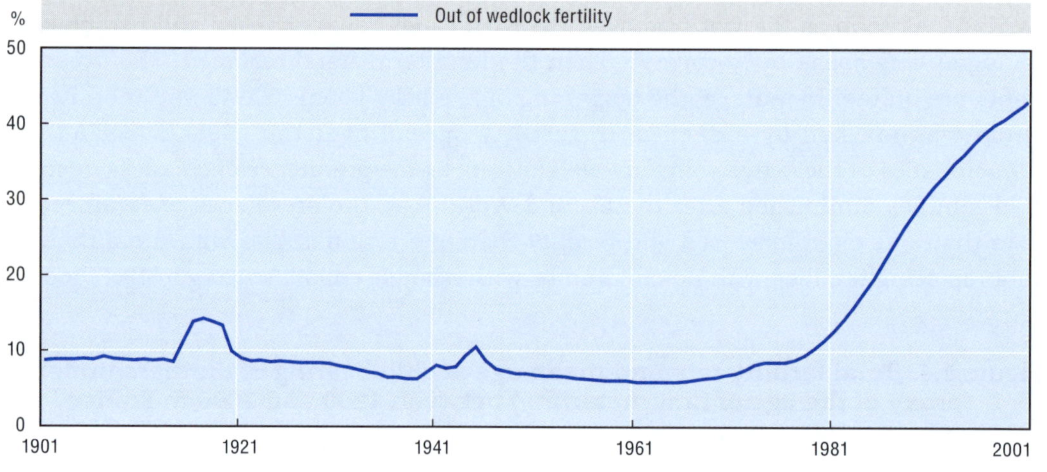

It is not our intention to explain how these trends are connected or were triggered – which is a difficult and still unfinished task – but to show that they are result of a combination of long periods of stability or latency and sudden changes that simultaneously affect some and perhaps all aspects of fertility. For example, because of the increasingly high age at childbearing, the fertility rate diminishes mechanically (exactly in equal proportion to the increase per time unit). Another more unexpected example, shown in Figure 1.6, is that the increase in twin births takes place at the same time as that of out-of-wedlock births and the age at first birth. This is neither a coincidence nor the effect of new assisted reproduction technologies, but once again a mechanical result of the higher age at childbearing, for the proportion of twin births increases with the mother's age.

Figure 1.6. **Proportion of twin births in France between 1900 and 2000**

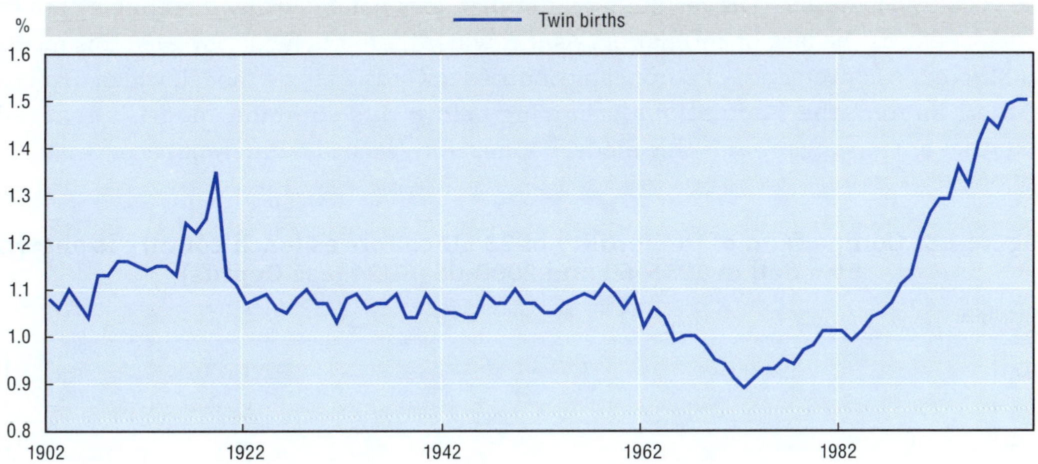

Other European examples: similarity without convergence

Is France's case representative of the other developed countries or is France on a different track? Looking at Figure 1.7 in which the trend of the fertility rate in selected developed countries has been superposed, one would be tempted to opt for the idea of diversity. Admittedly, the high fertility rates of the post-war period have disappeared everywhere, but at a very different pace. The beginning of the decline that started in France in 1965 came earlier in Finland (1950) and later in Spain and Ireland (1975) and later still in Latvia (1990). These few examples suggest that the form of political regimes is not unrelated to these time frames (death of Franco, fall of the Berlin Wall). They do not impose a level of fertility, but sustain it through a kind of inertia. It is also apparent that the countries' ranking by fertility rate varies broadly from the beginning to the end of the period.

Figure 1.7. **Trend of the total fertility rate in selected developed countries between 1950 and 2002**

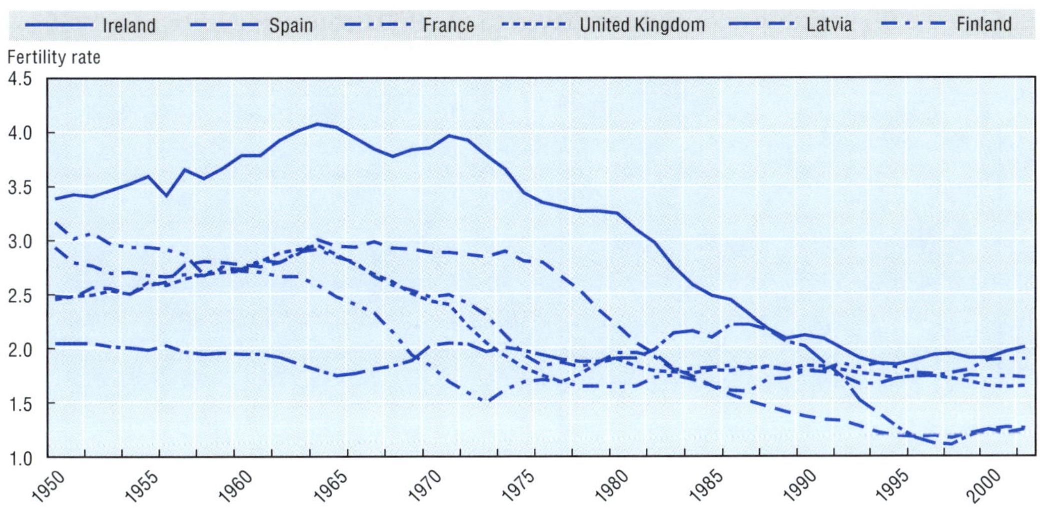

To show this more clearly, we have arranged the EU countries by fertility rate in 1950-55 and 2000-05 (Figure 1.8). The resulting scatter plot does not show any discernible pattern, which confirms the lack of correlation. As it is wider than it is high, however, this means that there is a convergence of European countries towards a single model, which deprives of their interest the fluctuations occurring before this common model is reached. Countries are moving towards this model haphazardly, each at a different pace.

Figure 1.8. **Comparison of the fertility of 23 EU countries (each country is shown by a dot) in 1955-60 and 2000-05 (EU24 less Cyprus)**

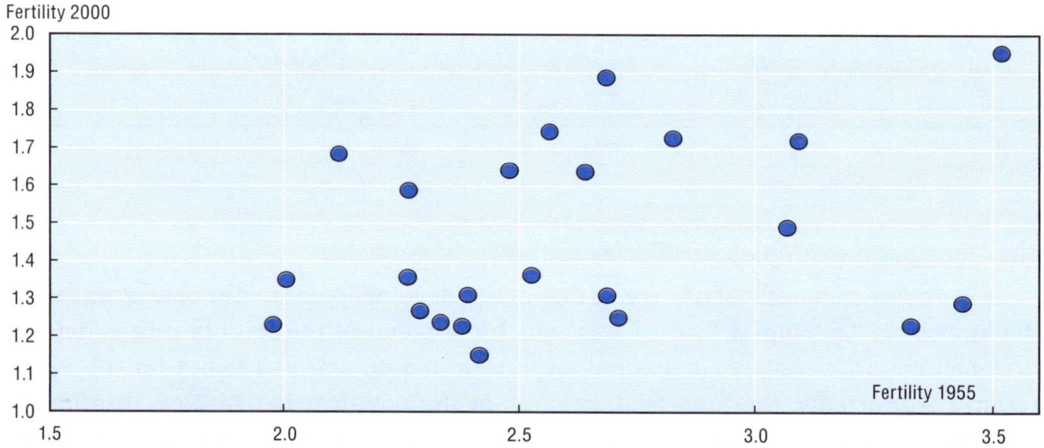

This hypothesis of convergence seems to be confirmed when the standard deviation of the fertility rates is calculated period by period (Figure 1.9). If we extrapolate the fairly linear trend, the differences in fertility should have disappeared in Europe by around 2025. However, this reasoning is made all other things being equal, *i.e.* without taking into account the drop in mean fertility. It is more accurate to follow the trend in the mean deviation, *i.e.* the standard deviation divided by mean fertility for the period. In this case,

Figure 1.9. **Variability of the fertility rate of 23 EU countries between 1950 and 2002 (EU24 less Cyprus)**

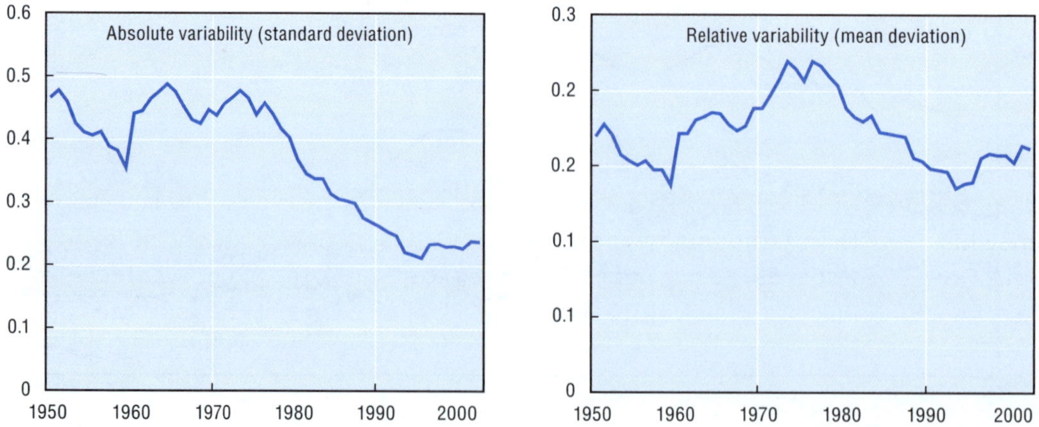

the trend shows no convergence. The mean deviation remains stable throughout the past half century. Its current value in 2000-05 is, for example, exactly the same as in 1955-60. For the time being, then, we must reject the idea of convergent European behaviour.

Geographic similarities and political differences

Might there at least be a geographic rationale for fertility rates? This time the answer is positive when we draw the map of fertility rates in Europe in 1950-55 and 2000-05 (Figure 1.10). During the first period, the countries of south-western and north-eastern Europe had higher fertility rates, while the countries of the central strip extending from the United Kingdom and Sweden to Italy and Greece had lower fertility rates. During the second period (2000-05), fertility was higher in a northern triangle with France at its bottom point and was lower to the east in the former communist countries and to the south. The autocorrelation coefficients calculated on the ranking of the 25 countries are respectively 0.35 and 0.55.

Figure 1.10. **Total fertility rate in 1955-60 and 2000-05 in EU countries**

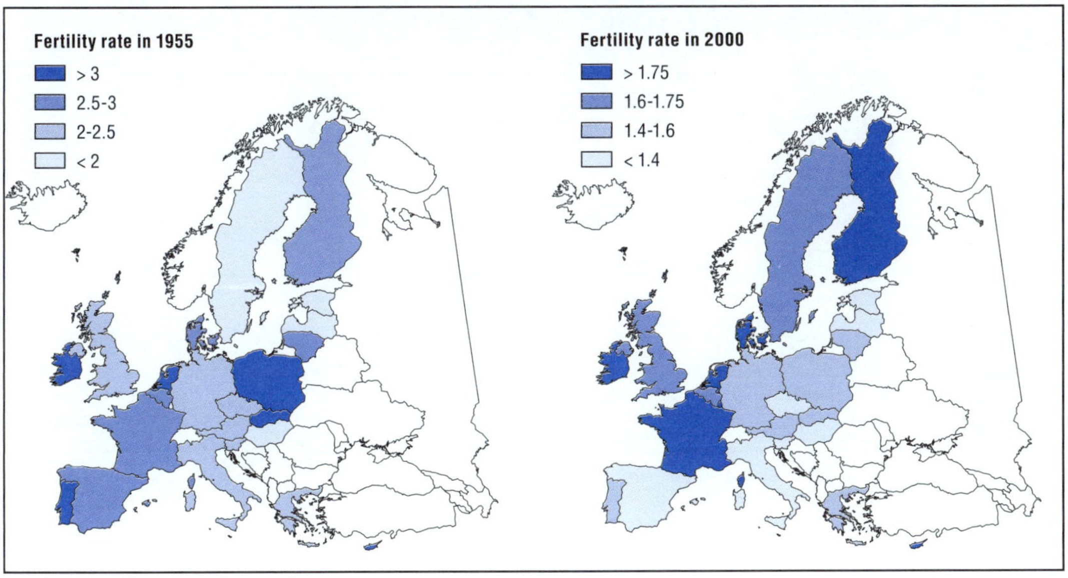

One way of verifying the similarity of trends in neighbouring countries is to show them in a group. This is done in Figure 1.11 for several north eastern countries (Latvia, Lithuania, the Slovak Republic, Poland) and for some Mediterranean countries (Spain, Greece, Portugal and Slovenia). In the first case, we see the stronger influence of the Catholic religion in Poland and the Slovak Republic which became part of the Soviet block somewhat later than Lithuania, while this influence is of course absent in Protestant Latvia. Once this initial difference has been taken into account, the major event took place in 1989 with the fall of the Berlin Wall. The common situation of the four "transition" countries then imposed a remarkably similar trend in their fertility rates.

The pattern for the Mediterranean countries is similar, but the political events took place 15 years earlier, *i.e.* the fall of the regime of the colonels in Athens, the death of

Figure 1.11. **Trend in the total fertility rate for groups of neighbouring countries**

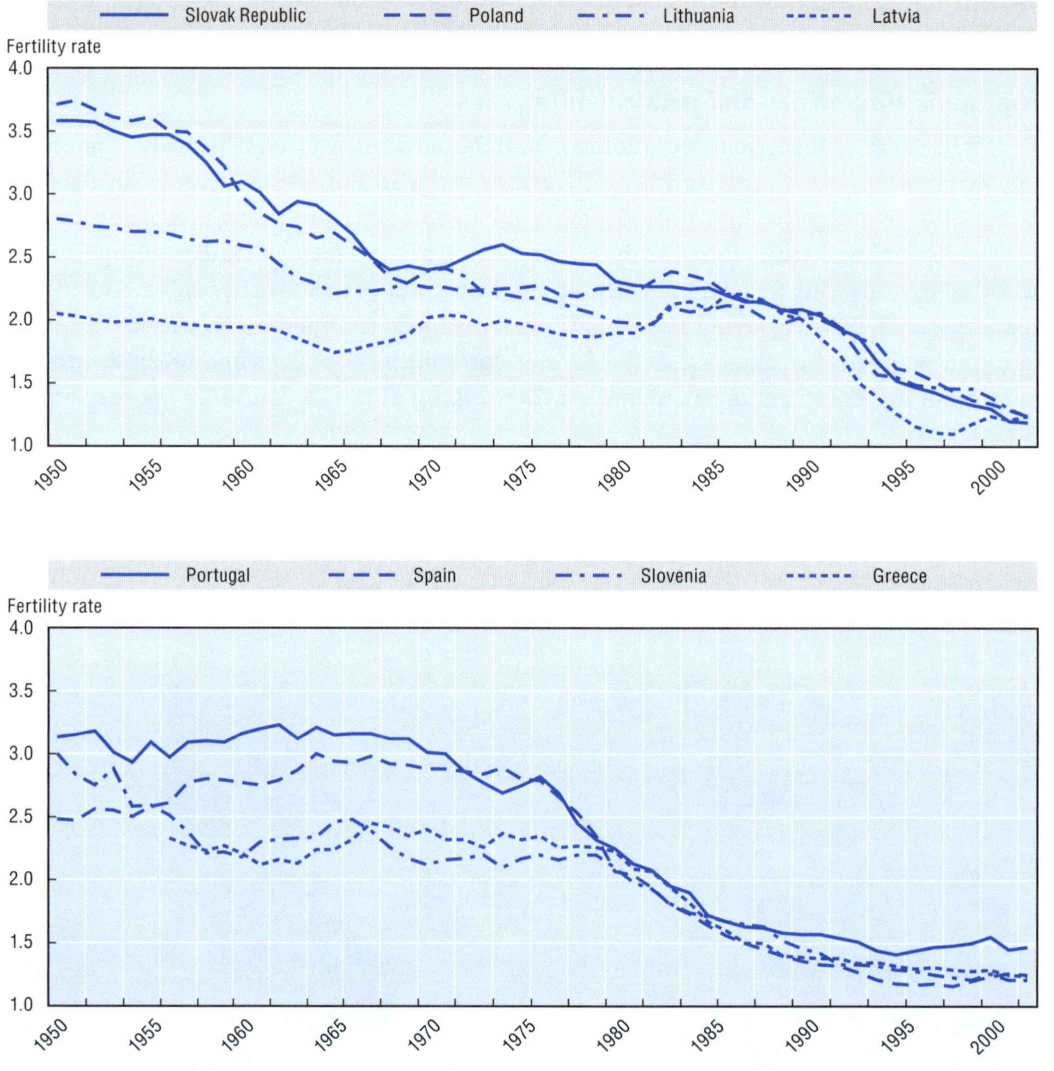

Franco in Madrid, the overthrow of Caetano in Lisbon and, to a lesser extent, the death of Tito for Ljubljana. More specifically, what these countries have in common is the concept of a blocked society: the political regime's rejection of change had the effect of preventing changes in fertility and thus in the organisation of the family. It then took a dramatic event, not to change demographic attitudes, but to enable society to adapt to a new set of circumstances, *i.e.* to readjust behaviour, bring it up to date and bring it into line with the economic and political situation. In order to understand these situations better and to be clearer about what is meant by "bring up to date" and "economic and political situation", instead of comparing countries that are close, we must compare countries that are very close in terms of their culture (religion, language, long-term history) but that have experienced different political regimes or legislative changes. In a sense, this is the biometric method of "matched tests" or pairings.

Three cases are especially interesting, *i.e.* West and East Germany, Romania and Bulgaria, and Sweden and Denmark.

West and East Germany

The only initial difference between West and East Germany was created in 1945 with the imposition of two radically different political regimes. In Figure 1.12, which shows the trend in the fertility rate year by year in both countries between 1950 and 2000 (the series have continued to be calculated by the Statistical Office in Wiesbaden since reunification), we see that between 1955 and 1975, fertility remained exactly the same in both countries. At the time, it was argued that this showed the importance of civil society and culture-specific behaviour, which thereby showed their resilience and, conversely, the inability of the State to control mentalities. In 1974, East Germany, more concerned than its neighbour about the declining fertility, passed pro-birth legislation that offered every mother a maternal salary for the three years following the birth of the child. The legislation was highly successful since fertility rose by 0.5 children, which is a significant increase, and this gap with West Germany was subsequently maintained. In fact, between 1965 and 1975, both countries had undergone the same changes as those that were discussed for France, for the introduction of modern means of contraception had made it possible to prevent unwanted births and had thus led to a drop in fertility. However, in 1974 in West Germany, the oil crisis had the effect, as in France, of delaying the age at childbearing and thus of keeping the fertility rate low. This age at childbearing rose since couples were having greater difficulty in finding work and housing and thus in settling down and starting a family. Since the origin of statistics, in particular thanks to the major study by Roger Schofield and Anthony Wrigley on England between 1550 and 1850, we know that during Kondratieff's depression phase real wages fall and delay the formation of couples and thus marriages and consequently fertility, which apparently falls. However, there was no reason for this mechanism to apply in East Germany where housing was granted to married couples who placed their names on a list. On the contrary, it was advantageous to put one's name on the list quickly and thus marry young. Similarly, since everyone of working age was provided with a job, there was no delay in entering working life. As of 1975, therefore, the difference in fertility between the two Germanies was based on

Figure 1.12. **Comparison of the trend in the total fertility rate in East and West Germany between 1950 and 2000**

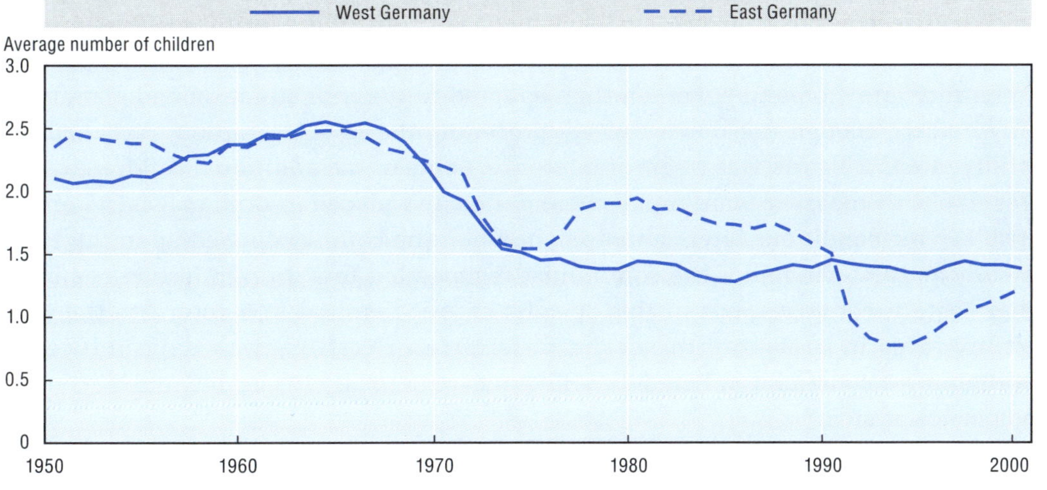

a difference in the timetable for starting a family. East German women continued to have their children very young until reunification (on average, they had their first child at the age of 24.5), while every year on the other hand, West German women postponed by approximately eight weeks the arrival of their first child (and consequently of subsequent children). As a result, by 1989 the age of women having their first child had risen in the West to 27 (today it is 29).

Still to be explained is the sudden upswing in fertility in East Germany in 1975. The immediate reason was, of course, the maternal salary law, which triggered a windfall effect. Women who were planning to have a child at a later date decided to do so earlier. This was exactly the opposite of what was happening at the same time in the West. As a result, the two demographic regimes suddenly veered in different directions, as the East adapted to the nature of work and housing under a communist regime. A development such as the availability of new contraception methods created a new situation in relation to the prior problem and risk of unwanted pregnancies. The Law of 1974 in the East was of a somewhat different nature. It led to an adjustment bringing fertility into line with the real situation. Before fertility became the target of government measures, it followed the same development on both sides of the Wall, but once a measure was introduced the long latency came to an end and the demographic regime responded accordingly. In 1989, with reunification, the situation again changed in the former East Germany, which was now subject to the same housing and employment constraints as in the West. The reaction was immediate and fertility plummeted as East German women adapted to the timetable (time lag) for establishing a family of West German women, who were now becoming pregnant later. The total deficit between the two rates (the surface between the two curves) is also practically the same as the total benefit that had preceded it between 1975 and 1989. Ultimately, both fertility rates seem destined to converge.

Romania and Bulgaria

Romania and Bulgaria have had a comparable history with the long Ottoman occupation, followed by authoritarian regimes, communism during the post-war period and now the transition and the entry of both countries into the European Union. Also, their respective fertility rates remained similar until Ceaucescu took a spectacular measure in 1968 (see Figure 1.13), when there was a virtually total ban on abortion, which had been almost the only available means of controlling fertility. Unprepared for this measure, Romanian women broke a record for births nine months later, doubling the fertility rate. Romanian women then adapted to the new situation and fertility fell fairly quickly, though not down to level preceding the new legislation, for which the fertility rate in Bulgaria was a sort of reference. Some of the additional children born as a result of this measure were rapidly abandoned and placed in orphanages, where the terrible living conditions later came to light when the country opened up in the 1990s. As early as 1990, the fall of the communist regimes led to a drop in fertility, as in the other Eastern countries, but in this specific case it resulted in a return to the same fertility rates in both countries. The difference in fertility was only induced by maintaining a constraint in Romania, while in East Germany it was due to the economic and political system.

Figure 1.13. **Comparison of the trend in the total fertility rate in Romania and Bulgaria between 1950 and 2000**

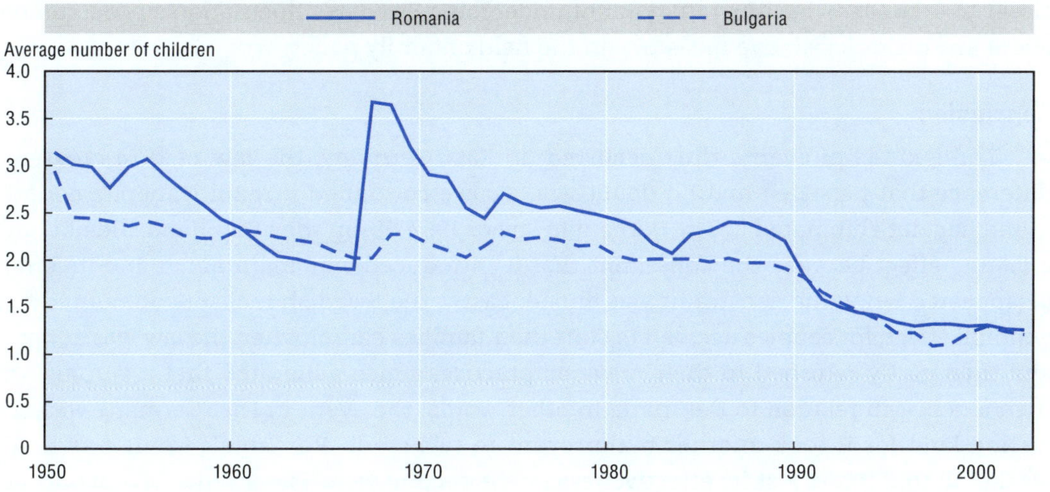

Sweden and Denmark

There is no need to stress all the political, cultural and economic characteristics shared by Sweden and Denmark. As a result, their fertility rates followed a very similar pattern until the early 1980s, as can be seen in Figure 1.14. In 1985 and 1986, however, Sweden adopted a number of measures designed to enable parents to stay at home when their children were very young. The fertility rate immediately soared. A number of countries, including France, thought that Sweden had found the magic formula for pro-natalism, but they were mistaken. A few years later, once the benefit of the measures had been reaped, the fertility rate fell below Denmark's, largely offsetting the gain in fertility achieved earlier. Then, at the end of the period, both countries returned to the same rate.

Figure 1.14. **Comparison of the trend in the total fertility rate in Norway, Sweden and Denmark between 1950 and 2000**

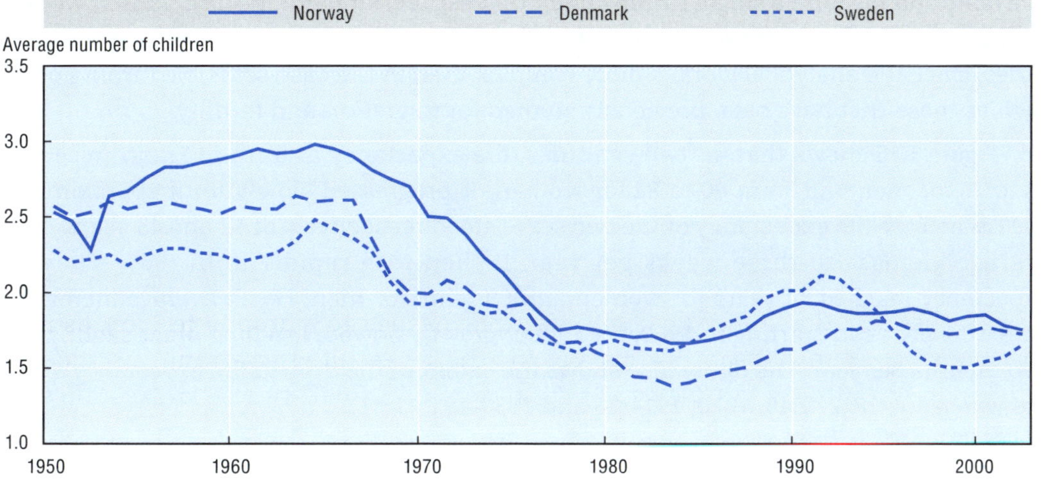

The trend in fertility in Norway shows even more clearly the singular nature of the Swedish experience – Norway differing from the other two Nordic countries but gradually drawing closer to Denmark's fertility rate without undergoing Sweden's fluctuation since it did not adopt any major legislative measures in the field of family policy.

Conclusion

Three kinds of events thus occurred: in East Germany, the law of 1974 created a difference that persisted and no doubt would have continued if reunification, a counter event, had not eliminated it. The Romanian law of 1967-68, on the other hand, did not have a lasting effect because the constraint that it introduced was maintained and its effect disappeared when the constraint was ended. Lastly, the Swedish measure amounted to a windfall effect, for couples decided to start their families earlier when the law was adopted and then partly returned to their previous practice, which generated first a surplus and then a deficit in relation to Denmark. In other words, the event in East Germany was of a lasting kind for it took another major event to reverse it. Romania's event was much weaker in that it had lost its effectiveness by the second year. The Swedish event was not of a lasting nature.

In the light of this analysis, it can be seen why predicting fertility trends means predicting future events, especially political events as they will often have a lasting influence. However, to borrow from Hannah Arendt, who devoted a good deal of her thinking to the concept of the event, by definition an event is unpredictable. Arendt sums this up with the following formula: the event creates its own past. The causes of an event, to the extent that they can be determined at all, can only be found after the event has occurred. Consequently, we cannot claim that this or that set of causes will trigger this or that event.

1.3. Mortality: a hidden turning point

The first section of this paper illustrated the case of relatively frequent turning points without major lasting effects, using the example of external migration. The second part identified turning points with effects that were lasting but sometimes less obvious and discussed them using examples of fertility trends. In this final section, we shall look at mortality and focus on a single turning point that escapes immediate observation. We shall confine ourselves to a single country, France, for which we have a very long statistical series, since the analytical work is more complex than in the case of visible turning points such as those that have been previously studied for migration and fertility.

Figure 1.15 shows that, in two centuries, life expectancy at birth in France rose from 38 to 75 for men and from 40 to 82 for women. It progressed slowly until approximately 1890, when the life expectancy of the two sexes stood respectively at 42 and 45 years, *i.e.* an average increase of three weeks per year. It then rose rapidly until 1960, when life expectancy reached 74 years for women and 68 years for men, *i.e.* an average increase of 5 months per year. Starting in 1960, the rate of growth slowed, levelling off at slightly over two months per year. The figure also shows the extent of the drop in life expectancy during the war years: 1812-1815, 1870, 1914-18 and 1939-45.

The chronology of the rising life expectancy is explained by the composite character of life expectancy, which takes into account the frequency of both child and old-age mortality. During the 19th century child mortality hardly diminished at all and then, around 1890, it

Figure 1.15. **Trend in life expectancy at birth from 1806 to 2000 in France**

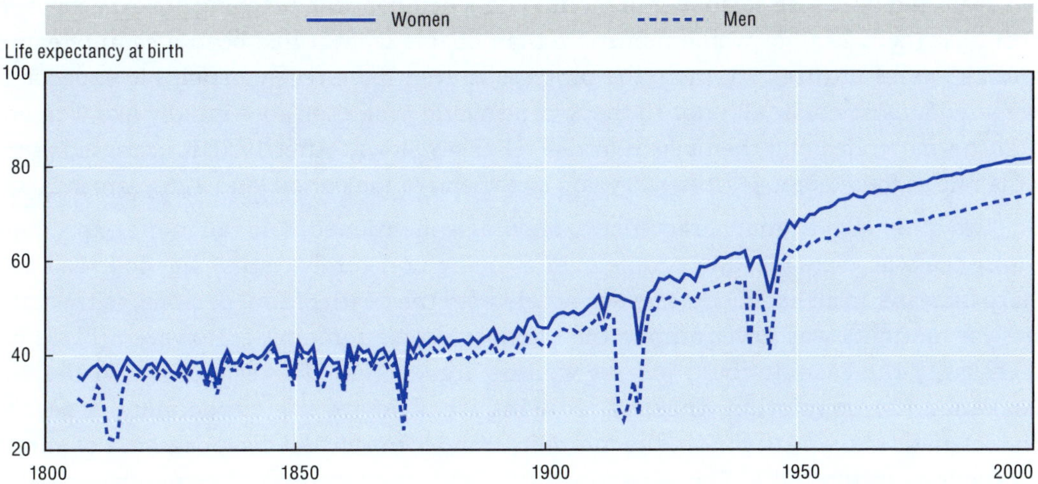

began to decline, falling from 200 per 1 000 to 10 per 1 000 in 1960; in other words, the risk of children dying during their first year fell twenty-fold. While one of five children did not reach the age of one under the July Monarchy (1830-1848), 99% of children did so at the beginning of the Fifth Republic (from 1958 until today). Consequently, describing the trend in mortality using life expectancy merely reflects the drop in infant mortality since it includes the same crucial period from 1890 to 1960. To determine the mortality trend at the opposite end of life, we must use a different approach.

An initial method consists of calculating life expectancy starting at a relatively advanced age, such as 60. This would show the average number of years that people who reach this age can expect to live. The trend in this life expectancy at 60 for men and women is shown in Figure 1.16. The picture that emerges is very different from that shown in Figure 1.15 for life expectancy at birth. Until the 1914 war, there was no increase in life expectancy at 60. It remained stuck at around 9 years. It then started to rise slowly for women only, reaching

Figure 1.16. **Trend in life expectancy at 60 from 1806 to 2000 in France**

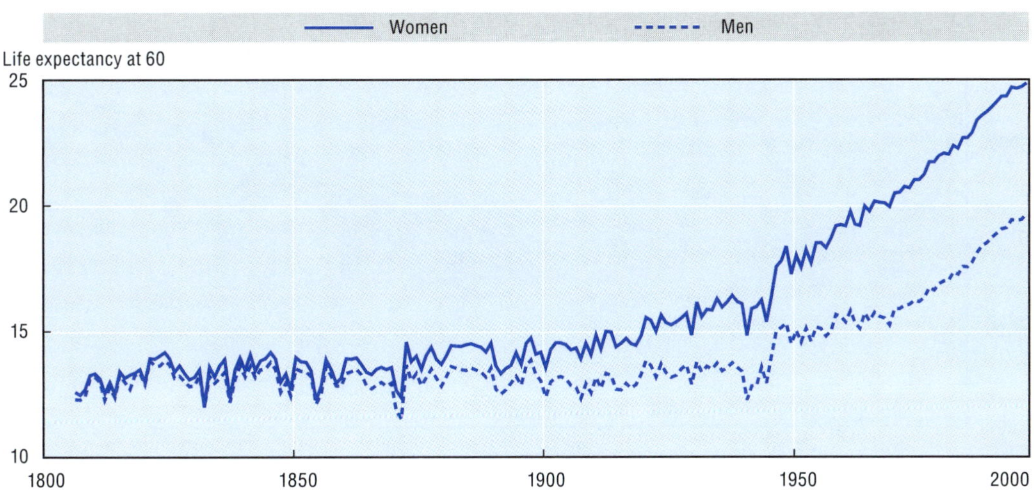

almost 12 on the eve of the Second World War. After the war ended, it suddenly jumped by two years and then rose steadily by a month and a half per year, reaching life expectancy at 60 of 25 years in 2000 for women, or more than double what it had been a century earlier (and 26.5 years in 2004). For men, the progress is even more recent. Their life expectancy increased almost not at all prior to the Second World War, then rose rapidly like women's after the war ended and then began to rise relatively slowly. After 1970, it increased at the same rate as for women, reaching 20 years by the end of the period (and 21.5 years in 2004).

Two other significant characteristics should be mentioned. The fall in life expectancy during the war years (despite people over 60 being non-combattants) was followed by a sharp increase. In all likelihood, the war accelerated the death of frail persons, so that after the war mortality was lower among the stronger people remaining. However, this is not necessarily the case. It could just as well be argued that the restrictions of the war weakened the population, thereby reducing its ultimate life expectancy. A second characteristic of the 1970 shift in the mortality trend is the virtual disappearance of annual fluctuations in mortality. These were very large in the 19th century and were already becoming smaller during the interwar period and after 1945, but as from 1970 they became imperceptible. This is an indication of a major regime shift. These fluctuations were caused by epidemics and cyclical variations in the environment (such as periods of very cold weather), the harmful effects of which may now be thought to be under control (which explains why there was such a strong emotional reaction to the consequences of the heat wave in the summer of 2003 in France, which took the people back to an earlier stage of mortality).

So two major changes in old-age mortality occurred around 1970: mortality began to decline at a faster pace and annual fluctuations disappeared. To understand these changes better, it is necessary to use more accurate data, *i.e.* the risks (or probabilities) of death at each age for each year. Figure 1.17 presents, in semi-logarithmic co-ordinates, the mortality curves (or tables) for female mortality, providing the values of these probabilities by age from 0 to 100 for five different years from 1806 to 1996.

Figure 1.17. **Trend in the age-specific female mortality risk at different ages (mortality table) for different years between 1806 and 1996 in France**

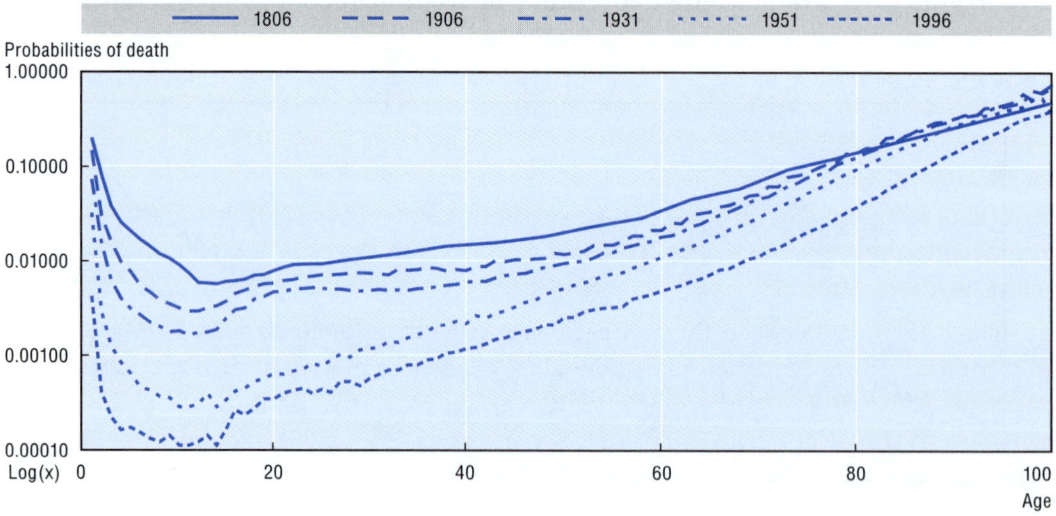

Immediately apparent is the sharp decrease in mortality among the young over the last two centuries. But another element that attracts attention is the highly regular growth of probabilities starting at the age of 50, and even 30 for the most recent mortality tables. Since the probabilities are represented by their logarithm, the linearity signifies that for each year of age after 30, the risk of mortality increases by a fixed proportion (in the range of 10%). An actuary, Benjamin Gompertz, was the first in 1824, to point out this remarkable trend which has since borne his name. Later, Makeham proposed improving the adjustment by adding a fixed risk to each age. In mathematical notation, the probability q(x) at age x may therefore be written:

$$q(x) = K\,(b)^{x} + A$$

Figure 1.18. **Adjustment of age-specific mortality risks of French women in 1960 by an exponential**[1]

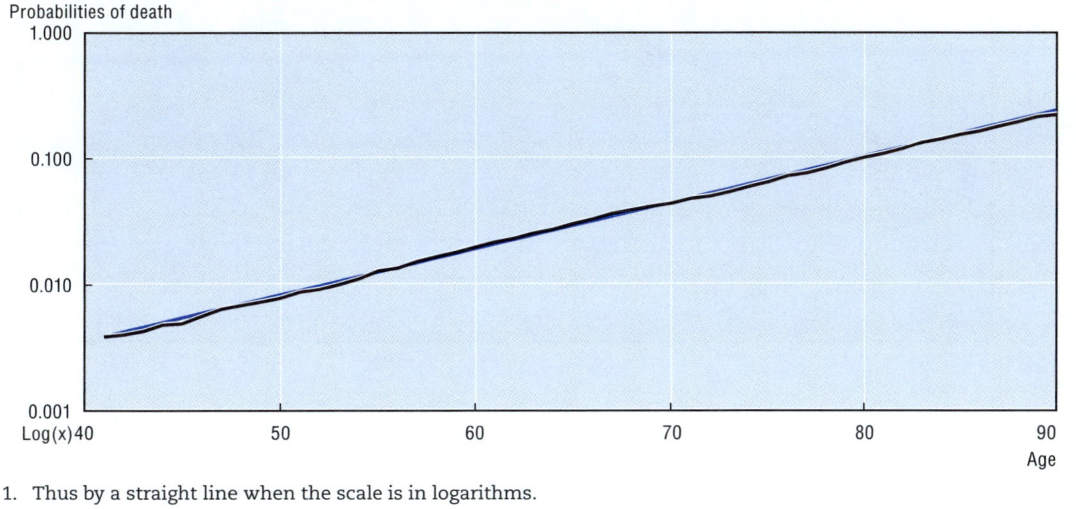

1. Thus by a straight line when the scale is in logarithms.

Figure 1.18 shows the extraordinary quality of the adjustment obtained in the case of the mortality risks experienced by French women between the ages of 40 and 90 in 1960. It is very rare to see such a close match in the social field. The advantage of the Gompertz-Makeham law is that it summarises a set of 50 risks (one per year from the age of 40 to 90) using three values, the constant K, the multiplicative factor b (close to 1.1 since we have seen that the annual increase was 10%) and the constant risk A. This latter is not relevant for old-age mortality, so we will only be concerned with the two initial coefficients K and b. We have estimated them for the value of A, which provided the best adjustment using the method of least squares on the logarithms. The trend of the two parameters since 1806 is interesting. Figure 1.19 shows the Gompertz lines corresponding to mortality risks before 1970 and after 1970.

The difference between the two periods could not be more obvious. Before 1970, the gradient of the lines (parameter b is their slope) increases in such a way that they seem to converge and intersect at an age of approximately 80. The older people grew, the less change there was in the risk of dying over time. This may be the source of certain beliefs in there being a maximum age or an age at which the Psalm of David says that it is normal to die. The fact that in the past there was a lower risk of dying after the age of 80 than in recent years

Figure 1.19. **Adjustments of mortality tables using Gompertz lines before and after 1976**

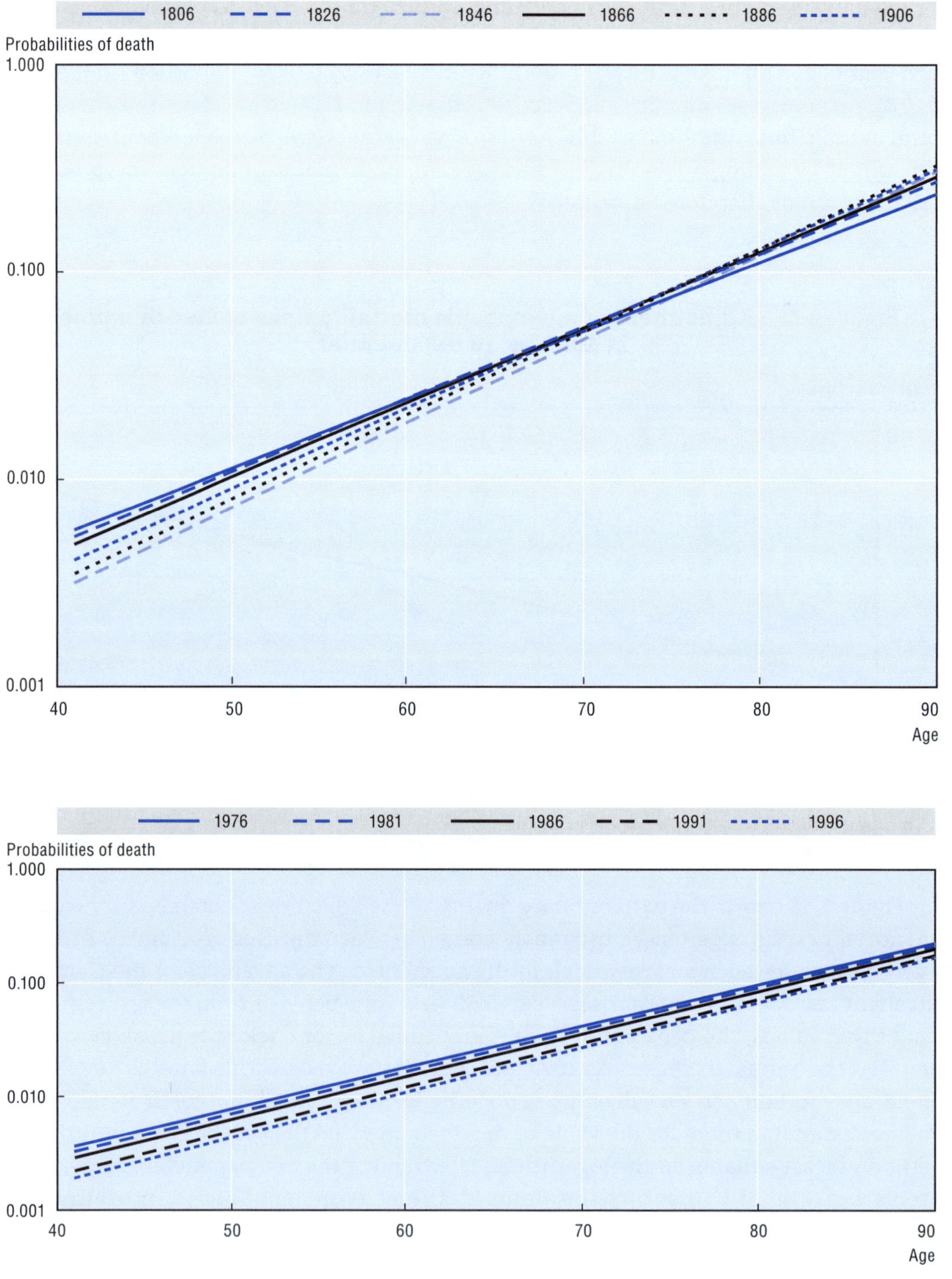

may be accurate (some, such as the probabilist Gumbel, contrasted mortality and longevity in the 1930s, thinking that they could explain the supposed presence of very old people in the past in countries with high mortality rates by a selection due to high mortality), but is much more likely to have been due to errors in recording the age of the oldest people who died at a time when civil records had not yet attained their current level of accuracy.

Be this as it may, up until 1970 the decline in mortality became proportionately lower as one advanced towards the biggest ages. However, everything is different after 1970. In figure 1.19, the Gompertz lines corresponding to mortality tables after this date now seem to be nearly parallel. This observation is of great importance. It means that mortality is declining uniformly at all ages and that the risk, whatever the figure put on it, is falling every year by a certain fraction, around 2%. This seems to be little but is actually a great deal when it is considered that, over a period of 35 years at this rate, the risk will be divided by 2. Another way of presenting these facts is to say that the mortality of people aged 60, 70 and 80 in 2000 is the same as the mortality of people 5 years younger in 1975, *i.e.* aged 55, 65 and 75 at that date.

There is a more accurate way of representing this change in old-age mortality around 1970. It suffices to represent each Gompertz line corresponding to a year by its two coefficients log(K) and b (we have chosen the logarithms of K because they are the coefficients of the line) and to consider these two coefficients as the two co-ordinates of a point located in a plane the horizontal axis of which measures slope b and the vertical axis the coefficient log(K). The result is shown in Figure 1.20. We have connected successive years in order better to identify the time path of these Gompertz lines. It can be seen that, before 1975, the points representing the Gompertz lines were themselves located along a line, which exactly expresses the intersection around a fixed point at about age 80, as shown in Figure 1.19. But suddenly, around 1975, this trend pattern no longer holds true. The path diverges horizontally from the line that it was following until then, which means that the slope is decreasing. This only lasts for a few years and, starting in 1980, another rectilinear path appears that is very clearly separate from the former one and much less inclined. This is exactly what we observed in Figure 1.19, where the slopes changed much more slowly while the coefficient K diminished rapidly.

Can this change in the mortality regime occurring around 1975 be explained? This is difficult as we do not know the biological or social reason that would explain the Gompertz law. Like the law of universal attraction that Newton observed but was unable to explain or justify, the Gompertz law, despite its universality (it is also valid for some of the animal kingdom), remains a mystery. Certain mathematical biology models indicate that it might be due to a gradual loss of competence in repairing errors in DNA replication coding and spontaneous mutations, but this is hardly useful from a practical standpoint and even less so for predicting the future mortality trend.

As a result, a turning point was concealed in the annual mortality tables. Unlike the turning points for fertility and migrations, this turning point cannot be related directly to political and economic events. It is therefore even more difficult to predict how long the situation corresponding to this turning point will last or when the next turning point will occur. This is unfortunate, for the trend in the two parameters K and b will affect the level of mortality at advanced ages in the coming years and is therefore relevant to any discussion of population ageing.

Figure 1.20. **The trend in the two parameters of the Gompertz laws adjusting age-specific mortality risks**

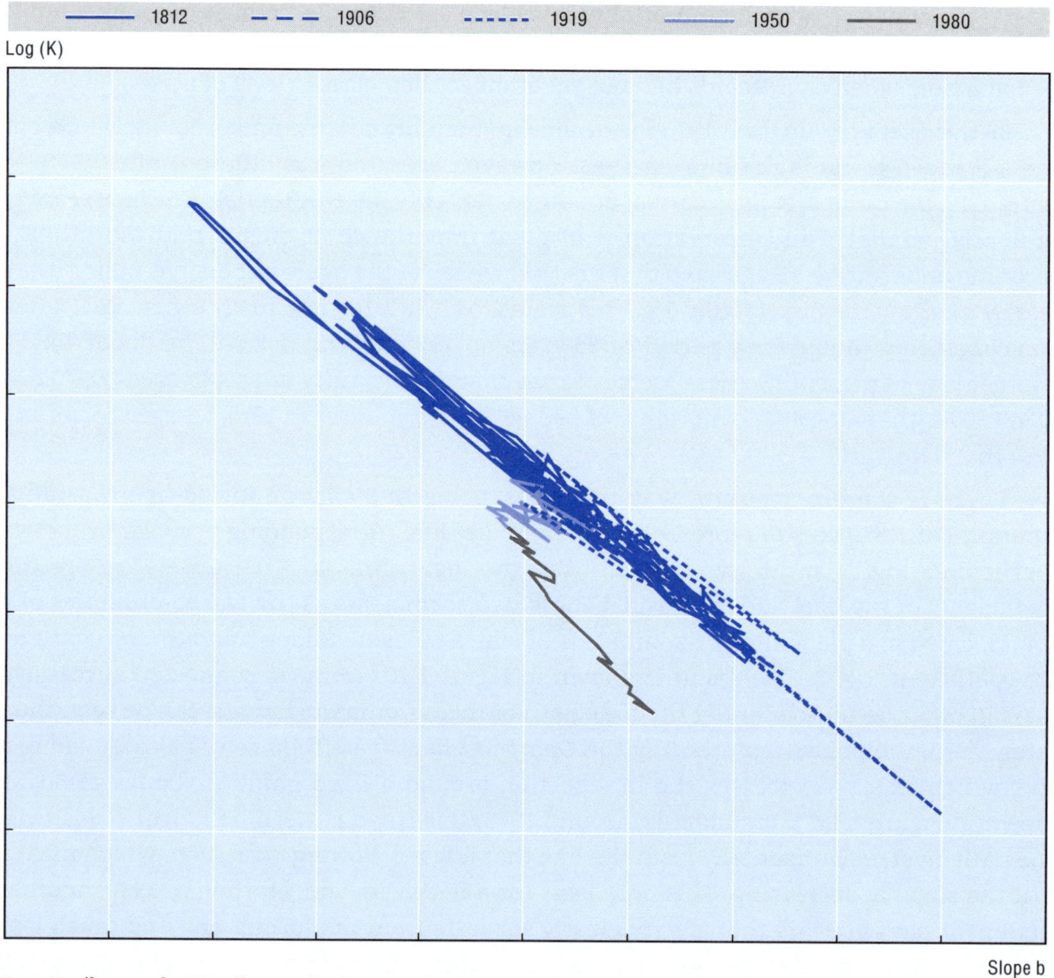

Note: Until around 1970, all mortality laws are in the same alignment, but they diverge from it and move in another direction, starting in 1980.

1.4. Conclusions

The conclusions of this brief study, which have been established on the basis of specific facts, are fairly negative about the possibilities of forecasting demographic trends. It is impossible to make a demographic forecast independently of an economic and political forecast. A long-term population forecast assumes implicitly that no event will occur. It drifts in an unreal world aptly illustrated by the migration projections conducted by the United Nations. Can political and economic events be predicted? Probably not. There remains one approach, *i.e.* using foresight and scenarios, assuming that this or that event will occur and deducing its impact on demographic patterns. This means forecasting possible rather than probable events, which cannot be foreseen.

References

Arendt, H. (1958), *The Human Condition*, Chicago University Press, Chicago.

European Commission (2005), *Mediterranean Migration*, 2005 Report of the CARIM, Florence.

INSEE (2005), *Les immigrés en France*, INSEE, Paris.

Jennissen, R. (2004), *Macro-economic Determinants of International Migration in Europe*, Dutch University Press, Amsterdam.

Le Bras, H. (2005), *La démographie*, Odile Jacob, Paris.

OECD (2005), *Trends in International Migration: SOPEMI – 2004 Edition*, OECD Publishing, Paris.

OECD (2006), *International Migration Outlook: SOPEMI – 2006 Edition*, OECD Publishing, Paris.

United Nations (1998), *World Population Monitoring 1997, Issues of International Migration and Development*, E 98 XIII/4, United Nations, New York.

United Nations (2006), *International Migration Report 2006*, United Nations, New York.

ISBN 978-92-64-04065-6
Higher Education to 2030
Volume 1: Demography

Chapter 2

What is the Impact of Demography on Higher Education Systems? A Forward-looking Approach for OECD Countries

by

Stéphan Vincent-Lancrin*

This chapter aims to evaluate the impact of demographic changes on the student population, on student-teacher ratios and expenditure in higher education and on the level to which the populations are educated. It shows that demographic changes are only one of the factors determining student enrolment trends, teaching staff numbers or costs in higher education. It also demonstrates that policy responses to falling student enrolments and rising enrolments in periods of expansion are often similar, albeit for sometimes different reasons. The investigation is based on forward-looking quantitative scenarios that provide a heuristic insight into these changes and their consequences, though without claiming that they can actually be forecast.

* OECD Centre for Educational Research and Innovation (CERI). Alexander A. Antonyuk (International Energy Agency and University of Oxford) carried out student enrolment projections in close collaboration with the author (see Annex 2.A1) who is grateful to him for his contribution and for their highly constructive discussions on certain demographic phenomena. The author also wishes to thank his colleagues William Thorn and Kiira Kärkkäinen for their comments, as well as Eric Charbonnier for his assistance with the data.

Demography has become a subject of concern in a growing number of countries. The population of some OECD countries is rapidly ageing, especially in Japan, Korea and Southern and Eastern Europe. By contrast, in countries such as Mexico and Turkey, the population is continuing to grow, in spite of a decrease in the fertility rate. While demographic issues have not featured prominently in debates on higher education in recent decades, ongoing demographic trends are giving rise to unprecedented concern. How far will the demography of higher education systems mirror that of the population as a whole? How is one to manage rising and falling student enrolment levels? What are the budgetary implications of such trends? What are the implications for the educational level of the population and the replenishment of teaching staff resources?

The present chapter seeks to evaluate the impact of demographic changes on the student population, student-teacher ratios and expenditure in higher education and on the level to which the populations are educated. It shows that demographic changes are far from decisive in determining student enrolment trends, teaching staff numbers or costs in higher education. It also demonstrates that policy responses to falling student enrolments and rising enrolments in periods of expansion are often similar, albeit for sometimes different reasons. The investigation is based on forward-looking quantitative scenarios that provide a heuristic insight into these changes and their consequences, though without claiming that they can actually be forecast. In a sense, these forward projections provide for a better understanding of recent trends by magnifying them.

The chapter is structured as follows. The first section offers projections of student enrolments in higher education in the case of two scenarios, showing that the expansion of systems seems set to continue in the decades ahead; Sections 2.2 and 2.3 examine more closely the impact of enrolment levels on total public expenditure in higher education and student-teacher ratios, respectively. Section 2.4 discusses the possible impact of these trends on academic staff recruitment. Section 2.5 indicates how the percentage of the population with higher education graduate qualifications might evolve in accordance with various trend scenarios, and the implications of such changes for the relative availability of graduate resources. Section 2.6 deals with the possible impact of these trends on broader participation and equity in higher education. Section 2.7 discusses various possible policy responses to the growth and contraction of student enrolment. The final section sums up the main conclusions of the chapter.

2.1. The impact of demography on student enrolment

The population of the OECD countries is ageing as fertility rates decrease and people live longer. The average percentage of the population aged over 65 in those countries is thus expected to rise from 14% to 21% between 2005 and 2030, and is already over 18% in some of them (Germany, Greece, Italy and Japan). The proportion of elderly non-working persons with respect to the total active population will thus increase on average from 26% to 42% between 2005 and 2030, with substantial proportions of non-working people in certain OECD

Figure 2.1. **Population projections for the 18-24 age group in 2015 and 2025**

(2005 = 100)

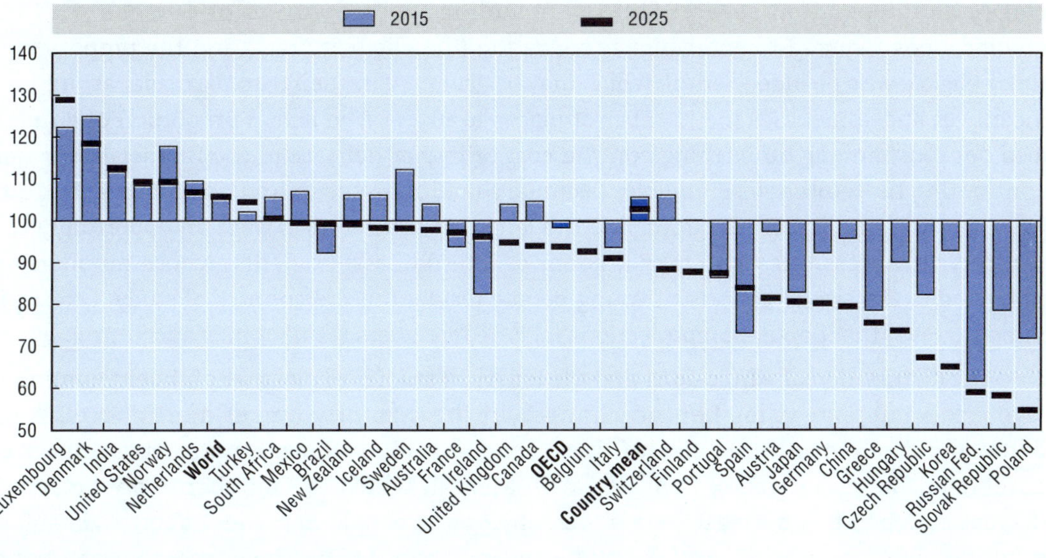

Source: United Nations, median projections (2006 revision).

countries (OECD, 2007a). According to UN median demographic projections (as revised in 2006), the 18-24 age group, which customarily accounts for the lion's share of student enrolments in OECD countries, will have fallen on average by 9% by 2025. This decrease will be gradual, as the 18-24 age cohort is expected to increase in 16 OECD countries in the period up to 2015, and in 10 up to 2020, but in just seven by 2025. Between 2005 and 2025, the number of young people aged 18-24 should rise by over 10% in two OECD countries (Denmark and Luxembourg), and is expected to fall by over 15% in 10 countries (Austria, the Czech Republic, Germany, Greece, Hungary, Japan, Korea, Poland, the Slovak Republic and Spain). Figure 2.1 summarises these trends and illustrates the demographic profile of a few other countries (Brazil, Russia, India, China and South Africa) (see Table 2.A2.1 for full details).

Sluggish trends in demography and student enrolments

All other things being equal, demography directly affects student enrolments in higher education because the size of younger age cohorts is a partial determinant of the number of students. Given that in OECD countries for which information is available, around 80% of students in higher education on average are aged less than 25, the relative impact of younger age cohorts has a major bearing on student enrolment levels. If rates of entry to higher education, together with survival rates, the average length of courses and other student-related factors (age, etc.) remain unchanged, countries in which those cohorts decrease in size will normally experience a fall in their student enrolments.

Yet the relationship between demography – or more specifically the size of the younger age cohorts – and higher education enrolment levels is a complex one. Student numbers depend on the access (or entry) rates of different cohorts in the population at different ages and, therefore, on the distribution of admissions and the duration of studies irrespective of whether the latter result in drop-out or a graduate qualification (see Annex 2.A1).

Several factors may offset decreases in cohort size, such as an increase in rates of access to higher education or a change in the length of studies. Where the structure of courses remains unchanged, studies may last longer because of a fall in drop-out rates, a growth in part-time student enrolments or an increase in the general level of education. Access rates clarify and depend on several factors, including the proportion of persons with the qualifications required to enter higher education (the eligibility rate) and the proportion of those eligible who do indeed enrol, which may be governed by their own particular aspirations, incentives and sometimes the number of places available. The actual proportion of entrants also depends, among other things on the cost of higher education, the financial pressures confronting those otherwise eligible, pecuniary (and non-pecuniary) advantages that they hope to gain from higher education and the length of their studies from an opportunity cost perspective. Access rates also take account of international students, whose numbers are unrelated to the size of cohorts of young people resident in the country of study (bearing in mind however that population projections include foreigners resident in that country).

The distribution of admissions and the length of studies explain why student enrolment levels to some extent lag behind changes in the size of younger age cohorts. A big demographic change in the size of these cohorts will not have a noticeable impact on enrolment for several years. Consider a situation in which the number of young people decreases. When this decrease gets under way, young people in earlier cohorts will still be entering higher education, and it will be several years before the succession of smaller cohorts finally affects the system (entering it gradually over a given period): this corresponds

Box 2.1. **The lagging impact of demographic changes on student enrolment**

Let us assume that 30% of a cohort enters the higher education system each year and that each student studies for three years. If cohorts increase before decreasing in size, the number of students will only begin to fall one year after the demographic change and at first no more than gradually before starting to follow the downward slope of the cohort curve. If entry rates are allowed to increase regularly by 2% during the first five years, from 30% to 40%, before being held constant in subsequent years, it is clear that two years will now elapse before any fall in enrolments is observed. This example will appear more or less striking depending on the precise figures selected and is intended merely to convey the persistence of the trends occurring over time: with sometimes longer courses of study, many different cohorts entering higher education over an extended period, and differing drop-out rates, etc., these effects may be more sustained.

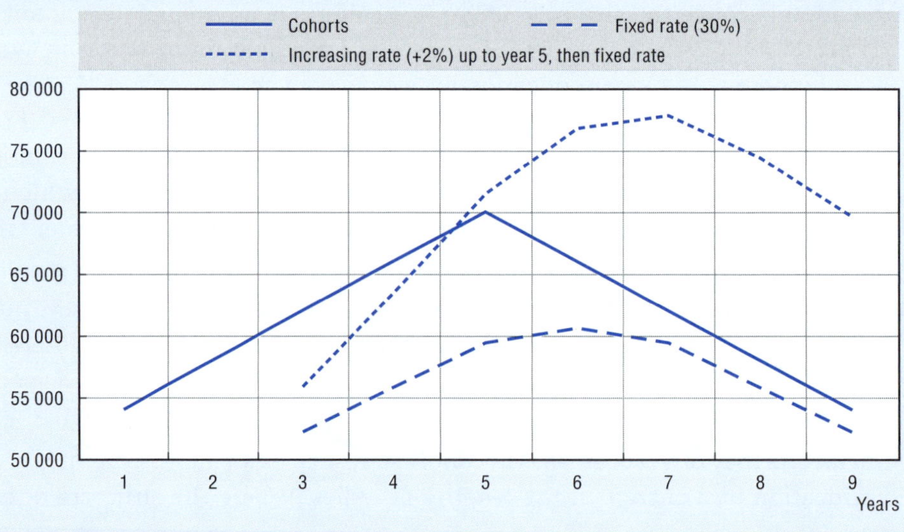

to the continued impact of past cohorts. The second reason for the time lag stems from past changes in entry rates: even if all students were to enter higher education at the same time, which is far from the case, their numbers could be reflected more in some cohorts than others in the system. Box 2.1 illustrates this with a simple hypothetical example.

Given this complexity, projections of future student enrolments have been made with effect from the entrance to the system of several cohorts of 17-year-olds over an extended period – in accordance with a model which, though simplified, captures some of this complexity (for the methodology, see Annex 2.A1).

The "status quo" scenario (scenario 1)

The first scenario considered is one of *status quo*. Table 2.1 sets out projections of student enrolments in the OECD countries if entry and survival rates remain as they were

Table 2.1. **Enrolment projections for tertiary students if entry rates remain at the 2004 level: scenario 1**

Thousands, full- and part-time

	Tertiary education (ISCED 5/6)				Index (2005 = 100)			Absolute difference		
	2005	2015	2020	2025	2015	2020	2025	2015	2020	2025
Australia	*1 025*	1 150	1 126	1 116	112	110	109	125	102	92
Austria	*244*	273	261	243	112	107	100	28	17	–1
Belgium	*390*	404	387	378	104	99	97	14	–2	–12
Canada	*m*	m	m	m	m	m	m	m	m	m
Czech Republic	*336*	361	307	286	107	91	85	25	–29	–50
Denmark	*232*	311	320	309	134	138	133	79	88	77
Finland	*306*	310	294	280	101	96	91	4	–12	–26
France	*2 187*	2 219	2 248	2 322	101	103	106	32	61	135
Germany	*2 269*	2 373	2 212	2 060	105	97	91	105	–57	–209
Greece	*647*	583	555	544	90	86	84	–63	–91	–102
Hungary	*436*	439	381	353	101	87	81	3	–55	–83
Iceland	*15*	18	17	16	117	110	107	3	2	1
Ireland	*187*	164	171	190	88	91	102	–23	–16	3
Italy	*2 015*	2 090	2 112	2 107	104	105	105	75	97	92
Japan	*4 038*	3 514	3 505	3 298	87	87	82	–524	–533	–740
Korea	*3 210*	2 921	2 613	2 115	91	81	66	–290	–597	–1 096
Luxembourg	*m*	m	m	m	m	m	m	m	m	m
Mexico	*2 385*	2,544	2 503	2 418	107	105	101	159	118	33
Netherlands	*565*	633	630	631	112	111	112	68	65	66
New Zealand	*240*	m	m	m	m	m	m	m	m	m
Norway	*214*	253	253	244	118	118	114	39	39	30
Poland	*2 118*	1 624	1 327	1 171	77	63	55	–494	–791	–947
Portugal	*381*	m	m	m	m	m	m	m	m	m
Slovak Republic	*181*	161	132	121	89	73	67	–20	–50	–61
Spain	*1 809*	1 382	1 348	1 467	76	74	81	–428	–462	–342
Sweden	*427*	559	504	478	131	118	112	132	78	51
Switzerland	*200*	244	230	212	122	115	106	44	31	13
Turkey	*2 106*	2 358	2 336	2 237	112	111	106	252	229	131
United Kingdom	*2 288*	2 445	2 290	2 252	107	100	98	157	2	–36
United States	*17 272*	19 287	19 082	19 256	112	110	111	2 015	1 810	1 984
OECD	***47 723***	**48 621**	**47 145**	**46 104**	**103**	**100**	**98**	**898**	**–578**	**–1 619**
Country mean					**104**	**100**	**96**			

m = missing.

Note: Estimates are based on the number of students enrolled both full-time and part-time, and on the entry and drop-out rates for 2004, as well as on the UN median population projections for 2000 (as revised in 2006). These estimates are not precise forecasts but projections intended purely as a guide. For the methodology, see Annex 2.A1.

in 2004. In this scenario, the changes are essentially demographic and depend solely on the size of the younger age cohorts (a simplified model in the sense that access to higher education terminates at the age of 28), and on changes in entry rates between 1998 and 2004. As has been noted, the impact of the increase in these rates is observed at a later stage when the distribution of individual entrance to higher education is taken into account, so this scenario in which entry rates are frozen is not strictly consistent with the demographic trends.

According to this scenario, countries would on average have 3% more students in 2015, with their numbers then falling back, but just gradually, to the same level in 2020 as in 2005, and then to 2% beneath the 2005 level in 2025. Because of the demographic changes anticipated, the higher education systems of several countries would contract in the years ahead, if there were no growth in their student access rates: the Czech Republic, Hungary, Japan, Korea, Poland, the Slovak Republic and Spain would experience a contraction of over 15% in 2025 compared to 2005. The decrease might already have reached this level in 2015 in Poland and Spain, and in 2020 in Korea and the Slovak Republic. In comparison to their current enrolment levels, Denmark, Iceland, Norway, Sweden and Switzerland would for their part experience an increase of over 15% by 2015, but only Denmark would still be in this position in 2025.

In highlighting a phenomenon that is essentially (though not exclusively) demographic, this scenario reveals that individual OECD countries exhibit very contrasting situations but that the overall picture remains fairly unspectacular.

The trend scenario (scenario 2)

The rise in entry rates may offset decreases in student enrolments or accelerate their growth. The "massification" of higher education in many countries did not always occur at a time of demographic growth: in the United States, the most recent major phase of expansion coincided with a decrease in the size of its younger age cohorts (Anderson and Cook, 2008).

Table 2.2 illustrates projections of student enrolments in higher education systems in accordance with a trend scenario. Rather than freezing rates of entry to higher education at their 2004 level, the rates are extrapolated linearly on the basis of the trends in each country between 2000 and 2004. Aside from the quality of the data available, one reason for selecting a short time series is to limit the perceived impact of the previous expansion of systems. In some countries such as Germany or France, this decision may have a bearing on the projections, because of renewed growth in participation during these years after a period of very little change. As previously, the survival rates are those for 2004, and the demographic projections those of the UN (as revised in 2006, for the median scenario). The underlying reasoning here is that rates of entry to higher education will increase in future years in countries in which they are fairly low, whereas countries that have already achieved "universal" participation are at saturation point so that the size of their cohorts is a more decisive factor. The upper limit on entry rates has been set at 90% in line with the principle that "universal" participation in higher education can never reach the same levels as in primary and secondary education – quite simply because the students concerned are young adults among whom a certain minimum proportion will always refuse to embark on non-compulsory education. While the ceiling has been set at a high level to accommodate significant potential for growth in the various countries, it in fact represents the prevailing level in Korea (in which,

Table 2.2. **Enrolment projections for tertiary students if entry rates continue to grow: scenario 2**

Thousands, full- and part-time

	Tertiary education (ISCED 5/6)				Index (2005 = 100)			Absolute difference		
	2005	2015	2020	2025	2015	2020	2025	2015	2020	2025
Australia	*1 025*	1 163	1 172	1 192	114	114	116	139	147	168
Austria	*244*	297	309	314	121	126	128	52	65	69
Belgium	*390*	393	377	368	101	97	94	4	–13	–22
Canada	*m*	m	m	m	m	m	m	m	m	m
Czech Republic	*336*	426	397	404	127	118	120	90	61	68
Denmark	*232*	325	335	323	140	144	139	93	102	91
Finland	*306*	324	316	307	106	103	100	18	10	1
France	*2 187*	2 372	2 549	2 776	108	117	127	185	361	589
Germany	*2 269*	2 731	2 840	2 911	120	125	128	462	571	642
Greece	*647*	604	616	650	93	95	101	–42	–31	4
Hungary	*436*	461	401	372	106	92	85	25	–35	–64
Iceland	*15*	18	17	17	119	113	110	3	2	1
Ireland	*187*	175	197	234	94	105	125	–11	10	47
Italy	*2 015*	2 239	2 405	2 569	111	119	127	224	390	554
Japan	*4 038*	3 714	3 857	3 765	92	96	93	–325	–182	–273
Korea	*3 210*	2 971	2 694	2 208	93	84	69	–239	–516	–1 002
Luxembourg	*0*	m	m	m	m	m	m	m	m	m
Mexico	*2 385*	3 062	3 307	3 468	128	139	145	677	922	1 083
Netherlands	*565*	701	746	793	124	132	140	136	181	228
New Zealand	*240*	240	240	240	m	m	m	m	m	m
Norway	*214*	269	277	271	126	129	127	55	63	57
Poland	*2 118*	1 742	1 482	1 343	82	70	63	–376	–636	–775
Portugal	*381*	m	m	m	m	m	m	m	m	m
Slovak Republic	*181*	182	163	162	100	90	89	0	–19	–19
Spain	*1 809*	1 457	1 466	1 646	81	81	91	–352	–343	–164
Sweden	*427*	570	516	489	134	121	115	143	89	62
Switzerland	*200*	264	269	266	132	135	133	64	70	66
Turkey	*2 106*	3 066	3 453	3 687	146	164	175	960	1 347	1 580
United Kingdom	*2 288*	2 594	2 528	2 578	113	110	113	306	240	290
United States	*17 272*	19 796	20 045	20 679	115	116	120	2 524	2 773	3 407
OECD	***47 723***	**52 538**	**53 354**	**54 412**	**112**	**113**	**116**	**4 815**	**5 632**	**6 689**
Country mean					**113**	**113**	**114**			

m = missing.

Note: Estimates are based on the number of students enrolled both full- and part-time, and on the entry and drop-out rates for 2004, as well as on the UN median population projections for 2000 (as revised in 2006). In the case of the United States, scenarios 1 and 2 are identical because entry rates in recent years have remained at a fixed upper level. The figures shown correspond to a "third" scenario in which entry rates increase very gradually by an annual average of 0.25%. These estimates are not precise forecasts but projections intended purely as a guide. For the methodology, see Annex 2.A1.

according to national data, around 80% of 18-year-olds enter higher education). The high level also compensates for the simplified perspective of the model in which access to higher education is limited to those aged 17-28.

In comparison with the first scenario, the situation changes very markedly (see Figure 2.2). On average, student enrolment levels in countries in 2005 would increase by 13% in 2015 and 2020, and by 14% in 2025 – with the growth in enrolments slightly higher in 2025 when expressed in terms of weighted averages. In the case of certain countries, the difference between the two scenarios is substantial. While in the first scenario a country like the Czech Republic would experience a 15% decrease in enrolments

Figure 2.2. **Trends in student enrolments between 2005 and 2025 on the basis of scenarios 1 and 2**

(2005 = 100)

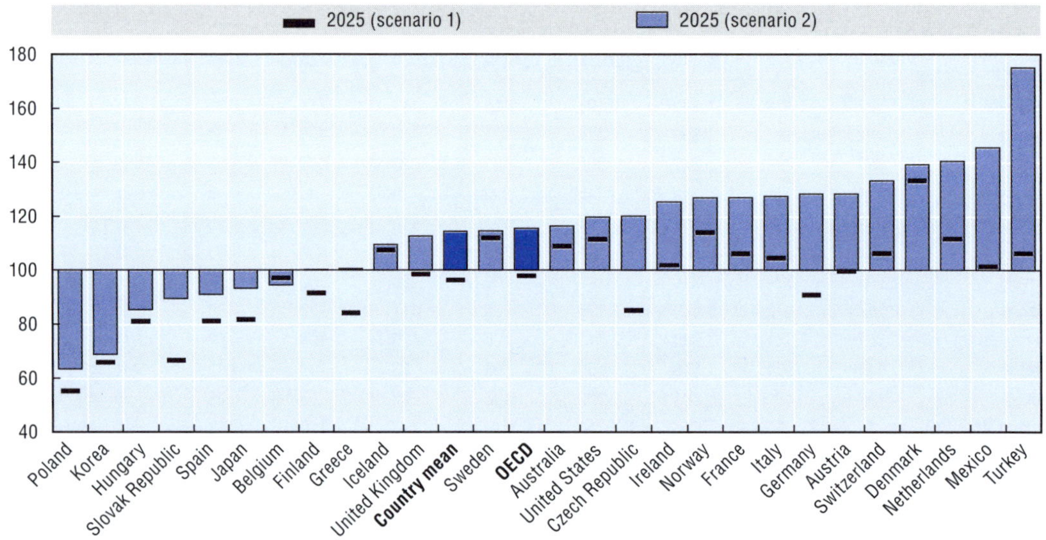

in 2025, in this trend scenario the system would continue to expand and could well grow by 20% in the years up to 2025. The scope in this country for greater participation in higher education thus remains a very significant factor. The difference is also considerable in Austria or Germany, for example, or indeed in the Slovak Republic, in which the decrease in enrolments remains very limited. In the United States, Korea, Poland or Sweden, the two scenarios barely differ because the rates of entry to higher education in these countries have changed very little in recent years, or because the rates were already high and therefore unlikely to grow strongly any further. In Germany, Mexico or Turkey, the growth in rates of entry to higher education is the main factor driving the growth in enrolments. In certain countries, such as Mexico and above all Turkey, growth will probably be more restrained however, simply because it is easier for systems to expand rapidly when they are small (relatively speaking) than when they are already large: linear extrapolation tends to accentuate long-term future growth when current growth is very fast. Nevertheless, in both these countries today, the demand for higher education easily exceeds the provision the system has to offer.

Figure 2.3 illustrates the continuous projected trends, country by country.

Why will expansion probably continue?

How far may recent trends reasonably be expected to continue? They might be affected by a change in higher education policy or labour market conditions. In countries in which the overall advantages enjoyed by graduates in terms of income-earning potential are relatively modest (or perceived to be so), a change in the economic fortunes of a country may immediately influence whether people decide to study. Thus Sweden experienced two small successive decreases in student enrolment (in 2004-05 and 2005-06) at a time of economic revival, although the model indicates that enrolments will increase. The continued growth of "massification" is also beset by many uncertainties. While countries such as Japan or Korea demonstrate that virtually universal participation in higher

Figure 2.3. **Size of cohorts of young people aged 17 and student enrolments according to the two scenarios: trends and country projections**

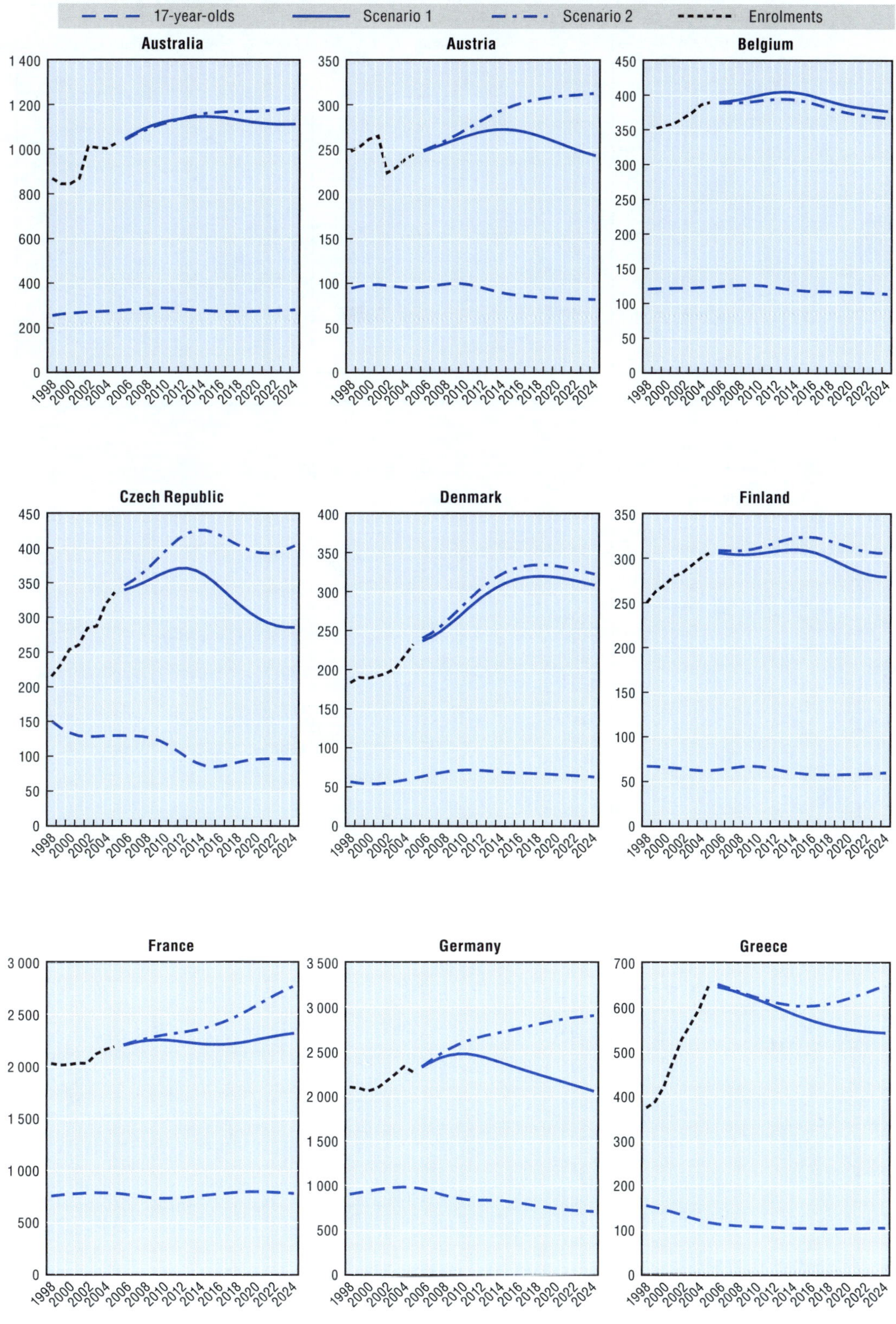

Source: OECD and UN Population Division (as revised in 2006).

Figure 2.3. **Size of cohorts of young people aged 17 and student enrolments according to the two scenarios: trends and country projections** *(cont.)*

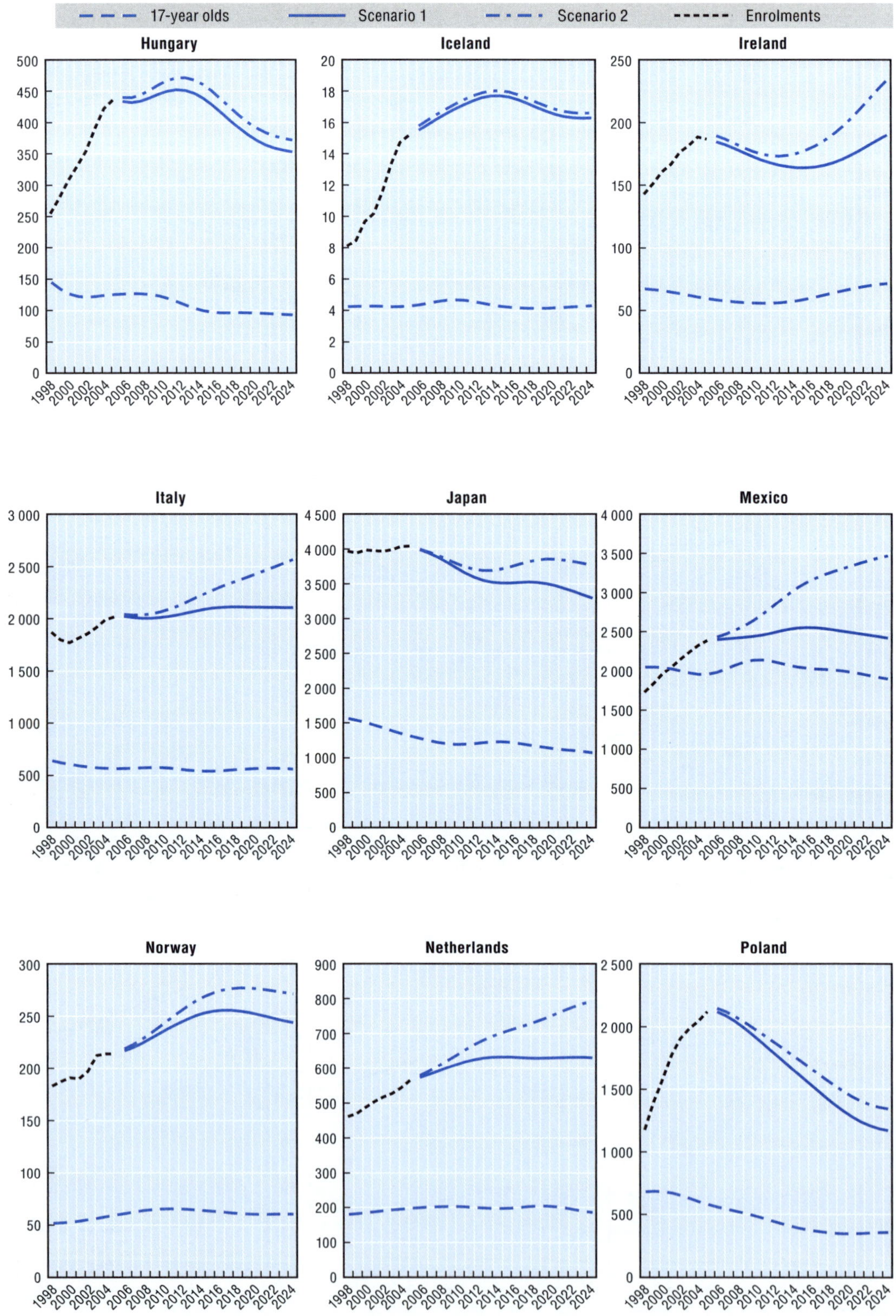

Source: OECD and UN Population Division (as revised in 2006).

Figure 2.3. **Size of cohorts of young people aged 17 and student enrolments according to the two scenarios: trends and country projections** *(cont.)*

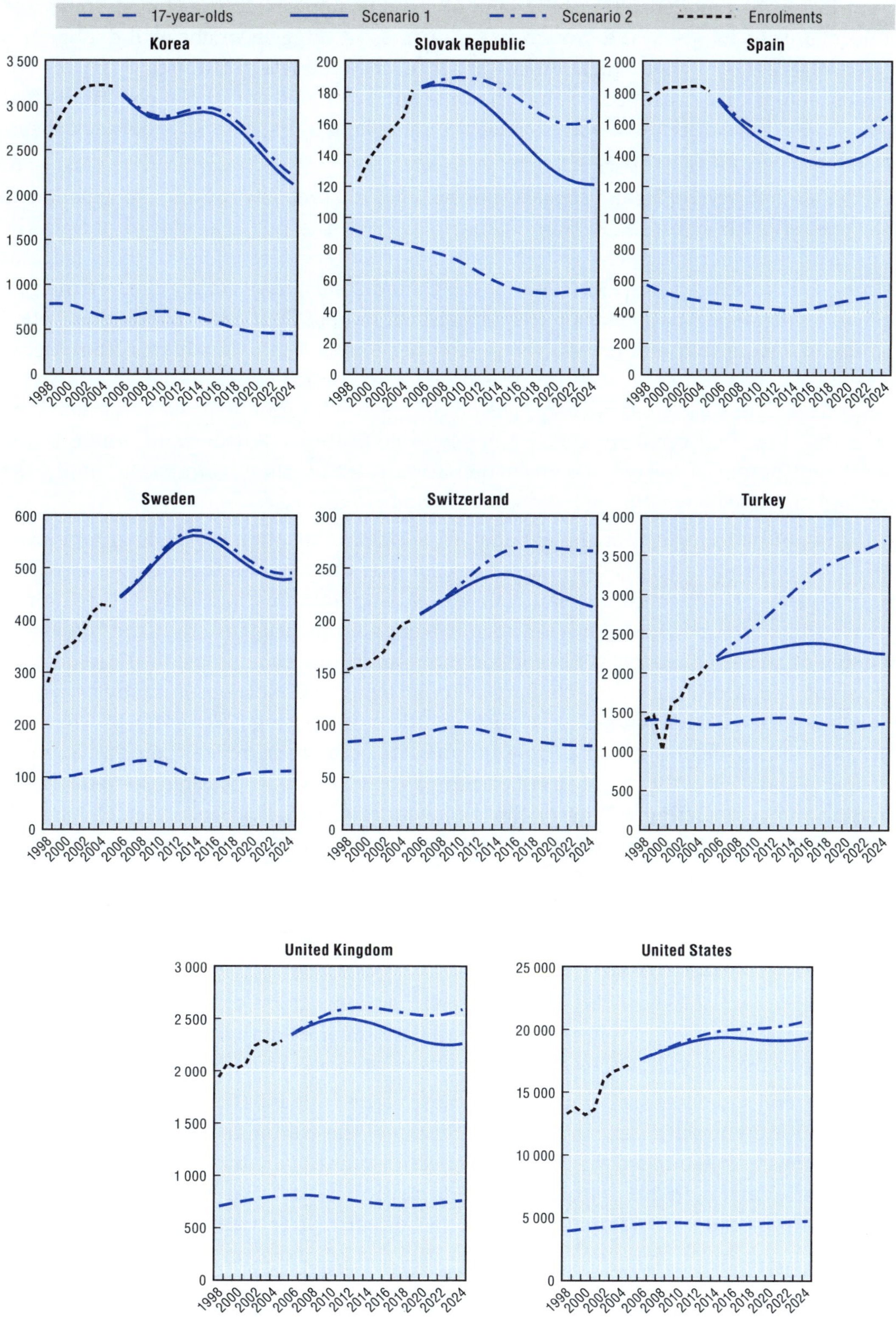

Source: OECD and UN Population Division (as revised in 2006).

education is possible, entry rates in other countries such as the United States have changed very little in recent years so that it is not unreasonable to suppose that other western countries might experience the same kind of stability. Conversely, the United States and other countries in which the growth in entry rates is sluggish might well deliberately increase access to higher education so that it reaches the levels of Korea or Japan. The trend scenario thus presupposes that the political, economic and social conditions that have shaped the earlier trend will exercise the same kind of impact in the decades ahead, though possibly for other reasons.

For all that, several factors suggest that systems will probably continue to expand and that scenario 2 is more likely than scenario 1. First, the political will to pursue the expansion of higher education systems exists in most countries. Many of them (such as Denmark, France, the United Kingdom or the United States) have set themselves the goal of broadening access or increasing the educational level of their adult population – often aiming to ensure that half an age group is either enrolled in or graduates from higher education. This stance is shaping the policies and strategies of higher education institutions, and suggests that the provision of higher education will not be rationed but encouraged by policy makers and the heads of institutions. Furthermore, there is still significant potential for growth in participation rates in many countries. Finally, the demand for higher education will probably continue to increase.

It might be thought that the expansion of higher education would lead to a lower return on investment for its graduates. For example, the bonuses they receive are often more modest in OECD countries than in the developing countries, in which participation in higher education is lower. However, recent trends do not suggest that the individual benefits of higher education are becoming more uniformly comparable to those possible for young people with a final secondary school leaving qualification: in many cases, the returns associated with degrees are changing little or increasing (OECD, 2007b). There are therefore strong incentives for people to graduate so as to increase their employment prospects and further their chances of earning a good living. It is possible that policies for funding and cost-sharing will lower these individual rewards, but the cases of Australia and the United Kingdom demonstrate that introducing and then increasing registration fees have had very little effect on student participation (Santiago *et al.*, 2008; Marks and McMillan, 2007). It is unlikely that in two decades the cost of higher education would be such as to discourage large numbers of students from pursuing their education at this level.

Tables 2.1 and 2.2 show the scale of growth or contraction of the higher education system in the two scenarios. The many simplified theories derived from the projection model mean that they should be used for guidance purposes rather than forecasting.

The trend estimates are comparable to those carried out at national level, where these exist (and are known to us). In the United States, the National Center for Education Statistics has thus estimated that the number of full-time or part-time students enrolled in higher education in 2014 would be 19.5 million[1] – a level comparable to the scenario 1 projection of 19.2 million in 2015. In Germany, projections have estimated that the student population would be 2.5 million in 2015 and 2.4 million in 2020, corresponding to comparable scales and rates of growth and then contraction.[2] In Hungary, projections put student enrolments by 2015, 2020 and 2030 at 520 000, 543 000 and 625 000 respectively.[3] This trend runs counter to the projections in our model which suggest that enrolments in

Hungary might fall because of a decrease in the size of the younger age cohorts and a tendency for higher education access rates to remain level. Inconsistencies of this kind serve as a reminder once more of the care required in interpreting estimates and projections, and of the significance of their underlying assumptions which contain simplifications not necessarily fully consistent with the circumstances of particular countries. Indeed, projections carried out on a country-by-country basis might well have produced slightly different results, if only because they could have reflected the potential impact of recent or publicly announced policies: as an example one might cite the admission of cohorts twice the normal size to higher education in Germany as a result of shortening general secondary education in the *Gymnasium* from nine years to eight between 2007 and 2014 in a majority of *Länder* (Gabriel, von Stuckrad and Witte, 2007).

In certain countries in which part-time study is a common occurrence, there may be a sizeable difference between the number of students enrolled full-time and part-time, and the number of full-time equivalent enrolments. Projections for the number of full-time equivalent enrolments are also annexed in Tables 2.A2.2 and 2.A2.3.

2.2. Impact on the budget for higher education

The ageing of the population has many implications for public expenditure and its distribution across various generations and age cohorts, as well as for the workforce. Many countries will have to contend with increasingly high dependence rates (expressed as the percentage of non-working persons with respect to the workforce): between 2005 and 2030, the dependence rate for the OECD is expected to rise from 26% to 42%, and from 36% to 54% in the case of the 15 initial European Union member countries (OECD, 2007a).

The ageing of the population might have an indirect impact on the funding of higher education: in societies in which a large proportion of the population and the electorate are elderly, education and higher education may appear to be a lower priority in terms of social options than in the past. Funding for pensions, health care and other services associated with ageing is a challenge that might lead to financial settlements prejudicial to public expenditure on higher education. In such a context, increasing public expenditure in this sector might be difficult. That said, it is also possible that elderly persons and policy makers will attach as much if not more importance to education and higher education than at present, either on altruistic grounds or because they stand to benefit indirectly from doing so (Poterba, 1998; Gradstein and Kaganovich, 2004). For example, the novel demands of an ageing society might change the priorities of governments and institutions, so that greater emphasis is placed on health disciplines, etc. Empirical research on this subject yields no firm conclusions. While, in Switzerland, educational expenditure is slowly coming to reflect demographic changes, the presence of an elderly population in the cantons has a distinctly negative impact on the level of educational funding (Grob and Wolter, 2007). In the United States, the elderly do not appear to have negative attitudes to education, and while a more elderly population is generally associated with lower levels of educational spending in the individual States, this does not apply to the "micro" level of districts (Poterba, 1997, 1998; Harris, Evans and Schwab, 2001).

In any event, increases or decreases in student enrolments have direct budgetary implications for all those with a stake in higher education. Expenditure on higher education depends on the level of enrolment and the cost of educational provision per student. In many countries, public-sector institutions receive grants on the basis of their enrolments or graduates (Santiago *et al.*, 2008). A decrease in enrolments may provide scope for increasing the funding per student, for example by lowering the student-teacher ratio. All other things being equal, it reduces the budgetary pressure on public expenditure. At institutional level and depending on its magnitude, it may result in an improvement in learning or working conditions – and thus may have a positive impact on the quality of higher education. However, a decrease in enrolments may also amount to a budgetary "crisis" if they become too low to support the costs incurred by institutions.

Given that in most OECD countries, education is still funded primarily from public sources (though Korea and Japan are two exceptions), the issue of the budget is primarily one of public expenditure, bearing in mind that it is politically easier to maintain a public budget at around the same level than to increase it significantly.

The budgetary impact of changes in student demography on the cost of higher education may be estimated in the two foregoing scenarios. This is a means of understanding how possible trends in student enrolment affect the cost of higher education and, in particular, funding from public sources. But it also provides an illustration of how the cost of education depends on several factors other than demography.

The budgetary projections are based on simple assumptions regarding trends in costs and the level of national resources. The first is that GDP and costs per student in higher education (at constant prices) both grow at similar moderate rates: the annual GDP growth rate has been set at 2%, and the rate of growth in expenditure per student attending higher education institutions at its average annual rate of 1.6% between 1995 and 2005 (in countries for which information was available). As countries are at different stages of investing or decreasing their investment, it may be considered that reasoning in terms of the average will minimise the seasonal effects involved.

Tables 2.3 and 2.4 show the impact of changes in student enrolments on the total budget earmarked for higher education in scenarios 1 and 2, as well as the corresponding breakdown into public and private expenditure if the distribution of costs between public and private sources were to remain the same as in 2005. Public expenditure on higher education institutions includes public grants to them, as well as transfers to families later passed on to institutions. Scenario 1 (*status quo*) would imply that total expenditure on higher education between 2005 and 2025 remained unchanged at 1.4% of GDP, with a slight increase to 1.6% by 2015. Public expenditure in countries would fall on average by 0.1 percentage points of GDP if cost-sharing between public and private sources of funding remained the same as in 2005. Scenario 2 (trend-related) would imply an average increase in expenditure between 2005 and 2025, to 1.6% of GDP, with a slight rise to 1.7% by 2015. The share of public expenditure would also increase slightly by 0.1 percentage points of GDP. However, this general tendency to stability belies differing trends between countries, with increases of 0.7 percentage points of GDP or more in Denmark, Mexico and the United States, and a decrease of 0.7 percentage points in Korea. While in most countries, the impact on public expenditure is similar to that on total expenditure, this is not so in some countries given the scale of their private contributions to the funding of higher education. Thus in the United States the total projected increase is relatively high (0.7 percentage points of GDP), although the rise in public expenditure (0.2 percentage points of GDP) remains close to the average for other countries.

Table 2.5 shows these same projections expressed as a percentage of total public expenditure (if this were to remain at the same current level as a proportion of GDP). It

Table 2.3. **Impact of scenario 1 on total expenditure for tertiary education institutions**

	Projected expenditure as share of projected GDP				Projected public and private expenditure as share of projected GDP							
	2005	2015	2020	2025	*2005*		2015		2020		2025	
					Public	*Private*	Public	Private	Public	Private	Public	Private
Australia	*1.6*	1.8	1.7	1.7	*0.8*	*0.8*	0.9	0.9	0.8	0.9	0.8	0.9
Austria	*1.3*	1.4	1.3	1.2	*1.2*	*0.1*	1.4	0.1	1.3	0.1	1.1	0.1
Belgium	*1.2*	1.3	1.2	1.2	*1.2*	*0.1*	1.2	0.1	1.2	0.1	1.1	0.1
Canada	*2.6*	m	m	m	*1.4*	*1.1*	m	m	m	m	m	m
Czech Republic	*1.0*	1.1	0.9	0.8	*0.8*	*0.2*	0.9	0.2	0.8	0.2	0.7	0.2
Denmark	*1.7*	2.4	2.4	2.3	*1.6*	*0.1*	2.3	0.1	2.3	0.1	2.2	0.1
Finland	*1.7*	1.8	1.6	1.5	*1.7*	*0.1*	1.7	0.1	1.6	0.1	1.5	0.1
France	*1.3*	1.4	1.4	1.4	*1.1*	*0.2*	1.2	0.2	1.2	0.2	1.2	0.2
Germany	*1.1*	1.1	1.0	1.0	*0.9*	*0.2*	1.0	0.2	0.9	0.2	0.8	0.1
Greece	*1.5*	1.5	1.4	1.4	*1.4*	*n*	1.5	0.1	1.4	0.0	1.3	0.0
Hungary	*1.1*	1.4	1.2	1.1	*0.9*	*0.2*	1.1	0.3	0.9	0.3	0.9	0.2
Iceland	*1.2*	1.5	1.4	1.3	*1.1*	*0.1*	1.4	0.1	1.3	0.1	1.2	0.1
Ireland	*1.2*	1.1	1.2	1.3	*1.0*	*0.1*	1.0	0.1	1.0	0.1	1.1	0.1
Italy	*0.9*	1.1	1.0	1.0	*0.6*	*0.3*	0.7	0.3	0.7	0.3	0.7	0.3
Japan	*1.4*	1.1	1.1	1.0	*0.5*	*0.9*	0.4	0.7	0.4	0.7	0.3	0.7
Korea	*2.4*	2.4	2.1	1.7	*0.6*	*1.8*	0.6	1.8	0.5	1.6	0.4	1.3
Luxembourg	*m*	m	m	m	*m*	*m*	m	*m*	m	m	m	m
Mexico	*1.3*	1.9	1.8	1.7	*0.9*	*0.4*	1.3	0.6	1.3	0.5	1.2	0.5
Netherlands	*1.3*	1.6	1.5	1.5	*1.0*	*0.3*	1.2	0.3	1.2	0.3	1.2	0.3
New Zealand	*1.5*	m	m	m	*0.9*	*0.6*	m	m	m	m	m	m
Norway	*1.3*	m	m	m	*1.3*	*m*	m	m	m	m	m	m
Poland	*1.6*	1.3	1.1	0.9	*1.2*	*0.4*	1.0	0.3	0.8	0.3	0.7	0.2
Portugal	*1.4*	m	m	m	*0.9*	*0.4*	m	m	m	m	m	m
Slovak Republic	*0.9*	0.9	0.7	0.6	*0.7*	*0.2*	0.7	0.2	0.5	0.1	0.4	0.1
Spain	*1.1*	1.0	0.9	1.0	*0.9*	*0.2*	0.8	0.2	0.7	0.2	0.8	0.2
Sweden	*1.6*	2.2	1.8	1.7	*1.5*	*0.2*	1.9	0.2	1.6	0.2	1.5	0.2
Switzerland	*1.4*	m	m	m	*1.4*	*m*	m	m	m	m	m	m
Turkey	*m*	m	m	m	*m*	*m*	m	m	m	m	m	m
United Kingdom	*1.3*	1.5	1.4	1.3	*0.9*	*0.4*	1.0	0.5	0.9	0.5	0.9	0.4
United States	*2.9*	3.5	3.3	3.3	*1.0*	*1.9*	1.2	2.3	1.2	2.2	1.2	2.2
Country mean	***1.4***	**1.6**	**1.4**	**1.4**	***1.1***	***0.4***	**1.2**	**0.4**	**1.1**	**0.4**	**1.0**	**0.4**

m = missing.

Note: In the case of all countries, annual growth in GDP and expenditure per student at constant prices have been set at 2% and 1.6%, respectively. Public expenditure includes transfers to households, which are subsequently passed on to institutions (*cf.* OECD, 2007b).

corresponds therefore to the national public commitment to direct expenditure on higher education following an increase in the budget – or, on the contrary, shows how the decrease in enrolments might unlock extra public resources whether for reinvestment in higher education or other publicly funded activities. Scenario 1 would represent scope for reinvestment of 0.3% of public expenditure on average, with the proportion of public expenditure on higher education falling from 2.5% to 2.2%. Scenario 2 would represent an average rise of 0.2% in public expenditure on higher education. Here again, countries exhibit significant differences. However, the impact of demographic changes would remain limited in a majority of countries.

Table 2.4. **Impact of scenario 2 on total expenditure for tertiary education institutions**

	Projected expenditure as share of projected GDP				Projected public and private expenditure as share of projected GDP							
	2005	2015	2020	2025	*2005*		2015		2020		2025	
					Public	*Private*	Public	Private	Public	Private	Public	Private
Australia	*1.6*	1.9	1.9	1.9	*0.8*	*0.8*	0.9	1.0	0.9	1.0	0.9	1.0
Austria	*1.3*	1.6	1.7	1.6	*1.2*	*0.1*	1.5	0.1	1.6	0.1	1.6	0.1
Belgium	*1.2*	1.3	1.2	1.2	*1.2*	*0.1*	1.2	0.1	1.2	0.1	1.1	0.1
Canada	*2.6*	m	m	m	*1.4*	*1.1*	m	m	m	m	m	m
Czech Republic	*1.0*	1.4	1.3	1.3	*0.8*	*0.2*	1.2	0.3	1.0	0.2	1.0	0.2
Denmark	*1.7*	2.5	2.5	2.4	*1.6*	*0.1*	2.4	0.1	2.5	0.1	2.3	0.1
Finland	*1.7*	1.8	1.7	1.6	*1.7*	*0.1*	1.8	0.1	1.7	0.1	1.6	0.1
France	*1.3*	1.5	1.6	1.7	*1.1*	*0.2*	1.3	0.2	1.4	0.2	1.4	0.2
Germany	*1.1*	1.3	1.3	1.3	*0.9*	*0.2*	1.1	0.2	1.1	0.2	1.1	0.2
Greece	*1.5*	1.5	1.5	1.6	*1.4*	*n*	1.5	0.1	1.5	0.0	1.5	0.1
Hungary	*1.1*	1.5	1.3	1.2	*0.9*	*0.2*	1.2	0.3	1.0	0.3	0.9	0.3
Iceland	*1.2*	1.7	1.5	1.5	*1.1*	*0.1*	1.5	0.1	1.4	0.1	1.3	0.1
Ireland	*1.2*	1.2	1.3	1.5	*1.0*	*0.1*	1.1	0.1	1.2	0.1	1.4	0.2
Italy	*0.9*	1.1	1.2	1.2	*0.6*	*0.3*	0.8	0.3	0.8	0.4	0.9	0.4
Japan	*1.4*	1.2	1.2	1.1	*0.5*	*0.9*	0.4	0.8	0.4	0.8	0.4	0.8
Korea	*2.4*	2.4	2.1	1.7	*0.6*	*1.8*	0.6	1.8	0.5	1.6	0.4	1.3
Luxembourg	*m*	m	m	m	*m*	*m*	m	m	m	m	m	m
Mexico	*1.3*	2.2	2.4	2.4	*0.9*	*0.4*	1.6	0.7	1.6	0.7	1.7	0.7
Netherlands	*1.3*	1.7	1.8	1.9	*1.0*	*0.3*	1.4	0.4	1.4	0.4	1.5	0.4
New Zealand	*1.5*	m	m	m	*0.9*	*0.6*	m	m	m	m	m	m
Norway	*1.3*	m	m	m	*1.3*	*m*	m	m	m	m	m	m
Poland	*1.6*	1.5	1.2	1.1	*1.2*	*0.4*	1.1	0.4	0.9	0.3	0.8	0.3
Portugal	*1.4*	m	m	m	*0.9*	*0.4*	m	m	m	m	m	m
Slovak Republic	*0.9*	1.1	0.9	0.9	*0.7*	*0.2*	0.8	0.2	0.7	0.2	0.7	0.2
Spain	*1.1*	1.0	1.0	1.2	*0.9*	*0.2*	0.8	0.2	0.8	0.2	0.9	0.2
Sweden	*1.6*	2.1	1.8	1.8	*1.5*	*0.2*	1.9	0.2	1.6	0.2	1.6	0.2
Switzerland	*1.4*	m	m	m	*1.4*	*m*	m	m	m	m	m	m
Turkey	*m*	m	m	m	*m*	*m*	m	m	m	m	m	m
United Kingdom	*1.3*	1.6	1.5	1.6	*0.9*	*0.4*	1.1	0.5	1.0	0.5	1.0	0.5
United States	*2.9*	3.5	3.5	3.6	*1.0*	*1.9*	1.2	2.3	1.2	2.3	1.2	2.3
Country mean	***1.4***	**1.7**	**1.6**	**1.6**	***1.1***	***0.4***	**1.3**	**0.4**	**1.2**	**0.4**	**1.2**	**0.4**

m = missing.
Note: See Table 2.3.

Can increases and decreases in the budget be attributed to changes in student demographic trends? Only up to a point. Table 2.6 indicates that demographic changes would account for an average increase of 0.16 percentage points of GDP between 2005 and 2025 in the trend scenario (compared to 0.25 altogether), and a decrease of 0.1 percentage points in scenario 1 (instead of very little change). Changes in costs are not related just to changes in the number of students, but also to trends in expenditure per student and in the level of national resources – and, in the case of public expenditure, to the relative share of public and private funding. The *relative* reduction in expenditure sometimes stems from its being expressed as a proportion of national assets. Figure 2.4 shows the difference between the growth in expenditure and in student enrolments in the trend scenario (scenario 2).

The budgetary projections shown should be interpreted with caution because of a series of limitations: once more, their purpose is primarily heuristic.

Table 2.5. **Impact of projections on total expenditure for tertiary education institutions, as share of public expenditure**

Public expenditure for tertiary education institutions as share of all public expenditure, 2005 and projections

	2005	Scenario 1			Scenario 2		
		2015	2020	2025	2015	2020	2025
Australia	*m*	2.5	2.4	2.3	2.7	2.6	2.7
Austria	*2.4*	2.7	2.5	2.3	3.1	3.2	3.1
Belgium	*2.2*	2.5	2.3	2.2	2.5	2.3	2.2
Canada	*3.5*	m	m	m	m	m	m
Czech Republic	*1.9*	2.1	1.7	1.6	2.6	2.4	2.4
Denmark	*3.1*	4.4	4.4	4.2	4.6	4.6	4.4
Finland	*3.3*	3.4	3.1	2.9	3.5	3.3	3.1
France	*2.1*	2.2	2.2	2.2	2.4	2.5	2.7
Germany	*2.0*	2.1	1.9	1.7	2.4	2.5	2.5
Greece	*m*	3.2	3.0	2.9	3.2	3.2	3.3
Hungary	*1.7*	2.2	1.8	1.7	2.3	1.9	1.8
Iceland	*2.6*	3.1	2.9	2.7	3.4	3.1	3.0
Ireland	*2.8*	3.0	3.1	3.4	3.2	3.5	4.1
Italy	*1.3*	1.5	1.5	1.5	1.6	1.7	1.8
Japan	*1.3*	1.0	1.0	0.9	1.1	1.1	1.0
Korea	*2.0*	2.1	1.8	1.5	2.1	1.9	1.5
Luxembourg	*m*	m	m	m	m	m	m
Mexico	*3.8*	m	m	m	m	m	m
Netherlands	*2.2*	2.7	2.6	2.6	3.0	3.1	3.3
New Zealand	*2.8*	m	m	m	m	m	m
Norway	*m*	m	m	m	m	m	m
Poland	*2.7*	2.2	1.8	1.5	2.4	2.0	1.9
Portugal	*1.9*	m	m	m	m	m	m
Slovak Republic	*3.5*	1.7	1.3	1.1	2.1	1.8	1.7
Spain	*2.3*	2.0	1.9	2.1	2.1	2.1	2.4
Sweden	*2.5*	3.4	2.9	2.7	3.3	2.7	2.7
Switzerland	*3.1*	m	m	m	m	m	m
Turkey	*m*	m	m	m	m	m	m
United Kingdom	*2.0*	2.2	2.0	2.0	2.4	2.3	2.3
United States	*2.7*	3.3	3.2	3.2	3.4	3.3	3.4
Country mean	***2.5***	**2.5**	**2.3**	**2.2**	**2.7**	**2.6**	**2.7**

m = missing.
Note: See Table 2.3.

There are many unknowns as regards the determining factors in the expenditure of higher education institutions. Some of it is linked to investment in infrastructure: if a country's past growth has been strongly tied to such investment, there is no reason why growth should continue if enrolments fall; conversely, if this is not the case, infrastructural investment may be expected to boost costs in countries about to experience sustained growth. Another share of expenditure – in fact the most important part – corresponds to the total wages bill of teaching and administrative staff, which is strongly related to the age of staff in salary systems based (mainly) on length of service. A major change in the age structure of staff might thus lead to an increase or decrease in institutional expenditure. The financial data shown also take account of staff retirement funds, thus incorporating a future-oriented budgetary factor.

A further limiting factor is that the reasoning here relates to expenditure finally allocated to higher education institutions. Yet indirect expenditure tied for example to

Table 2.6. **Impact of changes in enrolments on the budget for tertiary education institutions**

	Change in public and private expenditure for tertiary education institutions attributable to enrolment change as share of GDP						Change in public expenditure for tertiary education institutions attributable to enrolment change as share of all public expenditure					
	Scenario 1			Scenario 2			Scenario 1			Scenario 2		
	2015	2020	2025	2015	2020	2025	2015	2020	2025	2015	2020	2025
Australia	–0.02	–0.07	–0.07	0.14	0.13	0.18	–0.03	–0.10	–0.10	0.19	0.18	0.25
Austria	0.08	0.02	–0.07	0.29	0.35	0.37	0.16	0.04	–0.14	0.55	0.67	0.70
Belgium	0.01	–0.05	–0.08	–0.01	–0.06	–0.09	0.01	–0.09	–0.14	–0.01	–0.11	–0.16
Canada	m	m	m	m	m	m	m	m	m	m	m	m
Czech Republic	0.01	–0.17	–0.23	0.29	0.18	0.20	0.02	–0.31	–0.42	0.53	0.33	0.37
Denmark	0.58	0.63	0.53	0.70	0.74	0.64	1.05	1.14	0.96	1.27	1.35	1.16
Finland	0.06	–0.08	–0.12	0.11	0.02	–0.01	0.12	–0.15	–0.24	0.22	0.03	–0.02
France	0.03	0.05	0.09	0.14	0.24	0.38	0.05	0.08	0.15	0.22	0.39	0.60
Germany	0.05	–0.02	–0.09	0.23	0.27	0.30	0.10	–0.04	–0.17	0.42	0.50	0.55
Greece	–0.11	–0.18	–0.20	–0.13	–0.10	–0.01	–0.24	–0.38	–0.43	–0.27	–0.21	–0.03
Hungary	0.02	–0.18	–0.24	0.10	–0.11	–0.17	0.03	–0.28	–0.37	0.15	–0.17	–0.26
Iceland	0.14	0.04	0.01	0.28	0.17	0.14	0.29	0.09	0.02	0.57	0.36	0.29
Ireland	–0.09	–0.04	0.09	–0.03	0.12	0.37	–0.24	–0.11	0.24	–0.09	0.31	0.97
Italy	0.05	0.06	0.05	0.11	0.19	0.27	0.07	0.08	0.08	0.17	0.28	0.39
Japan	–0.15	–0.15	–0.21	–0.09	–0.04	–0.07	–0.14	–0.14	–0.19	–0.08	–0.04	–0.06
Korea	–0.20	–0.44	–0.81	–0.19	–0.41	–0.77	–0.17	–0.38	–0.71	–0.17	–0.36	–0.68
Luxembourg	m	m	m	m	m	m	m	m	m	m	m	m
Mexico	0.13	0.10	0.04	0.50	0.66	0.76	m	m	m	m	m	m
Netherlands	0.17	0.16	0.16	0.36	0.46	0.56	0.30	0.27	0.27	0.61	0.79	0.97
New Zealand	m	m	m	m	m	m	m	m	m	m	m	m
Norway	m	m	m	m	m	m	m	m	m	m	m	m
Poland	–0.43	–0.66	–0.75	–0.30	–0.49	–0.56	–0.72	–1.09	–1.23	–0.49	–0.80	–0.92
Portugal	m	m	m	m	m	m	m	m	m	m	m	m
Slovak Republic	–0.54	–0.75	–0.82	–0.35	–0.49	–0.48	–1.03	–1.45	–1.57	–0.67	–0.93	–0.92
Spain	–0.70	–0.72	–0.59	–0.63	–0.60	–0.42	–1.46	–1.49	–1.22	–1.31	–1.25	–0.87
Sweden	0.61	0.28	0.24	0.56	0.21	0.25	0.96	0.44	0.37	0.87	0.33	0.39
Switzerland	m	m	m	m	m	m	m	m	m	m	m	m
Turkey	m	m	m	m	m	m	m	m	m	m	m	m
United Kingdom	0.17	0.07	0.06	0.29	0.25	0.30	0.24	0.11	0.09	0.42	0.37	0.44
United States	0.29	0.21	0.28	0.36	0.36	0.51	0.28	0.20	0.27	0.34	0.35	0.49
Country mean	**0.01**	**–0.08**	**–0.10**	**0.13**	**0.11**	**0.16**	**–0.03**	**–0.18**	**–0.21**	**0.16**	**0.12**	**0.20**

m = missing.
Note: See Table 2.3.

student grants or loans is rising in public higher education budgets. One reason for not taking account of such indirect expenditure is the question of comparability and the fact that loans, which will be repaid at a later date, do not strictly speaking constitute expenditure. However, in the case of the Nordic countries, it is hard not to take this indirect expenditure into account, as it represents a major share of public expenditure and, to a large extent, real expenditure that will not be reimbursed.

Other budgetary projections are annexed (see Tables 2.A2.4 to 2.A2.7). They are based on the assumption that the total expenditure per student earmarked for higher education institutions would continue to grow in each country at the same rate as between 1995 and 2005, and that the GDP of countries would continue to grow at the same average rate as between 1995 and 2005 (all at constant prices). Public and private costs per student and national resources are thus extrapolated linearly country by country. The foregoing

Figure 2.4. **A comparison of the growth in the budget and in student numbers between 2005 and 2025 in scenario 2**

(2005 = 100)

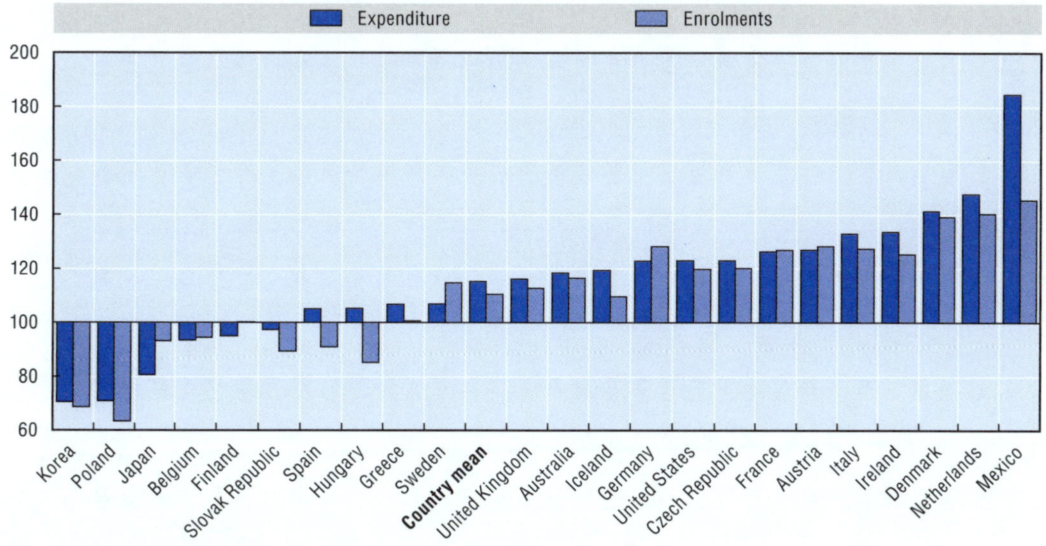

assumption enables one to understand what would occur if recent trends were maintained in the 20 countries for which all relevant data are available. (The projections for Belgium, France, Iceland and Korea are not included in the averages: they are based on the growth in costs per student between 2000 and 2005.) The results stand in much greater contrast than those in the budget scenario shown above.[4] In reality, decreases no less than increases can only correspond to transitional stages subsequent either to under-investment or, conversely, to a drive for sustained funding. These tables show that, in some countries, it will probably be hard to sustain the trends of the last decade in those ahead.

In conclusion, the projections in this section show that, on the basis of conservative assumptions, foreseeable demographic changes should not exert pressure on budgets limiting budgetary options or policy implementation in higher education to any significant extent.

2.3. Impact on student-teacher ratios

Another way of considering the impact of changes in the size of systems is in relation not to their budget but to the student-teacher ratio (*i.e.* the number of students for every teacher): at constant staffing levels, a decrease in student enrolments could lead to more favourable student-teacher ratios, with possible improvements in the quality of teaching, whereas an increase in enrolments might have the opposite effect. The expected negative impact of increases in the student-teacher ratio on quality presupposes that productivity in education remains constant, which is not necessarily so. It might indeed be hoped that innovations in teaching and administration result in greater productivity. In many cases, the expansion of higher education has gone hand in hand with an increase in student-teacher ratios (with larger classes and fuller lecture halls in first degree courses).

Table 2.7 shows how projected student enrolments would affect student-teacher ratios (assuming that teaching staff numbers remained constant). In scenario 1 (*status quo*), the student-teacher ratio in countries would fall on average by 1.9 students per teacher by 2025, whereas it would rise by 1.6 students by 2025 in scenario 2 (trend-based). Here

Table 2.7. **Impact of scenarios 1 and 2 on the student/teacher ratio (ISCED 5/6)**

	Student/staff ratio	Change in student/teacher ratio if same teaching staff as 2005						Teaching staff (FTE)	Additional teaching staff needed to keep student-teacher ratio at 2005 level (2005 = 100)					
		Scenario 1 (*status quo*)			Scenario 2 (trend)				Scenario 1 (*status quo*)			Scenario 2 (trend)		
	2005	2015	2020	2025	2015	2020	2025	*2005*	2015	2020	2025	2015	2020	2025
Australia	*20.7*	0.6	0.0	–0.1	2.4	2.4	2.9	*35 872*	103	103	100	111	111	114
Austria	*16.1*	0.9	0.1	–1.0	3.3	4.2	4.5	*15 223*	105	105	93	121	126	128
Belgium	*19.6*	0.3	–0.6	–1.0	0.1	–0.7	–1.1	*17 912*	102	102	95	101	96	94
Canada	*m*	m	m	m	m	m	m	*m*	m	m	m	m	m	m
Czech Republic	*20.7*	0.2	–3.2	–4.4	5.3	3.4	3.9	*15 755*	101	101	79	126	116	119
Denmark	*m*	m	m	m	m	m	m	*m*	m	m	m	m	m	m
Finland	*12.5*	0.4	–0.7	–1.0	0.7	0.0	–0.1	*17 940*	103	103	92	106	100	99
France	*16.7*	0.1	0.3	0.9	1.4	2.8	4.5	*130 970*	101	101	105	108	117	127
Germany	*12.4*	0.6	–0.3	–1.1	2.5	3.1	3.5	*178 086*	105	105	91	121	125	129
Greece	*30.6*	–2.2	–3.5	–4.1	–2.5	–2.0	–0.3	*21 119*	93	93	87	92	94	99
Hungary	*15.9*	0.1	–2.2	–2.9	1.0	–1.4	–2.1	*21 181*	101	101	82	107	91	87
Iceland	*10.7*	0.7	0.0	–0.3	1.8	1.0	0.8	*1 240*	107	107	97	117	109	107
Ireland	*17.0*	–1.9	–1.2	0.7	–1.0	1.1	4.7	*9 925*	89	89	104	94	106	128
Italy	*21.4*	0.9	1.1	1.1	2.3	4.1	5.8	*94 371*	104	104	105	111	119	127
Japan	*11.0*	–1.4	–1.5	–2.0	–0.9	–0.5	–0.8	*350 919*	87	87	81	92	96	93
Korea	*24.4*	–1.9	–4.2	–8.0	–1.9	–4.0	–7.7	*131 358*	92	92	67	92	84	69
Luxembourg	*m*	m	m	m	m	m	m	*m*	m	m	m	m	m	m
Mexico	*14.9*	1.0	0.7	0.2	4.2	5.7	6.7	*159 930*	107	107	101	128	138	145
Netherlands	*14.5*	1.6	1.5	1.5	3.5	4.7	5.9	*35 511*	111	111	111	124	132	141
New Zealand	*16.3*	m	m	m	m	m	m	*10 848*	m	m	m	m	m	m
Norway	*m*	0.0	0.0	0.0	0.0	0.0	0.0	*m*	m	m	m	m	m	m
Poland	*18.2*	–4.1	–6.6	–7.7	–2.7	–4.8	–5.7	*98 330*	77	77	58	85	74	69
Portugal	*m*	m	m	m	m	m	m	*28 824*	m	m	m	m	m	m
Slovak Republic	*16.2*	–2.0	–4.7	–5.6	0.1	–1.6	–1.6	*11 196*	87	87	65	101	90	90
Spain	*13.6*	–2.9	–3.1	–2.2	–2.3	–2.2	–0.7	*123 509*	79	79	84	83	84	95
Sweden	*8.9*	3.2	1.3	1.1	2.9	0.9	1.2	*33 010*	136	136	112	132	110	113
Switzerland	*18.2*	3.7	2.4	0.9	5.8	6.1	5.9	*9 755*	120	120	105	132	134	132
Turkey	*25.8*	3.2	2.9	1.7	11.6	16.3	19.1	*81 551*	112	112	107	145	163	174
United Kingdom	*18.2*	0.8	–0.4	–0.6	2.5	2.1	2.9	*93 439*	105	105	97	114	112	116
United States	*15.7*	1.9	1.6	1.9	2.2	2.3	3.1	*835 926*	112	112	112	114	115	120
OECD	***17.2***	**–0.5**	**–1.5**	**–1.9**	**1.0**	**1.1**	**1.6**	***2 563 698***	**102**	**102**	**93**	**111**	**110**	**113**
EU19	***17.0***	**–0.2**	**–1.4**	**–1.6**	**1.1**	**0.9**	**1.6**	***946 300***	**100**	**100**	**91**	**108**	**106**	**110**

m = missing.

Note: Student enrolments and the teaching staff are expressed in full-time equivalents (FTE).

again, there are significant variations between the two scenarios and from one country to the next. However, it is hard to reach general conclusions, bearing in mind that the impact on quality of one extra student per teacher is probably not the same for all initial class sizes (an increasing marginal diminution in quality probably occurs): in the case of countries with low student-teacher ratios, one extra student per teacher may not greatly affect quality; on the other hand, in countries in which the student-teacher ratio is already high, continuing to increase it may have a negative impact on the quality of provision (if teaching methods remain the same) or student performance. In particular, certain skills that are more readily imparted by teaching small groups of students would be hard to develop, such as the teamwork or communication skills that are regarded as essential in post-industrial economies (OECD, 2007e).

Figure 2.5. **Student-teacher ratios in each of the two scenarios in 2005 and 2025 if (full-time equivalent) teaching staff numbers were to remain at their 2005 level**

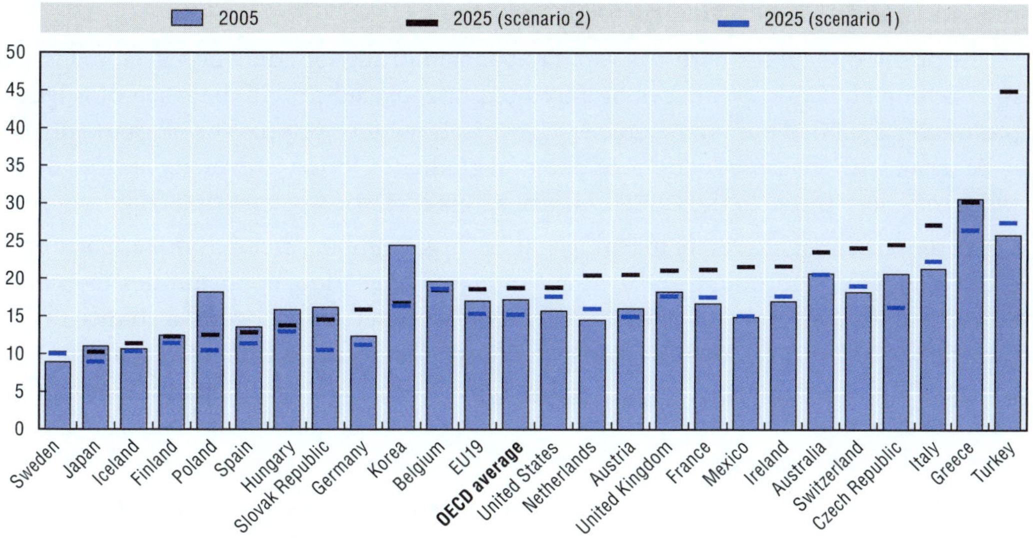

Note: Korea, the Netherlands, Switzerland: 2004 instead of 2005. The student-teacher ratio in Australia is possibly not comparable to that in the other countries. Student enrolment and teaching staff numbers are in full-time equivalents.

Source: OECD (except Australia: DEST, 2004).

As Figure 2.5 reveals, in the trend scenario, student-teacher ratios in certain countries could rise by over 3 students per teacher in the period up to 2025. This might apply to countries such as Australia, the Czech Republic, France, Ireland, Italy, Switzerland and Turkey, in which the student-teacher ratio exceeded the OECD country average in 2005 (17.2 students per teacher). Barring any revolution in teaching, quality will probably come under pressure in these systems if they do not increase their staffing. To cite an extreme case, student-teacher ratios in Turkey would soar (scenario 1 included): managing expansion there while the budget and quality changed very little would doubtless be a tall order. Mexico would also experience considerable pressure, even though its initial student-teacher ratio is lower. Other countries such as Greece and Korea would probably witness a decrease in their ratios, without them however falling below the current OECD country average. In the case of these countries, the decline in enrolment could be an unexpectedly welcome means of lowering the student-teacher ratio. Countries like Poland or Spain could use the decrease in their ratios to establish innovative teaching methods and perhaps raise their achievement rates (which would also slow down the fall in their student enrolments). Finally, in countries in which student-teacher ratios have changed little, ratios may be used as an adjustment variable to deal with changes in student enrolments.

Table 2.7 also indicates the order of magnitude of the increase or decrease in academic teaching staff that would be required if one wished to maintain the 2005 student-teacher ratio. It will be noted that these increases or decreases do not correspond to the number of teachers that should be recruited. For this to be determined, it is necessary to take account of the number of retirements and turnover among teaching staff, as well as the varied categories of teacher status. Changes in student enrolments in the trend scenario would lead to an average rise of 10% in the number of teachers in 2025 compared to 2005. In some countries, this increase would be quite big (Turkey, Mexico and the Netherlands), but would correspond to an average annual growth rate of 2-4%.

2.4. Impact on teacher recruitment requirements

One of the difficulties with the rapid expansion of higher education systems is that their teaching staff cannot always be recruited or replaced at will, because of a lack of appropriately qualified human resources. Conversely, where systems shrink markedly, one may be faced with "overproduction" of doctoral graduates if non-university sectors do not manage to absorb them. In the OECD countries, this scenario appears unlikely.

The retirement of academic teaching staff in large numbers creates both opportunities and challenges for institutions and systems of higher education: opportunities to improve the quality of teachers or the way their skills are distributed, but above all a chance to alter organisational or professional culture; challenges in terms either of recruiting large numbers of staff without making any quality concessions at a time when other institutions are doubtless in the same situation, or of retaining the best aspects of the organisational culture and its social capital.

The growth in student enrolments is conducive to changes in teaching staff and the employment of younger teachers (at constant student-teacher ratios): it enables the recruitment of new teachers who may be either young or different, without awaiting the departure of those already employed, and thus encourages some measure of responsiveness to social and academic changes. Permanent teaching staff either age or, as Willekens (2008) demonstrates, experience cyclic changes in their age structure. The percentage of non-statutory teaching staff increases, yet offers university heads, deans or ministries some degree of flexibility in managing their staff, though subject to the possible disadvantages of dual labour markets (Enders and Musselin, 2008).

One indicator of this potential problem lies in the average age of teachers in higher education.[5] As Willekens (2008) reveals, this is less the reflection of ageing in the population than the product of a particular employment system (characterised by tenure or "job security") combined with a change of size in the system at a constant student-teacher ratio. In most OECD countries, teachers in higher education are not that old on average, as Figure 2.6 indicates. Their average age is 45 in the 23 countries for which data are available. Italy is the only country in which the ageing of teaching staff is problematic, with an average age of 55 among these staff, 63% of whom have to be replaced by 2020 if their numbers are to remain constant, representing an average annual replacement rate of 4.2% (excluding replacements attributable to turnover).[6] France, Hungary and the Slovak

Figure 2.6. **Average age of teachers in higher education (2005)**

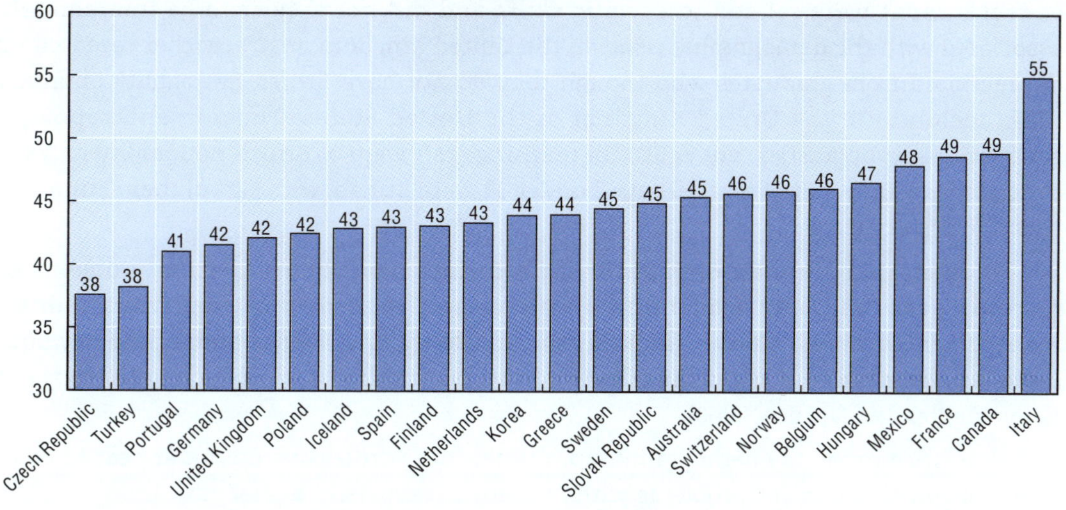

Note: Australia, Canada and the Czech Republic: 2000; Norway: 2004; Mexico: solely public education, 2004.
Source: OECD; Mexico: Bensusán and Ahumada Lobo (2006).

Republic are also experiencing a slightly difficult situation, with more than 40% of their teaching staff aged over 50 (and thus average annual replacement rates of 2.8-3% solely for those retiring). As retirement age and the regulations governing retirement vary from one country to the next, the problems posed by the age pyramid and the need to replace teachers differ depending on the regulations concerned. In the United States, in which retirement is no longer mandatory, the management of ageing involves for example the development of appropriate pension schemes (Clark, 2004).

In fact, the replacement and demography of teachers in higher education are more pertinent issues for individual academic subjects than for teaching staff as a whole. On the one hand, the age pyramid of teachers may vary markedly from one discipline to the next, sometimes for reasons peculiar to a particular field. Subjects with a strong practical dimension, such as education (in the sense of teacher training) or management, call for teachers who have acquired prior practical experience in their field, which means that the staff concerned are older on average than in the case of primarily research-oriented disciplines. On the other hand, certain subject areas may face greater problems in the recruitment or retention of teachers, depending on the level of competition from professional occupations in which the same basic skills are appreciated on the labour market. Finally, the recruitment of academic staff does not draw exclusively on trained human resources in the country concerned, but also on foreign graduates, especially in the English-speaking countries (Enders and Musselin, 2008).

A recent British study on the demography of the social sciences in the United Kingdom reveals the extent to which the position of teacher-researchers in the social sciences depends on the particular discipline (Mills *et al.*, 2007). While social sciences academics are older than their colleagues in the natural sciences, their age within each of the social sciences varies considerably: out of the 18 specific disciplines examined, academics were relatively more elderly in four sectors, namely education (over half of the staff aged over 50), social work (47%), social policy (42%) and management (41%), all of which are subjects with a dominant practical dimension. In the case of those that are research oriented, sociology and linguistics displayed the most elderly demographic profile, with 42% and 40% respectively of their staff aged over 50. Yet in the qualitative study, problems of retention or recruitment were related to specific skills and did not appear to be immediately associated with the demographic issue. In the United Kingdom, many teacher-researchers are recruited from graduates who though they do not have British nationality obtained their doctorate in the United Kingdom or the United States. Thus, in anthropology, economics and linguistics, under 70% of teaching staff were of British nationality in 2004. In economics, only 35% of teachers aged under 35 were British, with 32% of them European Union foreign citizens.

Another study in the Commonwealth countries also shows that the problems of recruiting and retaining academic staff are closely related to particular disciplines: management, business studies, information technology, and science and technology pose more problems because of openings in the private sector for doctoral graduates in these fields (Kubler and DeLuca, 2006).

Here once more, the demographics of the teaching profession do not appear to be of critical significance in any problems with recruiting teachers in higher education.

2.5. Impact on the percentage of higher education graduates in the population

An important quantitative aspect of demographic change has to do with its impact on the percentage of higher education graduates in the population (tertiary educational attainment).

The increase in the educational level of the population and, in particular, of its younger members is important for several reasons. Among them are a whole set of social reasons concerned with public health, criminality and individual and national welfare (OECD, 2007c; OECD, 2001). Then comes a further range of economic reasons: many models of economic growth demonstrate that the educational attainment of the population has a considerable bearing on national economic growth, because a good level of education has both a positive impact on worker productivity and is conducive to improved performance in terms of innovation. In countries at the highest level of economic development and closest to the "frontiers of knowledge", innovation is arguably even more important than in the remainder (Aghion and Howitt, 1998; OECD, 2006a; OECD, 2006b).

Next, there are two main considerations justifying interest in the education of young people: first, it is they who are generally best trained and educated, and the most likely to contribute to national innovation; the level of (formal) education of individuals changes little over their lifetime, notwithstanding attempts to develop policies for lifelong learning. This means that the political action most likely to raise the educational level of a population involves raising that of its young people. However, the percentage of graduates in the population is only really meaningful if the degrees they obtain are of sound quality: quantitative comparisons of educational level are based on the assumption that the quality of degrees both within and across countries is similar, although little conclusive information is yet available on this subject.[7]

What effect do the drive for expansion and the ageing of the population have on the overall educational level of the working population? Will the declared aim in certain countries of enabling 50% of their young age cohorts to obtain degrees be achieved? How will the relative level of education and training in countries develop if past trends persist (and population projections materialise)? And how are countries and regions going to

Table 2.8. **Proportion of graduates in the population, 2005 and projections**

	2005					2025 (30-year trend)					2025 (20-year trend)					2025 (10-year trend)				
	25-64	25-34	35-44	45-54	55-64	**25-64**	25-34	35-44	45-54	55-64	**25-64**	25-34	35-44	45-54	55-64	25-64	25-34	35-44	45-54	55-64
Australia	**32**	38	32	31	24	**42**	47	49	41	32	**41**	44	48	41	32	**43**	50	52	41	32
Austria	**18**	20	19	17	14	**27**	24	33	26	26	**27**	22	32	26	26	**26**	21	31	26	26
Belgium	**31**	41	33	27	22	**43**	53	47	41	34	**43**	54	48	41	34	**44**	55	48	41	34
Canada	**46**	54	50	43	36	**52**	66	57	47	40	**52**	66	57	47	40	**51**	62	55	47	40
Czech Republic	**13**	14	14	13	11	**16**	17	18	16	14	**16**	16	17	16	14	**15**	14	17	16	14
Denmark	**34**	40	35	32	27	**48**	48	58	47	41	**48**	47	58	47	41	**49**	50	60	47	41
Finland	**35**	38	41	34	27	**52**	49	62	48	47	**49**	43	59	48	47	**48**	39	57	48	47
France	**25**	39	25	18	16	**38**	52	43	38	23	**41**	59	47	38	23	**45**	69	53	38	23
Germany	**25**	22	26	26	23	**25**	24	29	21	25	**25**	24	29	21	25	**25**	24	29	21	25
Greece	**21**	25	26	19	12	**28**	37	32	24	23	**27**	32	29	24	23	**24**	25	25	24	23
Hungary	**17**	20	17	16	15	**22**	22	23	22	19	**22**	23	23	22	19	**22**	24	24	22	19
Iceland	**31**	36	34	29	21	**42**	48	45	38	36	**40**	43	42	38	36	**38**	39	40	38	36
Ireland	**29**	41	30	22	17	**44**	55	51	42	31	**46**	59	53	42	31	**47**	61	54	42	31
Italy	**12**	16	13	11	8	**18**	21	23	17	13	**17**	21	23	17	13	**18**	23	24	17	13
Japan	**40**	53	47	38	22	**60**	76	68	55	49	**58**	68	63	55	49	**57**	66	62	55	49
Korea	**32**	51	36	18	10	**57**	78	71	52	35	**60**	85	75	52	35	**59**	82	73	52	35
Luxembourg	**27**	37	27	22	19	**45**	47	56	45	33	**47**	51	59	45	33	**50**	58	63	45	33
Mexico	**15**	18	16	14	8	**22**	25	24	20	18	**21**	23	22	20	18	**21**	23	23	20	18
Netherlands	**30**	35	30	30	24	**40**	42	44	40	34	**39**	40	43	40	34	**41**	45	46	40	34
New Zealand	**27**	31	28	27	21	**32**	37	37	30	23	**30**	34	35	30	23	**32**	37	37	30	23
Norway	**33**	41	35	30	24	**42**	52	49	38	32	**42**	52	49	38	32	**43**	53	50	38	32
Poland	**17**	26	16	12	13	**25**	31	29	24	15	**27**	38	33	24	15	**30**	44	36	24	15
Portugal	**13**	19	13	10	7	**17**	26	21	15	10	**18**	27	22	15	10	**19**	32	25	15	10
Slovak Republic	**14**	16	13	14	11	**18**	19	19	18	15	**17**	18	19	18	15	**19**	23	22	18	15
Spain	**28**	40	30	22	14	**45**	56	51	44	33	**45**	58	52	44	33	**46**	59	53	44	33
Sweden	**30**	37	28	28	25	**34**	43	39	33	24	**35**	45	40	33	24	**39**	55	46	33	24
Switzerland	**29**	31	32	29	22	**38**	39	46	36	33	**36**	34	43	36	33	**35**	31	42	36	33
Turkey	**10**	12	8	9	7	**11**	14	13	11	5	**12**	14	14	11	5	**13**	19	16	11	5
United Kingdom	**30**	35	30	28	24	**39**	42	44	39	33	**39**	41	44	39	33	**41**	46	47	39	33
United States	**39**	39	40	39	37	**45**	41	47	45	46	**44**	39	46	45	46	**44**	40	46	45	46
Country average	**26**	**32**	**27**	**24**	**19**	**36**	**41**	**41**	**34**	**28**	**35**	**41**	**41**	**34**	**28**	**36**	**42**	**42**	**34**	**28**
EU19	25	**31**	**26**	**22**	**17**	31	**37**	**36**	**30**	**24**	32	**38**	**37**	**30**	**24**	33	**42**	**39**	**30**	**24**

compare in terms of their graduate numbers (and no longer just the percentage of graduates in their population)?

To throw further light on these questions, the educational level of the population and its various age groups have been projected with reference to past growth rates in this level. Projecting the number of graduates produced by domestic systems using the model adopted for student enrolment projections poses problems here, given that the level of incoming or outgoing migration, whether or not the migrants themselves are highly qualified, may have a telling impact on the educational level of the population, as too may the possible reclassification of previously obtained degrees.

The present study has thus somewhat relied on the fact that the educational level of the various age cohorts was, for the most part, already known in 2005: those aged between 35 and 44 in 2005 will be aged between 55 and 64 in 2025, etc. The educational level of a generation generally increases little over time, although to an extent which varies between countries. Data available on the educational level of the population in 1995 and 2005 (OECD, 1997 and 2007b) provide for a comparison of trends in the education of three generations during this decade (those aged between 35 and 44 in 1995 were aged between 45 and 54 in 2005, etc.), and thus to record changes in the higher education of these age cohorts over time. One may thus estimate the average growth in the educational level of these cohorts and take similar trends into account in the extrapolations, though with differences depending on the particular country.

Table 2.8 shows the tertiary educational attainment of the population in OECD countries in 2005, and projections for 2025 based on trends in the last 10, 20 and 30 years (scenarios referred to as T10, T20 and T30 respectively). Projections based on trends over the last ten years might be more relevant than those based on the last 20 or 30 years, but they are less reliable. The comparison with different scenarios is a reminder that they are no more than projections, and thus possible future scenarios. Figure 2.7 shows the percentage of graduates in the 25-64 age group of the population in 2005 and then the corresponding projections for 2025 in the three scenarios selected.

First, it will be noticed that there is little difference between the projected tertiary educational attainment levels in the three scenarios for the population aged 25-64. The percentage of graduates in the 25-64 age group in an OECD country lies between 35.5% and 36.1%, depending on the particular scenario, compared to an average 26% in 2005 – or an average increase of 10 percentage points. Even though the proportion of graduates in the youngest cohorts (aged 25-34 and 35-44) varies sometimes considerably from one scenario to the next, this has finally little bearing on the educational level of the total population. This clearly indicates the sluggishness of demographic changes and the influence of the oldest cohorts: many decades are required for a big change in the educational level of young people to impact significantly on the entire population.

Increases in tertiary educational attainment vary from one country to another on the evidence of changes over the last 10, 20 or 30 years, reflecting how it has tended to surge or slacken in past decades. Nevertheless, differences between most countries remain somewhat limited in all three scenarios, and especially in those for 20 and 30 years, in which the variation is no more than three percentage points (in France, Japan, Korea and Poland). The variation between the scenarios for 10 and 20 years is four percentage points at most (in France and Sweden). The greatest differences are apparent between the scenarios for 10 and 30 years, with variations between 4 and 7 percentage points (in

Figure 2.7. **Percentage of the population aged 25-64 who were graduates in 2005, and projections for 2025 based on trends in the last 10, 20 and 30 years**

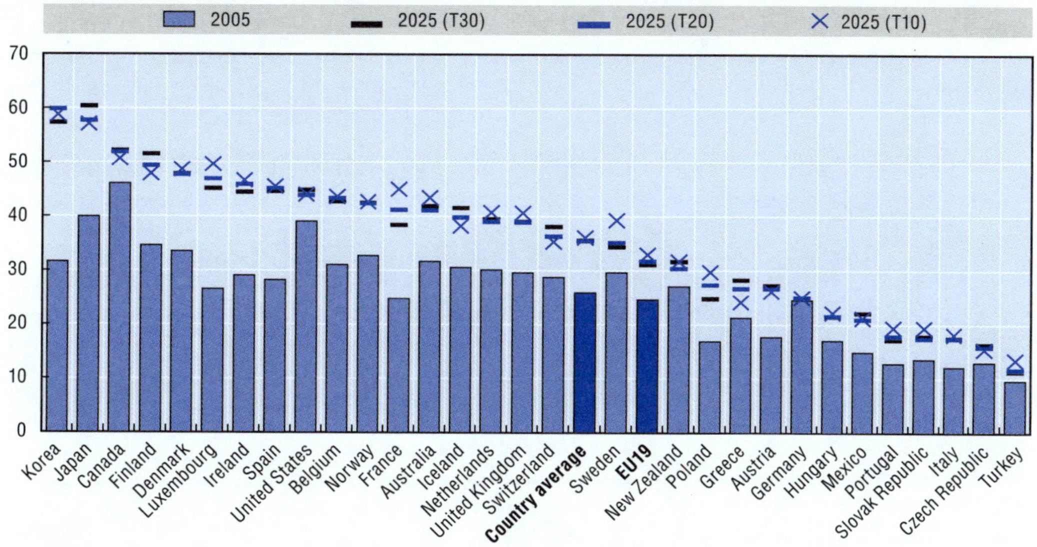

Note: Countries are classified in the descending order of the T20 scenario, corresponding to trends in the last 20 years.

Finland, France, Greece, Luxembourg, Poland and Sweden). Given differences in past growth rates, proportions of graduates in the populations of OECD countries would appear to be diverging rather than converging, with a standard deviation between them rising from 9 to 13 between 2005 to 2025 (in all three scenarios). This is partly attributable to the strong growth in provision in some countries (Japan, Korea and Canada), but also to the fact that growth has probably been underestimated in the case of emerging countries (Turkey, the Czech Republic, the Slovak Republic and Mexico), in which strong future economic growth will probably lead to more rapid growth than previously in the educational levels of their people in the decades ahead.

Depending on the particular scenario, 50% or more of the population aged between 25 and 64 would be graduates in three to four countries: this applies to Japan, Korea and Canada in all scenarios, and Finland in scenario T30. Japan and Korea would dominate with the greatest proportion of graduates. The United States would slightly lose its relative lead over the other OECD countries, as would Germany, because of weaker growth than the others. However, it should be noted that the proportion of graduates is not fully comparable across all countries: in those such as Germany which possess a dual apprenticeship system, non-tertiary post-secondary education (ISCED 4) may perform a role similar to the one played by some forms of higher education in other countries. Thus for men, an apprenticeship diploma (ISCED 4) in Germany has the same value (or income-earning capacity) on the labour market as a practically-oriented higher education qualification (ISCED 5B) awarded by a *Fachhochschule* (OECD, 2007b).

On observing the youngest cohorts, namely those consisting of people aged 25-44 whose tertiary educational attainment in the three scenarios differs, the differences are more marked (Figure 2.8). The proportion of graduates in the two youngest cohorts would again rise by 10 or 11 percentage points, with the proportion in this group in OECD countries increasing on average from 30% to 41-42% between 2005 and 2025. In the case of these (25-44) age cohorts, 13 countries would reach a proportion of graduates of 50% or over in at least one of the

Figure 2.8. **Percentage of the population aged 25-44 who were graduates in 2005, and projections for 2025 based on trends in the last 10, 20 and 30 years**

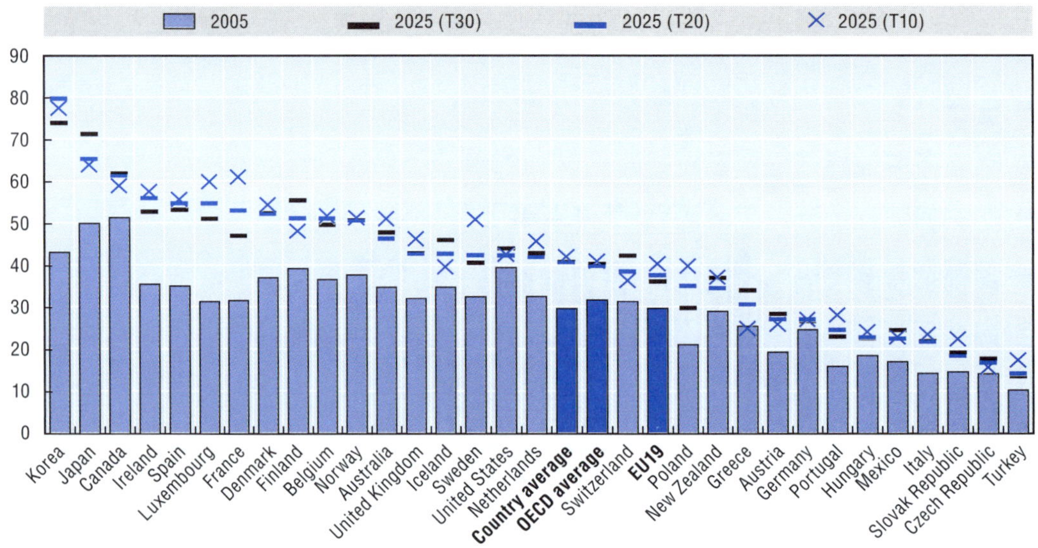

scenarios, and 9 of them would do so in all three. Here once more, country trends would diverge rather than converge, with a standard deviation rising from 11 to 16 between 2005 and 2025. The United States would lose more ground in terms of the relative educational levels of its younger age cohorts than in the case of its entire population of 25-64-year-olds.

What is the situation regarding the number of graduates available in the various countries? It would indeed appear that, depending on the size of populations and age cohorts, changes in the absolute number of graduates in a country may differ from trends in the educational level of the population. For example, although projections for the tertiary educational attainment of those aged 25-64 or 25-44 in Germany do not correspond to a decrease, its levelling out would be reflected in a fall of 8-9% in the number of graduates aged 25-64 depending on the particular scenario, and of 18-19% among those aged 25-44 (Figures 2.9 and 2.10). Or yet again, the strong growth in the tertiary educational attainment of the population in Japan might nevertheless be consistent with a decrease in the number of graduates aged 25 to 44, because of the diminishing size of the cohorts concerned. The situation is different in Korea, in which the projected decrease in the population will occur later than in Japan (Yonezawa and Kim, 2008). For the period up to 2025, Korea would thus witness a doubling in the number of its 25-64-year-old graduates compared to 2005, while the total number of its youngest graduates might rise by around 50%.

On the whole and in spite of ageing populations in some countries, the number of graduates will increase in almost all OECD countries, irrespective of the particular scenario, and in the case of both the 25-64 and 25-44 age groups. The average increase for countries would be 42-46% for those aged 25-64, depending on the scenario, and 23-29% for 25-44-year-olds (with weighted averages of 35-37% and 16-20%, respectively). There is still a difference between the graduate numbers and the graduate share. Notwithstanding an absolute increase in graduate numbers in the United States, and in particular a stronger increase than in the European Union, the former would account for a smaller share of all graduates in the OECD area than in 2005, both among those aged 25-64 and in the youngest

Figure 2.9. **Projected growth in the number of graduates aged 25-64**

(2005 = 100)

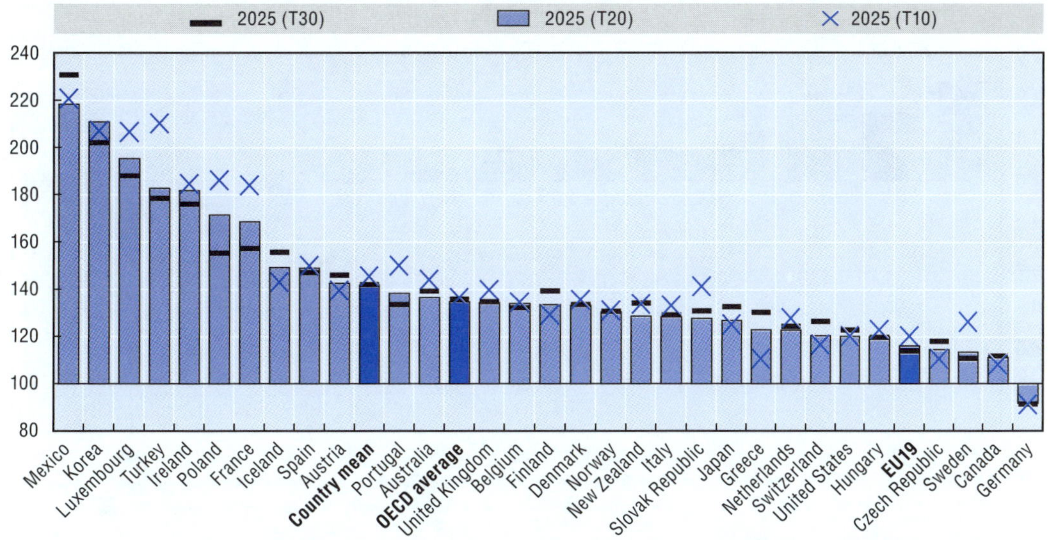

Figure 2.10. **Projected growth in the number of graduates aged 25-44**

(2005 = 100)

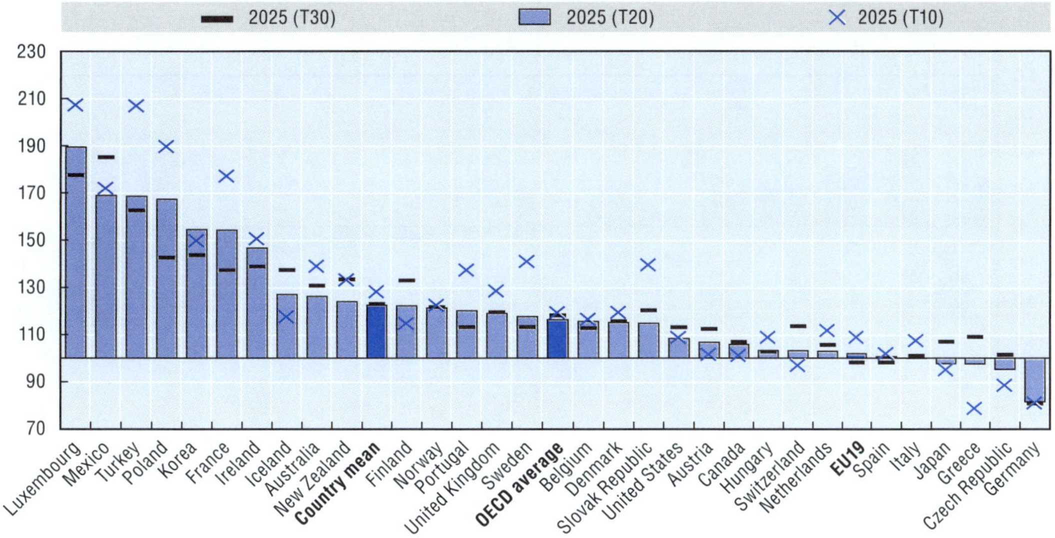

age cohorts (Figure 2.11). The projected growth in the number of graduates is indeed higher in many other member countries. Nevertheless, because of the shrinking size of younger cohorts in Europe, the European Union could experience a more marked decrease in the proportion of its graduates in the 25-44 age cohort (Figure 2.12).

However, the absolute number of graduates is not necessarily important, as most studies that associate growth with educational level focus on relative numbers. It might be thought that a larger stock of young graduates would result in a greater number of innovative ideas (Eberstadt, 2007), but much more is made of their significance in supporting the formation of a "critical mass".

Figure 2.11. **Loss or gain in the relative share of graduates aged 25-64 in the OECD area between 2005 and the three scenarios for 2025**

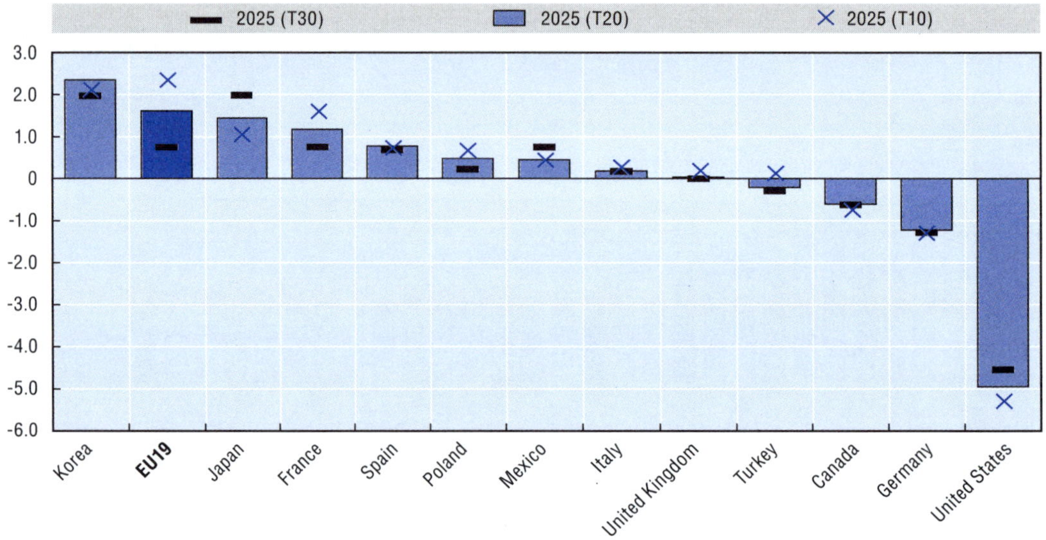

Note: Only countries in which the (positive or negative) change exceeds 0.1% in at least one of the scenarios are shown.

Figure 2.12. **Loss or gain in the relative share of graduates aged 25-44 in the OECD area between 2005 and the three scenarios for 2025**

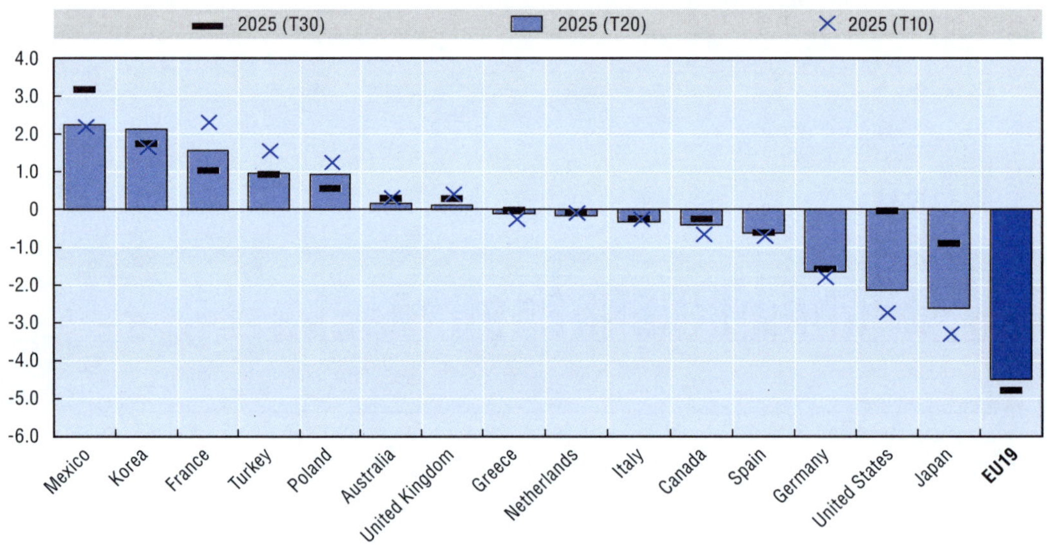

Note: Only countries in which the (positive or negative) change exceeds 0.1% in at least one of the scenarios are shown.

2.6. How will social inequality evolve in higher education?

Demographic changes are not merely quantitative but qualitative, and relate to the composition of the student population. The projections in the previous sections assume that in the decades ahead higher education will expand in some countries, such as Japan and Korea, to the point at which access will reach a maximum level tantamount to full participation. Given that higher education will probably continue to expand (in terms of participation if not enrolment), the key question is whether this can contribute to a lowering of social inequality in the sector and indeed be fuelled by such a trend. This section does not seek to provide an in-depth answer to this complex question which is already the subject of abundant research (see Vallet, 2003; Hout and DiPrete, 2004; Breen *et al.*, 2005; Santiago *et al.*, 2008), but aims to offer some summary material for further thought and discussion on trends observed in this area over past decades.

First, the very varied possible forms of inequality should be borne in mind, ranging from inequality between the sexes, inequalities between socio-economic, ethnic and religious groups, between immigrants and the remainder of the population, and between people from urban and rural communities and castes, etc. From one country to the next, the relevant bounds defining or governing the perception of inequalities differ, even though social inequalities may be more uniformly understood from an international standpoint (Hout and DiPrete, 2004). The variety of ways in which inequalities may be articulated or apparent in higher education should also be remembered: social inequalities may be embedded in access to or participation in higher education, but also in access to certain types of provision (elite institutions, etc.), certain disciplines or levels of study, or in attainment levels and the final award of qualifications, etc. Thus some types of inequality may diminish as others increase; or certain inequalities may be lessened among some groups while becoming more marked in others. Indeed, there is a very wide range of possible targets for anyone wishing to fight (or study) social inequality, and often they are shifting.

Next, the question of how inequalities change over time is itself fraught with a great many technical and theoretical problems. The measurement of social inequalities may indeed assume several appropriate forms which remain however quite distinct, so that ideally it helps to concentrate on monitoring an array of similarly focused indicators in order to establish whether inequalities have changed or diminished (Clancy and Goastellec, 2007). Given that society as well as its economic and social structures are changing, it is not always easy to judge how inequalities may also be changing: for example, what it means to come from a rural background today and what it meant 40 years ago are very different in real socio-economic terms, although one has to proceed as if this were not the case when studying inequalities over time.

Inequalities in access to higher education are the result of two combined influences, namely attainment at school and the decisions taken at each transitional point in education (Boudon, 1973, 1974). First of all, children from disadvantaged backgrounds often perform less well at school and are thus less likely to reach the level at which they would be eligible for higher education. This occurs for a variety of cultural, educational, nutritional, social or economic reasons as a result of which they do not confront these transitional stages in the same way as children from more privileged backgrounds (Field, Kuczera and Pont, 2007). Thus inequalities in higher education are partly the consequence of earlier schooling at primary and secondary levels, and they may be diminished (or increased) as a direct result of educational policies. For example, in Sweden as in France, the reform of lower secondary education appears to have been a crucial factor in lessening inequality (Erikson, 1996; Thélot and Vallet, 2000). Secondly, at all transitional stages in education and especially that of eligibility for higher education, children from disadvantaged backgrounds, whose achievement levels are the same as those of their more privileged peers, generally have fewer opportunities than they do to continue their studies, or to choose courses that are as ambitious, whether because of real or perceived financial pressures, or different aspirations, etc. (see for example Carnevale and Desrochers, 2003, on the United States, or Erikson and Jonsson, 1996, for Sweden, and Breen *et al.*, 2005, for a discussion of both factors).

The literature shows that as higher education has expanded, access to it has become more broadly based in most – perhaps even all – OECD countries, so that quantitative inequalities have been lessened: nowadays, a greater proportion of children from underprivileged backgrounds than 10, 20 or 30 years ago enter higher education (and obtain a qualification at that level). This applies to the 13 countries studied by Shavit and Blossfeld (1993) (western Germany, Hungary, Israel, Italy, Japan, the Netherlands, Poland, the Czech Republic, the United Kingdom, Sweden, Switzerland, Taiwan and the United States), but also to France (Vallet and Selz, 2007), Chile (Brunner, 2007), Spain (Ballarino *et al.*, 2008), Australia and Korea (Shavit, Arum and Gamoran, 2007), etc. This finding is often played down: yet it means that a child from a disadvantaged background is now more likely to enter higher education than at any time previously with consequently better prospects. Otherwise put and to paraphrase Rawls (1971): if we had to choose from behind a veil of ignorance the fairest society, in which the least privileged could be the most fortunate, we should be well advised to choose from those of today with their "massified" higher education rather than from those of the past, whether the past means 10, 20 or 50 years ago. As education is not simply a "positional good" whose value depends solely on the education of others but includes intrinsic personal benefits that are not exclusively economic (OECD, 2007c), this far greater openness is a sign of real social progress. It is probable that this will continue with the expansion of higher education in the decades ahead.

The second aspect of quantitative openness is apparent from the social make-up of students in higher education. While students from upper middle class backgrounds (or even higher in the social scale) accounted for a very high proportion of those in the system a few decades ago, their proportions have decreased although they remain over-represented. The upshot of this is that the student experience in higher education has changed qualitatively for those from all social backgrounds with a truly greater social mix – and varied consequences in terms of the real social capital of institutions. Figure 2.13 illustrates the situation in the case of the United States: the over-representation of students from the richest families has fallen in recent decades. The socio-economic composition of higher education systems has become much broader and closer to that of society. However, forms of social composition vary widely with types of institution: broadening of access has often begun in the least prestigious institutions, while the most prestigious, which give access to the dominant positions in society, have frequently retained a far more uniform social composition (Bowen, Kurzweil and Tobin, 2005; Shavit, Arum and Gamoran, 2007; Vallet and Selz, 2007).

While quantitative "democratisation" of higher education systems is well established, many sociologists do not equate it necessarily with lesser injustice, defined as inequality of educational opportunity. Expansion and increasingly open access have indeed been associated with a hierarchical stratification of systems (Duru-Bellat, 2006; Shavit, Arum and Gamoran, 2007), and it is possible that this works more to the advantage of children from the most privileged social backgrounds. In this respect, a decrease in inequality of opportunity and a fairer society only materialise when expansion offers greater benefits to the least fortunate rather than the most privileged (Shavit and Blossfeld, 1993; Shavit, Arum and Gamoran, 2007; Rawls, 1971). If education is regarded as a "positional good", a proportional rise in the educational level of all has nothing to offer those from the most

Figure 2.13. **Trends in the differing proportions of students who come from households in different quartiles of income distribution in the United States**

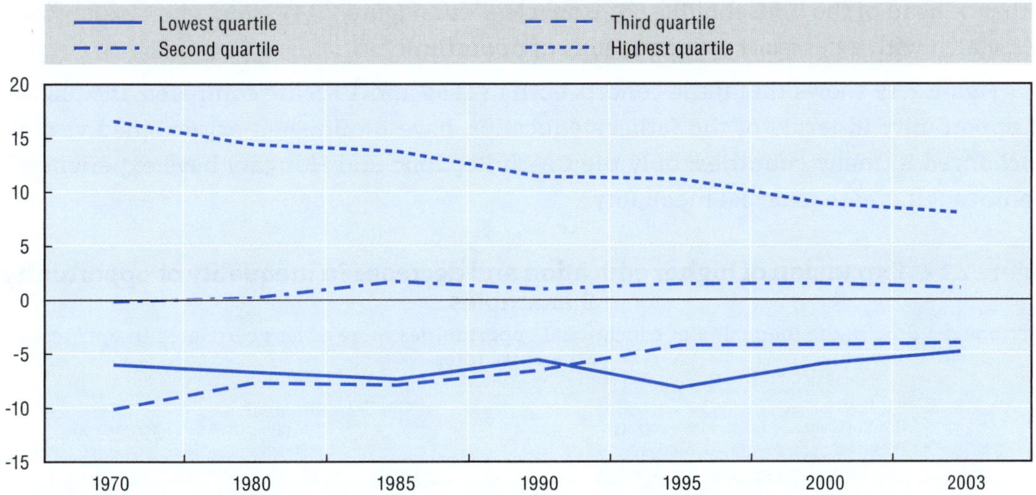

Note: Full representativeness occurs if the deviation in percentage points equals 0. A positive deviation of 15 points means that the group is over-represented and that it represents 15% more among the students than among the youth aged 18-23 years. It should be noted that students from the third quartile were under-represented more than those in the last quartile up to early 1990s.

Source: OECD (based on NCES data).

disadvantaged backgrounds, since differences in education between groups do not change (Duru-Bellat, 2006).

The influential book by Shavit and Blossfeld (1993) created the lasting impression that inequalities were more likely to persist than diminish during periods of expansion. It identified a lowering of inequality of educational opportunity in just two of the 13 countries studied (Sweden and the Netherlands) – and concluded that inequalities were "maximally maintained" until the participation of the most privileged group reached saturation point, etc. These findings have since been challenged or qualified by Shavit, Arum and Gamoran (2007), among others, who highlight the more inclusive or democratising effect of expansion on a system in which inequality of opportunity remains unchanged.

The most recent research shows that the influence of socio-economic background on access to higher education or the likelihood of graduating has in fact diminished in recent decades in many countries: besides the cases of Sweden and the Netherlands, studies have reached similar conclusions for Germany, France, Italy, Japan, Korea, Taiwan, the United States, Great Britain, Poland and Australia (Breen *et al.*, 2005; Shavit, Arum et Gamoran, 2007; Vallet and Selz, 2007). Yet there is no causal relationship or systematic association between expansion and a lowering of social inequalities of opportunity. Inequalities of opportunity in education have in fact increased in Ireland (Breen *et al.*, 2005) and Spain (Ballarino *et al.*, 2008), and levelled out in Switzerland (Buchmann *et al.*, 2007). They have also tended to grow in Eastern European countries by comparison with the Soviet era, as in the Czech Republic (Matějů, Řeháková and Simonová, 2007), Hungary, the Slovak Republic, Romania (Iannelli, 2003) and Russia itself (Breen *et al.*, 2005; Shavit, Arum and Gamoran, 2007). There is thus no firmly established relation between expansion and inequality of opportunity.

The examples of France, Germany and Australia reveal that the relation between expansion and a lowering of social inequality (measured in terms of the occupation of the father or head of the household) is far from clear-cut (Figure 2.14), even when expansion is associated with a decrease in inequalities of opportunity.

Figure 2.15 shows that if the cohorts born in 1955 and 1975 are compared, inequalities of opportunity in terms of the father's education have diminished or remained virtually unchanged in many countries: only the Czech Republic and Hungary have experienced a significant increase in social inequality.

Figure 2.14. **Expansion of higher education and decrease in inequality of opportunity: 3 examples**

Germany: A drop in the inequality of educational opportunities more or less correlated to the increase in the entry rates

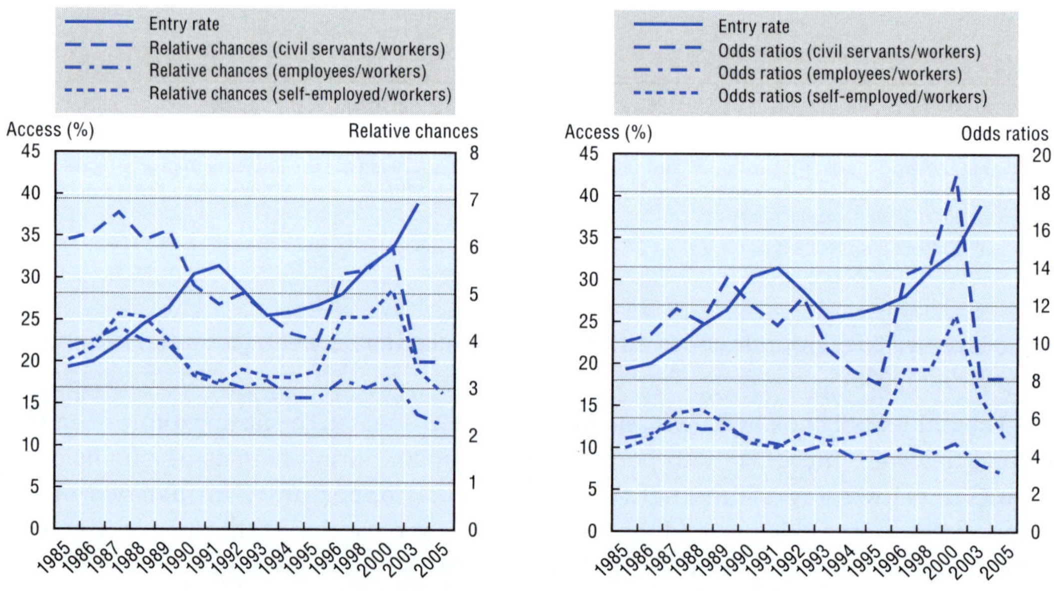

France: A rise in the entry rates and a decrease in the social inequality of educational opportunities

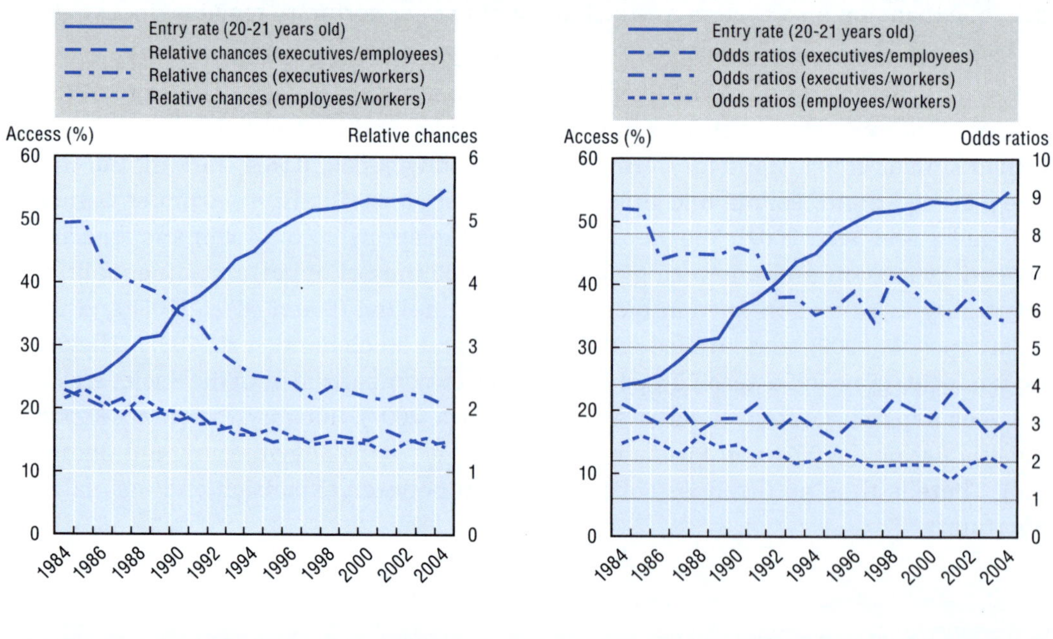

Figure 2.14. **Expansion of higher education and decrease in inequality of opportunity: 3 examples** *(cont.)*

Australia: An increase in the graduation rate at Bachelor level along with democratisation and an irregular decrease in inequality of educational opportunities

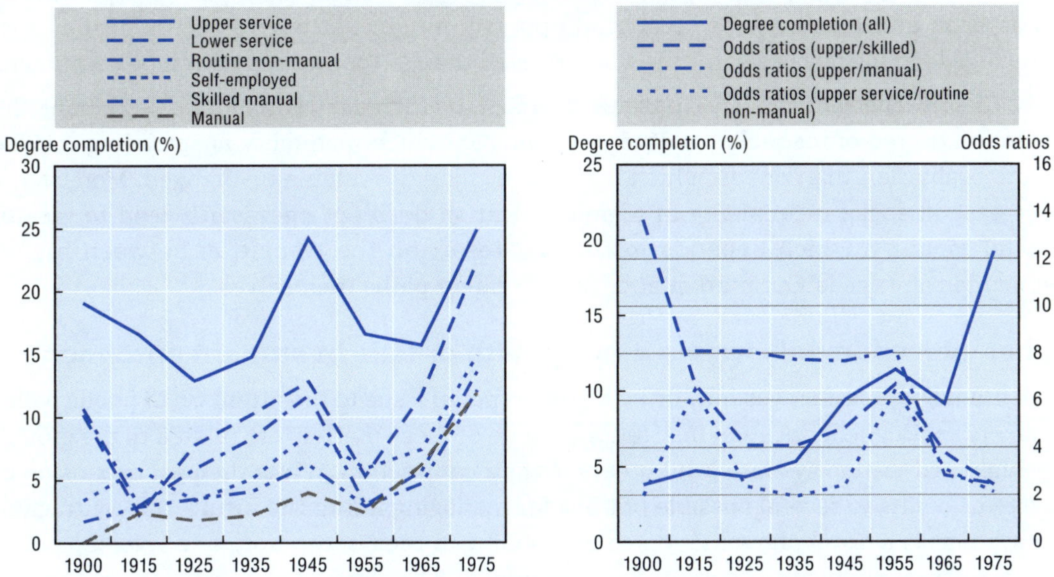

Source: Germany (*Statistische Ämter des Bundes und der Länder, Hochschulstatistik*; HIS-Hochschul-Information-System), France (Ministry of Education), Australia (Marks and McMillan, 2007).

Figure 2.15. **Trends in odds ratios for participation in higher education between people whose fathers have high and low levels of education respectively**

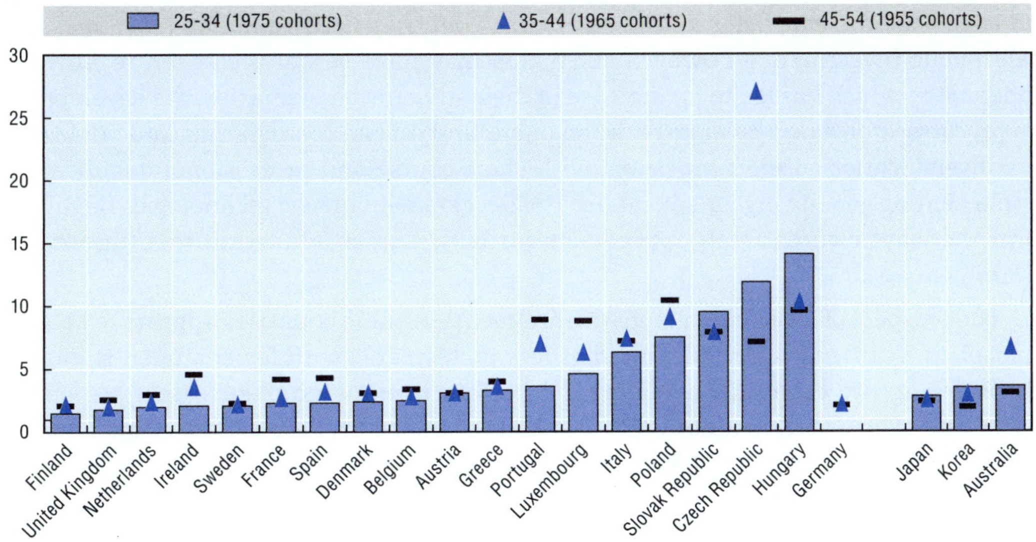

Note: Equality of opportunity is greater, the closer the odds ratios are to unity. An odds ratio of 2 means that it is twice as likely that a person whose father is educated to a high level (ISCED 5-6) will undertake higher education and that one whose father is relatively poorly educated (ISCED 0-2) will not do so, than the contrary. Odds ratios should not be confused with relative chances. In Australia, this applies specifically to cohorts born in 1961 (instead of 1955), 1965 and 1975. Data for Korea, Japan and Australia use different databases and are not necessarily comparable with each other, or with the other data.

Source: EOSS (2007); Australia: Marks and McMillan (2007); Japan and Korea: Ishida (2007).

On this basis it is possible that continued expansion of higher education is matched by a decrease in inequalities of opportunity, as has been observed in many countries in recent decades. However, given that this trend has occasionally discontinued or stagnated in the last ten years, the opposite might also occur. There is no causal relationship between expansion and equality of educational opportunity (except where access of the most privileged groups reaches saturation point), even though the two may often be correlated.

Clearly, the fact that inequalities decrease or increase tells us nothing about the absolute degree of inequality, so that a country in which inequality is spreading may be more egalitarian than one in which it is diminishing or remains unchanged. Moreover, a decrease in social inequalities in higher education does not necessarily lead to greater social mobility, which depends in the last resort on the transition between higher education and the labour market and then on career paths themselves.

2.7. Higher education policies *vis-à-vis* growth or falls in student enrolment

Demographic changes may bring certain types of issue to the attention of public policy makers and higher education institutions. Some of these matters are related to the growth of higher education systems, and others to their contraction. While the past expansion of systems points to several possible options for managing it into the future, the contraction of systems is a novel phenomenon corresponding to their saturation, or a levelling out of entry rates, as younger age cohorts become smaller. The previous sections suggest that the scale of the demographic problem will be limited in most OECD countries and that both major contractions and periods of strong growth will be very uncommon.

OECD countries have now acquired a certain amount of experience in managing the expansion of their higher education systems. Expansion has indeed been characteristic of the last 50 years of their development, albeit to a varying extent. In order both to encourage and cope with the expansion of their systems, countries have generally relied on large-scale public investment – however much this may have sometimes been regarded as inadequate – which has led to an increase in their student-teacher ratios, the development of a private sector, a new balance between public and private cost-sharing, and not least of all a diversification of their provision, with short-course and professional qualifications supplementing general higher education. The development of new technologies might also point the way towards fresh approaches for both higher education institutions and governments.

The prospect of a decline in student enrolments in some countries appears to be more unusual. In a sense, it might be viewed as less problematic: with fewer students, might it not be enough to close down institutions or discontinue courses which are under-subscribed? Would there not naturally be increased budgetary resources for improving the infrastructure and quality of higher education? The reality is more complex. Yet, as in the case of expansion, there are many possible ways forward even though the justification for them differs.

Diversification of student enrolment

One strategy of institutions for managing the fall in student enrolments is to attempt to halt it, by diversifying their intake and provision. This differentiated approach is possible given the existence of several "new" kinds of students:

- part-time students in countries in which this kind of participation remains uncommon.

- international students: their numbers have grown rapidly in the last ten years and institutions (and countries) are increasingly attempting to develop strategies for boosting their recruitment (OECD, 2006c).
- older less "traditional" students: in many countries, higher education institutions are offering easier access to courses for students with some professional experience or a family, who are seeking to retrain or obtain qualifications enabling them to change career or further their professional development. This process may or may not involve degree courses, or may lead to "certificates" awarded for evening or weekend classes.
- company employees: the provision of continuing education and training for people employed in firms, in such a way that the latter rather than their employees are the "client", is also expanding in some countries, even though it is not widespread in all OECD countries.
- retired people: the ageing of the population, with people living longer in good health, arguably creates a fresh demand for students from among the ranks of the retired whose desire to study is unrelated to their career development and envisaged more for its own sake. This would appear all the more likely if they already have a sound basic education.

While the diversification of enrolment may seem like a strategy for shoring up the fall in enrolments when higher education systems contract, it may also occur during expansion and indeed fuel it. It is thus more often viewed as a strategy for fair access and for diversity, and as a public service responsive to social demand, or a mechanism for diversifying the income of institutions.

Although institutions with falling enrolments have every reason to strive for diversification, this is often hard to achieve in practice in the short term.

The number of international students has grown strongly in the past decade, and countries and institutions have been increasingly active in seeking to attract them. In countries with low percentages of these students, recruiting them more intensively might arguably help to stem falling enrolments. Given that the past increase in international students has been included in the trends projected in Section 2.1, such compensatory action would correspond to an increase in the average admission rate of these students in the country concerned. Depending on the particular country, this approach appears more or less realistic. Not all countries are equally well placed to attract international students for a variety of reasons ranging from the reputation or climate of a country to its language or its openness to immigration (OECD, 2006c; Vincent-Lancrin, 2008; Marginson and van der Wende, 2007; Santiago *et al.*, 2008). This solution is not therefore universally applicable.

Turning to older students or retired people, as well as extending course provision for adults, may also appear to be ways of offsetting the decrease in the number of students who enrol when they leave school. For example, the American community colleges have devised strategies for adjusting to their demographic (and budgetary) circumstances by diversifying their various roles and provision. An increase in the average age of their students was observed just when the younger age cohorts were shrinking in size, as the colleges had given priority to recruiting less traditional students. With renewed expansion in the numbers of young people, a decrease in the average age of students is once again clearly apparent. Given that older students are statistically less likely to obtain their qualification, institutions might have fewer incentives to recruit them if substantial student flows are arriving from secondary education, especially whenever public expectations regarding student achievement are high (Bailey and Smith-Morest, 2007).

In practice however, the successful development of diversification may take time. Indeed, if higher education institutions lack the appropriate cultural reflexes or are faced with competition from a sector that specialises in the kind of provision just considered, they may find that there is inadequate demand for these new services. Furthermore, institutions themselves may have difficulty in adapting their provision to these new target groups, as a result of the organisational and cultural adjustments entailed or their perception of their own underlying purpose. From this angle, international students may be less of a challenge for institutions, as their expectations are often similar to those of "traditional" students.

Closures and mergers

For political and economic reasons, it is often hard to close higher education institutions, and especially those in the public sector. The first ones to face difficulty are often small private institutions or small public institutions with only a modest reputation located in rural or remote regions. Above all, the closure of public establishments in particular poses a political problem: the elected representatives of these regions or towns (and possibly other regions in similar circumstances) will tend to join forces to prevent these closures. While this may partly occur for reasons of form or prestige, local economic concerns are also an important issue. The fact that higher education institutions can make a major contribution to the economic vitality of their region (OECD, 2007d) is no less true if the latter is in economic decline. The presence of higher education institutions may encourage young people to remain in their region, or enable them to do so; moreover, through their teachers and students, not to mention their business purchases, institutions generate local economic activity the preservation of which is in the best interests of local leaders. These public players thus have legitimate reasons for seeking to sustain the activity of institutions, even if this is not very productive in national terms.

Mergers of institutions would thus appear to be more acceptable in the first instance, as they enable certain resources to be shared and savings achieved, while generally maintaining a variety of different locations. In conjunction with the forces of globalisation, which also stimulate merger for reasons to do with international visibility and the pooling of research funds, the likelihood that the student population will decrease should accentuate this trend in some countries.

Diversifying the higher education sector

The diversification of higher education may also be viewed in relation to demography, even though it constitutes a response to many other issues too, such as the appropriate matching of particular types of graduate to demand on the labour market, or research excellence. The division of labour between institutions or sub-sectors of higher education, or even courses within a single institution, has contributed to the expansion of higher education, and the management of that expansion.

To simplify matters, the various forms of diversification (or diversity) are of two main kinds, corresponding to the division between public and private institutions, or between general and professional (or long and short) higher education. General higher education is itself shared between institutions for research and for teaching, etc. Where systems are expanding, diversification provides a means of managing expenditure, broadening access to higher education and enhancing the performance of students. The cost of provision may indeed vary strongly from one type of institution to another, so that costs can be kept in check when the system is growing. Diversity may also help to satisfy more varied student demand, thereby attracting new groups of people into higher education and improving student achievement rates as long as institutions and students within the system are well matched – which also presupposes the existence of sound admissions and guidance systems. The main risk inherent in this diversity is that it can result in a hierarchy and real or perceived stratification, which may pose problems of equity (with inequality of opportunities). Where systems are contracting, diversification may be a way of limiting the decrease in enrolments, as a result of the potential effect of broadening student access. However, contraction may also lessen this diversity, with the disappearance of one or more of the least prestigious sectors.

Studies on private higher education suggest that the expansion of the private sector may often be viewed as a response – not necessarily anticipated – to restrictions on access to public higher education when the system is expanding (Levy, 2002; Teixeira and Amaral, 2007; Teixeira, 2009). For example, this has clearly been the case in Mexico, Portugal, Poland (Figure 2.16) and Chile. In Japan, private higher education has also contributed to expansion

Figure 2.16. **Student enrolment trends in the public and private sectors**

Japan: An expansion that benefited a traditionally dominant private sector

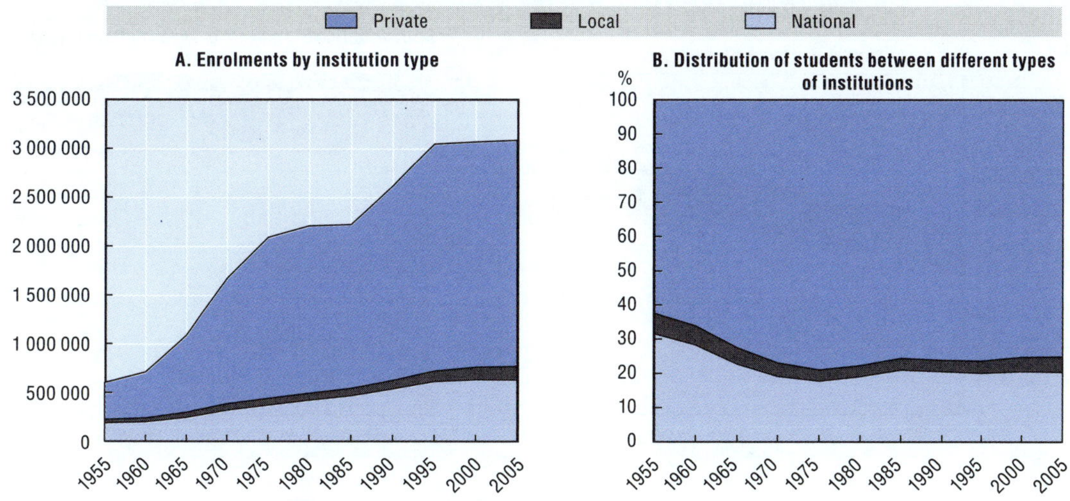

Mexico: An expansion drawing on the private sector

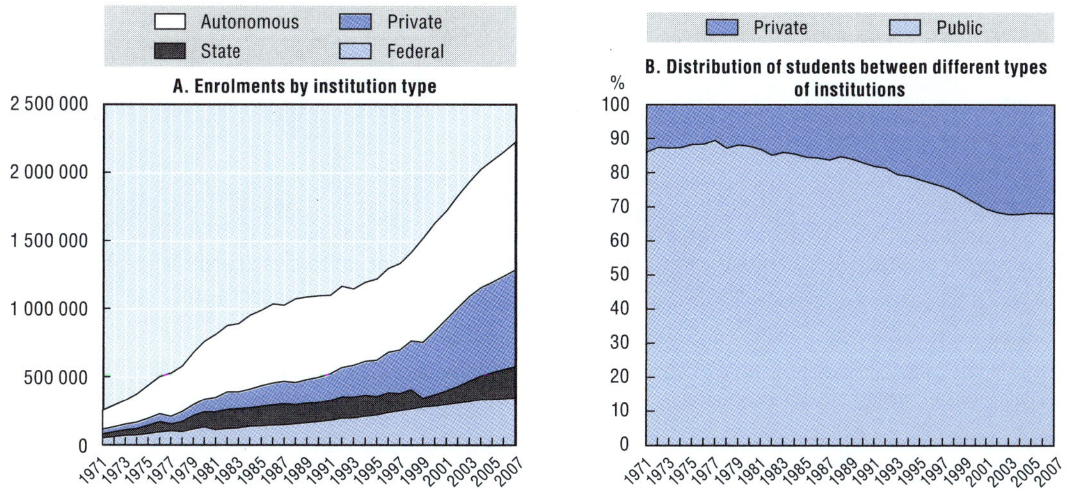

Figure 2.16. **Student enrolment trends in the public and private sectors** *(cont.)*

Portugal: An expansion drawing on the private sector and on the public polytechnics

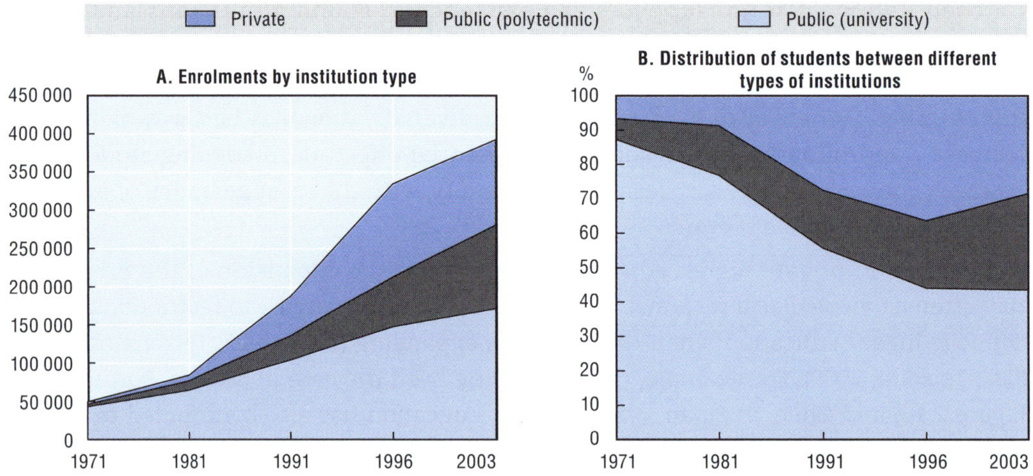

United States: An expansion with a relatively stable private sector during the recent decades

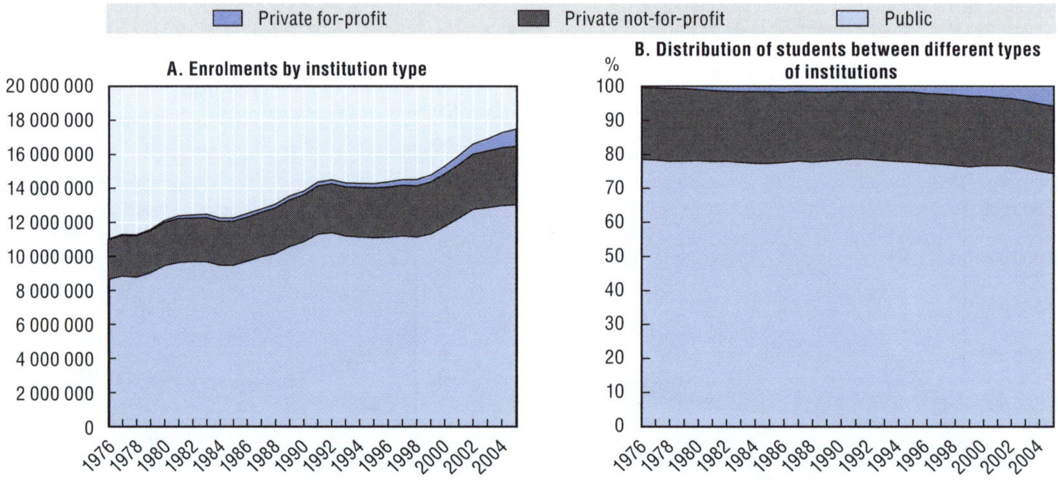

Poland: An expansion drawing on the private sector since the 1990s

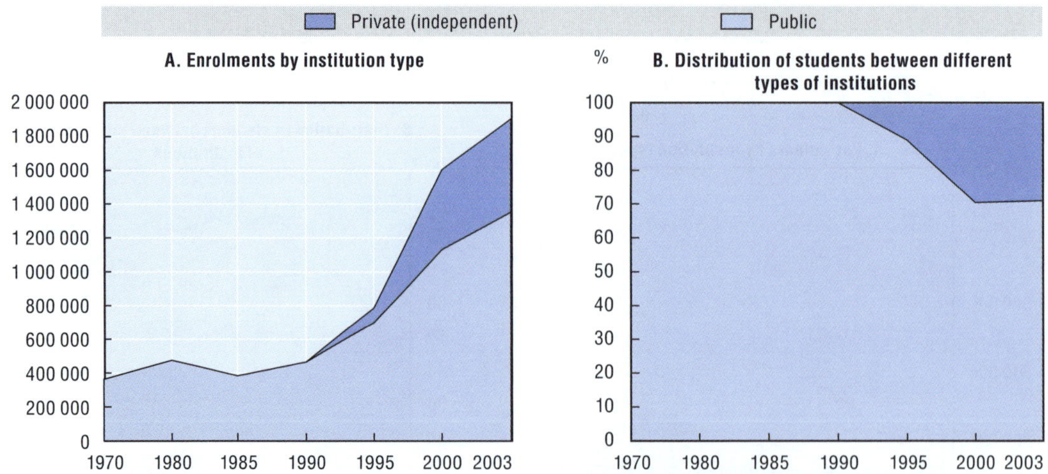

Source: MEXT (Japan), Ministry of Education (Mexico), NCES (United States), CSO (Poland), Teixeira and Amaral (2007) (Portugal).

but corresponds to a long established sector. In the United States, the expansion of the private sector has followed in the wake of increased student enrolment, rather than accentuating it. In most OECD countries, the expansion of higher education has not led to sustained expansion of the private sector, at least in the last two decades (Vincent-Lancrin, 2007).

From the standpoint of governments, the coexistence of a private sector has the merit of being far less costly than an entirely public system, even when private institutions are partly government dependent, and also of satisfying a social demand that governments cannot or do not wish to meet. This amounts to an attractive development option in countries in which systems are growing very fast. Where systems are contracting for demographic reasons, one of several open questions is whether this will affect the entire system or whether its impact on the public and private sectors will differ, leading in particular to the disappearance of the so-called demand-absorbing part of the private sector. It will thus be interesting to observe the development of the sector in the countries of Southern and Eastern Europe (such as Portugal and Poland), in which contraction can be anticipated.

Another aspect of diversification in systems corresponds to the main responsibilities of higher education institutions rather than whether they are publicly or privately owned. In this respect, the OECD countries reflect a wide variety of formally recognised possibilities, and countries confronted with such diversification have also reacted in a wide range of different ways in recent decades. Some of them have retained sectoral stability (Denmark), whereas others have granted priority to their universities (Germany and Hungary) and yet others – though to a variable extent – to institutions of professional or specialised education (Switzerland, Ireland, Poland and France) (Figure 2.17). While most systems are binary and distinguish between institutions of professional (short course)

Figure 2.17. **Expansion and diversification of systems**

France: A very diversified system that has been fairly stable between 1981 and 2004, whose expansion has partly relied on short tertiary educational programmes (STS and IUT)

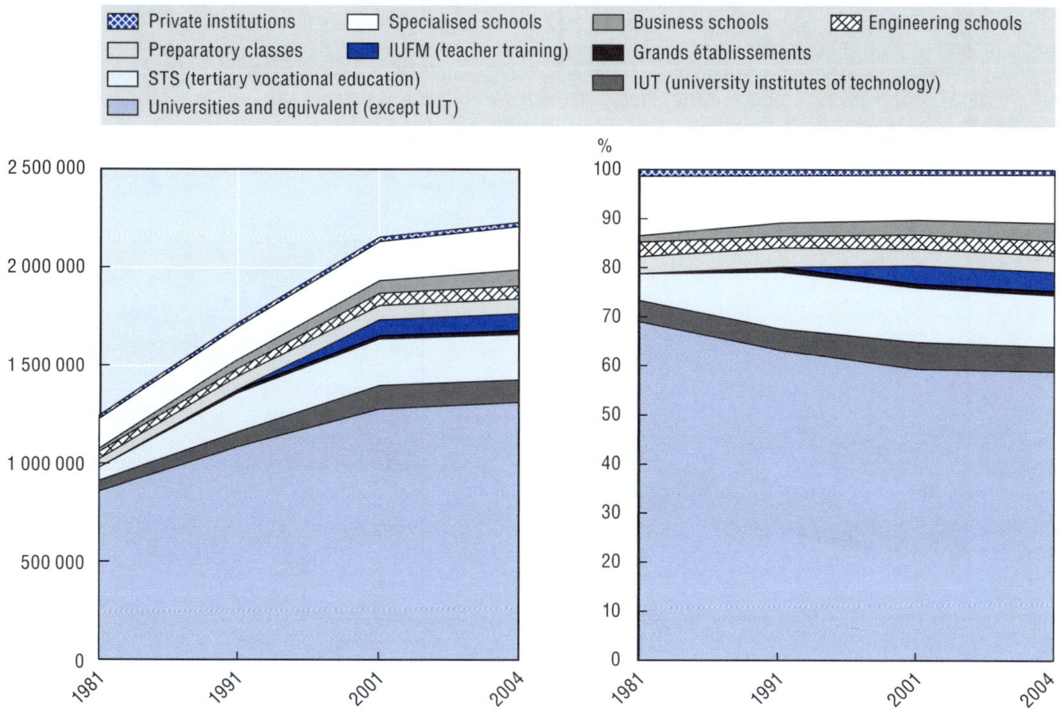

Figure 2.17. **Expansion and diversification of systems** *(cont.)*

Japan: An expansion that has first benefited junior colleges, before the university sector has regained its share with the stabilisation of enrolments

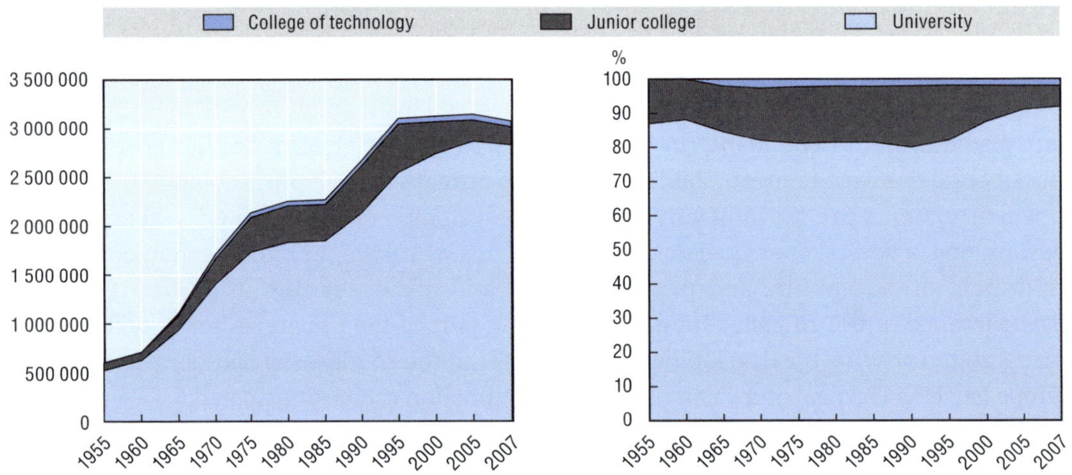

Germany: An expansion relying mainly on the university sector

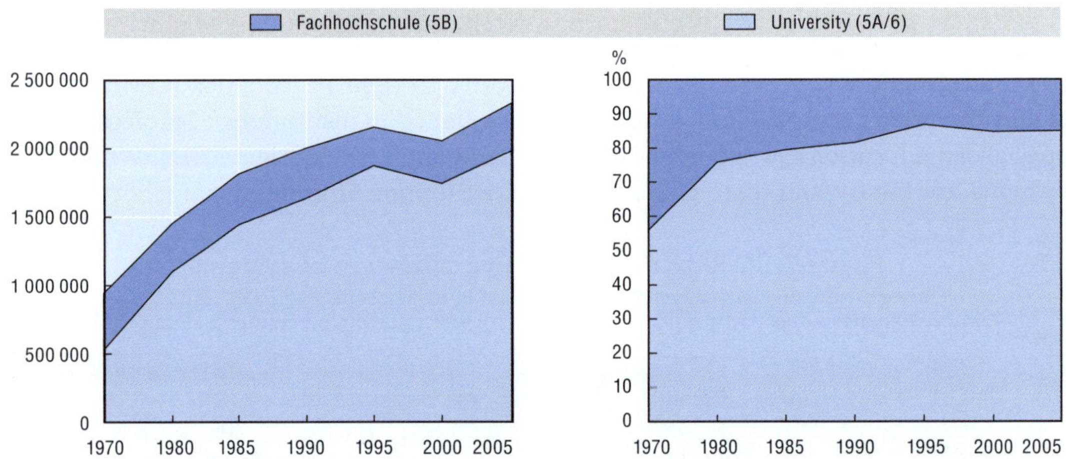

Denmark: An expansion keeping the share of the different sectors stable

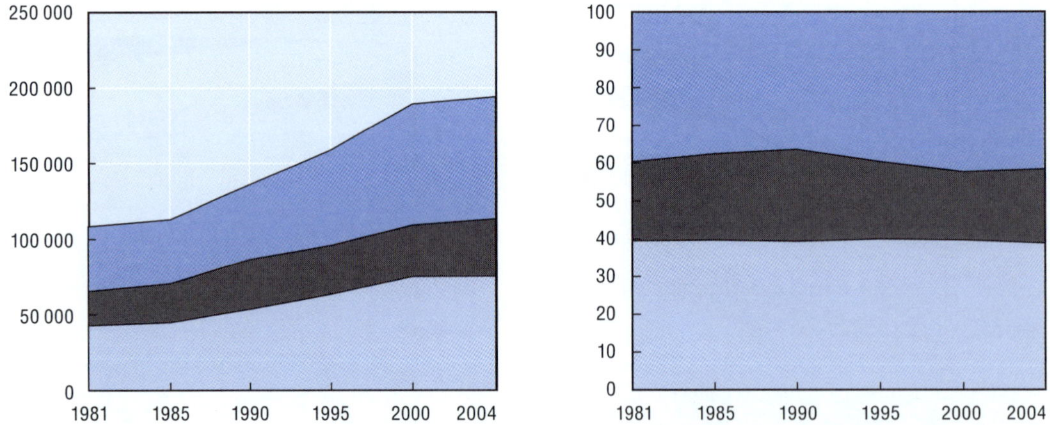

Figure 2.17. **Expansion and diversification of systems** *(cont.)*

Switzerland (awarded degrees): An expansion drawing on a slight growth of the non-university sector

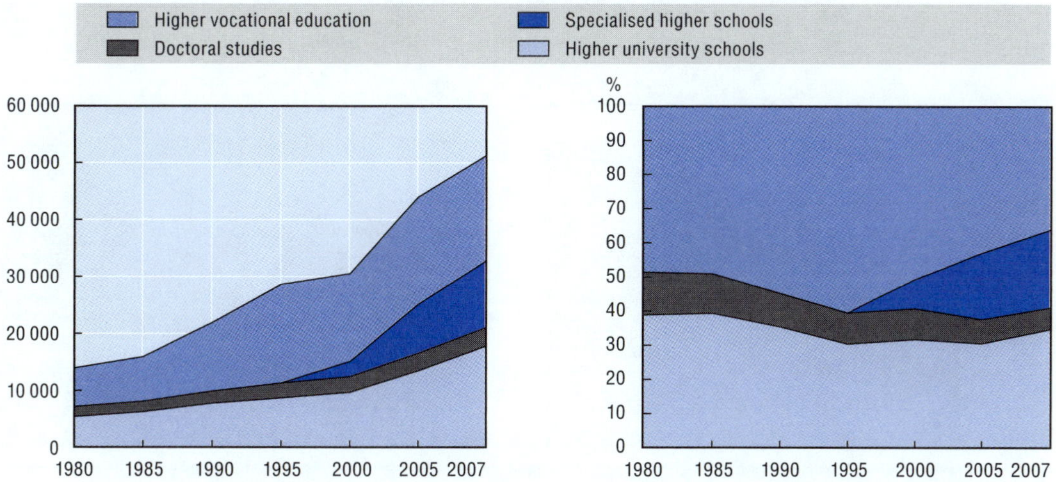

Hungary: A growth based on tertiary type-A education, without much formal differentiation

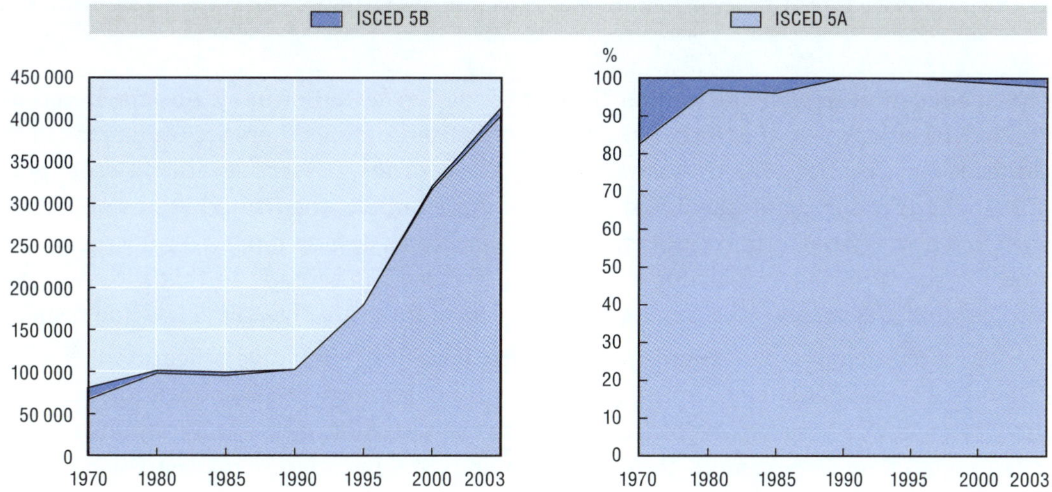

Ireland: A growth mainly based on the non-university sector

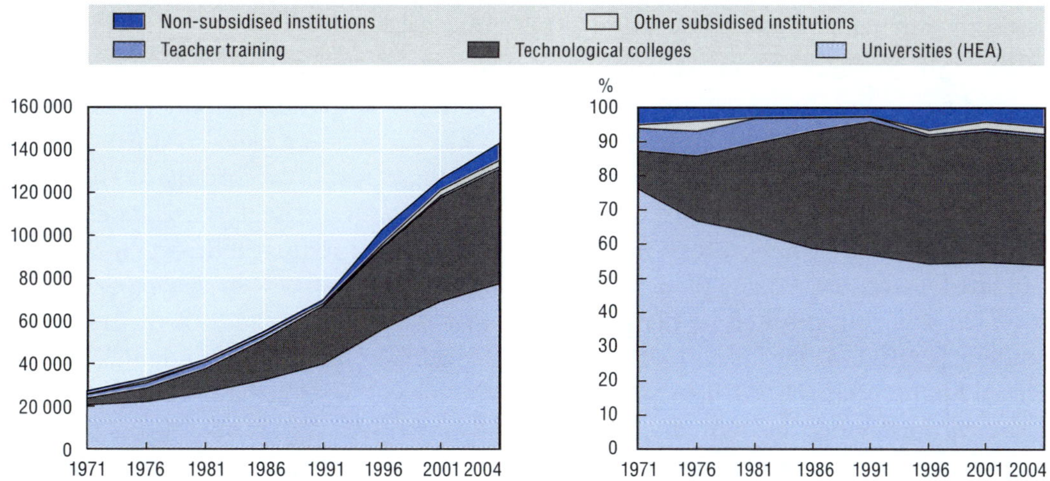

Figure 2.17. **Expansion and diversification of systems** *(cont.)*

Poland: A recent expansion keeping the structure of the system fairly stable

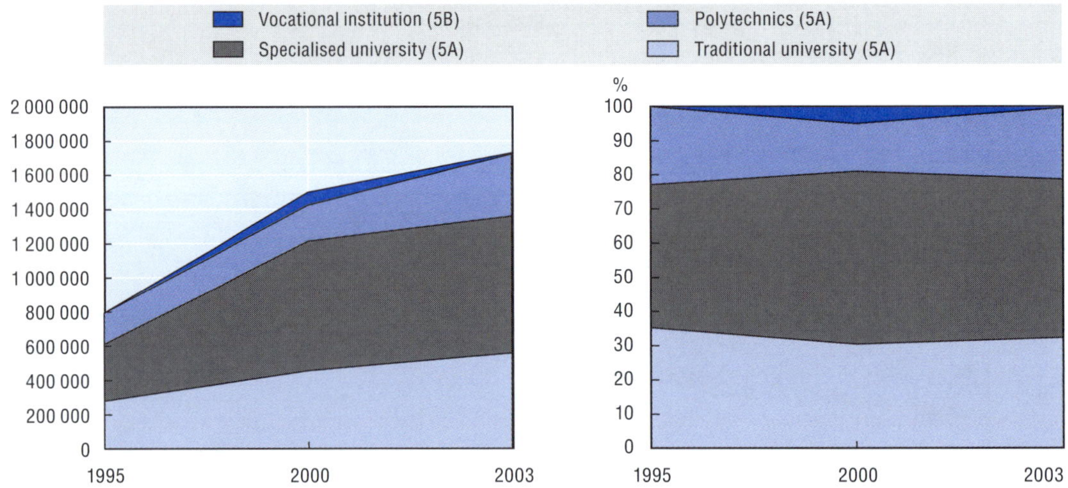

Source: France (Ministry of Education), Japan (MEXT), Germany (Federal Office of Statistics, Yearbook of East Germany for east German data up to 1990), Denmark (Statistics Denmark), Switzerland (Office fédéral de la statistique), Hungary (*Statisztikai Tájékoztató, Felsőoktatás*), Ireland (Department of Education and Science), Poland (CSO).

higher education and general (or long) higher education (as in Germany, Austria, Denmark, Finland, Ireland, Japan, the Netherlands and Switzerland, etc.), others are unitary (as in the United Kingdom since 1992, or Australia) or, on the contrary, possess several different types of higher education institutions and provision (for example, the United States or France). Over and above these formal distinctions, there is often a *de facto* if not a legally recognised stratification or division of labour within each of these sub-sectors, so that most systems may be studied from several different angles and all of them are diversified in some respects.

From the demographic standpoint, the first benefit of such diversification lies in the difference in cost per student in the different types of institution. Diversification may thus provide for lower cost expansion compared to the situation in a totally uniform higher education system. For example, the cost (or expenditure) per student may vary widely from one university to the next, depending on the level of its research commitment. In most OECD countries, the cost per student in (short) professional higher education (ISCED 5B) is lower than in general higher education (ISCED 5A) (OECD, 2007b).

Within general higher education, the difference in cost may be very variable, depending as a rule on an institution's research commitment. Although the British system is nominally a unitary one, the United Kingdom has witnessed a clear stratification of its institutions in terms of their research intensiveness: in 2007 according to the Higher Education Statistics Agency (HESA, 2008a and 2008b), 4 of the 170 higher education institutions in the United Kingdom accounted for 27% of its research expenditure and educated 4% of its students (and 7% of first degree students); 66% of the expenditure on research was concentrated in 19 institutions (21% of students and 29% of first degree students) and 80% in the first 32 (30% of students and 40% of first degree students). Similarly, only around 200 of the 6 000 higher education institutions in the United States are regarded as research universities. In Germany, the implicit hierarchy among universities is becoming increasingly explicit, with the "Excellence Initiative" (*Excellenzinitiative*) introduced by the Federal Ministry in 2006 in an effort to boost excellence in research by rewarding elite institutions on both a financial and honorary basis. Their research intensiveness is one of several criteria taken into account. France provides an example of another type of stratification with its *grandes écoles*, whose foremost concern is to train elites rather than undertake research: public expenditure per student both in the special classes preparing candidates for entry to the *grandes écoles* and within the *écoles* themselves is around twice that of the universities, with public expenditure per student in professional training courses lying somewhere between the two (Renaut, 2002).

The other benefit of system diversity is that it offers a means of satisfying the wide variety of educational goals and needs among the population. The emergence of short-course provision in higher education has contributed to its expansion in recent decades (Teichler and Bürger, 2008). In France, for example, the vocational baccalaureates and higher education programmes have made it possible to broaden access to higher education. This also applies to the United States community colleges with their two-year short courses mainly offering general education (Bailey and Smith-Morest, 2007).

If the diversification of provision both drives the expansion of systems and is a response to it, making it possible, among other things, to limit the cost of their higher education in comparison with the elite systems that often preceded them, one may well ask how a decrease in the size of systems will affect it. From one angle, countries seeking to check the fall in their enrolments will be able to continue to promote extensive differentiation within their systems, so that it becomes easier for greater numbers of students to enrol in them and do well. Furthermore, it is hard to see why countries would wish to deprive themselves of the other potential advantages of a differentiated system, in terms of relevance and excellence. On the other side, where there is a clear-cut stratification between different sectors, it is reasonable to enquire whether students in the least prestigious sector might not prefer to join the most prestigious sector if its places are less strictly limited. In Japan, it may thus be observed that the "junior colleges" sector is becoming steadily less attractive, essentially because women are increasingly deciding to go to university (Yonezawa and Kim, 2008). It might be considered that the decrease in student enrolments can only further this contraction. Yet this does not mean that the university sector will be less stratified. Since the number of places at the most prestigious universities will always remain extremely limited compared to the number of students, competition to secure admission to these institutions is unlikely to diminish.

For purpose-oriented diversification to result in higher participation and an increase in the number of qualifications awarded, it is important to establish transfer points between different courses, as well as the different types of provision and institution. This will enable students to select alternative options if they fail to progress in a particular branch or course of study, and free them from any obligation to terminate their studies rather than doing so when they wish. It is especially important for students to be able to transfer from short-course (or professional) education to long (or general) education, and *vice versa*. The development of modular courses and the possibility of accumulating credits for them over a long or indefinite period are also conducive to this kind of diversity and change the age profile of students. The diversification of systems of higher education or institutional provision at this level also presupposes a certain measure of diversification among teaching staff. Such diversity may make it easier to replace or recruit teachers by broadening the range of knowledge, expertise and experience that may be appropriate for this purpose.

It should be noted that the same diversity of purpose and costs may exist within an institution as within a system, so that the distinction between sectors is just one possible form of differentiation. However, the advantage of differentiating between the basic role of each sector is that it prevents institutions from drifting towards the university model, in which research is the foremost priority.

Public funding and cost-sharing

One of the most frequently emphasised effects of the expansion of higher education systems concerns the pressure it puts on public expenditure. It may indeed be the case that, for political or budgetary reasons, governments cannot continue to fund in an appropriate manner their higher education systems or to support systems for the least privileged students. Under these circumstances and to prevent any deterioration in the quality or equity of systems, one way of responding when they expand is to alter the share of costs borne by public and private sources, and to increase the share of private funding in the system, possibly by channelling some of the public expenditure into support for the least privileged students (Santiago *et al.*, 2008). The private financial sources correspond in most cases to the students themselves (and their families), even though institutions in certain countries (such as the United States, Canada, Hungary or Korea) manage to attract other forms of private funding on a significant scale.

An increased contribution from students and their families may have a negative impact on participation and equity if it is not paralleled by a student loans system; on the other hand, exclusively public funding with little financial support for families may sometimes limit access to higher education to a greater extent than a system in which the most affluent families contribute more (Santiago *et al.*, 2008; Johnstone, 2006). It is not our purpose here to engage in the complex debate on cost-sharing in higher education, but simply to note that the increase in private funding represents one possible pragmatic response to the expansion of higher education systems. However, there are limits to this solution, since if students have to bear excessively high private costs, this could in principle lead to decreased student participation or possibly even to downward pressure on birth rates in some countries (Yonezawa and Kim, 2008).

If one way of responding to the expansion of systems involves increasing the funding of higher education from private sources, does the opposite apply when student enrolments fall? Maybe but not necessarily. From the standpoint of institutions, a lowering of registration fees may constitute an appropriate response for them, as they can then activate competitive pricing to their own advantage to attract students into a more competitive environment. From the system point of view, the contraction of systems in absolute terms will probably correspond to their expansion or levelling out in relative terms, so that budgetary resources will not necessarily become available (see, for example, the projections for Japan in Table 2.4). Besides, in countries in which a culture of private funding is well entrenched, it is unlikely that governments will change their policy. In countries like Korea or Japan, in which fairly high registration fees exist alongside only modest student financial support, the budgetary windfall resulting from contraction might reasonably be reinvested by lowering registration fees and increasing financial support, especially if the private cost of education in those countries does indeed limit their birth rate.

As already noted, it has to be borne in mind that the relation between expansion or contraction and public expenditure is far from automatic, as the public cost of higher education depends also on the growth in costs per student, on economic growth and on the public investment that countries are politically willing to make in higher education. In many OECD countries in which the number of pupils in primary and secondary education is going to decrease for demographic reasons, the expansion in higher education might possibly be funded by reinvesting the savings achieved at those levels. Conversely, if in other countries the cost per student continues to rise faster than the level of their national resources, the contraction of systems might be paralleled by a sharp increase in the public cost of higher education and prompt the public authorities to redistribute the share of costs borne by public and private sources. In all cases, political considerations will be decisive.

The attainment, quality and number of graduates

Policies concerned with access to higher education have long sought to encourage access rather than enhance student performance. As is demonstrated by changes in policy such as those clearly apparent at the ministerial meeting on education in 2006 (OECD, 2006d), or again changes in attitudes to access regarding persons with disabilities (Ebersold, 2008), many OECD countries today pay greater attention to the achievement or graduation rates of students. It is all the more important that governments should seek to improve student attainment levels now that their societies are ageing. Despite an increase in the educational level of the population, some countries will witness a decrease in the total number or relative proportions of their graduates, especially among the younger age groups, and improving the attainment rates of their students may be one way of limiting it. In certain countries, in which the proportion of graduates in the population is relatively low compared to higher education participation rates, improving student achievement rates may also be a means of increasing graduate numbers. Student attainment is related to teaching quality in higher education, as well as to the quality of student guidance and supervision, and the way in which paths of study between different levels and types of course are structured. It should be noted here that the balance between flexibility and firmness in the structure of these study paths is important: too rigid a system which fails to provide for easy transfer between branches or disciplines, or from one institution to another, or in which students are unable to opt for alternative courses without starting their studies again from scratch, or to discontinue and then return to their studies, will tend to result in high drop-out rates, given that some students who would like to change direction or to continue their studies cannot do so easily; on the other hand, excessively flexible study paths may produce the same outcome, in this case because incentives for students to complete their studies within a given period are too weak (as may be the case in the United States).

Quality assurance and the recognition of qualifications

Because of the circumstances in which it originated, it is often thought that quality assurance is of special importance in the expansionary phases of higher education systems. Quality assurance was indeed first developed as a response to the diversification and expansion of higher education (Lewis, 2009). The proliferation of providers and forms of provision is thought to increase the risk that the quality of courses and qualifications will be compromised. It is thus becoming essential to achieve at least minimum quality standards to ensure that public money is spent efficiently or protect the various interests with a stake in higher education, including students and employers. While many countries have tended to restrict the use of quality assurance and accreditation to the private sector in their system, the likelihood that quality standards will slip is just as great in public higher education institutions.

However, quality assurance is no less important in periods of contraction. This is doubtless one of the reasons why Japan and Korea have undertaken major reforms in the area of quality assurance in recent years (Yonezawa and Kim, 2008; Santiago *et al.*, 2008). Where institutions are closed or courses discontinued, it is vital for the students affected to be able to pursue their studies in another institution without sacrificing the benefits of their previous coursework. To this end, governments have to further the recognition of qualifications, credits and previously completed courses. While quality assurance and academic recognition are two distinct mechanisms, quality assurance unquestionably promotes mutual recognition and confidence among institutions. This is why, for example, the two go hand in hand in the Bologna Process in Europe (OECD, 2004).

E-learning

New information and communication technology may also have an important part to play in managing access to higher education when student enrolments are either expanding or contracting. Its key asset in this respect is that it can make participation in higher education more flexible. In this context, e-learning is thus used primarily to deliver entire courses (in virtual universities) or, in institutions offering conventional classroom provision, to deliver certain courses or modules by distance means (OECD, 2005). In either case, this enables students to study at home and spend less time on the campus and in classrooms. On the one hand, therefore, e-learning may be used to broaden access to higher education for those who would be unable to study if they had to attend all their lectures on campus, whether prevented from doing so for health reasons (Ebersold, 2008), or because they lived in remote areas, or had to meet family or professional obligations. Potentially, if not always in practice, it thus provides an opportunity to broaden the scope for student participation in institutions and systems which wish to do so, for example because of falling enrolments. On the other hand, e-learning may also provide a better way of managing the expansion of student enrolment, by limiting the amount of face-to-face provision and, by the same token, the cost of physical infrastructure and use of buildings, or even staff costs.

Numerical impact, geographical distribution and variations over time

In certain cases, as discussed in Section 2.1, it is likely that growth (or contraction) of the system will cause little concern, either because the numbers involved are relatively small or because it is evenly distributed geographically. Regardless of their size, all OECD countries could cater, with no great difficulty, for an increase of 30 000 or even 60 000 students: if this intake could not be spread across existing institutions, a few new establishments would be enough to accommodate it. The creation of one or two million extra places in 10 or 20 years could be a challenge even for the biggest countries if it were concentrated on just a small section of their territory. The nature of the challenge is thus essentially related to the distribution of these new students across the area they occupy – as a given country might well experience simultaneously a surge in prospective enrolments in some regions and a marked contraction in others. Another organisational difficulty is linked to a possible increase followed by a decrease in student enrolment, given that this kind of variation over time may pose planning problems (Gabriel, von Stuckrad and Witte, 2007). Germany, for example, is experiencing both problems. Some *Länder* will witness a fall in their enrolments while others will experience a sharp increase. Furthermore, enrolments will first rise and then later fall.

2.8. Summary

The main conclusions of this chapter may be summed up as follows:

- Demography is only one of several factors determining the size of higher education systems: decreases in the size of younger age cohorts do not necessarily lead to a fall in student enrolments and may sometimes go hand in hand with the expansion of systems.
- Except in just a few countries, demographic changes should on the whole have a fairly limited impact on the size of higher education systems in the OECD area, whether the scenario is one that maintains the *status quo*, or the continuation of past trends in participation. Broadening of access to higher education is likely to continue, without preventing decreases in student enrolment in some countries.
- The projections carried out illustrate the relative sluggishness in the dynamics of demography as regards, on the one hand, the time lag between changes in the numerical strength of younger age cohorts and changes in the size of systems and, on the other, the impact that more elderly cohorts have on the proportion of graduates in the population: that proportion did not therefore differ radically in the scenarios considered, despite the very different growth rates they depicted.
- While changes in the size of higher education systems increase total costs in the sector, they should not necessarily result in greater pressure on national public expenditure or on the investment of national resources in higher education: in fact increases in costs are partly unrelated to changes in student enrolments, which leaves policy makers with some room for political manoeuvre.
- If past trends persist, the proportion of graduates in the 25-44 age group of the population will exceed or be close to 50% in many countries. The countries with easily the greatest proportion of graduates will be Japan, Korea and Canada. The United States will concede its relative advantage to a minor extent and the European Union (19 countries) will come close to equalling it for the 25-64 age group. By contrast, the United States will slightly increase its lead over the European Union in terms of the youngest graduates.
- The expansion of higher education has often been associated with the growth of far more inclusive access, meaning an increase in the probability that the least privileged groups in society (but also the remainder) will enter higher education. The make-up of the student population may thus reflect more faithfully the social composition of the population as a whole. While expansion does not necessarily lead to more equal opportunities among the different groups, this is what has occurred in most countries in the course of recent decades. It is possible that this will continue as expansion is pursued, but the association between expansion and inequality of opportunity is far from systematic. It is thus hard to predict the impact of continued expansion on inequalities of opportunity, even if it is likely to support efforts to increase the inclusiveness of systems still further.
- Changes in the size of higher education systems partly depend on policies in this sector, and particularly on those concerned with access, while also exerting a reciprocal influence on them, for example as regards cost-sharing or the diversification of systems. Responses to these changes and strategies for dealing with them do not basically differ whether higher education is contracting or expanding. The main issues confronting policies for higher education concerned with access, quality, its various purposes or objectives and the funding of systems, or the way in which all these issues are addressed, do not appear to be radically affected by any change in the size of systems,

even though geographical variations or changes over time may pose specific problems. The nature and management of student demography are just one aspect of more general concerns regarding appropriate relations between higher education and the labour market, or again globalisation or policy in the field of science and innovation, etc.

Notes

1. *Cf. http://nces.ed.gov/programs/digest/d04/tables/dt04_173.asp*
2. Estimates of the Standing Conference of the Ministers of Education and Cultural Affairs of the *Länder* in the Federal Republic of Germany (*KultusministerKonferenz*): *http://www.kmk.org/statist/home.htm.*
3. Data provided by the *Statisztikai Tájékoztató, Felsőoktatás.*
4. In Australia for example, GDP per capita, like GDP per student, has grown more rapidly than expenditure on higher education institutions in the last decade, so that the increase in student enrolments would correspond to a lowering of expenditure as a percentage of GDP if past trends continued – to a level of 0.6% which corresponds to long-term national projections of public expenditure on universities (Australian Treasury, 2007). In Hungary, expenditure per student fell whereas there was a strong growth in GDP; in Ireland, GDP also rose much faster than expenditure per student in higher education. Conversely, in Portugal and Spain, expenditure per student in higher education grew more rapidly than GDP, with the result that even the projected big fall in enrolments in Spain would not prevent the increase in expenditure on higher education if the past trend continued.
5. The average age of teachers does not however give a clear idea of the replacement problem, as the distribution of teachers across different age groups may vary while their average age remains the same.
6. Retirement age has been arbitrarily set at 65 in all calculations.
7. In 2008, the OECD initiated a feasibility study for an international comparison of higher education learning outcomes in OECD countries: *www.oecd.org/edu/ahelo.*

References

Aghion, P. and P. Howitt (1998), *Endogenous Growth Theory*, MIT Press, Cambridge, MA.

Anderson, E. and B. Cook (2008), "Access to Post-secondary Education in the United States: Past, Present and Future Perspectives", *Higher Education to 2030, Volume 1: Demography*, OECD Publishing, Paris.

Australian Treasury (2007), *Intergenerational Report 2007, www.treasury.gov.au/igr.*

Bailey, T. and V. Smith-Morest (eds.) (2007), *Defending the Community College Equity Agenda*, John Hopkins University Press, Baltimore MD.

Ballarino, G., F. Bernardi, M. Requena and H. Schadee (2008), "Persistent Inequalities? Expansion of Education and Class Inequality in Italy and Spain", *European Sociological Review.*

Bensusán, G. and I. Ahumada Lobo (2006), "Sistemas de jubilación en las instituciones públicas de educación superior y composición por edad del personal academic", ANUIES, *Revista de la Educación Superior*, Vol. XXXV (2), No. 138, pp. 7-35.

Boudon, R. (1973), *Education, Opportunity, and Social Inequality: Changing Prospects in Western society*, Wiley, New York.

Boudon, R. (1974), "Educational Growth and Economic Equality", *Quality and Quantity*, Vol. 8, pp. 1-10.

Bowen, W. G., M.A. Kurzweil and E.M. Tobin (2005), *Equity and Excellence in American Higher Education*, University of Virginia Press, London.

Breen, R., R. Luijkx, W. Müller and R. Pollak (2005), "Non-persistent Inequality in Educational Attainment: Evidence from Eight European Countries", paper prepared for the Start-Up Workshop of the EDUC Research Theme of the 6th EU Framework Network of Excellence "Economic Change, Quality of Life and Social Cohesion (EQUALSOC)", Mannheim, Germany, 2-3 December.

Brunner, J.J. (2007), "Chile's Higher Education System: A Comparative Political Economy Focus", *http://mt.educarchile.cl/mt/jjbrunner/archives/HE_Chile_021107.pdf.*

Buchmann, M., S. Sacchi, M. Lamprecht and H. Stamm (2007), "Switzerland: Tertiary Education Expansion and Social Inequality", Y. Shovit, R. Arum and A. Gamoran (eds.), *Stratification in Higher Education: A Comparative Study*, Stanford University Press, Stanford.

Carnevale, A. and D.M. Desrochers (2003), *Standards for What? The Economic Roots of K-16 Reform*, Educational Testing Services, Princeton, NJ.

Clancy, P. and G. Goastellec (2007), "Exploring Access and Equity in Higher Education: Policy and Performance in a Comparative Perspective", *Higher Education Quarterly*, Vol. 61(2), pp. 136-154.

Clark, R.L. (2004), "Changing Faculty Demographics and the Need for New Policies", paper prepared for the TIAA-CREF Conference on "Recruitment, Retention and Retirement: The Three Rs of Higher Education in the 21st Century", New York City, 1-2 April.

Duru-Bellat, M. (2006), *L'inflation scolaire. Les désillusions de la méritocratie*, Seuil, Paris.

Ebersold, S. (2008), "Adapting Higher Education to the Needs of Disabled Students: Developments, Challenges and Prospects", *Higher Education to 2030, Volume 1: Demography*, OECD Publishing, Paris.

Eberstadt, N. (2007), *Demographic Exceptionalism in the United States: Tendencies and Implications*, American Enterprise Institute.

Enders J. and C. Musselin (2008), "Back to the Future ? The Academic Professions in the 21st Century", *Higher Education to 2030. Volume 1: Demography*, OECD Publishing, Paris.

Erikson, R. (1996), "Explaining Change in Educational Inequality – Economic Security and School Reforms", R. Erikson and J. Jonsson (eds.), *Can Education be Equalized? The Swedish Case in Comparative Perspective*, Boulder, Colorado, pp. 95-112.

Erikson, R. and J.O. Jonsson (1996), "The Swedish Context: Educational Reform and Long Term Change in Educational Inequality", *Can Education be Equalized? The Swedish Case in Comparative Perspective*, Boulder, Colorado, pp. 65-93.

European Observatory on the Social Situation (EOSS) (2007), *Network on Social Inclusion and Income Distribution*, Applica.

Field, S., M. Kuczera and B. Pont (2007), *No More Failures*, OECD Publishing, Paris.

Gabriel, G., T. von Stuckrad and J. Witte (2007), "Up and Down We Wander: German Higher Education Facing the Demographic Challenge", manuscript for the UNESCO-CEPES project "Demographics and Higher Education in Europe: An Institutional Perspective".

Gradstein, M. and M. Kaganovich (2004), "Aging Population and Education Finance", *Journal of Public Economics*, Vol. 88, pp. 2469-2485.

Grob, U. and S. Wolter (2007), "Demographic Change and Public Education Spending: A Conflict between Young and Old?", *Education Economics*, Vol. 15(3), pp. 277-292.

Harris, A.R., W.N. Evans and R.M. Schwab (2001), "Education Spending in an Aging America", *Journal of Public Economics*, Vol. 81, pp. 449-472.

HESA (2008a), "Students in Higher Education Institutions, 2006-2007", London.

HESA (2008b), "Resources of Higher Education Institutions, 2006-2007", London.

Hout, M. and T.A. DiPrete (2004), "What We Have Learned: RC 28's Contribution to Knowledge about Social Stratification", working paper, University of California, Berkeley.

Iannelli, C. (2003), "Parental Education and Young People's Educational and Labour Market Outcomes: A Comparison across Europe", I. Kogan and W. Müller (eds.), *School-to-Work Transitions in Europe: Analyses of the EU LFS 2000 Ad Hoc Module*, Mannheimer Zentrum für Europäische Sozialforschung, Mannheim.

Ishida, H. (2007), "Japan: Educational Expansion in Inequality in Access to Higher Education", Y. Shovit, R. Arum and A. Gamoran (eds.), *Stratification in Higher Education: A Comparative Study*, Stanford University Press, Stanford.

Johnstone, D.B. (2006), *Financing Higher Education: Cost-sharing in an International Perspective*, Boston College Center for International Higher Education, Boston.

Kubler, J. and C. DeLuca (2006), *Trends in Academic Recruitment and Retention: A Commonwealth Perspective*, Association of Commonwealth Universities, London.

Levy, D.C. (2002), "Unanticipated Development: Perspectives on Private Higher Education's Emerging Roles", PROPHE Working Paper No.1.

Lewis, R. (2009), "Quality Assurance in Higher Education – Its Global Future", *Higher Education to 2030. Volume 3: Globalisation*, OECD Publishing, Paris.

Marginson, S. and M. van der Wende (2007), "Globalisation and Higher Education", OECD Education Working Paper No. 8, OECD, Paris.

Marks, G. and J. McMillan (2007), "Australia: Changes in Socioeconomic Inequalities in University Participation", Y. Shovit, R. Arum and A. Gamoran (eds.), *Stratification in Higher Education: A Comparative Study*, Stanford University Press, Stanford.

Matějů, P., B. Řeháková and N. Simonová (2007), "The Czech Republic: Structural Growth of Inequality in Access to Higher Education", Y. Shovit, R. Arum and A. Gamoran (eds.), *Stratification in Higher Education: A Comparative Study*, Stanford University Press, Stanford.

Mills, D., A. Jepson, T. Coxon, M. Easterby-Smith, P. Hawkins and J. Spencer (2007), *Demographic review.*

OECD (1997), *Education at a Glance: OECD Indicators,* OECD Publishing, Paris.

OECD (2001), *The Well-Being of Nations: The Role of Human and Social Capital*, OECD Publishing, Paris.

OECD (2004), *Internationalisation and Trade in Higher Education*, OECD Publishing, Paris.

OECD (2005), *E-learning in Tertiary Education. Where Do We Stand?,* OECD Publishing, Paris.

OECD (2006a), *Cross-border Tertiary Education: A Way towards Capacity Development*, OECD Publishing, Paris.

OECD (2006b), "Encouraging Innovation", *Economic Policy Reforms: Going for Growth* 2006, OECD Publishing, Paris.

OECD (2006c), "The Internationalisation of Higher Education: Towards an Explicit Policy", *Education Policy Analysis: Focus on Higher Education 2005-2006 Edition*, OECD Publishing, Paris.

OECD (2006d), "Key Documentation from the Meeting of OECD Education Ministers, June 2006", *Education Policy Analysis: Focus on Higher Education 2005-2006 Edition*, OECD Publishing, Paris.

OECD (2007a), *OECD Factbook 2007*, OECD Publishing, Paris.

OECD (2007b), *Education at a Glance: OECD Indicators*, OECD Publishing, Paris.

OECD (2007c), *Understanding the Social Outcomes of Learning*, OECD Publishing, Paris.

OECD (2007d), *Higher Education and Regions Globally Competitive, Locally Engaged*, OECD Publishing, Paris.

OECD (2007e), *PISA 2006: Science Competencies for Tomorrow's World*, OECD Publishing, Paris.

Park, H. (2007), "Korea: Educational Expansion and Inequality of Opportunity for Higher Education", Y. Shovit, R. Arum and A. Gamoran (eds.), *Stratification in Higher Education: A Comparative Study*, Stanford University Press, Stanford.

Poterba, J.M. (1997), "Demographic Structure and the Political Economy of Public Education", *Journal of Policy Analysis and Management*, Vol. 16 (1), pp. 48-66.

Poterba, J.M. (1998), "Demographic Change, Intergenerational Linkages, and Public Education", *American Economic Review*, Vol. 88(2), pp. 315-320.

Rawls, J. (1971), *Théorie de la justice*, Seuil, Paris.

Renaut, A. (2002), *Que faire des universités ?*, Bayard, Paris.

Rogers, A. (1986), "Parameterized Multistate Population Dynamics and Projections", *Journal of the American Statistical Association*, Vol. 81(393), pp. 48-61.

Santiago, P., K. Tremblay, E. Basri and E. Arnal (2008), *Tertiary Education for the Knowledge Society*, OECD Publishing, Paris.

Shavit, Y., R. Arum and A. Gamoran (2007), *Stratification in Higher Education: A Comparative Study*, Stanford University Press, Stanford.

Shavit, Y. and H.-P. Blossfeld (eds.) (1993), *Persistent Inequality: Changing Educational Attainment in Thirteen Countries*, Westview Press, Boulder (CO).

Teichler, U. and S. Bürger (2008), "Student Enrolments and Graduation Trends in the OECD Area: What Can we Learn from International Statistics?", *Higher Education to 2030, Volume 1: Demography*, OECD Publishing, Paris.

Teixeira, P. (2009), "Privatisation and Mass Higher Education: Lessons from Experience?", *Higher Education to 2030, Volume 3: Globalisation*, OECD Publishing, Paris.

Teixeira, P. and A. Amaral (2007), "Waiting for the Tide to Change? Strategies for Survival of Portuguese Private HEIs", *Higher Education Quarterly*, Vol. 61(2), pp. 208-222.

Thélot, C. and L.-A. Vallet (2000), "La réduction des inégalités sociales devant l'école depuis le début du siècle", *Économie et Statistiques*, Vol. 334 (4), pp. 3-32.

Vallet, L.-A. (2003), "State of The Art and Current Issues in Comparative Educational Stratification Research", *http://83.145.66.219/ckfinder/userfiles/files/pageperso/vallet/Changequal-5.pdf*.

Vallet, L.A. and L. Selz (2007), "Évolution historique de l'inégalité des chances devant l'école : des méthodes et des résultats revisités", *Éducation et Formations*, Vol. 74, pp. 65-74.

Vincent-Lancrin, S. (2007), "The Crisis of Public Higher Education: A Comparative Perspective", Working Document CSHE.18.07, *http://cshe.berkeley.edu/publications/docs/ROPS.Vincent-Lancrin.Crisis.CSHE.18.pdf*.

Vincent-Lancrin, S. (2008), "Student Mobility, Internationalization of Higher Education and Skilled Migration", *World Migration Report 2008*, IOM.

Willekens, F. (2008), "Demography and Higher Education: The Impact on the Age Structure of Staff and Human Capital Formation", *Higher Education to 2030, Volume 1: Demography*, OECD Publishing, Paris.

Wissenschaftsrat (2006), *Empfehlungen zum arbeitsmarkt- und demographiegerechten Ausbau des Hochschulsystems*.

Yonezawa, A. and T. Kim (2008), "The Future of Higher Education in a Context of a Shrinking Student Population: Policy Challenges for Japan and Korea", *Higher Education to 2030, Volume 1: Demography*, OECD Publishing, Paris.

ANNEX 2.A1

Model Description

by

Alexander A. Antonyuk*

In this document we adopt the terminology used in Rogers (2005) that describes the double exponential function of Coale and McNeil. This function, when integrated (summed in our discrete case) to any age x and then multiplied by the size of the group that will ever experience an event, *e.g.* enter higher education, yields the proportion of the group who have already experienced the event (*e.g.* entered higher education) at each age.

We take the same approach to model three key events in tertiary education: entry to tertiary education, survival on the course (or discontinuing the study), and graduation. For each of those we defined parametric functions. We fixed the shape and the mean of the entry and discontinue ("drop-out") functions for all countries to values approximately equal to the average for OECD countries. Then we fitted graduation functions for each country individually.

Parameter fitting was done by comparing output to observed data. For fixed *input* to the model we used:

- UN demographic data and median projections (as revised in 2006), namely the size of the 17-year-old cohorts for each country and for each required year.
- OECD estimates of entry and discontinue rates prior to 2004.

The *output* of the model was compared to the OECD data on the number of enrolled students in 2004. Thus, for each country we varied the mean of the graduation function (keeping the shape fixed) and found the parameters that produced output which is very close to the observed enrolment data in 2004.

Figure 2.A.1 shows an example of the three functions. Note that the area under the curves does have a simple interpretation unlike the transition rate curves in multi-state modelling (Willekens, 2008). For example, consider the entry rate curve. In the figure it has the area of 0.6, which is the sum of the function values for all ages. This means that 60% of the cohort will enter tertiary education at some point in their life. Also, we can deduce from the figure that approximately 24% of the cohort will start tertiary education by the age of 18 (2% at 16, 6% at 17, and 16% at 18).

* Alexander A. Antonyuk is a statistician at the International Energy Agency.

Once all three distributions are established the number of students (from a given year cohort) enrolled in a course is calculated as follows. The number is cumulative and is calculated from the previous year *x–1*:

$$Enrolled(x) = Enrolled(x-1) + Cohort\_Size*Entry(x) - Total\_Discontinue*Discontinue(x) - Total\_Graduate*Graduate(x),$$

where *Entry(x)*, *Discontinue(x)* and *Graduate(x)* are the values of the parametric functions at year x, and *Total_Discontinue* and *Total_Graduate* are the total number of people in the cohort who will ever discontinue the course and graduate respectively. They are easy to calculate once we know the *Entry_Rate* and *Survival_Rate* for the cohort:

$$Total\_Discontinue = Cohort\_Size*Entry\_Rate*(1 - Survival\_Rate),$$
$$Total\_Graduate = Cohort\_Size*Entry\_Rate*Survival\_Rate.$$

The model was designed to allow us to take into account the timing of changes (*e.g.* following a change in government policy) and the dynamics of the changes in demographics. For instance, while predicting enrolments in 2015, the model can account for a change in entry rates in 2010, which will only affect subsequent years.

Figure 2.A1.1. **Age functions used in the model**

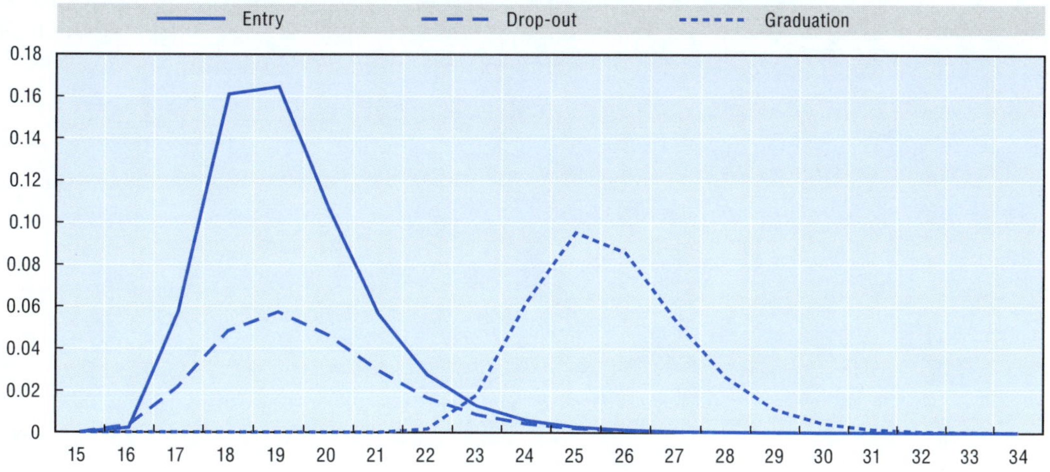

The projections have then been corrected by comparing the model output with the value actually observed in 2005.

For ISCED 6 tertiary courses, there are not enough data to carry out the same analysis so we used a simpler method to predict enrolment and attainment for these advanced degrees. We calculated the ratio of the number of students enrolled in 5A and 5B courses to that in level 6 courses in 2004. Thus we used the more detailed model to predict the 5A and 5B numbers and then calculated level 6 numbers based on those predictions. We believe that the assumption of constant ratio is quite realistic, since the ratio probably does not change very quickly and very significantly.

The reasons for having adopted such a model are the following: the availability of data, so that the model uses entry and survival rates that are available in the OECD education database; the ease of interpretation of the Coale and McNeil function; the possibility (necessity) to use an automated fitting procedure for the 30 analysed countries, given that the trial and error approach used in other research was not possible given time constraints.

The limitations and assumptions of the model are the following:

- the real patterns (shapes of the curve) of entry, survival and graduation can be to some degree different from the ones we used;
- there are no entry and survival rates estimates before 2000, so we assumed that before 2000 they were the same as in 2000;
- we assumed no mortality for people before the age of 64, which should not introduce much discrepancy for OECD countries;
- the entry function assumes that no one in a cohort enters tertiary education after the age of 28.

The whole analysis was done in exactly the same way for Type A and Type B tertiary education, and for the full-time and part-time and full-time equivalent enrolments.

Two types of projections have been made: a *status quo* scenario that freezes entry rates at the 2004 level, and a trend scenario that allows entry rates to grow according to a linear extrapolation, with growth capped at 90%.

ANNEX 2.A2

Supplementary Tables

Table 2.A2.1. **Population projections for the 18-24 age group in 2015 and 2025**

2005 = 100

	1995	2005	2015	2020	2025
Australia	96	100	104	100	98
Austria	109	100	97	86	81
Belgium	106	100	100	95	93
Canada	92	100	105	97	94
Czech Republic	125	100	82	67	67
Denmark	126	100	125	124	118
Finland	93	100	100	92	88
France	105	100	94	96	97
Germany	96	100	92	87	80
Greece	112	100	79	77	76
Hungary	125	100	90	78	74
Iceland	96	100	106	100	98
Ireland	94	100	82	85	96
Italy	141	100	94	91	91
Japan	132	100	83	83	81
Korea	119	100	93	81	65
Luxembourg	107	100	122	126	129
Mexico	101	100	107	104	100
Netherlands	114	100	110	109	107
New Zealand	96	100	106	102	99
Norway	113	100	118	115	109
Poland	89	100	72	59	55
Portugal	120	100	86	88	88
Slovak Republic	101	100	79	64	58
Spain	124	100	73	76	84
Sweden	105	100	112	95	98
Switzerland	101	100	106	98	88
Turkey	93	100	102	105	104
United Kingdom	95	100	104	99	95
United States	88	100	108	106	109
OECD	**102**	**100**	**98**	**95**	**94**
Country mean	**107**		**98**	**93**	**91**
Brazil	85	100	92	96	99
China	112	100	96	88	80
India	84	100	112	113	113
Russian Federation	84	100	62	54	59
South Africa	87	100	106	104	101
World	**90**	**100**	**105**	**104**	**106**

Source: UN Population Division, median projections (as revised in 2006).

Table 2.A2.2. Scenario 1: observed and projected enrolments in tertiary education (FTE) under current conditions

Thousands

	Total tertiary (ISCED 5/6)				Index (2005 = 100)			Absolute difference		
	2005	2015	2020	2025	2015	2020	2025	2015	2020	2025
Australia	*742*	763	740	739	103	100	100	21	–2	–3
Austria	*244*	258	246	228	105	101	93	13	2	–16
Belgium	*351*	357	341	334	102	97	95	6	–10	–18
Canada	*m*	m	m	m	m	m	m	m	m	m
Czech Republic	*326*	329	275	256	101	85	79	4	–50	–69
Denmark	*208*	275	282	272	132	136	131	67	74	64
Finland	*224*	230	212	205	103	95	92	6	–12	–18
France	*2 187*	2 201	2 229	2 304	101	102	105	14	42	116
Germany	*2 203*	2 305	2 150	2 003	105	98	91	102	–54	–200
Greece	*647*	600	572	561	93	88	87	–47	–75	–86
Hungary	*336*	339	290	275	101	86	82	3	–46	–61
Iceland	*13*	14	13	13	107	100	97	1	–0	–0
Ireland	*169*	150	157	176	89	93	104	–18	–12	7
Italy	*2 015*	2 100	2 123	2 118	104	105	105	85	108	103
Japan	*3 871*	3 364	3 357	3 152	87	87	81	–507	–514	–719
Korea	*3 210*	2 960	2 652	2 154	92	83	67	–251	–558	–1 057
Luxembourg	*m*	m	m	m	m	m	m	m	m	m
Mexico	*2 385*	2 544	2 503	2 417	107	105	101	159	118	33
Netherlands	*515*	572	568	570	111	110	111	57	53	55
New Zealand	*177*	m	m	m	m	m	m	m	m	m
Norway	*184*	221	220	211	120	119	115	37	35	27
Poland	*1 788*	1 385	1 142	1, 034	77	64	58	–403	–646	–754
Portugal	*m*	m	m	m	m	m	m	m	m	m
Slovak Republic	*181*	159	129	118	87	71	65	–23	–52	–63
Spain	*1 678*	1 318	1 289	1 411	79	77	84	–360	–388	–267
Sweden	*295*	399	339	331	136	115	112	105	44	36
Switzerland	*178*	214	201	186	120	113	105	36	24	8
Turkey	*2 106*	2 366	2 342	2 246	112	111	107	259	236	140
United Kingdom	*1 705*	1 783	1 665	1 653	105	98	97	79	–39	–52
United States	*13 126*	14 730	14 431	14 735	112	110	112	1 604	1 306	1 610
OECD	***41 064***	**41 935**	**40 472**	**39 702**	**103**	**99**	**97**	**872**	**–592**	**–1 362**
Country mean					**103**	**98**	**95**			

m = missing.

Table 2.A2.3. **Scenario 2: observed and projected enrolments in tertiary education (FTE) under recent trends**[1]

Thousands

	Total tertiary (5A, 5B, 6)				Index (2004 = 100)			Absolute difference		
	2005	2015	2020	2025	2015	2020	2025	2015	2020	2025
Australia	*742*	827	827	847	111	111	114	85	85	105
Austria	*244*	295	308	312	121	126	128	51	63	68
Belgium	*351*	354	338	331	101	96	94	2	–13	–20
Canada	*m*	m	m	m	m	m	m	m	m	m
Czech Republic	*326*	409	379	387	126	116	119	83	53	62
Denmark	*208*	289	296	285	139	142	137	81	88	77
Finland	*224*	237	225	221	106	100	99	13	1	-3
France	*2 187*	2 373	2 550	2 777	108	117	127	185	362	590
Germany	*2 203*	2 656	2 764	2 831	121	125	129	453	561	628
Greece	*647*	593	605	639	92	94	99	–53	–42	–7
Hungary	*336*	358	307	292	107	91	87	22	–29	–44
Iceland	*13*	15	14	14	117	109	107	2	1	1
Ireland	*169*	158	179	215	94	106	128	–10	11	47
Italy	*2 015*	2 236	2 402	2 566	111	119	127	221	387	551
Japan	*3 871*	3 563	3 701	3 605	92	96	93	–308	–170	–266
Korea	*3 210*	2 965	2 688	2 202	92	84	69	–246	–522	–1 008
Luxembourg	*m*	m	m	m	m	m	m	m	m	m
Mexico	*2 385*	3 052	3,297	3 457	128	138	145	667	912	1,073
Netherlands	*515*	640	681	726	124	132	141	125	166	211
New Zealand	*177*	m	m	m	m	m	m	m	m	m
Norway	*184*	235	240	235	128	131	128	51	56	51
Poland	*1 788*	1 525	1 321	1 232	85	74	69	–262	–467	–556
Portugal	*m*	m	m	m	m	m	m	m	m	m
Slovak Republic	*181*	182	163	163	101	90	90	1	–18	–18
Spain	*1 678*	1 393	1 409	1 589	83	84	95	–284	–269	–88
Sweden	*295*	389	325	333	132	110	113	95	31	38
Switzerland	*178*	234	238	235	132	134	132	56	60	58
Turkey	*2 106*	3 056	3 436	3 667	145	163	174	950	1 329	1 560
United Kingdom	*1 705*	1 943	1 904	1 972	114	112	116	238	199	267
United States	*13 126*	15 001	15 061	15 733	114	115	120	1 875	1 935	2 608
OECD	***41 064***	**44 979**	**45 657**	**46 869**	**110**	**112**	**115**	**3 915**	**4 593**	**5 805**
Country mean					**112**	**112**	**115**			

m = missing.

1. Estimates are based on the number of students enrolled both full- and part-time, and on the entry and drop-out rates for 2004, as well as on the UN median population projections for 2000 (as revised in 2006). In the case of the United States, scenarios 1 and 2 are identical because entry rates in recent years have remained at a fixed upper level. The figures shown correspond to a "third" scenario in which entry rates increase very gradually by an annual average of 0.25%. These estimates are not precise forecasts but projections intended purely as a guide. For the methodology, see Annex 2.A1.

Table 2.A2.4. **Impact of scenario 1 on total expenditure for tertiary education institutions: other budgetary projections**

	Projected expenditure as share of projected GDP				Projected public and private expenditure as share of projected GDP							
					2005		2015		2020		2025	
	2005	2015	2020	2025	*Public*	*Private*	Public	Private	Public	Private	Public	Private
Australia	*1.6*	1.3	1.1	1.0	*0.8*	*0.8*	0.6	0.7	0.6	0.6	0.5	0.5
Austria	*1.3*	1.5	1.5	1.4	*1.2*	*0.1*	1.4	0.1	1.4	0.1	1.3	0.1
Belgium	*1.2*	1.1	0.9	0.8	*1.2*	*0.1*	1.0	0.1	0.9	n.	0.8	n.
Canada	*2.6*	m	m	m	*1.4*	*1.1*	m	m	m	m	m	m
Czech Republic	*1.0*	0.6	0.4	0.2	*0.8*	*0.2*	0.5	0.1	0.3	0.1	0.2	0.0
Denmark	*1.7*	2.5	2.5	2.4	*1.6*	*0.1*	2.4	0.1	2.4	0.1	2.3	0.1
Finland	*1.7*	1.4	1.2	1.1	*1.7*	*0.1*	1.4	0.0	1.1	0.0	1.0	0.0
France	*1.3*	1.2	1.1	1.1	*1.1*	*0.2*	1.0	0.2	1.0	0.2	0.9	0.2
Germany	*1.1*	1.1	1.0	0.9	*0.9*	*0.2*	1.0	0.2	0.9	0.1	0.8	0.1
Greece	*1.5*	1.8	1.8	1.8	*1.4*	*n*	1.7	0.1	1.7	0.1	1.7	0.1
Hungary	*1.1*	0.7	0.4	0.3	*0.9*	*0.2*	0.6	0.2	0.3	0.1	0.2	0.1
Iceland	*1.2*	1.2	1.0	1.0	*1.1*	*0.1*	1.1	0.1	1.0	0.1	0.9	0.1
Ireland	*1.2*	0.7	0.7	0.7	*1.0*	*0.1*	0.7	0.1	0.6	0.1	0.6	0.1
Italy	*0.9*	1.2	1.3	1.3	*0.6*	*0.3*	0.9	0.4	0.9	0.4	0.9	0.4
Japan	*1.4*	1.2	1.3	1.2	*0.5*	*0.9*	0.4	0.8	0.4	0.8	0.4	0.8
Korea	*2.4*	2.0	1.6	1.2	*0.6*	*1.8*	0.5	1.5	0.4	1.2	0.3	0.9
Luxembourg	*m*	m	m	m	*m*	*m*	m	m	m	m	m	m
Mexico	*1.3*	1.5	1.4	1.3	*0.9*	*0.4*	1.1	0.5	1.0	0.4	0.9	0.4
Netherlands	*1.3*	1.2	1.1	1.0	*1.0*	*0.3*	1.0	0.3	0.9	0.2	0.8	0.2
New Zealand	*1.5*	m	m	m	*0.9*	*0.6*	m	m	m	m	m	m
Norway	*1.3*	m	m	m	*1.3*	*m*	m	m	m	m	m	m
Poland	*1.6*	0.9	0.7	0.5	*1.2*	*0.4*	0.7	0.2	0.5	0.2	0.4	0.1
Portugal	*1.4*	0.0	0.0	0.0	*0.9*	*0.4*	0.0	0.0	0.0	0.0	0.0	0.0
Slovak Republic	*0.9*	0.6	0.4	0.3	*0.7*	*0.2*	0.5	0.1	0.3	0.1	0.2	0.1
Spain	*1.1*	1.2	1.2	1.4	*0.9*	*0.2*	0.9	0.2	1.0	0.2	1.1	0.3
Sweden	*1.6*	1.7	1.2	1.1	*1.5*	*0.2*	1.5	0.2	1.1	0.1	1.0	0.1
Switzerland	*1.4*	m	m	m	*1.4*	*m*	m	m	m	m	m	m
Turkey	*m*	m	m	m	*m*	*m*	m	m	m	m	m	m
United Kingdom	*1.3*	1.3	1.2	1.1	*0.9*	*0.4*	0.9	0.4	0.8	0.4	0.8	0.4
United States	*2.9*	3.6	3.5	3.6	*1.0*	*1.9*	1.2	2.3	1.2	2.3	1.2	2.3
Country mean	***1.4***	**1.3**	**1.2**	**1.1**	***1.1***	***0.4***	**1.0**	**0.3**	**0.9**	**0.3**	**0.8**	**0.3**

m = missing.

Note: GDP and educational expenditure per student at constant prices have been projected linearly on the basis of the 1995 and 2005 trends. For Belgium, France, Iceland and Korea, the figures are based on the trends per student between 2000 and 2005. Public expenditure includes transfers to households, which are subsequently passed on to institutions.

Table 2.A2.5. **Impact of scenario 2 on total expenditure for tertiary education institutions: other budgetary projections**

	Projected expenditure as share of projected GDP				Projected public and private expenditure as share of projected GDP							
					2005		2015		2020		2025	
	2005	2015	2020	2025	*Public*	*Private*	Public	Private	Public	Private	Public	Private
Australia	*1.6*	1.5	1.3	1.2	*0.8*	*0.8*	0.7	0.7	0.6	0.7	0.6	0.6
Austria	*1.3*	1.7	1.8	1.9	*1.2*	*0.1*	1.7	0.1	1.7	0.1	1.8	0.1
Belgium	*1.2*	1.0	0.9	0.8	*1.2*	*0.1*	1.0	n.	0.9	n.	0.8	n.
Canada	*2.6*	m	m	m	*1.4*	*1.1*	m	m	m	m	m	m
Czech Republic	*1.0*	0.8	0.5	0.3	*0.8*	*0.2*	0.6	0.1	0.4	0.1	0.3	0.1
Denmark	*1.7*	2.6	2.6	2.5	*1.6*	*0.1*	2.5	0.1	2.5	0.1	2.4	0.1
Finland	*1.7*	1.5	1.3	1.1	*1.7*	*0.1*	1.4	0.0	1.2	0.0	1.1	0.0
France	*1.3*	1.3	1.3	1.3	*1.1*	*0.2*	1.1	0.2	1.1	0.2	1.1	0.2
Germany	*1.1*	1.3	1.3	1.3	*0.9*	*0.2*	1.1	0.2	1.1	0.2	1.1	0.2
Greece	*1.5*	1.8	1.9	2.0	*1.4*	*n*	1.7	0.1	1.8	0.1	1.9	0.1
Hungary	*1.1*	0.8	0.4	0.3	*0.9*	*0.2*	0.6	0.2	0.4	0.1	0.2	0.1
Iceland	*1.2*	1.3	1.1	1.0	*1.1*	*0.1*	1.2	0.1	1.0	0.1	1.0	0.1
Ireland	*1.2*	0.8	0.8	0.9	*1.0*	*0.1*	0.7	0.1	0.7	0.1	0.8	0.1
Italy	*0.9*	1.3	1.5	1.6	*0.6*	*0.3*	0.9	0.4	1.0	0.4	1.1	0.5
Japan	*1.4*	1.3	1.4	1.4	*0.5*	*0.9*	0.4	0.9	0.5	0.9	0.5	0.9
Korea	*2.4*	2.0	1.7	1.3	*0.6*	*1.8*	0.5	1.5	0.4	1.2	0.3	1.0
Luxembourg	*m*	m	m	m	*m*	*m*	m	m	m	m	m	m
Mexico	*1.3*	1.8	1.8	1.8	*0.9*	*0.4*	1.3	0.6	1.3	0.6	1.2	0.5
Netherlands	*1.3*	1.4	1.3	1.3	*1.0*	*0.3*	1.1	0.3	1.0	0.3	1.0	0.3
New Zealand	*1.5*	m	m	m	*0.9*	*0.6*	m	m	m	m	m	m
Norway	*1.3*	m	m	m	*1.3*	*m*	m	m	m	m	m	m
Poland	*1.6*	1.0	0.8	0.6	*1.2*	*0.4*	0.8	0.3	0.6	0.2	0.5	0.2
Portugal	*1.4*	0.0	0.0	0.0	*0.9*	*0.4*	0.0	0.0	0.0	0.0	0.0	0.0
Slovak Republic	*0.9*	0.7	0.5	0.4	*0.7*	*0.2*	0.6	0.2	0.4	0.1	0.3	0.1
Spain	*1.1*	1.3	1.4	1.6	*0.9*	*0.2*	1.0	0.3	1.1	0.3	1.3	0.3
Sweden	*1.6*	1.6	1.2	1.1	*1.5*	*0.2*	1.4	0.2	1.1	0.1	1.0	0.1
Switzerland	*1.4*	m	m	m	*1.4*	*m*	m	m	m	m	m	m
Turkey	*m*	m	m	m	*m*	*m*	m	m	m	m	m	m
United Kingdom	*1.3*	1.5	1.4	1.3	*0.9*	*0.4*	1.0	0.5	0.9	0.4	0.9	0.4
United States	*2.9*	3.7	3.7	3.8	*1.0*	*1.9*	1.3	2.4	1.3	2.4	1.3	2.5
Country mean	***1.4***	**1.5**	**1.4**	**1.4**	***1.1***	***0.4***	**1.1**	**0.4**	**1.0**	**0.4**	**1.0**	**0.4**

m = missing.

Note: See Table 2.A.4.

Table 2.A2.6. **Impact of projections on total expenditure for tertiary education institutions as share of public expenditure: other budgetary projections**

Public expenditure for tertiary education institutions as share of all public expenditure, 2005 and projections

	2005	Scenario 1			Scenario 2		
		2015	2020	2025	2015	2020	2025
Australia	*m*	1.9	1.6	1.4	2.0	1.8	1.6
Austria	*2.4*	2.9	2.8	2.6	3.3	3.5	3.6
Belgium	*2.2*	2.0	1.7	1.5	2.0	1.7	1.5
Canada	*3.5*	m	m	m	m	m	m
Czech Republic	*1.9*	1.2	0.7	0.4	1.5	0.9	0.6
Denmark	*3.1*	4.5	4.5	4.3	4.7	4.8	4.5
Finland	*3.3*	2.7	2.3	2.0	2.8	2.4	2.2
France	*2.1*	1.9	1.8	1.7	2.1	2.0	2.1
Germany	*2.0*	2.1	1.9	1.7	2.4	2.4	2.4
Greece	*m*	3.7	3.7	3.7	3.7	3.9	4.2
Hungary	*1.7*	1.1	0.7	0.4	1.2	0.7	0.4
Iceland	*2.6*	2.5	2.2	2.0	2.7	2.4	2.2
Ireland	*2.8*	2.0	1.8	1.9	2.1	2.1	2.3
Italy	*1.3*	1.8	1.9	1.9	1.9	2.1	2.3
Japan	*1.3*	1.1	1.1	1.1	1.2	1.3	1.3
Korea	*2.0*	1.7	1.4	1.1	1.7	1.4	1.1
Luxembourg	*m*	m	m	m	m	m	m
Mexico	*3.8*	m	m	m	m	m	m
Netherlands	*2.2*	2.2	1.9	1.7	2.4	2.3	2.2
New Zealand	*2.8*	m	m	m	m	m	m
Norway	*m*	m	m	m	m	m	m
Poland	*2.7*	1.6	1.1	0.9	1.7	1.3	1.1
Portugal	*1.9*	m	m	m	m	m	m
Slovak Republic	*3.5*	1.2	0.7	0.5	1.4	1.0	0.9
Spain	*2.3*	2.5	2.5	2.9	2.7	2.8	3.4
Sweden	*2.5*	2.6	1.9	1.7	2.5	1.9	1.7
Switzerland	*3.1*	m	m	m	m	m	m
Turkey	*m*	m	m	m	m	m	m
United Kingdom	*2.0*	2.0	1.8	1.7	2.1	2.0	2.0
United States	*2.7*	3.4	3.4	3.4	3.5	3.5	3.7
Country mean	***2.5***	**2.2**	**2.0**	**1.8**	**2.4**	**2.3**	**2.2**

m = missing.
Note: See Table 2.A.4.

Table 2.A2.7. **Impact of changes in enrolments on budget for tertiary education institutions: other budgetary projections**

	Change in public and private expenditure for tertiary education institutions imputable to enrolment change as share of GDP						Change in public expenditure for tertiary education institutions imputable to enrolment change as share of all public expenditure					
	Scenario 1			Scenario 2			Scenario 1			Scenario 2		
	2015	2020	2025	2015	2020	2025	2015	2020	2025	2015	2020	2025
Australia	–0.02	–0.05	–0.05	0.10	0.09	0.11	–0.02	–0.07	–0.06	0.14	0.12	0.15
Austria	0.09	0.02	–0.08	0.31	0.39	0.42	0.17	0.04	–0.16	0.59	0.74	0.80
Belgium	0.01	–0.04	–0.05	0.00	–0.04	–0.06	0.01	–0.07	–0.10	–0.01	–0.09	–0.11
Canada	m	m	m	m	m	m	m	m	m	m	m	m
Czech Republic	0.01	–0.07	–0.06	0.16	0.07	0.05	0.01	–0.13	–0.11	0.30	0.13	0.10
Denmark	0.59	0.64	0.55	0.71	0.77	0.66	1.07	1.17	1.00	1.29	1.39	1.21
Finland	0.05	–0.06	–0.09	0.09	0.01	–0.01	0.09	–0.11	–0.16	0.17	0.02	–0.01
France	0.03	0.04	0.07	0.12	0.20	0.29	0.04	0.06	0.11	0.19	0.32	0.46
Germany	0.05	–0.02	–0.09	0.23	0.27	0.30	0.10	–0.04	–0.17	0.41	0.50	0.55
Greece	–0.13	–0.22	–0.26	–0.15	–0.12	–0.02	–0.28	–0.47	–0.55	–0.32	–0.25	–0.03
Hungary	0.01	–0.06	–0.06	0.05	–0.04	–0.04	0.01	–0.10	–0.09	0.08	–0.06	–0.06
Iceland	0.12	0.03	0.01	0.22	0.13	0.10	0.24	0.07	0.02	0.46	0.27	0.20
Ireland	–0.06	–0.02	0.05	–0.02	0.07	0.20	–0.16	–0.07	0.13	–0.06	0.18	0.54
Italy	0.05	0.07	0.07	0.13	0.24	0.35	0.08	0.10	0.10	0.19	0.35	0.51
Japan	–0.17	–0.18	–0.26	–0.10	–0.05	–0.09	–0.15	–0.16	–0.23	–0.09	–0.04	–0.08
Korea	–0.16	–0.34	–0.61	–0.16	–0.32	–0.58	–0.14	–0.30	–0.53	–0.14	–0.28	–0.51
Luxembourg	m	m	m	m	m	m	m	m	m	m	m	m
Mexico	0.11	0.08	0.03	0.41	0.51	0.56	m	m	m	m	m	m
Netherlands	0.14	0.12	0.11	0.28	0.33	0.38	0.24	0.20	0.19	0.49	0.58	0.65
New Zealand	m	m	m	m	m	m	m	m	m	m	m	m
Norway	m	m	m	m	m	m	m	m	m	m	m	m
Poland	–0.31	–0.41	–0.42	–0.21	–0.31	–0.32	–0.51	–0.68	–0.70	–0.35	–0.51	–0.53
Portugal	m	m	m	m	m	m	m	m	m	m	m	m
Slovak Republic	–0.36	–0.43	–0.41	–0.23	–0.28	–0.24	–0.69	–0.82	–0.78	–0.44	–0.53	–0.46
Spain	–0.87	–0.95	–0.82	–0.78	–0.80	–0.59	–1.82	–1.98	–1.72	–1.63	–1.66	–1.22
Sweden	0.47	0.19	0.15	0.42	0.14	0.15	0.73	0.30	0.23	0.66	0.23	0.24
Switzerland	m	m	m	m	m	m	m	m	m	m	m	m
Turkey	m	m	m	m	m	m	m	m	m	m	m	m
United Kingdom	0.15	0.06	0.05	0.26	0.22	0.26	0.22	0.09	0.08	0.38	0.33	0.38
United States	0.30	0.22	0.30	0.37	0.38	0.55	0.29	0.21	0.29	0.35	0.36	0.52
Country mean	**0.00**	**–0.06**	**–0.07**	**0.11**	**0.10**	**0.14**	**–0.02**	**–0.12**	**–0.15**	**0.12**	**0.10**	**0.18**

m = missing.

Note: See Table 2.A.4.

ISBN 978-92-64-04065-6
Higher Education to 2030
Volume 1: Demography

Chapter 3

Demography and Higher Education: The Impact on the Age Structure of Staff and Human Capital Formation

by

Frans Willekens*

This chapter first highlights major demographic trends in the OECD area and compares them to trends in other major areas of the world. It then presents a simulation to show how the ageing of staff in higher education is an outcome of two processes – ageing in place and evolution of the student population – demonstrating the importance of a cohort perspective in investigating the relation between demography and the future of higher education. The paper then looks at human capital produced by higher education in terms of the contribution to the labour market of tertiary education graduates in person-years. It concludes by speculating on the role of demographics as a driver of change in higher education.

* Netherlands Interdisciplinary Demographic Institute (NIDI), The Hague.

3.1. Introduction

Demography affects the future of higher education in two important ways. The first is the demand for education. A decline in fertility has an immediate effect on the number of births and, with a certain delay, on the recruitment base for higher education. The second is the ageing of lecturers and researchers in institutions of higher education, which is only partly due to the ageing of the population. In fact, more people than ever survive to the age of retirement, but a major reason for the ageing of staff is past patterns of recruitment and replacement (turnover). The rapid growth of institutions of higher education in the 1960s and 1970s to accommodate the baby boom generation and the increase in participation rates led to extensive recruitment of personnel. The baby boom was then followed by a baby bust, and the need for new personnel was minimal because the necessary staff was already in place and was ageing.

This paper first highlights major demographic trends in the OECD area and compares them to trends in other major areas of the world. It then presents a simulation to show how the ageing of staff in higher education is an outcome of two processes: namely, ageing in place and evolution of the student population. The combination of a declining student population and a staff that is ageing in place leaves little room for recruitment, and this has been a problem for many institutions of higher education in the OECD area. What the simulation shows is the importance of a cohort perspective in investigating the relation between demography and the future of higher education. The cohort perspective is addressed in the third of these sections. Education is an investment in human capital and increases future labour productivity and future income. The measurement of human capital and assessment of the impact of human capital on economic growth have been, and continue to be, the subject of many studies. A number of these studies advocate a cohort perspective rather than a period or cross-sectional perspective. The fourth section therefore measures human capital produced by higher education in terms of the contribution to the labour market of graduates from higher education in person-years. This concept of human capital is related to the income-based approach to human capital measurement but is much simpler. A concluding section speculates on the role of demographics as a driver of change in higher education.

3.2. Major demographic trends in the OECD area

The OECD area is quite heterogeneous. It includes high-fertility countries such as Mexico and Turkey and countries with very low fertility such as Italy and the Czech Republic. Trends in total fertility rates (TFR) have changed dramatically over the last 30 years, declining from an average of 2.4 children per woman in 1970 to 1.6 in 2000. Most of this decline took place between 1970 and 1985. In southern European countries, the decline started later but was much faster. In Central Europe, the decline was also remarkably rapid, dropping from around replacement level in the mid-1980s to a TFR of around 1.3 at the beginning of the 21st century. This very rapid decline can be attributed in part to postponement of the first birth from about age 24 in 1970 to between 27 and 30 at the turn of the century. When women become mothers at a later age, the decline is temporary and fertility increases after a period of low fertility. In most countries, fertility remains low but some countries, most notably the United States and the Nordic countries, have experienced a recovery. Countries such as Japan and Italy, however, have not seen a recovery and fertility is very low (1.3 or lower). For a description of fertility trends in OECD countries, see Sleebos (2003).

A comparison of the decline in fertility in the OECD area with the decline in two very large non-member countries, China and India, leads to an interesting observation (Figure 3.1): both have experienced a decline in fertility and are converging towards the European fertility rate. In China, the decline has been extremely rapid, owing in part to the one-child policy. In India, the decline has been slower but regional differences are marked. Fertility declined rapidly in southern India and several areas have a TFR of near or below replacement level. In northern India, most states continue to experience high fertility. Overall, by 2025, China, India, North America and Europe are projected to have closer levels of fertility rates.

Figure 3.1. **Total fertility rates, selected regions of the world**

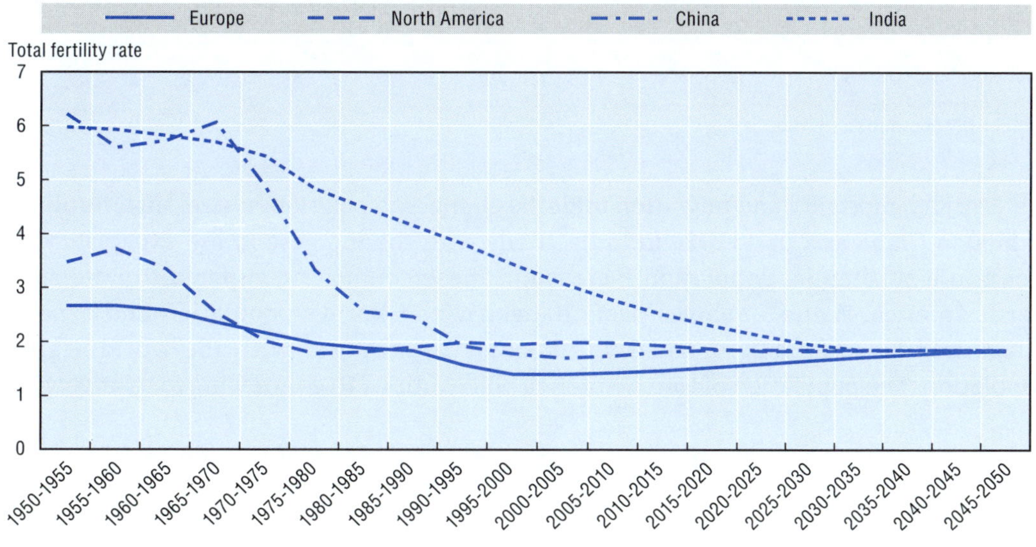

Source: UN Population Division.

In the OECD area, life expectancy has been increasing, from around 65 for males and 70 for females in 1950 to 70-75 for males and 78-80 for females at the turn of the century. Japan enjoys the highest life expectancy, 78.6 for males and 85.6 for females. The United Nations expects life expectancy in OECD countries to increase further to 78-80 for males and 83-85 for females around 2050. Life expectancy at 65 is increasing too. In 2003, average life expectancy for a person 65 years old across OECD countries stood at 15.9 for males and 19.3 for females, an increase of more than three years since 1970. The increase is expected to continue. The OECD projects that in 2040 average life expectancy at 65 in the OECD area will reach 18.1 years for males and 21.6 years for females. China and India are catching up. They started from life expectancy of about 40 for males in 1950 and of 42 (China) and 38 (India) for females. Until the first half of the 1980s, females in India had a shorter expected lifetime than males. Currently, however, females are living longer than males, in India as in other countries of the world. Figure 3.2 shows the long-term trend in life expectancy for several areas of the world, again a convergence pattern.

Figure 3.2. **Life expectancy at birth, selected regions of the world**

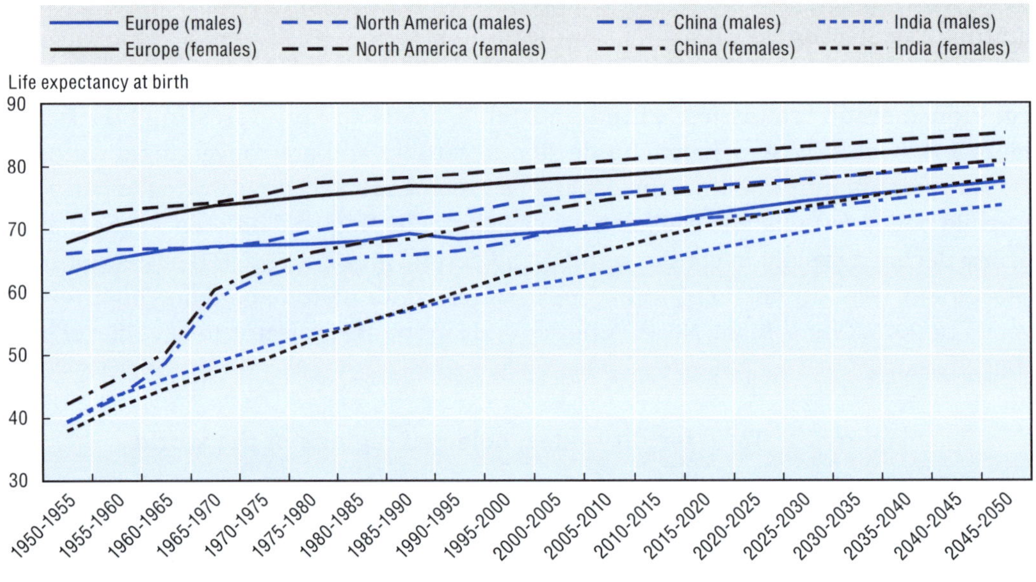

Source: UN Population Division.

Fertility, mortality and migration underlie changes in population size. High fertility up to 1990 in China and up to 2025 in India, along with the increase in life expectancy, will result in a substantial population increase in these countries compared to Europe and North America. Figure 3.3 shows past changes in the world's population and expected future trends. Around 2030, India will become the country with the world's largest population. The population of North America will continue to grow owing to relatively high

Figure 3.3. **Total population, selected regions of the world**

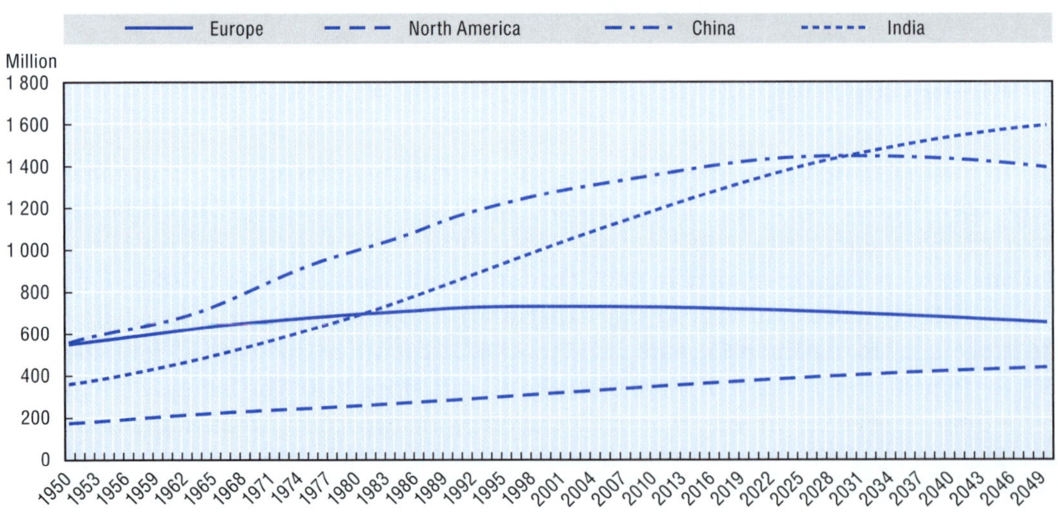

Source: UN Population Division.

fertility. In Japan, the population was expected to peak in 2006 and then move into a period of decline. According to the United Nations, Europe's population reached a peak in 2003.

The combination of the decline in fertility and the increase in life expectancy results in an ageing population. Today the elderly (65+) account for between 15% and 20% of the population in many OECD countries. The increase in the share of the elderly is most rapid in countries that experienced rapid declines in fertility, such as Japan and Korea. In 2030 the population aged 65+ is projected to reach 30% in Japan and Italy. For a recent account of demographic changes in OECD countries, see Gonand (2005).

Ageing of the population is not restricted to OECD countries. It is occurring in many parts of the world, including China and India. Throughout history, humankind has searched for the secrets of longevity and for ways that allow couples to have the number of children they want. Today, people live longer than ever before, and reliable and safe family planning methods are widely available. However, these major achievements pose new challenges and require society to adjust to the new realities. Smaller families and longer lives imply an increase in the old-age dependency ratio unless pension reform restores the balance between working life and retirement, labour market policies lead to more effective use of human capital, and health policies help to achieve more active ageing. The achievements of the past have enabled people to take more control over their lives. The challenge of the future will be to extend that control while maintaining a balance between individual and social responsibilities.

3.3. Ageing in the higher education sector

The overall population of lecturers, researchers and other personnel in higher education is ageing, a trend that will continue. The main reason is not the ageing of the general population but recruitment associated with the tenure system. This section uses a simple simulation model to demonstrate the effect of: *i)* declining enrolments in higher education as a result of the decline in fertility; *ii)* a recruitment policy that links new recruitments to the size of the student population; and *iii)* the tenure system in higher education which has led to the ageing that characterises the educational sector in general.

Assume an institution of higher education with a ratio of one staff member for 15 students.[1] Recruitment policy seeks to maintain that ratio. A student population of 45 000 means a staff of 3 000. Assume that in the base year the composition of the staff is as follows: about one-quarter (24%) are between 50 and 64; about one-third (32%) are between 40 and 49; and the rest (44%) are under 40. The youngest staff member is 29. Of the employees aged 50-64, one out of six is assumed to be over 60. The staff members of a given age group are distributed uniformly over the ages in the age group. Hence, there are 120 staff members for each year of age for the age group 29-39, 96 for the age group 40-49, 60 for the age group 50-59, and 24 for the age group 60-64. Assume further that no staff member dies, no one leaves before retirement at age 65, and there is no problem for replacing them.

Three scenarios are considered: constant enrolment, declining enrolment and increasing enrolment

First scenario: constant enrolment

When enrolment remains fixed at 45 000, staff size remains constant and retiring staff members are replaced through recruitment. In an attempt to maintain a young workforce, new recruits are 29 years of age. During the first five years, 24 persons retire each year. After this initial period, the figure increases to 60 retirements a year over the following ten years, to 96 in the subsequent ten years and to 120 in the next period. The age composition of the staff is shown in Figure 3.4.

Figure 3.4. **Number of staff members, by age group: constant enrolment scenario**

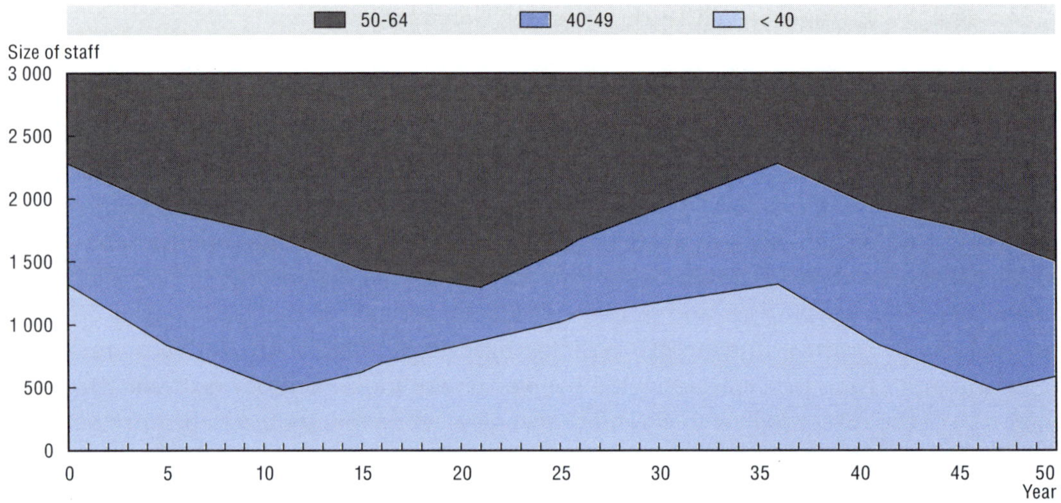

The total number of employees remains fixed but the age structure changes significantly over time. The share of employees less than 40 years of age declines from 44% in the base year to 16% after 11 years. When the large cohorts of employees below 50 start to retire, recruitment of young employees increases substantially and the share of young members of the staff starts to increase. Initially, the increase comes at the cost of the age class 40-49. After 21 years, only 14% of the workforce is in their forties while 57% are 50 or older. Then, 36 years after the introduction of the recruitment policy, the composition of the workforce is the same as in the initial period: 44% are below 40, 32% are between 40 and 49, and 24% are 50 or over. During the years that follow, the pattern observed initially is repeated. The scenario with constant enrolment and a recruitment policy that is fully determined by replacement of retiring staff members by young persons shows that a remarkable change in age structure may result.

Second scenario: declining enrolments

Consider a scenario in which enrolment decreases by 300 each year. After 50 years, enrolment declines from 45 000 initially to 30 000. As a consequence, the staff is reduced from 3 000 to 2 000, or 20 staff members a year. The reduction is obtained by not replacing all retiring employees. The number being replaced in a given year is the number retiring minus 20. As a result of the change in enrolment and the recruitment policy, the share of employees under 40 years of age declines from 44% initially to 9% after 11 years. In that year, those aged 50 or more account for 47%. The proportion of those aged 50+ increases further to 66% after 21 years. In that year, 25% of the staff is under 40 and only 9% are between 40 and 49. Figure 3.5 shows the changing age structure.

Figure 3.5. **Number of staff members, by age group: decreasing enrolment ratio**

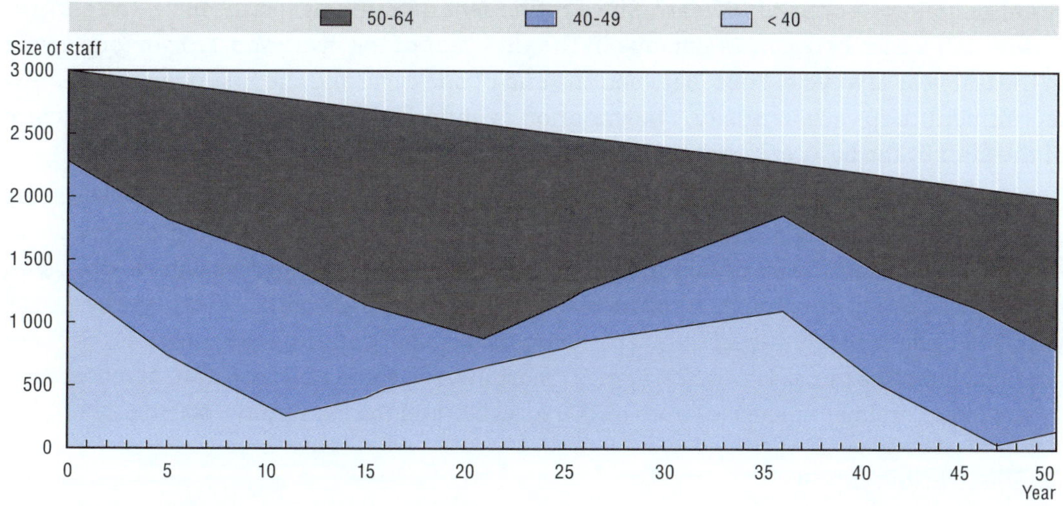

Third scenario: increasing enrolments

In the third scenario, assume that the enrolment increases by 300 students a year. This is a linear increase from 45 000 in the base period to 60 000 after 50 years. After 11 years, the staff under 40 years of age reaches a minimum of 22% which compares favourably with the 16% in the constant enrolment scenario and the 9% in the decreasing enrolment scenario. After 21 years, the proportion of those aged 50+ reaches a maximum of 50% (see Figure 3.6).

These simple simulations illustrate vividly the consequences of student enrolments and recruitment policy on the age structure of the workforce in institutions of higher education. Although the figures are arbitrary, the results of such restrictions on institutions of higher education (student/staff ratio and staff stability) are real. When the staff is stable and ages in place, its age structure varies, even when enrolment remains constant. When

Figure 3.6. **Number of staff members, by age group: increasing enrolment scenario**

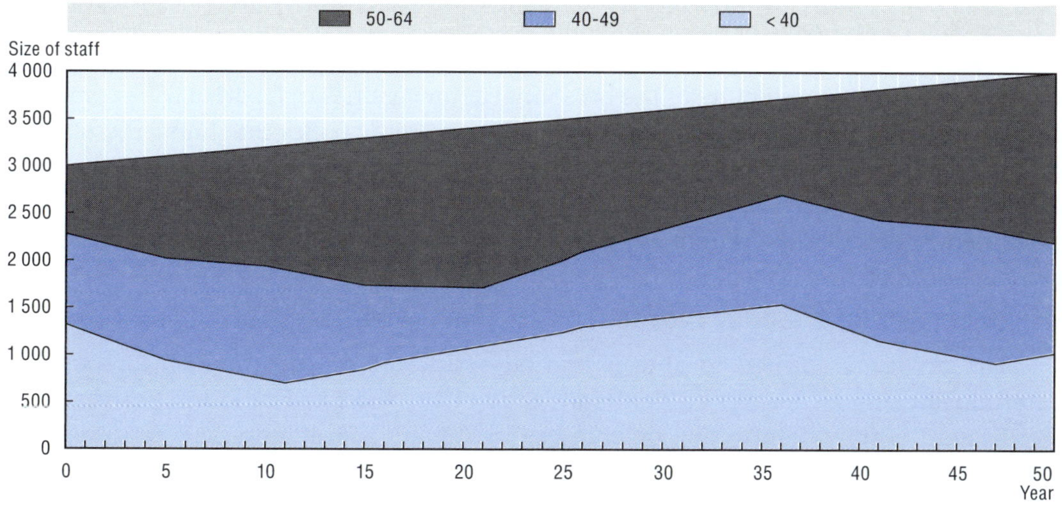

enrolment is constant, staff members retire at 65, and retirees are replaced by young persons (aged 29), and the share of senior staff (50-64) varies between 24% and 57%. The variation follows a cycle of 36 years. Since retirement determines recruitment, the entry of young staff varies between 24 persons in the first year of the cycle and 120 persons a year in the last year of a cycle. Thus, between the end of one cycle and the first phase of the next recruitment drops substantially. The variation is entirely determined by the age structure of the staff in the base year and the recruitment and retirement policies.

In sum, enrolment affects recruitment and hence the age structure of the staff. The share of senior staff reaches a maximum of 66% when enrolments decline and of 50% when enrolments increase. To maintain a more or less balanced age structure with a strict staff replacement policy, enrolments must increase. For instance, if enrolments increase by 1 000 a year, the cycle is barely perceptible. The share of the junior staff (those under 40) declines gradually from the initial 44% to 32% after 50 years and the share of senior staff increases from 24% to 39%. Enrolment increases from 45 000 to 95 000 and the staff from 3 000 to 6 333.

An illustration: Japan

The theoretical model is illustrated using data on Japanese universities.[2] In Japan, university enrolments increased from 1.7 million in 1972 to 3.8 million in 2005. The increase was rapid in the 1970s and levelled off after 1995. The number of staff in higher education increased from 118 000 in 1972 to 171 000 in 1981 and 318 000 in 2005. The staff-student ratio was 14 in 1972, 12 in 2005 and varied between 12 and 15 in the intervening years. Table 3.1 shows the enrolment and staff data for a number of years. Between 6% and 9% of the staff are 65 or older.

Table 3.1. **Student enrolments and staff at universities in Japan**

	Enrolments	Staff				
		Total	< 40	40-49	50-64	65+
1972	1 684 296	117 799	46 648	32 636	28 706	9 809
1981	2 561 463	171 245	65 333	47 235	45 402	13 275
1987	2 636 489	195 490	65 624	53 346	64 024	12 496
1990	3 243 962	211 261	61 950	65 661	69 653	13 997
1996	3 731 804	259 735	71 253	78 955	87 419	22 108
2002	3 727 519	307 097	73 221	87 563	119 090	27 223
2005	3 764 386	317 641	74 065	93 768	121 930	27 878

The observed age structure of the personnel at universities in Japan may be compared with the age structure that would result under a recruitment policy that limits recruitment to young people. The number of recruitments is determined by the retirement of staff and changes in student enrolments. To obtain annual data on enrolments, a trend model was estimated to describe the enrolment data. Several models were tried and the quadratic model performed best. The model is:

Enrolments (t) = 1 656 769 + 103 964 t – 1 145 t^2 ($R^2 = 0.95$) where t is the year since 1972.

The model is applied to obtain annual estimates of enrolments. The staff is determined using a constant student/staff ratio of 15. The fixed ratio implies that staff recruitment is fully determined by changes in student enrolments and retirement of personnel. The age at retirement is not known but it is known that about 7% of the staff are 65 or older. For the illustration, it is assumed that retirement occurs at 65.

The baseline age structure (in 1972) was determined from data on personnel by five-year age groups. A uniform distribution of ages within the five-year age groups is assumed. In 1972, 43% of the staff members below 65 years of age were less than 40 years of age; 30% were aged 40-49 and 27% were aged 50-64. About 2% were younger than 25, 10% were older than 25 but less than 30, and 16% were aged 30-34. Recruitment is limited to young people. In the theoretical model, recruits are 29 years old. The recruitment pattern of Japanese universities is assumed to be as follows: 15% of the recruits are below 25, 60% are aged 25-29 and 25% are aged 30-34. Figure 3.7 shows the changing age composition of personnel at Japanese universities predicted by a model incorporating a policy that restricts recruitment to young people. The observed age pattern is shown in Figure 3.8. The predicted age structure of personnel is relatively close to the observed age structure. It implies that, in Japan, staff follows enrolments and the recruitment policy of Japanese universities is not much different from the policy assumed in the theoretical model.

Figure 3.7. **Predicted number of staff members at universities in Japan, by age group**

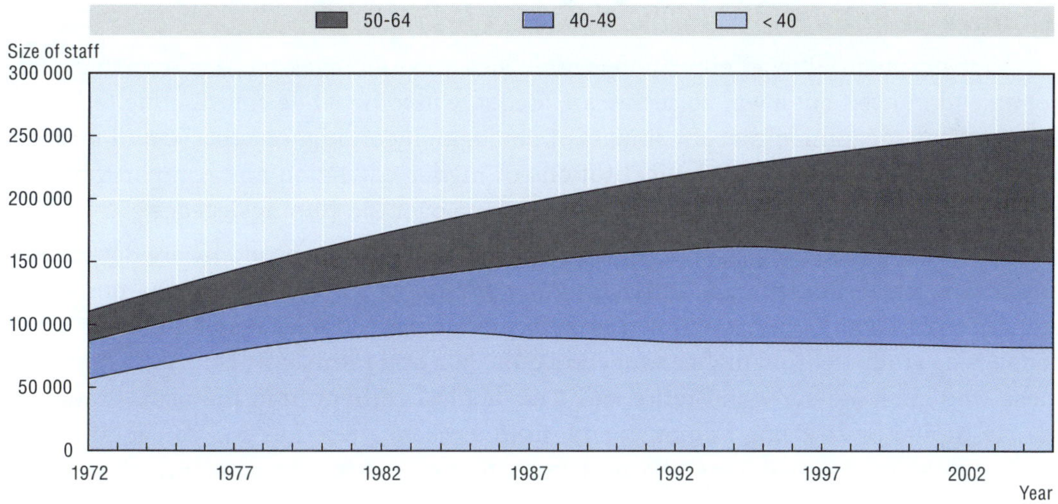

Figure 3.8. **Observed number of staff members and enrolments at universities in Japan, by age group**

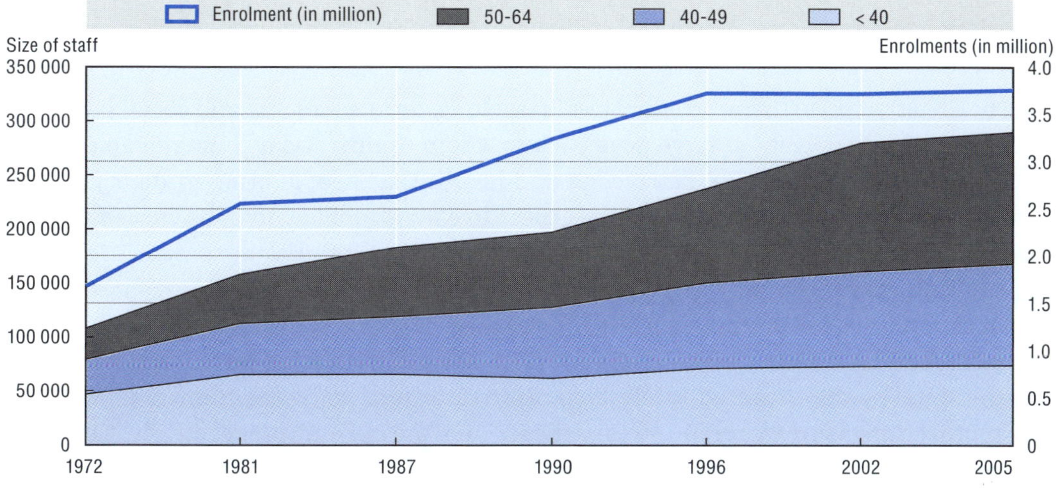

Conclusion

Ageing of teachers and researchers in higher education is a fact of life. To avoid the detrimental effects commonly associated with ageing personnel, the focus must shift from the age structure of personnel to the human capital of personnel. Teachers and researchers change over the course of their career and as they age, and institutions need to prepare for an ageing personnel. If, as is generally accepted, productivity declines with age, the decline is not only due to growing older, it is also an effect of the changing portfolio of tasks and responsibilities that constitute a job. What is needed is a life-course paradigm in personnel planning, with programmes designed to maintain knowledge and skills. It is also necessary to identify the jobs that fit persons of a given age and competence. If an optimal match is not feasible, competences and/or jobs must change because ageing is inevitable. If institutions of higher education are unable to introduce the necessary adjustments in human capital and jobs, flexible retirement schemes may help alleviate the negative consequences of an ageing staff.

3.4. Trends in human capital and higher education in the OECD area and in China and India

To many people, higher education is often viewed as an investment in human capital, not an end in itself but a way to secure an adequate income while contributing to society at large. This section looks at the impact of demography on higher education in terms of the human capital generated by institutions of higher education and compares human capital formation in the OECD area, India and China over the coming decades.

The contributions of institutions of higher education to the economy are determined not by how much human capital they produce (capital stock) but also by the number of years in which that human capital is used in productive activities (capital flow). That is, people who graduate from higher education quite late and retire early contribute less than those who graduate early and retire late. This analysis differs from the usual studies of human capital by studying human capital from a *cohort perspective* and considering how much human capital members of a birth cohort contribute to the economy during their entire working life. This contribution is defined in terms of the human capital generated by institutions of higher education. Therefore, the human capital contributed to the economy by a given birth cohort depends on the proportion entering higher education, the age of entry, the proportion graduating and the age of graduation, and the number of years of working life. The human capital a person contributes may vary over time as a result of depreciation and/or continued education (lifelong learning). In this study, such changes are disregarded.

The idea that investment in education has a long-term economic and social payoff for the individual and society at large goes back to Adam Smith. Today, human capital – the skills, capabilities, experience, knowledge and health that people bring to their jobs and that enhance their productivity and permit them to earn a good income – is viewed as a key determinant of international competitiveness. The concept is thus quite broad. There is no single definition of human capital and no unique way to measure it. Measurement of human capital is based on three general approaches. The first is cost-based and estimates human capital by the cost of producing it. The second is income-based and estimates human capital by the expected future income stream from using the human capital. The first approach measures capital retrospectively and the second prospectively. The third approach is education-based and measures human capital in terms of education output indicators such as literacy rates, enrolment rates, drop-out rates, repetition rates, average years of schooling in the population and test scores. The rationale for this method is that education is a key aspect of human capital formation and that measures of levels of education can be (and are generally) used as proxies for human capital. For a recent overview of conceptual and measurement issues, see Le, Gibson and Oxley (2005) and Wössmann (2005).

This study measures human capital generated by higher education by the number of years graduates of institutions of higher education participate in the labour force. The human capital contributed by graduates of higher education is measured in person-years. If one person contributes an average of 30 years, 100 graduates contribute 3 000 person-years of human capital generated by institutions of higher education. Since each year in the labour force may be associated with an income or wage level, this duration-based approach is related to the income-based approach. Like the latter, it is a prospective measure of human capital.

Assumptions and specifications of the model

A detailed investigation of the impact of demography on the creation of tertiary-level human capital is beyond the scope of this paper. Therefore the following assumptions are made. First, all graduates are gainfully employed and receive an income. In this simple model, unemployment does not exist, although it may easily be introduced. Second, graduates of institutions of higher education remain in the labour force until they retire at the age of 65. Early withdrawal from the labour force, owing to disability or early retirement, for example, is not considered. Taking unemployment, early withdrawal and early retirement into account would provide a way to measure the "waste" of human capital produced by institutions of higher education if the measurement of human capital is restricted to gainful employment.

The impact of demography on higher (or tertiary) education and the human capital it generates is studied here by comparing the OECD area to China and India. To determine the effect of education on the human capital of a birth cohort, four stages of life are distinguished; the period before tertiary education, the period during which young adults engage in tertiary education, the period following drop-out from tertiary education; and the period in the labour market after graduation from tertiary education. These stages are referred to as states, and the four states define the state-space or multistate approach[3] that is used here to determine the effects of higher education on human capital. The events (or *transitions* from one state to another) considered are entry into tertiary education, drop-out and graduation.

The contribution of higher education to human capital formation depends on: *i)* the size of the population; *ii)* the recruitment base, *i.e.* the population that meets the requirements for entering higher education (*e.g.* completed secondary education); *iii)* the rate of entry into higher education; *iv)* the drop-out rate; and *v)* the graduation rate.

The recruitment base is assumed to consist of all the members of a birth cohort. Hence, the rate of entry into tertiary education is the ratio of the number of persons entering higher education at a given age to the number of persons that have not (or not yet). In technical terms, this is the *population at risk*. A person who has entered higher education leaves either by graduating or by dropping out. These are competing events.

Moreover, mortality is neglected and it is assumed that all members of the birth cohort survive to the highest age considered in the simulation.

The level of entry into higher education and the rate at which young adults leave higher education are indicated by the transition rates. In this study, transition rates differ by age and the age-specific rates differ by region (OECD and China-India). Transition rates are generally estimated from empirical observations on the number of transitions during a given period and the duration at risk of a transition (see Annex 3.A1), but these data are not available for this study. As an alternative, a parameterised approach is followed. Its specification is given in the annex. Parameterisation involves specification of a parametric model of transition rates that adequately captures empirical regularities. Transition rates are plausible if the changes they generate are comparable to observed changes. To compare the model output and the empirical evidence, a few indicators are used. According to OECD data, almost every second person (47%) will enter general higher education programmes during his/her lifetime; the percentage of the population aged 25 to 34 that has attained tertiary education is 28% (OECD average for 2001); and on average, a 17-year-old in OECD countries can expect to receive 2.5 years of tertiary education (OECD, 2004). For China, a 10% rate of entry into tertiary education was assumed. The drop-out rate is assumed to be lower than in the OECD, about 0.5%. India was then assumed to have similar characteristics as China.

Projections under current conditions

The parameters used in the model approximate the real ones. The states occupied by cohort members at different ages are shown in Figure 3.9. In the OECD area, according to the model, 43.3% of the birth cohort enters tertiary education, *i.e.* fewer than the actual 47%, and 5% of those who enter leave higher education before completion. On average, cohort members spend 2.1 years in tertiary education, close to the observed 2.5 years. Figure 3.9 shows the time spent in the different states up to age 40. Persons graduating from tertiary education spend the period between graduation and age 40 in the labour market. This represents 15.84 years, which implies graduation at age 24. Between age 40 and 65, tertiary education graduates contribute 25 years if they do not die or retire early. Of the members of the birth cohort, 56.5% never enter tertiary education, 2.2% enter and drop out, and 41.1% enter and graduate. This means that, on average, a member of the

Figure 3.9. **States occupied by birth cohort at successive ages, OECD**

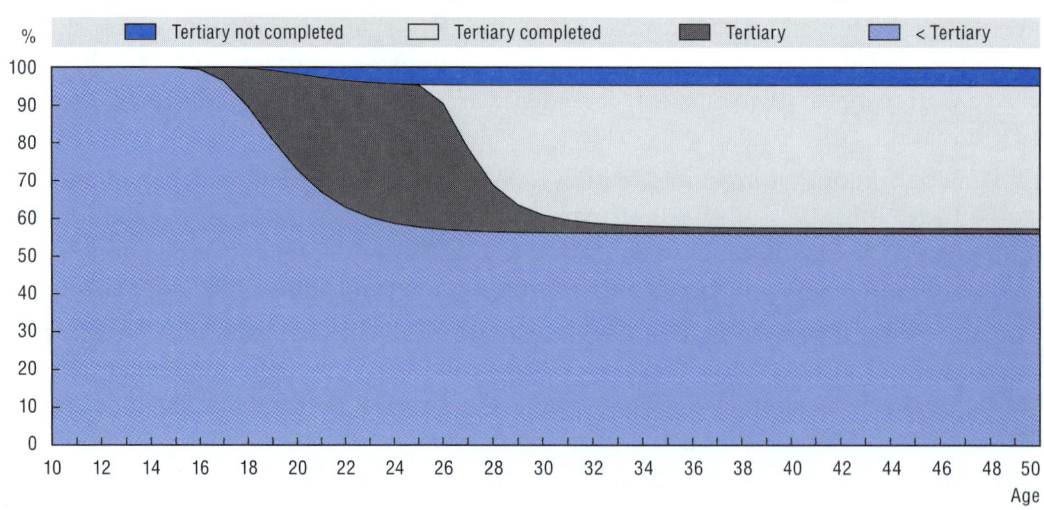

entire birth cohort contributes 6.4 years to the labour market as a highly educated person before reaching the age of 40 and 10.3 years between age 40 and retirement at age of 65. On average a member of the full cohort spends 0.4 years as a highly educated person between dropping out of tertiary education and the 40th birthday.

In China, as shown in Figure 3.10, the picture is very different. Of the cohort members, only 10.1% enter higher education. The human capital produced by higher education is therefore low if measured in terms of the number of years a member of a birth cohort contributes to the labour market as a highly educated person. In China and India, because an average cohort member is much less likely than in OECD countries to enter tertiary education, the contribution to the labour market after graduation from tertiary education is limited. (It is assumed that the transition rates that apply to China also apply to India.) On average, a member of the birth cohort spends 0.5 years in tertiary education and contributes 1.6 years of skills and knowledge obtained in higher education to the labour market before reaching the age of 40 (Figure 3.10). The average contribution between age 40 and 65 is 2.5 years.[4] The low value is the consequence of the low probability of enrolment into higher education.

Figure 3.10. **States occupied by birth cohort at successive ages, China-India**

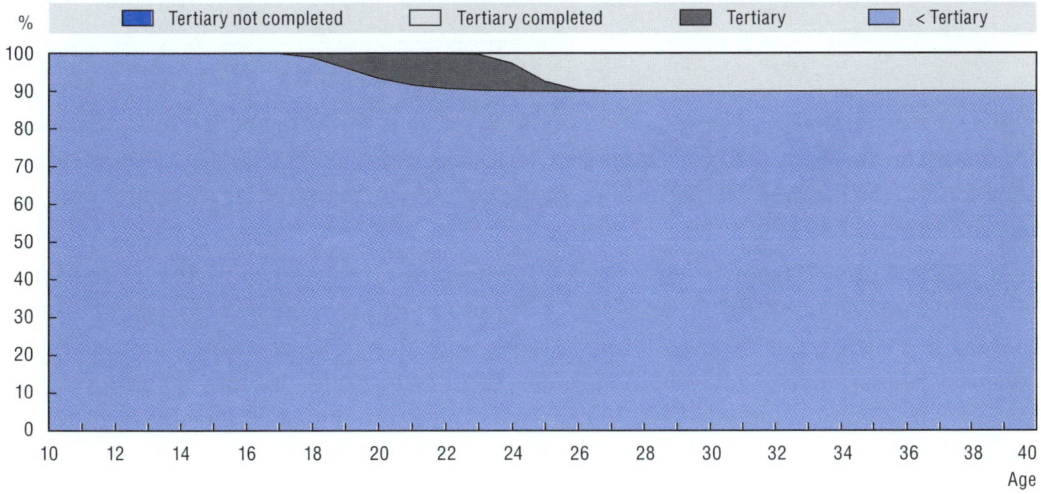

However, the picture changes dramatically when the contribution of an average cohort member is multiplied by the size of the birth cohort. In the period 2000-04, 17.6 million children were born in China annually compared to 4.4 million in North America and 7.4 million in Europe. In India, the annual number of births was 25.8 million. If the transition rates are the same in Europe and North America, the members of a birth cohort in North America who complete tertiary education contribute 73.8 million person-years of human capital before reaching the retirement age of 65.[5] In Europe the contribution is 123.4 million person-years.[6] In China, the birth cohort contributes 72.5 million person-years of skills and knowledge obtained in higher education to the labour market.[7] In India, the contribution is 106.2 million person-years. It is interesting to note that in China a birth cohort contributes about the same human capital to the labour market as in North America. The low entry into higher education is offset by the large size of the birth cohort. This analysis clearly demonstrates that size matters.

Projections under different conditions

If enrolment in tertiary education in China reached 40%, *i.e.* the level in OECD countries, the birth cohort would contribute 294.7 million person-years.[8] In India, it would contribute 432 million person-years of knowledge and skills acquired in tertiary education. With enrolment in higher education at 40% in each of the four regions, China would contribute four times more high-level human capital to the economy than North America and 2.4 times more than Europe, and India would contribute close to six times more than North America and 3.5 times more than Europe. These figures demonstrate that in semi-developed countries like China and India, fertility is a very important variable in human capital. Table 3.2 summarises the results.

Table 3.2. **Future contribution of tertiary educated human capital by the cohort born in 2000-04**

	Scenario 1 (current conditions)	Scenario 2 (current OECD conditions in China and India)
	Million person-years	Million person-years
Europe	123.4	123.4
North America	73.8	73.8
China	72.5	294.7
India	106.2	432.0

The institutions of higher education in China today contribute about the same amount of human capital with tertiary education to its economy as the institutions of higher education in North America. Institutions of higher education in India contribute only 16% less than comparable institutions in Europe.

A slight increase from 10.1% to 11.5% in the rate of entry into higher education in China and India would result in an amount of human capital equivalent to that currently observed in North America and Europe, where more than 40% of a cohort enters higher education. Higher rates of entry would produce tertiary-educated human capital exceeding that in North America and Europe if their rate of entry remains at its current level. With a rate of entry into higher education of slightly over 20%, *i.e.* half the current rate in major OECD areas, China and India would produce twice the tertiary-educated human capital. This could allow China and India to become poles of innovation if they continue to emphasise engineering and science.

These scenarios are for birth cohorts of sizes observed in 2000-04. A decline in fertility results in smaller birth cohorts and hence a reduction in person-years of tertiary-educated human capital unless smaller cohorts are offset by higher rates of entry into higher education. In China and India, because of the low enrolment rates, fertility decline does not have much effect, however. For instance, a decline of 1% in the number of births is offset by increasing the rate of entry into higher education from 10.1% to 10.2%. A 1% decline in cohort size in China and India combined reduces the number of births by 433 000 and the tertiary educated human capital by 1.8 million person-years, if the rate of entry into tertiary education remains constant. To maintain human capital in China and India at the previous level, at least three policy options are available: *i)* family policies that increase fertility; *ii)* educational policies that increase the rate of entry into higher education; and *iii)* migration policies that attract knowledge workers to China and India. The effect on

 HIGHER EDUCATION TO 2030 – VOLUME 1: DEMOGRAPHY – ISBN 978-92-64-04065-6 – © OECD 2008

human capital of a 1% decline in numbers of births (by 433 000) is offset by immigration of 43 800 graduates of higher education if they are the same age as native graduates of higher education (24 years).

Similarly, OECD countries can choose between family policies that increase fertility, policies that promote entry into higher education, policies that reduce drop-out and immigration policies that are attractive to knowledge workers. Preventing a student from dropping out has the same effect on tertiary-educated human capital as attracting a tertiary-educated immigrant. One less birth reduces the tertiary-educated human capital by 16.8 person-years.[9] A 1% fertility decline reduces the human capital by 2.0 million person-years. The decline can be offset by immigration of 48 000 persons with tertiary education, provided each immigrant contributes 40.84 years of human capital.

3.5. Conclusion

Demography affects the future of higher education in important ways. In many OECD countries low to very low levels of fertility result in a continued decline in the number of young adults. Institutions of higher education are responding by increasing participation rates and by organising mid-career programmes and higher education for seniors. Demographic change and the increased emphasis on lifelong learning, in view not only of employability but also as part of personal (human) development, represent opportunities for institutions of higher education. Enrolments of young adults in higher education will reach maximum levels and further increases in enrolments will necessitate targeting other age groups, in particular mid-career and senior people.

To demonstrate the effect of enrolment levels on the staff size and the age composition of staff in institutions of higher education, a simulation study was carried out. The study shows important cycles in the age structure of the personnel as a result of recruitment and retirement policies. The extent of the variation in age structure depends on changes in enrolments. The cycles are less marked when enrolments increase rapidly. The simulation illustrates the problems associated with maintaining an optimal age composition of the workforce in institutions that are characterised by the tenure system as it exists today. The simulation model is able to replicate current trends in the age structure of personnel at institutions of higher education, as demonstrated by Japan where ageing of higher education personnel was very low in periods of rapid expansion of enrolments and high in periods when the growth in enrolments levelled off.

Ageing of teachers and researchers in higher education is here to stay. Institutions can respond by adopting a life-course paradigm in personnel planning with much greater attention to matching competences and job requirements. Jobs need to fit the age and competence of individuals. If matching is not successful and training programmes or greater flexibility in job requirements cannot remedy the situation, flexible retirement schemes may help alleviate the negative consequences of an ageing staff. The life-course paradigm provides a holistic framework that integrates many current labour market policies and points to new policies that affect time use, activity patterns, personal development and human capital development throughout the life cycle.

The contribution of higher education to the economy may be measured by the human capital contributed to the labour market by graduates of institutions of higher education. Education is a most important element of labour quality. Ho and Jorgenson (1999) found that in North America almost all of the trend in labour quality improvement during the period 1948-95 can be attributed to the rise in average levels of educational attainment. They expect this trend to continue well into the 21st century. This study measures human capital not only in terms of educational attainment but also in terms of the time spent in employment before retirement. It measures the person-years of skills and knowledge obtained in higher education contributed to the economy. In the OECD area, an average person is estimated to contribute 16.9 years of tertiary education-based human capital to the labour market before retirement at the age of 65. In China, the average is 4.1 years. The difference is largely attributable to differences in participation in higher education (above 40% in the OECD area and 10% in China). A graduate of an institution of higher education contributes about the same number of years of tertiary education-based human capital (about 40 years), irrespective of the country of residence (and in the absence of early retirement). The picture becomes very different when the contribution is not expressed per capita but for the entire birth cohort. In the current decade, 17.6 million children are born in China each year, 25.8 million in India, 4.4 million in North America and 7.4 million in Europe. China's large birth cohort combined with the low entry rate into higher education results in about the same person-years of tertiary education-based human capital as in North America where higher education is more widespread (72.5 million person-years in China and 73.8 million person-years in North America). If India had China's entry rate into higher education today (10%) and the retirement age was 65 as in most other countries, a birth cohort would contribute 106.2 million person-years of tertiary education-based human capital to the Indian economy. If in China and India, enrolments in higher education reached the levels in OECD countries today and fertility changed little, a birth cohort in China would contribute 295 million person-years of tertiary education-based human capital to its economy and a birth cohort in India would contribute 432 million person-years, or three and five times more, respectively, than a birth cohort in North America.

Demographics is expected to be a strong driver of change in higher education in the OECD area. Institutions of higher education already respond to fertility decline by increasing enrolment rates for non-traditional categories of students and by diversifying the supply of educational programmes. Declining enrolments result not only in excess personnel but also in wider swings in the age structure of the personnel.

While institutions of high education diversify to maintain current activity levels, they also continue to need to generate the human capital and produce the knowledge and skills necessary for continued technological and economic advancement. There appears to be, however, a degree of public disenchantment with the role played by the university, owing, perhaps in part, to the need for immigrant knowledge workers. One means to respond to such concern might be the development, for each field of study, of a *human capital index* to measure the impact on the economy and society at large of the knowledge and skills generated by that field of study. A human capital index could measure the relative scarcity of specific human capital in society. Institutions with different fields of study could be characterised by a composite human capital index. Government funding of institutions of higher education could use the (composite) human capital index in addition to the more traditional funding criteria. The human capital index could help ensure that institutions of higher education continue to contribute to meeting the needs of their society.

Notes

1. The actual average ratio in an OECD country was 15.4 in 2002 (OECD, 2004).
2. The data are official Japanese data provided by the OECD secretariat: the data for 1972 and 2005 have been adjusted by the Secretariat.
3. For a brief overview of multistate models and key references, see Willekens (2003).
4. $0.101 \times 25 = 2.525$.
5. $4.423 \times 6.4 + 4.423 \times 0.411 \times 25 = 73.8$.
6. $7.354 \times 6.4 + 7.354 \times 0.411 \times 25 = 123.4$.
7. $17.566 \times 1.6 + 17.566 \times 0.101 \times 25 = 72.5$.
8. $17.566 \times 6.4 + 17.566 \times 0.411 \times 25 = 294.7$.
9. $0.411 \times (15.85 + 25)$.

References

Gonand, F. (2005), "Assessing the Robustness of Demographic Projections in OECD Countries", Economics Department Working Papers No. 464, ECO/WKP(2005)51, OECD Publishing, Paris.

Ho, M.S. and D.W. Jorgenson (1999), "The Quality of the US Work Force, 1948-95", *www.ksg.harvard.edu/cbg/ptep/laborjbes.pdf*.

Le, T., J. Gibson and L. Oxley (2005), "Measures of Human Capital. A Review of the Literature", New Zealand Treasury Working Papers 05/10, November, New Zealand Treasury, Wellington.

OECD (2004), *Education at a Glance – OECD Indicators 2004*, OECD Publishing, Paris.

Rogers, A. (1986), "Parameterized Multistate Population Dynamics and Projections", *Journal of the American Statistical Association*, Vol. 81(393), pp. 48-61.

Sleebos, J.E. (2003), "Low Fertility Rates in OECD Countries. Facts and Policy Responses", OECD Social, Employment and Migration Working Papers No. 15, OECD Publishing, Paris.

Vincent-Lancrin, S. (2004), "Building Futures Scenarios for Universities and Higher Education: An International Approach", *Policy Futures in Education*, Vol. 2(2), pp. 245-263.

Willekens, F. (2003), "Multistate Demography", in P. Demeny and G. McNicoll (eds.), *Encyclopedia of Population*, revised edition, Macmillan Reference USA, New York, pp. 681-684.

Wössmann, L. (2005), "Specifying Human Capital", *Journal of Economic Surveys*, Vol. 17(3), pp. 239-270.

ANNEX 3.A1

Methodology

This annex explains the concept of a transition rate and specifies the assumptions that have been made in the multistate simulation model of Section 3.4.

A transition rate is the rate at which individuals transfer between functional states or stages of life. For instance, entry into higher education is a transition and the propensity of a young adult to enter higher education (entry rate) is the transition rate. The rate of leaving higher education because of drop-out or graduation is a transition rate as well. The formal definition of a transition rate is the ratio between the number of transitions during a given period and the duration of exposure to the risk of a transition. The latter is equivalent to the time spent in a state (state of origin) during the period considered.

The transition rates are described by a double exponential distribution. The double exponential distribution is a skewed distribution that has been used by several authors to describe profiles of transition rates. The double exponential model is:

$$f(x) = a \exp\{-\alpha(x-\mu) - \exp[-\lambda(x-\mu)]\}$$

where α, λ and μ are parameters and a is a scaling factor to assure that $f(x)$ is a density function (area under the curve is unity). The parameter μ positions the unimodel curve on the age axis, whereas λ and α reflect the steepness of its ascending and descending sides, respectively. If $\alpha > \lambda$, the mode of the function is smaller than μ. If $\alpha < \lambda$, the mode is larger than μ. If $\alpha = \lambda$, the function is the Fisher-Tippett distribution which is an extreme value distribution with a steep ascending slope and a slower descending slope (see *e.g.* *http://mathworld.wolfram.com/ExtremeValueDistribution.html*). Examples of the double exponential distribution are shown in Figure 3.A1.1. Table 3.A1.1 gives the parameters. Model 1 is the Fisher-Tippett distribution. The first distribution is positioned around age 25 and the second around age 30. Both have the same downward slope (α). The upward slope is higher in the second distribution (λ). The area under the curve is different.

Table 3.A1.1. **Parameters of the double exponential distribution**

Parameter	Model 1	Model 2
a	0.3001	0.3366
μ	25	30
α	0.3	0.3
λ	0.3	0.5
CF	1.0	1.0

Figure 3.A1.1. **Double exponential distribution**

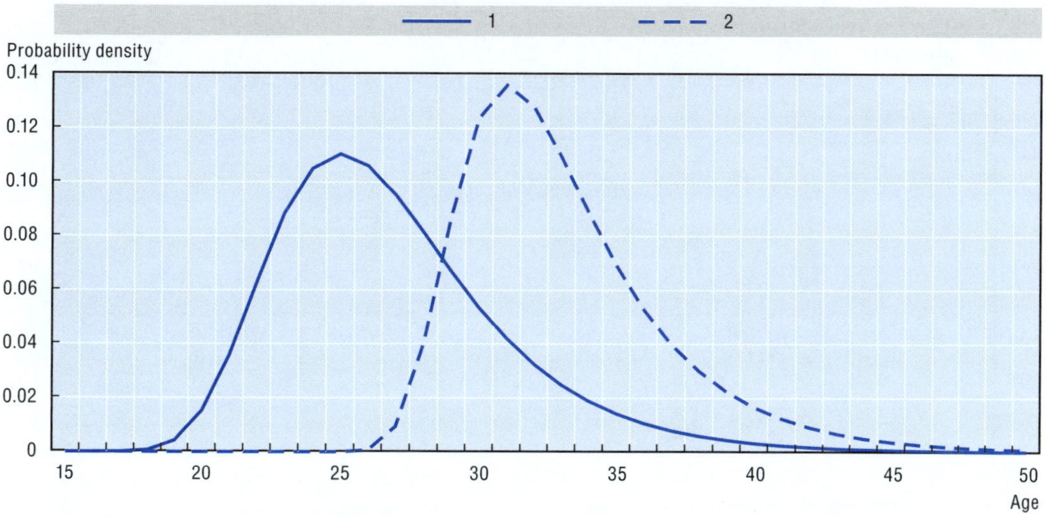

To determine the parameters of the double exponential distributions describing the transition rates among the states considered in this paper, an iterative procedure based on trial and error was used. The aim was to obtain transition rates that would result in known characteristics of the tertiary education. To derive parameter values, information presented by Vincent-Lancrin (2004) was used. In the OECD area almost every second person (47%) will enter general higher education programmes during his/her lifetime (Vincent-Lancrin, 2004, p. 247). In addition, 28% of the population aged 25 to 34 has attained tertiary education (OECD average for 2001). A further relevant piece of information is that on average in OECD countries, a 17-year-old can expect to receive 2.5 years of tertiary education.

For China, a much lower rate of entry into tertiary education was assumed; namely 10%. The drop-out rate is assumed to be lower than in the OECD, about 0.5%. Table 3.A1.2 shows the parameters of the double exponential model for the OECD area and Table 3.A1.3 shows the parameters for China.

The transition rates are shown in Figures 3.A1.2 and 3.A1.3.

Table 3.A1.2. **Parameters of the double exponential distribution, OECD**

Parameter	Entry into tertiary education	Graduation	Drop-out
a	1	1	1
μ	18.5	28.0	19.5
α	0.8	1.2	0.8
λ	0.8	0.4	0.5
Area	0.8	2.0	0.1

Table 3.A1.3. **Parameters of the double exponential distribution, China**

Parameter	Entry into tertiary education	Graduation	Drop-out
a	1	1	1
μ	18.5	28.0	19.5
α	0.8	1.2	0.8
λ	0.8	0.4	0.5
Area	0.15	2.0	0.01

Figure 3.A1.2. **Transition rates, OECD area**

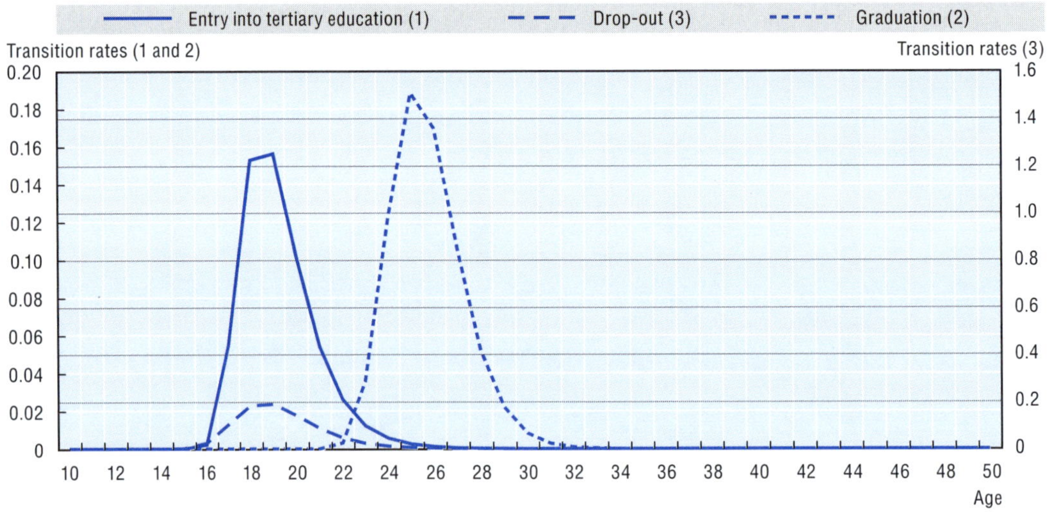

Figure 3.A1.3. **Transition rates, China**

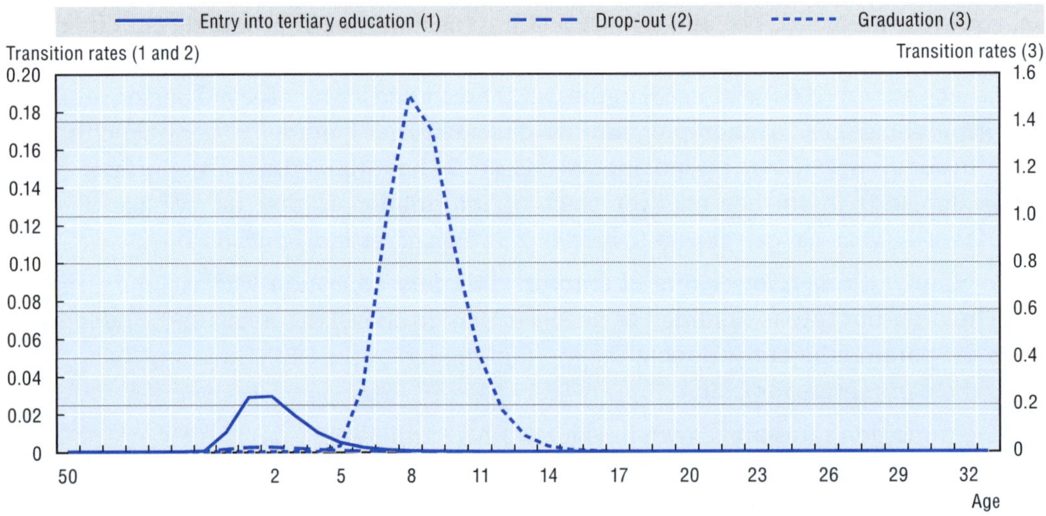

ISBN 978-92-64-04065-6
Higher Education to 2030
Volume 1: Demography

Chapter 4

Back to the Future? The Academic Professions in the 21st Century

by

Jürgen Enders* and Christine Musselin**

This chapter addresses the impact of changes in higher education on the academic profession in the past, present and possible future. We start by arguing that the growth of the academic profession implied increased differentiation. We then examine the ongoing transformation of working and employment conditions in the academic workplace, which challenges its traditional power structure. Finally we look at the restructuring of the international academic community. One of our conclusions is that demographic changes are likely to play a minor role in the reshaping of the academic profession.

* Centre for Higher Education Policy Studies, University of Twente, the Netherlands.
** Centre for Organisation Sociology (Centre de sociologie des organisations), Sciences Po and National Center for Scientific Research (Centre national de la recherche scientifique, CNRS), France.

4.1. Introduction

Among the various sectors of production and service in modern societies and the institutions in charge of them, higher education has usually been perceived as peculiar in several respects: a relatively open set of multiple goals; a loose mechanism of coercion, controlled and steered from above; and a high degree of fragmentation and strong influence of the principal workers – the academic professionals – on the determination of goals, the management and administration of institutions and the daily routines of work. In addition, in terms of the interrelations between different sectors of production and services, the academic profession has been considered as one of the most influential in shaping other sectors. This is underscored, for example, by references to the academic profession as the "key profession" or to the "triumph of the academic man" (Perkin, 1969; Jenks and Riesman, 1968).

While this view has always been contested and has partly functioned as a myth, public debate and academic reflection on the academic profession now stress the disappearance of a (golden) age of contentment and serenity. We find complaints that the concept of a single academic profession may be an illusion, that the academic profession can hardly cope with the tensions it has to live with, and that it is endangered. For about three decades it has been widely assumed that the academic profession feels increasingly embattled, and the available literature suggests that the sense of crisis has grown (see for example Kogan, Moses and El-Khawas, 1994; Kingsley, 1997; Farnham, 1999; Enders, 2001; Altbach, 2000). Concern about the academic profession is obviously entangled with the massification of higher education and the long-standing secular trend towards a "knowledge society". The transformation of higher education and the changing nature and role of knowledge in society are accompanied by changes in higher education and its interrelationships with society that are a mixed blessing for the academic profession (Enders and Teichler, 1997).

- Over the last few decades, there has been a decline in the socioeconomic status of higher education alongside its expansion and the "scientification" of society. While the expansion of higher education was influenced by the expected need for highly qualified manpower, the economy did not follow. Consequently, the process of expansion has often been regarded as too expensive. Today, the private benefits of higher education are stressed whereas the public benefits were underscored in the past. And some observers are starting to talk about over-education.
- As scientific knowledge and highly qualified expertise have grown in importance, higher education and the academic profession are losing their exclusive and central role as the main producer of scientific knowledge and technology. Higher education faces growing competition from other research sectors and institutions, and its performance is more and more compared to that of other suppliers of tertiary education.
- There is increasing tension between the traditional modes of teaching and bodies of knowledge and the established forms of communication between students and

academic teachers, on the one hand, and the competences, life and learning styles, professional expectations and careers of students, on the other. This raises questions about the future conceptualisation of study programmes as well as the role of academic teaching and teachers.

- The growing importance of science-based knowledge and technology to society is accompanied by a great deal of ambivalence about the impact on future developments. On the one hand, expectations regarding the usefulness and practical impact of science and technology have increased. On the other, modern societies are more and more aware that science-based knowledge and technology can be risky in social, technological and ecological terms. Insofar as higher education is considered one of the main sources of the further development of society, it is blamed for some of the negative consequences of science-based innovations.
- The cosmopolitan approach to higher education and its research function in the 20th century has been one of the sources of globalisation. It seems indeed reasonable to argue that the academic profession was among the first global players. However, the effect of economic, political, social and scientific globalisation on the function of higher education is far from straightforward. National systems compete more and more on international markets and highly innovative research is increasingly conducted across the traditional boundaries of systems, disciplines and institutions. New information and communication technologies influence the distribution and dissemination of knowledge as well as the meaning of the words "knowledge" and "science".

This list is by no means exhaustive. The examples may, however, suffice to show that higher education and research have to cope with conflicting pressures. These pressures are not recent but seem to be embedded in long-term secular trends in modern societies. Neither are they a national phenomenon. At present, the higher education systems in most highly developed countries are undergoing a difficult process of change that affects the position of the academic profession.

The following discussion addresses the impact of such drivers of change on selected features of the academic profession in the past, present and possible future. Four main transformations of the changing profile of the academic profession are examined. We start by arguing that the growth of the academic profession implied increased differentiation. We then examine the ongoing transformation of working and employment conditions in the academic workplace which challenges the traditional power structure. Finally we look at the restructuring of the international academic community. In discussing the "academic profession", we rely on a rather broad definition that includes academic staff working in universities and other higher education institutions in different ranks, with different contracts and at different stages of their career. Thus, we consider not only the "professoriate", as the traditional core of the academic profession, but other faculty groups as well.

4.2. The changing profile of the academic profession

Growth and internal differentiation of the academic profession

In the 20th century higher education has grown into a mass system and a mature enterprise. Some time after World War II, various phenomena in highly developed countries contributed to a political climate which made possible a substantial boost in expenditure for higher education and research and encouraged an increase in the numbers of students in higher education institutions (Schofer and Meyer, 2004): a belief that blue-sky research best serves society's needs for scientific and technological innovation; a boom in the economics of education, *i.e.* the belief that substantial investment in education is required to ensure economic growth; a readiness to reduce inequality of opportunity in education; and probably the radical student protest of the late 1960s as well.

Expansion in world higher education has been dramatic, especially after about 1960. Nowadays higher education worldwide enrols more than 100 million students. In the OECD area, almost every second young person (17-25 years old) enters some kind of higher education programme. Between 1991 and 2001, participation in higher education for the age group 25-34 increased from 21% to 30% for the 19 OECD countries for which data were available for both years; in 2001, the participation rate in the OECD area amounted to 28% on average (Vincent-Lancrin, 2004). Enrolment and participation rates are considerably lower in many transition and developing countries, although many have experienced and/or are experiencing considerable growth in their higher education sectors. As a result, these countries typically have enrolment rates that approximate those of highly developed countries only a few decades earlier.

Further, the overall growth of the higher education sector has fuelled the "massification of academic research" (Vincent-Lancrin, 2006) and increased expenditure on R&D in the higher education sector. In the OECD area, trend data on R&D indicate significant growth in expenditure on R&D overall as well as in the higher education sector during the past two decades. While industry remains the most important performer, the share of R&D performed by the higher education sector has increased over this period.

These developments have left their imprint on both the quantitative and qualitative profile of the academic profession. Most obviously, the growth and diversification of higher education have meant growth and diversification of the academic profession as well. The massification of higher education has led to a rise in faculty numbers, sometimes in a relatively uncontrolled way which has affected quality in the profession. Of course, growth in academic staff was most impressive in times of dynamic expansion of higher education and increased funding. In many countries, these conditions are no longer present or are less so. Nevertheless, expansion of the academic profession has not yet come to a halt. For the last 20 years, OECD data indicate an increase of 127% (full-time equivalent) in growth of the number of higher education staff defined as "researchers". Available data on overall academic staff numbers for a selected number of countries covering the last ten years show a diversified picture (see Figure 4.1). For countries such as Austria, Germany and the Netherlands, there has been a rather small increase in academic staff numbers over the last decade, whereas the academic profession has grown considerably in countries such as Finland, France or Sweden.

Overall expansion has also led to a rising share of female staff in the academic profession. In comparison with their representation among higher education students and graduates, however, women are still underrepresented. In 2003, female academic staff accounted for about 25% of the academic staff in Austria, about 30% in Germany, the Netherlands and France, and about 40% in Finland, Sweden, Flanders and the United Kingdom (see Figure 4.2). In all countries for which such data are available, women remain less likely to climb up the academic career ladder and hold a professorial position: the proportion of women in the professoriate ranges from less than 10% (the Netherlands), to about 15% (Sweden, the United Kingdom) to 20% (Finland). Important variations among disciplines may be hidden behind this average.

Figure 4.1. **Changes in the number of academic staff**

(FTE, 2000 = 100)

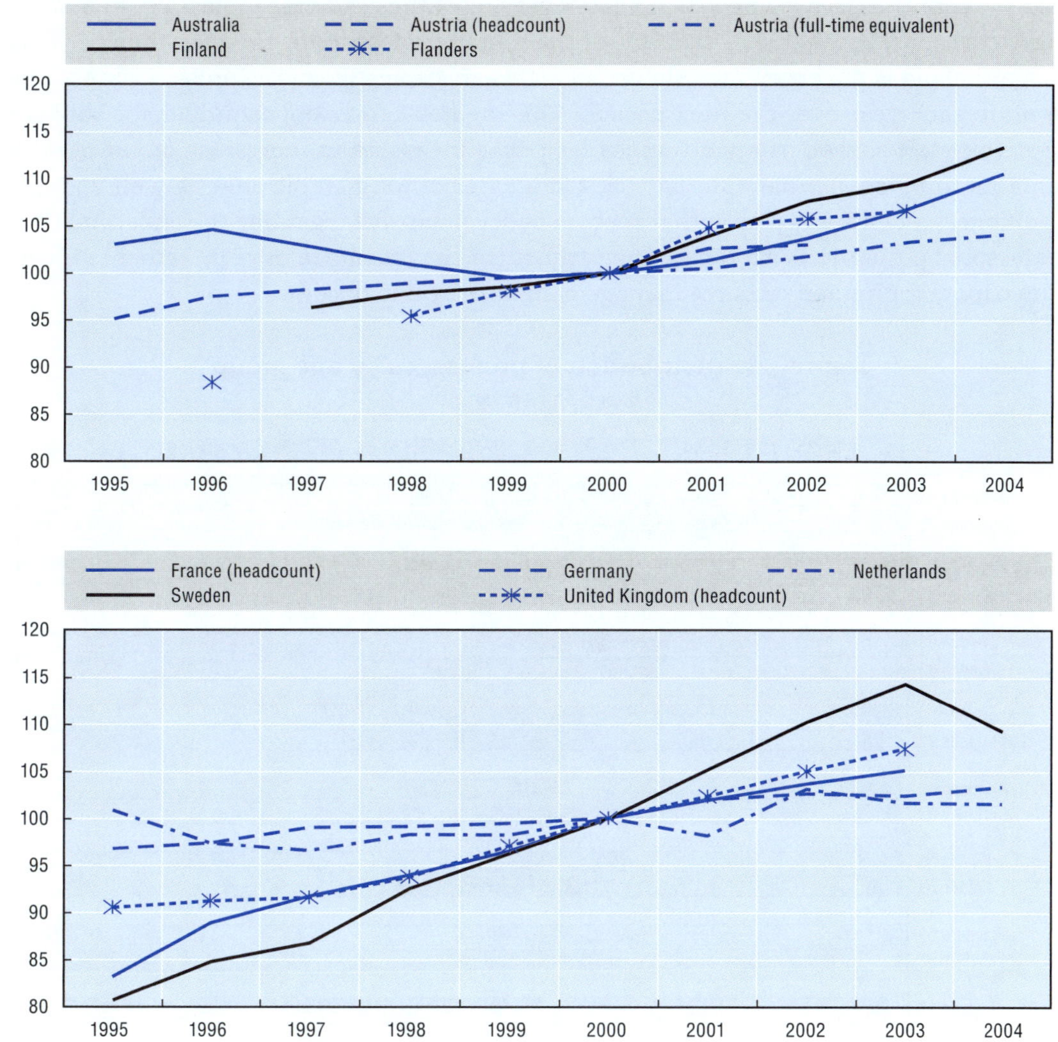

Source: *CHEPS International Higher Education Monitor.*

Figure 4.2. **Female academic staff as a percentage of total academic staff**

(FTE, 2003)

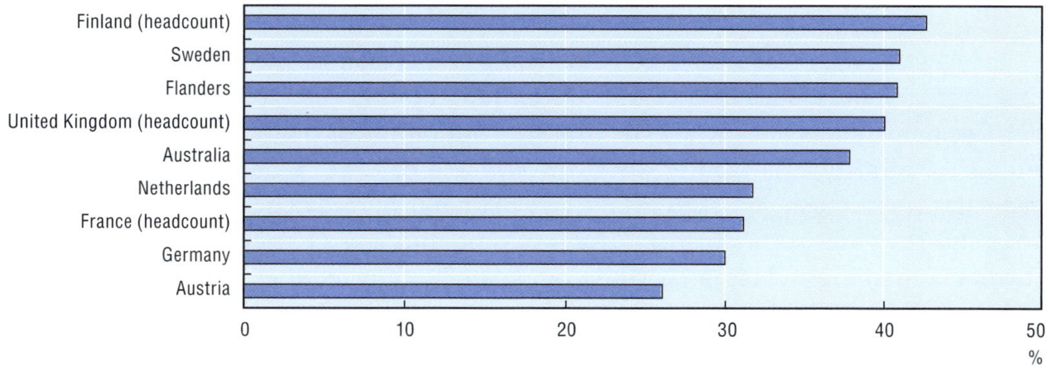

Source: *CHEPS International Higher Education Monitor.*

Faster and slower growth cycles in the academic profession have had an impact on the age structure of the academic profession. Data on the age structure of the professoriate in selected countries (see Figure 4.3) indicate a greying of the academic profession. In most of these countries, between 40% and 60% of the overall professoriate are older than 55 years of age; Finland is the exception. Altogether, between 4% and 6% of the professoriate is due to retire each year over the next decade. This creates career opportunities for younger academic staff as well as opportunities for policy measures to reorganise or cut back. It remains to be seen what role participation rates among traditional as well as non-traditional students will play with respect to policy measures regarding the replacement of professorial positions. What is clear, however, is that increasing rates of retirement provide ample room for human resource management in the years to come.

Figure 4.3. **Distribution of professors by age group**

Based on headcount

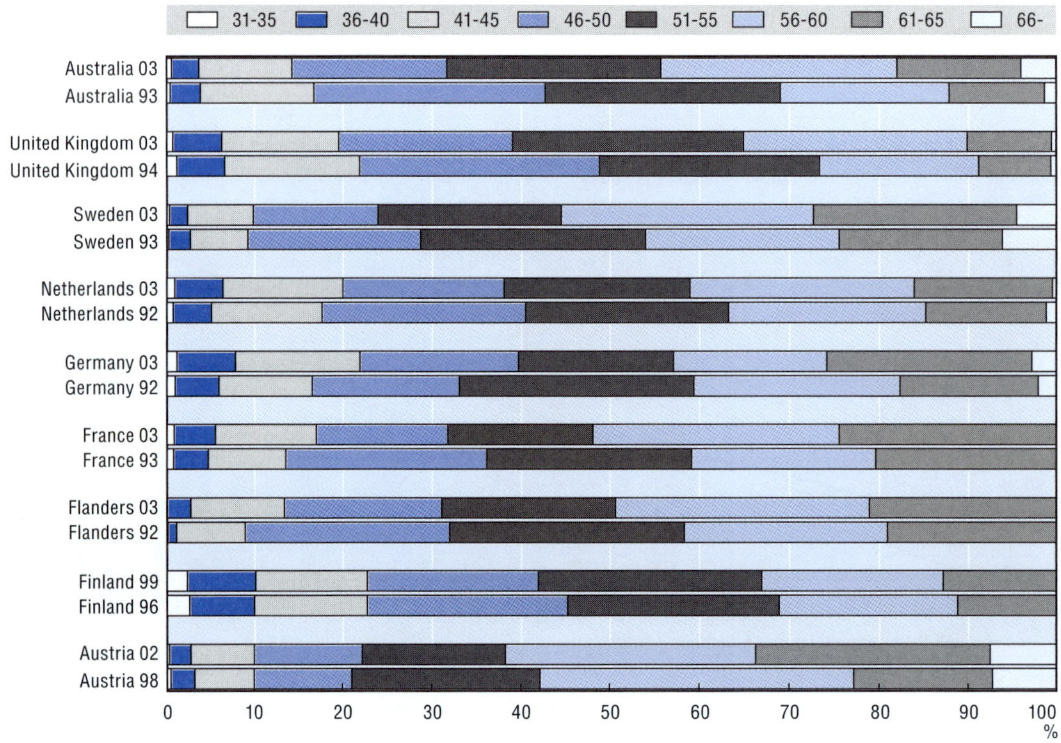

Source: *CHEPS International Higher Education Monitor.*

In any case, with resources either stabilising or increasing slowly, change is expected to take place through substitution and concentration rather than through overall growth. This development has already affected the size and profile of the academic profession as well as matters such as faculty workload and use of time, productivity and output. Academics are increasingly asked to take care of their own research funding, and the more successful they are in this respect, the less time and energy they have for their core activities of teaching and research. Often, adequate funding requires diverse sources, each of which has a stake in the expected outcomes and products of the academic enterprise. A further development concerns the disconnection of funding for research and teaching.

While resources for teaching have been reduced on a per student basis, research funding is more subject to market-like influences (see for example Chen, 2002).

Massification has resulted in greater differentiation of academic sectors, institutions and job roles. There is room for debate about the extent to which such diversity is an unavoidable response to the massification of higher education and the extent to which it is due to governmental regulation or institutional responses to market forces (Scott, 1995). Traditionally, diversity basically meant a division of work in terms of institutions' primary functions of either teaching or research, or a combination of both, through forms of governance and funding that worked as incentives and constraints. Recent forces, such as globalisation and regionalisation, however, encourage much finer and more flexible differentiation of institutions which may well lead to greater volatility and fuzziness within and across systems (Meek *et al.*, 1996; Nowotny, Scott and Gibbons, 2001; Bleiklie, 2003).

Enabling or limiting academics' time and resources for research and teaching is one of the most common means of specifying sectoral or institutional missions, and this can create new divisions within the academic profession or underline old ones. More and more faculty face the fact that the "gold standard" that once applied can no longer be taken for granted. The academic profession is becoming less homogenous in terms of the resources available, and the gap between the "haves" and the "have-nots" seems to widen, as reflected by the rise in untenured staff, teaching-only staff or research-project personnel (Gappa, 2002). Massification and diversification have also meant that the privileges once enjoyed by members of the academic profession in an elite higher education system have increasingly come under pressure (Trow, 1972). Traditionally, job roles in academia tended to encompass teaching and research, management and service, although with differing emphasis, while the division of work within the profession mainly took place via increasing specialisation of fields of knowledge. Today academics are more likely to concentrate on management or on teaching and research, while teaching and research themselves represent a further division of work.

At the same time, new opportunities for entrepreneurial academics have appeared in areas and activities beyond traditional job roles on the academic home turf. As historians have shown, technology transfer from universities to industry and other users of research results, such as the military or the health-care system, has always been part of the academic world. However, since the 1960s, it has become more prevalent. Priority setting to promote technologically promising scientific developments, attempts to forecast scientific breakthroughs with a strong application potential, and a general emphasis on "relevance" and "strategic research" are now familiar phenomena (Irvine and Martin, 1984; Rip, 2004). More and more academics face a situation in which they are asked to move from the circumscribed world of academia to a complex world of blurring boundaries and a growing emphasis on the quasi-entrepreneurial role of academics (Henkel, 2000; Kingsley, Owen-Smith and Powell, 2001). Finally, recent developments in new interdisciplinary fields of inquiry challenge traditional disciplinary boundaries and invite new forms of interaction in fields such as biotechnology, nanotechnology or the cognitive sciences. The technology-driven dynamics of such sciences allows for new forms of co-operation not only across the traditional academic disciplines but also between academia and other research providers and users.

For the coming decades, OECD figures indicate a decrease in the number of young domestic students in most OECD countries (Vincent-Lancrin, 2004). For our ageing societies the projected decline in younger people may lead to a continuous decrease in the traditional university-age population. This is a serious threat for higher education in times where funding is increasingly related to numbers of students and graduates. Opportunities to compensate for such a demographic trend are available. They include increasing overall participation rates, increasing demand by non-traditional and elderly students, and catering on the international market. Especially in transition and developing countries, demand is increasing and supply is still limited. There is already a growing market for non-traditional higher education in highly developed countries as well as rises in enrolments of international students on campus, through foreign branch campuses, joint ventures and franchise arrangements, and online teaching and learning. In consequence, the need has arisen to reconsider study programmes and the role of academic teaching and teachers in order to adapt to new types of students and transformed teaching conditions. In a global perspective, the academic profession in the 21st century may be one in which the main mission of academics will be to train a diversified student body in an institutional context that is likely to further diversify as well.

In this evolving framework, it seems likely that "cutting-edge research" will be more concentrated in certain centres of excellence and relevance and that some academics will mainly dedicate their efforts to it, while other types of research[1] will be carried out by the mainly-teaching staff. Second, traditional disciplinary academic work is likely to persist but is likely to be increasingly accompanied by new forms of interdisciplinary co-operation that are driven by the internal dynamics of scientific discovery as well as by changing expectations as regards the contribution of research to application. Third, job roles and work tasks are likely to be more differentiated and aligned on those of the business sector owing to the blurring of boundaries between academia, on the one hand, and other sectors and stakeholders in society, on the other.

Transformation and diversification of conditions of work and employment

Higher education and research systems almost everywhere have undergone two major changes which affect, in one way or another, the management of academic staff as well as their work and employment conditions. The first concerns the constructing of universities as organisations (Brunsson and Sahlin-Andersonn, 2000) and their transformation from collegial communities of academics into an organisation with a hierarchy (de Boer and Goedegebuure, 2001). Accordingly, university leaders have been encouraged to become managers and to develop strategic management (Rhoades and Sporn, 2002). The second change deals with the modification of funding mechanisms, through the introduction of lump-sum or global budgets for higher education institutions, output-based criteria in the allocation process, further competition through project-based or programme-based funding for research, private funding, *e.g.* through tuition (fees) or public-private co-operation. Both of these changes have strongly impinged upon academics' working conditions but also traditional contractual arrangements.

These overall trends notwithstanding, conditions of work and employment still depend heavily on national patterns. Status, salary structures, forms and rules of collective bargaining, career paths and employment relationships are affected first and foremost by national settings, history and each country's economic situation. As a consequence, the same practices may have very different meanings in different contexts.[2] The degree to which conditions of work and employment are part of the social fabric must be taken into account, even though our argument is often couched in general terms.

To describe the ongoing transformations, four dimensions are discussed: academics-university relationships; contractual arrangements and "permanence" models; salary setting and salary structures; and the division of work.

More institutional affiliation and more mobility at the same time: the contradictory forces affecting academics-university relationships

In a Carnegie Foundation study of 14 countries at the beginning of the 1990s, academics always declared that their affiliation to their discipline was stronger than their affiliation to their institution. The strength of their affiliation to their institution varies however (only 34% of Germans considered their institution "very important" or "fairly important", compared to 95% of Chileans).[3] Interestingly, the two dimensions are not negatively correlated: both can be high. This international study did not tackle the reverse perspective, namely the kind of relationship developed by institutions with their academics. Do university managers conceive of their institutions as shelters for highly qualified individuals to whom they offer support for their activities? Or, at the other extreme of the continuum, do they behave like employers who provide income and working conditions to knowledge workers who in return have to meet production objectives in terms of number and quality of teaching, numbers and reputation of publications, etc.? While no study has documented the evolution of the level of affiliation to the discipline or to the institution since the Carnegie study, there is plenty of evidence that many countries have moved away from the shelter-like mode and towards the employer-like mode. This has had several sources. First is the move towards more institutional autonomy which has led in many countries to delegating the management of positions and staff from the state level to the university. Such transfers have taken place for instance in the Netherlands where faculty members are no longer appointed by the ministry but by the rector of the university (de Weert, 2004), in Italy with the reform of national competitions (Boffo, Moscati and Vaira, 2004), and recently in Japan with the reform of the national universities (Oba, 2005). Second, the expansion of assessment procedures at the national or institutional level has emphasised and publicised (sometimes widely) the quantity and quality of each academic's performance: the most spectacular case is probably the introduction of the Research Assessment Exercise in the United Kingdom, with its regular publication of rankings for each department according to the research production of its staff and distinguishing between those who are recognised as active in research and the others (see for example Henkel, 2000; Harley, 2002). Third, the introduction of staff management techniques in universities (evaluation, personal development, etc.) has been expanded and has led some authors to conclude that academics are becoming "managed professionals" (see for example Slaughter and Leslie, 1997; Rhoades and Slaughter, 1997). Even if these techniques are more often associated with Anglo-Saxon universities, the idea that universities have to develop their own staff management devices pervades France's recent law to reform the research system, adopted in April 2006, which foresees the creation by each university of a procedure for evaluating its staff and labs.

Such changes have modified universities' internal relationships and have created an employment relationship between each institution and its staff. In parallel, even in very egalitarian countries, many higher education institutions began differentiating themselves from one another,[4] exhibiting their singularity and developing stronger institutional identities (branding) and expecting their staff to adhere to their strategies. Both of these trends have combined to strengthen but also transform the nature of academics' affiliation to their institution.

At the same time two other changes move in the opposite direction. First, institutional stability has become suspect. In many countries (Japan, Norway, Portugal, Spain), most academics' careers developed within a single institution, but this model is now widely criticised. Inbreeding is frowned upon and institutional mobility is promoted, thus encouraging faculty members to become more mobile. For the last decade there are, unfortunately, few comparative data, either over time or among countries that provide evidence of an effective increase in institutional mobility and a decrease in inbreeding. Some recent statistics on Japan (Yamanoi, 2006) give an idea of the strength of the process: in 1954, 98% of the faculty members at the University of Tokyo graduated from this institution; they were still almost 90% in 1984, but only 78% in 2003. Moreover, this shift in favour of institutional mobility is evident in many policy documents, and some institutions in countries where mobility is traditionally rare are trying to promote new practices. Spain has for example forbidden public universities to give a first permanent job to their former doctoral students.

Second, involvement in formal international or national networks or multiple affiliations has become frequent and is valorised. In Europe, the number of academics involved in European or international projects has increased steadily as the European Commission and individual countries have developed policy instruments encouraging international research projects. As a result many academics are more than ever engaged in strong relationships with partners from other organisations (including non-academic ones), thus weakening the institutional affiliation individual universities try to build with their staff.

If the traditional pattern of universities as shelters for self-regulated academics is weakening, the emerging pattern includes some contradictions, as it simultaneously aims at reinforcing academics' affiliation to their institution but also promotes mobility and flexibility. This tension is expected to increase in the coming years.

Permanence: a model for the happy few? Restructuring the contractual arrangements

The differentiation of the academic profession which derived from massification produced a diversification of career patterns. Until recently, academic careers were everywhere based on a two-stage process, with a first period characterised by apprenticeship, selection and time-limited positions, and the second beginning with access to a permanent position. From one country to another, within this overall pattern three very different career models developed and are still very frequent.

The first is the tenure model, which is typical of the US system. It is based on an early, severe selection of young PhDs, among whom some are offered tenure-track positions, *i.e.* time-limited posts[5] leading, at the end of a certain period of time, to a tenure procedure to decide whether they will be offered a tenured position.[6] This model is described by economists as an "up or out" system (O'Flaherty and Siow, 1992, 1995).

The second could be qualified as a "survivor" model and is typical of countries in which the Humboldtian and chair-system tradition is strong. Up to the 2001 reforms, it was characteristic of Germany. After their PhD, candidates for an academic career must go through various trials to provide evidence of their talents and wait many years to obtain a permanent position.[7] Only those overcoming the long period of selection and "tournaments" (Lazear and Rosen, 1981), *i.e.* competitions involving many candidates among whom only one or a few are maintained, have a chance to survive.

The third model can be described as a "protective pyramid" and is (was) frequent in many public systems of higher education (Italy, Spain, France). In these countries, access to a permanent position occurs quite early after a highly selective tournament. There then exist different categories of permanent positions organised hierarchically with procedures allowing promotion of some from one category to another. There is no assurance that those entering the pyramid can rise to the top: this very much depends on the growth rate of the overall pyramid and the age/seniority of those on the top.

Up until now, these three models are still the most frequent, and few countries have tried to abandon their traditional model (see the case of Germany in Box 4.1).

Box 4.1. **An unusual case of shift from one permanence model to another: Germany**

In 2001, without abandoning the "survivor" model which still exists in parallel, Germany introduced a new category of positions, called the *Juniorprofessoren*. Two main arguments pushed this reform forward. First, the fact that many young scholars were suspected of leaving Germany to escape the long and uncertain selection process leading to professorship. Second, assistantship was criticised for its negative impact on the innovation capacity of young scholars: on the one hand, being dependant on the professors, they could not develop their own research autonomously and be creative; and on the other, the preparation of the *Habilitation* (an obligatory exercise for becoming a professor) was described as deadening and ill-adapted to the requirements of modern research. This led to the progressive suppression of the *Habilitation* (to be achieved by 2009) and the creation of *Juniorprofessoren*. The latter are in two respects comparable to US tenure track positions: they are time-limited (three years), can be renewed once, and provide the opportunity to apply for a permanent position after the sixth year without passing the *Habilitation*. Academics in these positions, albeit non-permanent, do not work as assistants for the permanent professors: they are autonomous. However, there is no tenure process as in the United States: at the end of the six years, *Juniorprofessoren* must apply for the open professor positions and go through the usual German recruitment process.

Even if rarely abandoned, each of these models has been subjected to strong criticism[8] during the last decades. A common claim concerns the lack of flexibility due to permanence: it entrenches highly specialised staff whose domains of competence may quickly become irrelevant owing to the rapid transformation of science; it deprives institutions of efficient means of managing their staff (more so when it occurs early); and it is given (and with it, better salaries) when the person's scientific productivity is about to decrease.

Different methods have been introduced to counteract these weaknesses. One consists in creating posts that delay access to tenure-tracks positions (model 1) or to permanent positions (model 2) and that provide highly qualified and productive scientific manpower. This leads to an increase in the number of post-doctoral positions in the countries concerned, in particular in the life sciences, but is becoming more common in most scientific disciplines. According to Stephan (2006), the number of individuals working in post-doctoral positions rose from 23 000 in 1991 to 30 000 in 2001. In other countries, new positions were explicitly created as a means of transition towards a permanent job. For instance, in Germany the fixed-term C2 professor positions were introduced in the face of a lack of C3 (permanent) professor positions.

A second category of measures, typically for countries with a tenure system,[9] leads to the expansion of time-limited and part-time teaching positions, *i.e.* of non-tenure-track positions. According to Ehrenberg (2005), part-time and full-time non-tenured positions represented around 43% of the academic population in the United States in 1975, but reached 64% in 2003: as a result, the majority of faculty members no longer occupy tenured positions. In Australia, the number of casual positions more than doubled between 1990 and 2001 (Robinson, 2005). In the United Kingdom, the numbers of both fixed-term contracts and part-time staff have increased. The former represented 39% of the academic staff in 1994 and 44.8% in 2003, while the latter were about 12% in 1995 and rose to nearly 18% in 2002 (Court, 1998; Robinson, 2005). In a number of countries, the rise of private for-profit institutions contributes to this trend in academic appointments: they generally recruit their academic personnel from public universities but offer them few full-time or long-term contracts and operate on the contract system. Short-term contracts, part-time teachers paid by the hour and lack of social benefits characterise the employment conditions of many faculty in these institutions.

A third group of measures consists in developing new incentives on the internal labour market of each university (Musselin, 2005a). In countries with a tenure system, this has taken, for instance, the form of "tenure by objectives" or "post-tenure review" but many other devices have been implemented. In the two other models it appears more difficult to introduce such measures, but they are slowly appearing. In Germany for instance, a merit-based component has been introduced in the salary of newly recruited professors since 2001; in France bonuses are allocated to those who show a strong commitment to teaching, to research or to administrative responsibilities.

Other solutions consist in progressively reducing or abandoning the traditional permanent situations. New types of contracts are offered to those acceding to a "permanent" position. For example, in 1988 the British announced the suppression of tenure (Court, 1998). In Austria, for instance, new professors are no longer civil servants but have a time-unlimited contract (Pechar, 2004). Similar changes have been introduced in Japan's public universities (Yamanoi, 2003).

Traditional contractual arrangements and career paths have thus been criticised everywhere and new methods have been developed. Some are only improvements of existing arrangements (for instance when internal labour markets tend to strengthen and exert more control over academic staff), but others promote completely new contractual situations as well as new career paths which are more flexible, less structured and do not lead to permanence. Segmentation labour economists (Doeringer and Piore, 1971) would probably conclude that this leads to the creation of new secondary markets that reduce the chances of accessing the primary ones as the number of permanent or permanent-track positions decreases. Stephan (2006), for instance writes that "the probability that a young person trained in the biomedical sciences in the United States holds a tenure track position has declined considerably in recent years, going from 10.3% to 6.9%" from 1993 to 2001.

The pattern based on a two-stage dynamic is no longer the only one available for the academic profession, as traditional permanent positions tend to diminish in percentages and as career tracks that do not lead to permanence are developing. The contingent positions tend to develop as alternative career tracks, less secure, distinct from the traditional two-stage tracks and with few paths for going from one to another. Ehrenberg observes that some American institutions have begun organising career development for casual staff (Ehrenberg, 2005).

Setting the salaries of academics: national diversity and increasing international differentiation

There are important symbolic elements in rewards for academics, in terms of reputation, distinctions, etc. Nevertheless, there are economic elements as well, which make it possible to speak of "prices" of academics. The composition of these elements, the way they are set, and their differences from one academic to another are strongly linked to national habits and context.

In some countries, compensation of academics consists solely of their salaries, while in others it also includes special working conditions, or even personal benefits (special loan to buy a house close to the university for instance). Practices vary significantly.[10] In some countries the salary component is negotiated at the national level and is part of a fixed scale that allows for little if any negotiation. In others, national collective bargaining fixes the overall evolution of salaries but each institution then decides, within this framework, what each academic will receive. In still others, salaries are determined through negotiations between each institution and its staff. The negotiation of the other components (special working conditions, personal benefits) is less regulated and therefore less visible and more closely linked to individual institutions and negotiations. This is probably why this aspect of the academic's compensation is becoming more prevalent, notably in countries where the negotiation of salaries is restrained by a bureaucratic scale. In France, for instance, some universities are beginning to play with these components in order to become more attractive (especially to foreign academics).

As a whole, this suggests that valorisation of academic work is handled very differently from one place to another on the basis of national practices and rules and that there are no harmonised international markets.

This heterogeneity (or tendency to individualised treatment), which seems to be increasing,[11] strongly limits possibilities for comparisons within a single country and *a fortiori* among countries. There are few available data on personal benefits and on special working conditions.[12] It is therefore necessary to focus on the salary aspect, even if it is only one part of academic compensation. Four main trends can be traced.

- The relationships between academic and non-academic salaries within a country are linked to the degree of massification of higher education – and thus to the size of the academic profession. In countries where the rate of access to higher education has increased, academic salaries tend to become less attractive, and there is a growing gap between these salaries and those of PhD holders working in the non-academic sector. In one survey of salaries of academic staff carried out for the Commonwealth Universities, J. Kubler and L. Roberts conclude that in these countries "all academic wages compare poorly with the private sector... Moreover evidence... indicates that academic salaries have not grown in step with salaries in other parts of the public sector" (Kubler and Roberts, 2004-05; Ehrenberg, McGraw and Mrdjenovic, 2005).
- Within a country salary variations among academics tend to increase with the introduction of more individualised assessment and performance measurement

(Slaughter and Leslie, 1997). But this depends heavily on the societal context: salary structures are regulated first of all by the rules of individual countries and are linked to the specific status of the academic profession. Therefore, in countries where academics are civil servants, their salaries depend first on salary rates for all civil servants; in countries (the Netherlands, the Nordic countries) where the gap between lowest and highest salaries is traditionally moderate even in the productive sector, the same holds true for academic salaries; while in countries built on less egalitarian social contracts, the increased differentiation experienced by all wage earners in the last decades is also valid for academics. In this last case, there are important gaps between the lowest and highest salaries, but also growing differences among disciplines according to the social value they are accorded by the non-academic sector.

- Third, the discrepancies among countries in terms of academic salaries have tended to increase. This is linked to variations in economic development but also to the variations mentioned above, *i.e.* when the non-academic salary structure becomes more differentiated, academic salaries also do. In this case, there is an increasing gap with countries where overall growth has been less strong and/or where differentiation remains moderate, and/or when public rules define the salary structure. Moreover, the share of non-salary components in academics' compensation is often greater in the first group of countries than in the others and such components tend to increase as well. As a result, some countries' comparative advantage has increased quite radically in the last years while other, even developed, countries cannot compete with the compensation offered by the former. Moreover, this can widen the gap among sectors within the same country: in the United States the academic wage offered by the public research universities cannot be as attractive as that offered by private ones; in France, the conditions (and incentives) proposed by the private not-for-profit business *grandes écoles* are far more interesting than the salaries offered by French universities and other public *grandes écoles*.
- Multi-affiliation develops when regular employment does not provide sufficient income. This has long been the case in Latin America where relatively few academics traditionally work as full-time university employees and many faculty members either have several academic positions at different institutions or teach part-time at a university in addition to their primary work obligations. Faculty members sometimes work on an hourly basis with meagre salaries or without pay, often while working towards their Master or PhD (Marquis, 2002; Balbachevsky and da Conceicao Quinteiro, 2002). This has become more and more frequent in the previous Eastern Bloc. In Poland and Russia, many full-time employees receive relatively low salaries and seek supplementary part-time contracts in order to have a reasonable income.

From academic activity to academic work and a new division of labour

This last section deals with academic activities and the organisation of work, which have undergone two main changes.

In the past, academics were involved in research and teaching[13] (along with administrative responsibilities and tasks) and were largely responsible for organising their time and managing the relative weight accorded to each task. With the diversification of career paths and the restructuring of contractual arrangements, only part of the profession still functions in this way. Many academics are now recruited to carry out only one of the two activities (research or teaching) and are expected to accomplish precise tasks. This is particularly, but not only, the case for contingent staff. As stressed by Finkelstein, "full-time faculty are now hired as teaching-only or even lower-division/introductory courses teaching-only; or in natural sciences and the professions, research-only or clinical-only; or even primarily administrative roles in programme development and management" (Finkelstein, 2003). They thus come closer to being "academic workers".

This goes along with the increasing control over academic activities. The pressure for relevance and for short-term results facilitates the development of institutional or national devices to measure individual or collective performance as well as the introduction of incentives to encourage certain types of behaviour (and discourage others). In some cases, methods from the non-academic sector (such as the keeping of time sheets on one's activity) have even been introduced in order to better control the activities carried out and the time spent on them. The academic profession itself has professionalised and somewhat standardised its methods and outputs. All this directly affects the choices and work of academics. When the number of papers published each year in international journals and with a high impact factor becomes a main (and easy to calculate) indicator of performance, involvement in risky research projects with a long-term perspective for publication is no longer attractive. Or, when the main supervisor of each new PhD is offered a bonus, as in some institutions in the Netherlands, academics respond readily to such incentives. Indeed, some universities are finding it difficult to pay the bonuses, as they underestimated staff response. This reveals an ongoing transformation of the academic profession, which is now considered less as an occupation and more as a job.

The division of work is also affected. On the one hand, the divide between teaching and research, and between academics and academic workers, has increased. On the other, higher education institutions have become more interventionist in terms of allocation of work, and regular individual negotiations are used to set the tasks and duties of each academic, which reduces self-determination. There is a sensible shift in academic activity from a craft activity (where "either one worker makes the whole object or supervisors co-ordinate the work of specialists" [Granovetter and Tilly, 1988]) to a more "industrialised" activity.

We expect this evolution to continue and be generalised in the coming decades. The division of work is expected to increase and to become more formalised and institutionalised, leaving less initiative to the individual responsibility of each academic. On the one hand, the teaching and research divide will widen. Fewer academics will be involved equally in both, as specialisation in teaching or in research will be more frequent. The division of work within each group will be more structured than it is today. In teaching, for instance, development of curricula may become separate from the delivery of courses: this may already be the case for e-learning (Miladi, 2005) and may spread to more traditional teaching situations. In research, a new division is already observed between proposal writers, research managers, experimenters, etc., and it will intensify.

The reinforced division of work should increase the diversity of work and employment conditions. Specific conditions will be set for different categories of tasks. This is already the case for non-permanent staff who tend to be more and more specialised (either in teaching or in research) and recruited for quite specific tasks.

Today, the allocation of work of permanent staff is still self-regulated. However, the divide between teaching and research is already more externally structured: in some countries academics negotiate how they allocate their time with university managers, while in others, higher education institutions are opening teaching positions on the one hand and research positions on the other. Self-regulation is expected to diminish in this respect.

This increasing division of work will probably provoke a growing differentiation in salaries, reflecting the hierarchy that will be established among the different categories of tasks and of staff and also among their respective "prices".

Will academic work become less attractive? There is no clear evidence of this. Many of the changes experienced by academics today are comparable with those observed on non-academic labour markets (see for example Osterman, 2002). Therefore, even if the academic profession may seem less attractive today than in the past, the issue at stake tomorrow is much more the relative attractiveness of academic and non-academic work.

Challenges to the power of the guild and growing demands for accountability

Many of the changes described above are congruent with the transformation of the nature of universities. In a nutshell, they reveal the shift from universities as interest organisations towards a model that is closer to (but not the same as[14]) "work organisations", with a stronger division of work, the introduction of more wage-earner-like employment relationships, and more professional and managerial university leaders. Academics are expected not only to contribute to science and to the development of their discipline, they are also expected to contribute to the overall performance of their university/organisation. This is emphasised by the development of institutional evaluation. In business schools, for instance, accreditation agencies such as EQUIS or the AACSB, which first developed in specific regions (Europe for the first and the United States for the second) but have tended to become international, provide their labels to the institutions they assess and not to single programmes. They therefore encourage each institution to expect results from all its members and to ask them to conform to the accreditation criteria. The same happens (and will intensify) with the recent diffusion of international rankings, such as the Shanghai ranking and the ranking issued by *Times Higher Education*. Both assess and rank institutions, thus emphasising overall performance.

The reinforcement of the institutional level modifies the status of academic production as shown by the increasing relevance of issues relating to the ownership of academic products. On the one hand, there is often a shift from views and practices in which these products (teaching and research) were considered as the property of individual academics to views and practices in which the higher education institutions have ownership. On the other hand, the transformation of academic goods into products whose circulation and diffusion is restricted by property rights provokes debate about the nature of academic goods, and initiatives launched against publishing houses such as open archives and open journals are gaining ground.

At the individual level, more diversified types of control have been introduced (see the case of France in Box 4.2). Traditionally, control over academic activities mainly consisted in assessment of research production and was often voluntary. Once they reached permanence or tenure, academics would be free not to apply for new positions, submit papers to journals or go to conferences.

Such a situation still exists in some countries but it has become rarer. Many countries have developed systematic assessments, for research as well as for teaching, sometimes directly linked to funding mechanisms, such as the Research Assessment Exercise in the

Box 4.2. **The progressive regression of voluntary evaluation in France**

Faculty members in French universities have long been able to escape any form of evaluation. Only those desiring a promotion, sending a paper to a journal, answering a call for proposal or asking for one of the bonuses created at the beginning of the 1990s faced some form of evaluation.

In 1997, the ministry introduced the evaluation of teaching. Implementation has been uneven but has become more frequent.

The four-year contracts signed between the ministry and each institution relating to its research strategy led to the evaluation of the research activities of faculty members involved in research labs receiving funding in this way. According to an administrative report, this concerns about 80% of permanent academics.

Under new measures of the recent act for research (April 2006), all faculty members working in universities should be regularly evaluated by their institution under the supervision of a national agency for the evaluation of higher education and research. If such regular assessment procedures are new to university teachers, they have been applied for many years to researchers in national research institutions such as the CNRS.

United Kingdom, while higher education institutions that are in charge of the management of their positions and staff are creating their own evaluation devices. In some cases, this involves norms concerning the number of papers published each year in international journals or the number of patents available for licensing.

It is nevertheless important to note that these assessment processes still generally rely on external peer reviews: this is the case for the British Research Assessment Exercise, for the Spanish research assessment, etc. As a result, external peer reviews regain vitality and legitimacy; they are taken seriously by university leaders who use them as a lever for change, redistribution or decision within their own institution. In a study on hiring and staffing decisions, Musselin (2005b), for instance observed that in three German mathematics departments, decisions made at the university level to cut positions were informed and justified by evaluations led by peers of the discipline.

In parallel, however, non-academic forms of evaluations have developed: greater control over the carrying out of teaching duties, stricter supervision of expenses, incentive mechanisms in the allocation of budget, etc. More attempts are being made to discipline behaviour and to restrict self-determination in the use of time and money. One can therefore speak of both a diversification and intensification of the scope of control and of the types of control on individual academics.

Rather than a loss of academic power (as is often stated), there is a general expansion of the forms and sources of control that are being superimposed on traditional professional assessment mechanisms. Instead of simply undergoing peer evaluation, academics are increasingly exposed to various types of external peer reviews, to institutional assessment devices, to national evaluation procedures and to competitive international ratings as well. These different devices are not only more numerous, they also cover an ever larger array of tasks: scientific publications of course, but also involvement in technology transfer, amount of research contracts, teaching, etc.

For the future, then, there are two main issues. The first is the generalisation of the trend towards specialisation and diversification described above. Today, the diversification and intensification of control over academics still does not concern some countries, but this is expected to change as the academic profession diversifies and employment arrangements change. Moreover, in the same country, the span and intensity of control is likely to vary more among different segments of the profession. Academics with international reputations and careers will probably still benefit from considerable freedom and be more concerned by peer reviews than by other forms of assessment. However, a larger part of the academic population will certainly be more constrained in their day-to-day teaching or research activities and also more engaged in collective duties. In this segment, those with time-limited and single-task contracts should be even more dependent and controlled.

Second, the maintenance of professional power in its present form is under pressure. As noted, external peer review is still very strong. The research on hiring mechanisms mentioned above also concludes that in France, Germany and the United States the recruitment of colleagues and in particular the evaluation of applications and applicants for vacant positions are in the hands of academics (Musselin, 2005b). Some domains remain under academic control. External peer review is even gaining in importance and is used as a legitimate instrument for change by university managers. But this is not the only side of the issue. First, there is a tendency to mix different types of assessments and assert different kinds of control over issues which were previously free of control or only submitted to peer assessment. This is the case, for example, of the routine management of academic staff. Second, even when decisions are in the hands of academics, they often no longer rely on "pure" academic criteria but incorporate other kinds. This is sometimes done to increase the chances of achieving a goal: for instance, the defence of a new curriculum may gain in legitimacy if it can be demonstrated that there is a need for such training on the job market. However, it has also become part of the "normal" way of dealing with some issues: for instance, in many countries, the ability to develop contractual research is considered an important criterion when recruiting a professor. Finally, the involvement of non-academic stakeholders in decision-making bodies (university councils, research councils, etc.) may further diminish the guild power, if it strengthens the principle of shared governance on which their participation relies today.

Centres and peripheries: the international academic community

Higher education has many variants, and the situation of academic staff varies considerably across and within countries. A country's economic and political power, its size and geographic location, its dominant culture, the quality of its higher education system and the international role played by its language have to be taken into consideration when it comes to inclusion in or exclusion from the international academic community. In analysing the results of an international survey on the academic profession undertaken in the 1990s (Boyer, Altbach and Whitelaw, 1994), four types of approaches to internationalisation can be identified which reflect the different contexts set out above.

In some countries, generally less developed economically, academics may wish to be partners in international communication and co-operation but face problems because they tend not to be considered partners on equal terms. This is certainly a central problem for many senior academics in developing countries which are also experiencing a growing "digital gap". International flows mainly involve junior staff from these regions who contribute to a growing international orientation on their home turf owing either to academics who return home or to emigrants who retain a certain commitment to, and support for, their home countries.

In other countries, generally developed but small, international communication, co-operation and recognition are considered indispensable. Except in a very small number of fields of study, academics are not respected in their home country unless they have international visibility. Academics from such countries gain access to international networks without major difficulties; the national system seems to be perceived as either too small or too limited to strive only for national visibility.

In larger countries such as Germany, France, Spain or Japan, academics in many fields can strive for either more national or more international visibility. International co-operation and communication are highly valued by most academics. But the country's own academic tradition, the networks in the scientific community on the home turf, academic communication and publication in the country's language still play an important role and support a certain insularity of their faculty as well.

Finally, for many years in the United States and to some extent the United Kingdom, internationalisation mainly meant hosting foreign students and academics and considering research from other countries only if published in English, and often only in "international" publications in these two countries. Being at the centre of the world academic system places faculty in a powerful and comfortable position in terms of international contacts and recognition. However, it also encourages a very insular approach that will probably last only as long as this dominance is not endangered.

Nowadays, global trends are expected to play an increasingly important role and a further push towards the internationalisation of higher education seems to be in the making (Sassen, 1996; Scott, 1998; OECD, 2004b). International mobility of students and academic staff seems to be rising, new technologies connect scholarly communities around the world in new ways, and English has become the new lingua franca of most international communities. New regulations concerning comparability of degrees and mutual recognition, such as those of the European Union, and the growth of virtual universities, off-campus providers and internationally active study programmes foster the internationalisation of teaching and learning (Teichler, 1999; van der Wende, 2001). There is an international market for academics, for members of the professoriate as well as for junior staff, even if it is still limited in scope. Academia contributes to internationalisation and is at the same time affected by increasing "globalisation" within and beyond higher education. "Internationalisation" would here imply greater exchange and mobility of faculty across national borders while "globalisation" refers to trend towards worldwide standardisation, with a consequent loss of national identities and traditions.

As regards growing international exchange and mobility of faculty, there is little doubt that there is a strong positive bias. The European Commission's policy stresses the need for inter-European co-operation and exchange and encourages mobility as an instrument to give a European dimension to academic careers. The OECD is another important advocate of academic mobility and exchange in the service of higher education, the economy and society simultaneously. The OECD was probably also among the first to investigate the rise of a truly global labour market for R&D in which national borders play a diminishing role (OECD, 2004a). Equally important, the growing awareness of the important role of international intake for the competitiveness of US higher education and research fosters a strong internationalisation discourse.

In addition, the information technology revolution is speeding up scientific research and communication worldwide and sharpens the need for up-to-date information as well as the search for the latest competitive advantage in a globalising scientific working environment. All this is still in the early stages and the impact on higher education and the academic profession will be felt everywhere. In the developing world, access to such resources and exchange channels is relatively recent and for many academics still sporadic. The issue of access is central if new technologies are to be used to help overcome the traditional isolation of academics in the developing world instead of increasing their peripherality (Altbach, 2002).

There is also some evidence that international academic mobility and exchange is growing. Certain indicators, such as joint publications and joint patent applications by researchers residing in different countries, research projects carried out by international teams and/or supported by international funds demonstrate the increase in cross-border research collaboration (Vincent-Lancrin, 2006; Guellec and Cervantes, 2002). In many highly developed countries the share of foreign doctoral candidates has risen but varies considerably: about 2% in New Zealand, 5% in Australia, 9% in the United Kingdom, 18% in Finland and the United States, 22% in Spain. As regards visiting faculty, the United States plays a leading role as receiving country with a considerable growth rate over the last ten years (and a slight decline after 9/11/2001). In Europe, the United Kingdom, followed by France, Germany and the Netherlands are main receiving countries for researchers. For China a massive increase in foreign experts working in higher education has been reported, and in Japan the inflow of faculty for long-term appointments has increased (Guellec and Cervantes, 2002; Institute for International Education, 2006; OECD, 2005; Luiten-Lub, van der Wende and Huisman, 2005).

Empirical evidence suggests that junior as well as senior faculty use such international experience in different ways (Sveva, 2001; Enders and Mugabushaka, 2004; Musselin, 2005c). There is certainly a pool of researchers and teachers, top academics in certain fields, who are truly global and of strategic importance for research universities and national governments. Second, many junior faculty use temporary international experience (especially at top universities) to increase their standing and career opportunities when returning home. Third, for another group of the internationally mobile, working in another country is a "second best" solution, owing to a lack of career opportunities at home. Finally, academics' international mobility also includes those who go from "poor to rich" and hope to stay, at least for a while, in the new country.

The academic world is still clearly hierarchical and research universities in the industrialised world set the standards for the international science system. International mobility, whether of academics or students, is predominantly a South-to-North phenomenon even though there are efforts towards an exchange on more equal terms. There is significant movement also between the industrialised countries – especially to the United States as host for a temporary stay of junior staff – and some South-to-South movement as well.

Recent developments on the global job market for scientists and engineers suggest that this picture is likely to change (Freeman, 2005). Data show that the overall share of science and engineering graduates from European and Asian universities, especially from China, is growing while US production is stagnating and increasingly relies on foreign-born faculty. Increasing numbers of scientists and engineers in low-income countries, such as

China and India, create opportunities to catch up with the North in certain fields of scientific discovery and innovative products and processes. Relocation of R&D facilities, offshoring of highly skilled work from the North to the South, and socioeconomic and technological improvements in certain low-income countries contribute to these countries' advances on the global market. While it is premature to forecast the effects of such developments in the long term we may conclude that there are signs of a move towards a more polycentric world of scientific excellence with the United States one of its heartlands.

4.3. Conclusions and outlook

Today, the academic profession finds itself living in interesting times. While each academic system is embedded in its own national traditions, there are some common realities: increasing financial constraints, processes of differentiation within massified higher education systems, demands for accountability and responsiveness to societal needs, market-like approaches to higher education, and rising international co-operation and competition. Higher education has become a mature service industry and the academic profession has become a large and complex profession with many faces. Obviously, there are many unanswered questions about the future of the academic profession. We live in times of uncertainty about the future development of higher education and its place in society and it is therefore not surprising to note that the future of the academic profession seems uncertain, too. Nevertheless, it seems worth having a final look at our findings and offering some conclusions.

In sum, we argue that the traditional consensus among faculty in modern universities about what it means to be a professional in the higher academic strata is under pressure. The consensus stressed the following points: research is supposed to be a prominent focus of academic work and knowledge is pursued for its own sake; the effort to advance the frontiers of knowledge is best organised in academic disciplinary units; reputation is established by national and international peer groups of scholars; and quality is assured by peer review and academic freedom. Recent experience shows that these defining notions of the academic career are not a given and are likely to be contested in various ways.

On the one hand, the national boundaries of academic careers are weakening. First, we observe a growing international market for faculty and growing competition for talent. Academic labour markets are likely to become more international than in the past. Nowadays, the baby boom generation of faculty moves towards retirement but important fields suffer from a shortage of PhD students on their home turf, with the result that they hire candidates from other countries, making the market for young talent increasingly international. The internationalisation of academia is also seen in the increasing importance of articles in international journals as performance criteria.

Second, we observe blurring boundaries between traditional academic roles and quasi-entrepreneurial roles. The traditional academic criteria of excellence also tend to be accompanied by new criteria of success. Academics are, for example, increasingly expected to raise their own research funding, and success in leveraging funding becomes more and more important for both the institution and the individual faculty member. Expectations regarding the "relevance" of academic work for other sectors and stakeholders in society are rising, and spin-offs and market-like activities tend to become part of the academic reward system.

Third, recent developments have created new positions and career lines around the traditional academic career ladder. As in other organisations that seek more flexible forms of employment, these more or less peripheral positions around the core of the profession offer limited prospects for climbing the traditional career ladder. Career management of new groups of staff and new forms of contractual arrangements have become more important. In addition, new divisions of work within the main areas of work have appeared. Universities tend to break up the teaching-research nexus and to professionalise their management. Different units are created for teaching and research, money flows through different channels for teaching and research, and staff may be assigned more exclusively to research, teaching or management.

On the other hand, there are signs that academic careers are becoming more closely bound to the institution. First, measures are taken to reorganise universities by aligning academics' activities more closely with the interests of their institution. Local expectations regarding commitment and contribution to the institution are rising. The growing need to profile individual universities and to commit faculty to the mission of the institution calls for a new organisational identity among faculty. Teamwork within and across institutional units is increasing, and the "group", in addition to the individual scholar, becomes an important unit for measuring success.

Second, within universities, academics are losing part of the traditional guild power that protected their autonomy and "idiosyncrasy". Priorities in teaching and research are increasingly set by professional management. Also, recent measures taken to steer and control the professional agenda of academics (prescription of work portfolios, performance contracts, time sheets, etc.) tend to limit the freedom of individual academics more than in the past. Various phenomena such as growing expectations as regards regular attendance of faculty at their workplace, assignment of staff to specific tasks and projects with prescribed time budgets, and use of time sheets indicate that management technology is being introduced into the academic workplace.

Various drivers thus affect academic careers in multiple and sometimes ambiguous ways. This may mean in effect a narrowing gap between career models in academia and the corporate world (see for example Kleinman and Vallas, 2001; Menger, 2002). Corporate career models seem to adopt more and more elements that traditionally played a defining role in the academic world. In turn, universities have adopted certain elements of the traditional corporate models of professional work. This also implies that the university is no longer unlike other organisations, or at least it is less unlike. This further implies that looking at the future of the academic profession means simultaneously looking at the future of corporate work and corporate workers, as the latter are expected to control and produce more and more knowledge as part of their own professional activity.

Notes

1. See for instance the typology proposed by Laredo and Mustar (2000) which shows that research activities and strategies are more heterogeneous and diverse than it is often said and that various types of research activities, commitments to research, and research-based relationships to the local environment may be observed.
2. For instance, being a permanent academic teaching in different institutions or working simultaneously in a firm has different causes in developing and in developed countries. In the first case, multiple affiliations are the only way to survive for low-income academics; in the second it exemplifies the emerging model of boundary-less careers and polycentric affiliations.

3. The study concerned: Australia, Brazil, Chile, England, Germany, Hong Kong (China), Israel, Japan, Korea, Mexico, the Netherlands, Russia, Sweden and the United States (Boyer, Altbach and Whitelaw, 1994).
4. This can take rather different forms. In some countries (Spain and France for instance), universities are encouraged to stress their particularities and their specific orientations in their strategic plans, while in others (as in Germany or China for instance), some institutions are identified as "elite institutions" and allocated funding, thus establishing a hierarchy and promoting vertical differentiation.
5. In the United States, where this model prevails, young academics on tenure tracks generally experience two three-year contracts before they pass the tenure procedure.
6. In most cases, with the exception of a few highly reputed institutions whose policy is to exceptionally give tenure to those they recruit on tenure tracks, the chance of receiving tenure is very high (more than 70% in the United States according to Chait, 2002; this includes the highly reputed institutions mentioned above).
7. In Germany, where this model prevailed, the average age of access to a first permanent position was 42 in 2000.
8. For a review of the on-going situation and debates in the US system, see Chait (2002).
9. In the United States, the tenure model is overwhelming (85% of all universities have tenure agreements, and almost 100% of the research universities) but in the last years the percentage of academics recruited on tenure tracks has diminished and is today below that of those recruited on adjunct, post-docs or part-time positions. This trend remains relatively rare in research universities, however.
10. For a description of academic price setting in Germany and the United States, see Musselin (2005a).
11. In countries where salaries cannot be negotiated, one observes increasing negotiation on working conditions or housing. In France for instance, salaries are set according to a national income scale which is the same for all disciplines and institutions. However, some universities have found support from local authorities to provide better housing to their new faculties. Others have negotiated with the ministry to have part of the budget they get for their four-year contract dedicated to start-up funds.
12. A recent Australian study commissioned by the Australian Department of Education (DEST) has shown how the decline in salaries for academic staff has led to the rise of other non-monetary benefits in employment negotiations: see Horsley and Woodburne (2003).
13. Research and teaching should be understood broadly. Teaching includes all activities linked to training, from teaching class, to preparing courses, organising internships, using new technologies, conceiving e-learning curricula, tutoring groups, etc. Research not only concerns experimentation and writing papers, but also technology transfer, project writing, networking with other research colleagues, etc.
14. As argued by Musselin (2004), academic activities possess two characteristics whose simultaneous presence makes universities specific: they are loosely coupled activities on the one hand and unclear technologies on the other. These two characteristics remain central even if recent trends tend to lower loose coupling and to make the productive technologies clearer.

References

Altbach, P.G. (ed.) (2000), "The Changing Academic Workplace: Comparative Perspectives", Center for International Higher Education, Boston.

Altbach, P.G. (2002), "Centers and Peripheries in the Academic Profession: The Special Challenges in Developing Countries", *The Decline of the Guru: The Academic Profession in Developing and Middle-income Countries*, Center for International Higher Education, Boston College, Chestnut Hill, MA, pp. 1-22.

Balbachevsky, E. and M. Conceicao Quinteiro (da) (2002), "The Changing Academic Workplace in Brazil", in P.G. Altbach (ed.), *The Decline of the Guru: The Academic Profession in Developing and Middle-income Countries*, Center for International Higher Education, Boston College, Chestnut Hill, MA, pp. 77-110.

Bleiklie, I. (2003), "Hierarchy and Specialisation: on the Institutional Integration of Higher Education Systems", *European Journal of Education*, Vol. 38(4), pp. 341-356.

de Boer, H. and L. Goedegebuure (2001), "On Limitations and Consequences of Change: Dutch University Governance in Transition", *Tertiary Education and Management*, Vol. 7(2), pp. 163-180.

Boffo, S., R. Moscati and M. Vaira (2004), "The Academic Workplace. Country Report Italy", in J. Enders and E. de Weert (eds.), *The International Attractiveness of the Academic Workplace in Europe*, Materialen und Dokumente, Hochschule und Forschung, Francfort on Main, pp. 243-263.

Boyer, E.L., P.G. Altbach and M.J. Whitelaw (1994), "The Academic Profession: An International Perspective", Carnegie Foundation for the Advancement of Teaching, Princeton, N.J.

Brunsson, N. and K. Sahlin-Andersonn (2000), "Constructing Organisations: The Example of Public Reform Sector", *Organisation Studies*, Vol. (21)4, pp. 721-746.

Chait, R.P. (ed.) (2002), *The Questions of Tenure*, Cambridge, Harvard University Press.

Chen, X. (2002), "The Academic Profession in China", in P.G. Altbach (ed.), *The Decline of the Guru: The Academic Profession in Developing and Middle-income Countries*, Center for International Higher Education, Boston College, Chestnut Hill, MA, pp. 111-140.

Court, S. (1998), "Academic Tenure and Employment in the UK", *Sociological Perspectives*, Vol. 41(4), pp. 767-774.

Doeringer, P.B. and M.J. Piore (1971), *Internal Labor Markets and Manpower Analysis*, Heath Lexington Books, Lexington.

Ehrenberg, R.G. (2005), "The Changing Nature of the Faculty and Faculty Employment Practices", working paper, Cornell Higher Education Research Institute.

Ehrenberg, R.G., M. McGraw and J. Mrdjenovic (2005), "Why do Field Differentials in Average Faculty Salaries Vary across Universities?", working paper, Cornell Higher Education Research Institute.

Enders, J. (ed.) (2001), *Academic Staff in Europe. Changing Contexts and Condition*, Greenwood, Westport, CT.

Enders, J. and A.-M. Mugabushaka (2004), *Wissenschaft und Karriere*, Deutsche Forschungsgemeinschaft, Bonn.

Enders, J. and U. Teichler (1997), "A Victim of their Own Success? Employment and Working Conditions of Academic Staff in Comparative Perspectives", *Higher Education Policy*, Vol. 34(1), pp. 347-372.

Farnham, D. (ed.) (1999), *Managing Academic Staff in Changing University Systems. International Trends and Comparisons*, Society for Research in Higher Education and Open University Press, Buckingham.

Finkelstein, M. (2003), "The Morphing of the American Academic Profession", *Liberal Education*, Association of American Colleges and Universities, Fall, *www.aacu.org/liberaleducation/le-fa03/le-sfa03feature.cfm*.

Freeman, R.B. (2005), "Does Globalisation of the Scientific/Engineering Workforce Threaten US Economic Leadership?", NBER Working Paper No. 11457, Cambridge, MA.

Gappa, J.M. (2002), "Academic Careers for the 21st Century: More Options for New Faculty", in J.C. Smart and W.G. Tierney (eds.), *Higher Education: Handbook of Theory and Research*, Agathon Press, New York, pp. 425-475.

Granovetter, M. and C. Tilly (1988), "Inequality and Labor Processes", in N. Smelser (ed.), *Handbook of Sociology*, Sage Publications, Newbury Park, CA, pp. 175-221.

Guellec, D. and M. Cervantes (2002), "International Mobility of Highly Skilled Workers. From Statistical Evidence to Policy Formation", *International Mobility of the Highly Skilled*, OECD Publishing, Paris, pp. 71-98.

Harley, S. (2002), "The Impact of Research Assessment Exercise on academic Work and Identity in UK Universities", *Studies in Higher Education*, Vol. 27, pp. 187-205.

Henkel, M. (2000), *Academic Identities and Policy Change in Higher Education*, London/Philadelphia.

Horsley, M. and G. Woodburne (2003), *Australian Academic Salaries Time Series Project 1977-2002*, Australian Centre for Organisational, Vocational and Adult Learning.

Institute for International Education (2006), *Data on US international education*, New York, IIE.

Irvine, J. and B. Martin (1984), *Foresight in Science. Picking the Winners*, Frances Pinter, London.

Jenks, C. and D. Riesman (1968), "The Triumph of the Academic Man", A.C. Eurich (ed.), *Campus 1980: The Shape of the Future in American Higher Education*, Delacorte Press, New York, pp. 92-115.

Kingsley, J. (1997), "The American Academic Profession", *Daedalus*, Vol. 126(4).

Kingsley, J., J. Owen-Smith and W.W. Powell (2001), "Careers and Contradictions: Faculty Responses to the Transformation of Knowledge and Its Uses in the Life Sciences", S. Vallas (ed.), *The Transformation of Work. Research into the Sociology of Work*, Vol. 10, JAI Press, pp. 109-140.

Kleinman, D.L. and S.P. Vallas (2001), "Sciences, Capitalism, and the Rise of the 'Knowledge Worker': The Changing Structure of Knowledge Production in the United States", *Theory and Society*, Vol. 30(4), pp. 451-492.

Kogan, M., I. Moses and E. El-Khawas (1994), *Staffing Higher Education: Meeting New Challenges*, London and Bristol.

Kubler, J. and L. Roberts (2004-2005), *Academics Staff Salary Survey*, Association of Commonwealth Universities.

Laredo, P. and P. Mustar (2000), "Laboratory Activity Profiles: an Exploratory Approach", *Scientometrics*, Vol. 47(3), pp. 515-539.

Lazear, E.P. and S. Rozen (1981), "Rank-Order Tournaments as Optimum Labor Contracts", *Journal of Political Economy*, Vol. 89(5), pp. 841-864.

Luiten-Lub, A., M.C. van der Wende and J. Huisman (2005), "On Cooperation and Competition: A Comparative Analysis of National Policies for Internationalization of Higher Education in Seven Western European countries", *Journal of Studies in Higher Education*, Vol. 9(2), pp. 147-163.

Marquis, C. (2002), "Universities and Professors in Argentina: Changes and Challenges", in P.G. Altbach (ed.), *The Decline of the Guru: The Academic Profession in Developing and Middle-income Countries*, Center for International Higher Education, Boston College, Chestnut Hill, MA, pp. 53-76.

Mayer, K.U. (2000), *Wissenschaft als Beruf oder Karriere?*, presented at the conference on "Wissenschaft zwischen Geld und Geist", Max-Planck-Institut für Wissenschaftsgeschichte, Berlin, 16-18 November.

Meek, L., L. Goedegebuure, O. Kivinen and R. Rinne (1996), *The Mockers and Mocked: Comparative Perspectives on Diversity, Differentiation and Convergence in Higher Education*, Pergamon, Oxford.

Menger, P.-M. (2002), *Portrait de l'artiste en travailleur. Métamorphoses du capitalisme*, Seuil, Paris.

Miladi, S. (2005), "L'organisation de l'enseignement en ligne : contraintes et limites", presented at the international conference "L'information numérique et les enjeux de la société de l'information", Tunis, 14-16 April.

Musselin, C. (2004), "Are Universities Specific Organisations?", conference "Towards a multidiversity ? Universities between national traditions and global trends in higher education" organised by the Institute for Science and Technology Studies, Bielefeld, November.

Musselin, C. (2005a), "European Academic Labor Markets in Transition", *Higher Education*, Vol. 49, pp. 135-154.

Musselin, C. (2005b), *Le marché des universitaires. France Allemagne, États-Unis*, Presses de Sciences Po, Paris.

Musselin, C. (2005c), "Towards a European Academic Labor Market? Some Lessons Drawn from Empirical Studies on Academic Mobility", *Higher Education*, Vol. 48, pp. 55-78.

Nowotny, H., P. Scott and M. Gibbons (2001), *Re-Thinking Science: Knowledge and the Public in an Age of Uncertainty*, Polity Press, London.

Oba, J. (2005), "The Incorporation of National Universities in Japan: Initial Reactions of the New National University Corporations", *Higher Education Management and Policy*, Vol. 17(2), pp. 97-118.

OECD (2004a), *OECD Science, Technology and Industry Outlook*, OECD Publishing, Paris.

OECD (2004b), *Internationalisation and Trade in Higher Education: Opportunities and Challenges*, OECD Publishing, Paris.

OECD (2005), *Education at a Glance – OECD Indicators 2005*, OECD Publishing, Paris.

O'Flaherty, B. and A. Siow (1992), "On the Job Screening, Up or Out Rules and Firm Drowth", *Canadian Journal of Economics*, Vol. 25(2), pp. 346-368.

O'Flaherty, B. and A. Siow (1995), "Up or Out Rules in the Market for Lawyers", *Journal of Labor Economics*, Vol. 13(4), pp. 709-735.

Osterman, P. (2002), "Changing Work Organisation in the United States", contribution for the Conference "Transforming the Democratic Balance among State, Market and Society: Comparative Perspectives on France and the Developed Democracies", Harvard University, April.

Pechar, H. (2004), "The Changing Academic Workplace: From Civil Servants to Private Employees", J. Enders and E. de Weert (eds.), *The International Attractiveness of the Academic Workplace in Europe*, Materialen und Dokumente, Hochschule und Forschung, Francfort on Main.

Perkin, H. (1969), *Key Profession: A History of the A.U.T.*, Routledge and Palmer, London.

Rhoades, G. and S. Slaughter (1997), "Academic Capitalism, Managed Professionals, and Supply-Side Higher Education", *Social Text*, Vol. 51, pp. 9-38.

Rhoades, G. and B. Sporn (2002), "New Models of Management and Shifting Modes and Costs of Production: Europe and the United States", *Tertiary Education and Management*, Vol. 8(1), pp. 3-28.

Rip, A. (2004), "Strategic Research, Post-modern Universities and Research Training", *Higher Education Policy*, Vol. 17, pp. 153-166.

Robinson, D. (2005), "The Status of Higher Education Teaching Personnel in Australia, Canada, New Zealand, the United Kingdom and the United States", *International Higher Education and Research Conference*, Melbourne, December.

Sassen, S. (1996), *Losing Control? Sovereignty in an Age of Globalisation*, Columbia University Press, New York.

Schofer, E. and J. Meyer (2004), "The World-Wide Expansion of Higher Education in the Twentieth Century", Contribution presented at the international conference "Towards a multiversity? Universities between national traditions and global trends in higher education", University of Bielefeld, November.

Scott, P. (1995), *The Meanings of Mass Higher Education*, Open University Press, Buckingham.

Scott, P. (ed.) (1998), *The Globalisation of Higher Education*, The Society for Research in Higher Education and Open University Press, Buckingham.

Slaughter, S. and L.L. Leslie (1997), *Academic Capitalism: Politics, Policies, and the Entrepreneurial University*, John Hopkins University Press, Baltimore.

Stephan, P. (2006), "Job Market Effects on Scientific Productivity", paper presented at the Sciences Po seminar on higher Education, February, *www.cso.edu/fiche_rencontre.asp?renc_id=46*.

Sveva, A. (2001), "International Mobility of PhDs", *Innovative People: Mobility of Skilled Personnel in National Innovation Systems*, OECD, Paris, pp. 243-260.

Teichler, U. (1999), "Internationalisation as a Challenge for Higher Education in Europe", *Tertiary Education and Management*, Vol. 5(1), pp. 5-23.

Trow, T. (1972), "The Expansion and Transformation of Higher Education", *International Review of Education*, Vol. 18, pp. 61-82.

Vincent-Lancrin, S. (2004), "Building Future Scenarios for Universities and Higher Education: an International Approach", *Policy Futures in Education*, Vol. 2(2), pp. 245-263.

Vincent-Lancrin, S. (2006), "What is Changing in Academic Research? Trends and Futures Scenarios", OECD-CERI Working Paper, Paris.

de Weert, E. (2004), "The Academic Workplace. Country Report The Netherlands", J. Enders and E. de Weert (eds.), *The International Attractiveness of the Academic Workplace in Europe*, Materialen und Dokumente, Hochschule und Forschung, Francfort on Main, pp. 290-309.

van der Wende, M.C. (2001), "Internationalisation Policies: About New Trends and Contrasting Paradigms", *Higher Education Policy*, Vol. 14(3), pp. 249-259.

Yamanoi, A. (2003), *A Study of the Non-tenure System for Faculty Members in Japan*, Research Institute for Higher Education, Hiroshima University, Hiroshima.

Yamanoi, A. (2006), "The Japanese Academic Marketplace and Academic Productivity", contribution presented at the conference on "Quality, Relevance and Governance in the Changing Academia: International Perspectives", RIHE, University of Hiroshima, February.

ISBN 978-92-64-04065-6
Higher Education to 2030
Volume 1: Demography

Chapter 5

Student Enrolments and Graduation Trends in the OECD Area: What Can we Learn from International Statistics?

by

Ulrich Teichler and Sandra Bürger*

This chapter aims to disaggregate the recent expansion of tertiary education. It looks to what extent the increasing number of students in recent years reflects changes in the definition of the sector, its composition, entry rates, demographic developments and successful completion of study programmes. It also examines how this expansion affects graduation rates and the educational attainment of the population. As a conclusion, it discusses the richness and the limitations of the available statistical information for interpreting the future.

* International Centre for Higher Education Research, University of Kassel, Germany.

5.1. Introduction

Over a period of about five decades, there has been a substantial increase in study beyond secondary education. It has been accompanied by a lively debate about the changing demands of the economy, about the needs of society and the general impact of an increasing number of highly educated citizens, about changes in access to higher education and in the composition of the study body and about the changing character of higher education as a consequence of the increase in enrolments.

The aim of this chapter is not to participate in the general debate on the changing function of tertiary education in the context of expansion, but to analyse in some depth various elements of the process. Expansion may be broadly measured by the rise in the absolute numbers of students, but more detailed and more disaggregated information is needed to understand the changes that have occurred.

First, the *definition of the sector* plays a role. Reports shortly after World War II indicating that only about 3-5% of the relevant age group were awarded a post-secondary degree in the highly developed countries generally referred only to *universities*. Even in the 1960s, little attention was paid to post-secondary institutions that were not considered on equal terms with universities, for example in the areas of engineering education and teacher education (see OECD, 1970/71). Around 1970, the term *higher education* seems to have become commonly accepted as a term signalling basic elements of university education and education at other types of higher education institutions; in highly developed countries at that time, about 20% of the relevant age group on average enrolled in higher education programmes. Increasing emphasis was placed on issues of institutional composition and thus on signs of increasing "diversification" (see, for example, OECD, 1983). In the 1980s and 1990s, international bodies, notably the OECD, but also to a certain extent UNESCO and the European Commission, took the lead in coining the term *tertiary education* in studies on recent developments in education beyond the secondary level. The term "tertiary" as opposed to "higher" suggests that there is more to education in the third stage than what is conveyed by the terms used for traditional, vertically stratified education systems which point to certain curricular characteristics and quality levels. Over this period, enrolment rates increased to more than 50%, and it was predicted that in the first decades of the 21st century more than three-quarters of an age group would receive some tertiary education in many highly developed countries (OECD, 1998).

Second, *institutional composition* is an important element in the analysis of the expansion process. There are *functional definitions* of institutional composition, and most attention has been paid by scholars and politicians to a developmental theory of the US higher education researcher Martin Trow (1974): up to an enrolment rate of about 15%, there is only "elite higher education". Beyond that point, "mass higher education" emerges and, when enrolment surpasses 50%, there is "universal higher education". Trow sees the coexistence of these segments as protecting the elite sector to preserve quality and serve the most talented students in the best possible way. In addition, *types of institutions and*

 HIGHER EDUCATION TO 2030 – VOLUME 1: DEMOGRAPHY – ISBN 978-92-64-04065-6 – © OECD 2008

programmes were presented, often in terms of a dichotomy between universities and "non-university higher education", "short-cycle higher education", "the alternative sector", "applied higher education", etc. Further, *years of study* and *levels of study programmes* were often viewed as a gold standard for comparing systems and programmes as well as students' attainment. As the underlying concepts were controversial and the institutional arrangements continued to vary substantially by country, UNESCO and the OECD developed in the 1990s a typology based primarily on years of study and levels of study programmes and also taking into account the type of study programmes – in OECD terms "*tertiary-type B*" and "*tertiary-type A*" education. In addition, data are available on *fields of study*, a topic not addressed in this analysis.

Third, the *socio-biographic composition* is important for identifying those benefiting from and those disadvantaged by the expansion process. *Parents' educational attainment*, *parents' socio-economic status* and *ethnicity* are often referred to as socially distributive background variables; however, these indicators are measured differently in different countries. International statistics most often give information based on uncontroversial definitions of students' *age* and *gender*.

Fourth, information about *new entrants* is in various respects more interesting than information on overall student enrolments. While the total number of students is influenced by the varying duration of study programmes, the number of new entrants indicates how many persons participate in tertiary education. Changes in the number of students reflects, on the one hand, *demographic developments*: an increase in the number of births is likely to lead some years later to a rise in new entrants and a demographic downturn is likely to lead to a decline. On the other hand, an increase in the number of new entrants may be due to relatively higher participation in tertiary education: the *entry rate* is defined as the share of new entrants in all persons of the relevant age group.

Fifth, the number of *graduates* indicates how many persons are fully qualified in terms of tertiary education and are "delivered" to society. This number is also affected by demographic developments, and the *graduation rate* indicates the share of those who have successfully completed tertiary education programmes in their entire age group. The graduation rate is lower than the earlier new entry rate, because some students drop out: *success rates* establish a link between entry rates and graduation rates. Moreover, the annual number of graduates affects the educational composition of the population, usually measured as *educational attainment of the adult population*, or more specifically in OECD statistics as the rate of 25-64-years-olds having attained tertiary education.

Sixth, *international student mobility* plays a role in the expansion or contraction of tertiary education. Available statistics refer to national higher education, and in the past one could assume that most students were citizens of the country in which they studied. In recent years, however, the number of *foreign* students and students *studying abroad* and the number of students who are *inwardly mobile* or *outwardly mobile* for the purpose of study affect enrolment figures in some highly developed countries to such an extent that student mobility can no longer be viewed as marginal.

The aim of this chapter is to disaggregate the recent expansion of tertiary education on the basis of the kinds of sources of information described above. To what extent does expansion of the number of students in recent years reflect changes in the definition of the sector, its composition, entry rates, demographic developments and successful completion of study programmes, and how does it affect graduation rates and the educational attainment of the population? The analysis focuses on OECD data on western European countries and on Japan, while at times referring to other OECD member countries and occasionally to other parts of the world. It addresses changes from the early 1990s to nowadays.

In addition, this chapter discusses the richness and the limitations of the available statistical information. Compilations such as the annual OECD publication, *Education at a Glance*, indicate the wealth of information available. A detailed analysis, however, also points to the limitations of such information, which may be due to controversial concepts, the variety of definitions, data collection practices in individual countries and the degree of willingness, on the part of individual countries and international bodies that collect statistics from individual countries, to include or exclude certain dimensions when collecting data.

5.2. Enrolment trends

As the foregoing indicates, the most noticeable trend in higher education in recent decades appears to be its expansion, often referred to as the "massification" of higher education. International statistics provide three measures of this expansion: enrolment numbers, enrolment rates and entry rates. This section suggests that the growth in enrolment rates in higher education has been less related to demographic factors than to the lengthening of courses of study and the availability of new short programmes of study, in some cases following the upgrading of vocational programmes to tertiary educational programmes. Demographic developments might however play a more important role in the future.

Overall student numbers

The quantitative expansion of tertiary education is often described in terms of the absolute number of students enrolled. Trends in *overall enrolment of students* can be clearly identified if the definition of the sector has not changed over time or if changes of definition are clearly indicated. Japan, for example, collects educational data according to fairly stable definitions and is thus a suitable case for analysis. The number of students at universities and junior colleges in Japan increased from about 240 000 in 1950 to about 3 million in 2000, *i.e.* by a factor of more than twelve in 50 years. In addition, more than half a million persons were enrolled in other tertiary education institutions in 2000, primarily the institutions of vocational training that were upgraded to tertiary education institutions in 1978.

Leaving aside all changes in definitions, the tertiary student population worldwide may be estimated to have grown over five decades from less than 10 million in the 1950s to about 183 million in 2006 according to the most recent UNESCO data (UNESCO, 2007).

Table 5.1 shows overall student enrolments in tertiary education throughout the world from 1980 to 1995 as presented in an analysis for the UNESCO World Conference on Education 1998. The number of students in the "more developed regions" only increased from 23 million in 1980 to 25 million in 1985, but then increased at a somewhat faster pace to 29 million in 1990 and 34 million in 1995. UNESCO has recently changed its political-geographic definitions, but recent data suggest that the overall number of students in the "more developed regions" reached 39 million in 2006. However, overall student enrolments in highly developed countries increased in the 1980s and in the 1990s at a slower rate than in other parts of the world.

 HIGHER EDUCATION TO 2030 – VOLUME 1: DEMOGRAPHY – ISBN 978-92-64-04065-6 – © OECD 2008

Table 5.1. **Number of tertiary education students (in thousands) by world region, 1980-2006**

	1980	1985	1990	1995	2006[1]
WORLD TOTAL	51 160	60 296	68 665	81 745	139 395
More developed regions :	23 321	25 053	29 050	34 346	38 963
North America	13 517	13 887	15 628	16 438	18 814
Asia/Oceania	2 910	2 929	3 512	5 318	5 363
Europe	6 895	8 237	9 910	12 589	14 786
Countries in transition	11 317	10 882	10 716	10 790	19 298
Less developed regions :	16 523	24 361	28 899	36 610	81 135
Sub-Saharan Africa	563	906	1 365	1 926	3 182
Arab States	1 487	2 017	2 449	3 143	6 060
Latin America/Caribbean	4 930	6 364	7 353	8 121	15 635
Eastern Asia/Oceania	5 266	9 120	10 600	14 333	36 735
Southern Asia	4 063	5 535	6 456	8 004	17 162
Least developed countries	664	1 033	1 181	1 712	2 089

1. In case of missing value for the year 2006, data for 2004 or 2005 are used when available.
Note: The grouping is based on the country groupings undertaken by UNESCO in the 1990s.
Source: UNESCO (1998, 2006 and 2007).

Available OECD data make it possible to estimate that total tertiary education enrolments in European member countries in 2000 (*i.e.* including some in Central and Eastern Europe) increased in the period under consideration here, *i.e.* from the early 1990s until 2006, from about 11 million to about 13 million. This is far below the world average for overall expansion of student numbers.

Growth in enrolments is best described on the basis of annual *growth rates*. During the 1950s the number of students in higher education grew at an annual rate of 5% on average in European OECD member countries; during the 1960s the average rate increased to almost 8% (Pellegrin, 1974). The pace was similar in the early 1970s. It should be borne in mind, however, that in some countries part of the growth took place through the upgrading of institutions that were formerly not considered higher education institutions and mostly not included in higher education statistics. From the mid-1970s to the mid-1980s, the average growth rate in European OECD member countries was below 2%; there were substantial differences among individual countries, with stagnation and moderate decline in some.

Between the mid-1980s and early 1990s, the OECD (1998) observed a new period of "massification" of "tertiary education" (including vocational tertiary education). However, average annual growth of somewhat more than 3% was well below that of the early post-war decades. Table 5.2 suggests that annual growth rates varied substantially among European OECD member countries: about one-third grew at less than 3%, one-third at between 3% and 4%, and one-third at more than 4%.

From 1996 to 2006, the period primarily examined here, average annual growth of students enrolled in tertiary education in western European countries levelled off to about 1.7%. Table 5.2 shows:

- A decline in two countries.
- Annual growth of less than 1% in four countries.
- An increase of between 1% and 3% in five countries.

Table 5.2. **Growth rates in absolute numbers of student full-time enrolment in tertiary education in selected OECD countries, 1985, 1996 and 2006**

1996 = 100

	1985	1996	2006
Western Europe			
Austria	77	100	107
Belgium	67	100	93
Denmark	72	100	116
Finland	60	100	83
France	64	100	105
Ireland	51	100	140
Italy	67	100	114
Netherlands	79	100	122
Norway	53	100	109
Spain	54	100	101
Sweden	94	100	114
Switzerland	79	100	142
Turkey	31	100	175
United Kingdom	50	100	121
Central and eastern Europe			
Czech Republic	m	100	181
Hungary	m	100	182
Poland	m	100	190
Other countries			
Australia	56	100	149
Canada	76	100	65
Japan	60	100	101
United States	87	100	132

m = missing.
Note: 1997 for Turkey and 1998 for Poland.
Source: OECD Education Database.

Similarly, enrolments declined in Canada, increased marginally in Japan and grew in Australia and the United States.

With the exceptions of Ireland and Switzerland, higher growth rates were observed only in those European countries with a lower enrolment rate among the respective age group in the early 1990s, *i.e.* Turkey and the new OECD members in Central and Eastern Europe.

In sum, expansion of higher education in terms of overall student numbers continued both in western Europe overall and all OECD members from the early 1990s until the most recent years for which data are available. However, the increase was smaller than that in all other parts of the world. Moreover, developments were quite heterogeneous in western Europe, with marginal growth in some cases and a decline in others. Overall expansion of higher education in terms of student numbers can no longer be viewed in terms of a more or less consistent pattern across the highly developed countries.

Entry and enrolment rates

Relative numbers of new entrants or of all students enrolled are often more useful than absolute numbers. When analysing and assessing the expansion of tertiary education, issues such as opportunities for study or the impact of expansion on the proportion of highly qualified persons among the adult population are of interest and can be more readily observed in relative terms. Two ways of presenting the relative expansion of higher education are often used:

- *enrolment rates:* the number of students enrolled in tertiary education, compared, as a rule, to the overall population of the age group typically engaged in tertiary education;
- *entry rates:* the number of new entrants compared to the population of the typical age for entering tertiary education.

The UNESCO and the World Bank frequently publish enrolment rates. For example, the statistical background information for the UNESCO World Conference on Higher Education 1998 presented two indicators of this kind (UNESCO, 1998). First, the number of students per 100 000 inhabitants was calculated. From 1980 to 1995, it increased by almost 25% worldwide from 1 151 to 1 434. In rounded figures, it grew by 34% in "more developed countries" from 3 100 to 4 100; it declined by 12% in "countries in transition" from 3 000 to 2 600; it increased by 65% in "less developed countries" from 500 to more than 800, and by 77% in "least developed countries" from less than 200 to about 300.

Second, UNESCO calculated the "gross enrolment ratio" as the percentage of students among young people within five years of the country's normal secondary education leaving age. From 1980 to 1995, the enrolment ratio increased in "more developed countries" from 37.2% to 59.6%; in "countries in transition" from 33.6% to 34.2%; in "less developed countries" from 5.1% to 8.8%; and in "least developed countries" from 1.8% to 3.2%.

Since then, these figures have increased further. For 2006, the gross enrolments rates were 70% in North America and western Europe, 57% in Japan, 73% in Australia and 31% worldwide (UNESCO, 2007).

A comparison of the various growth figures over the period of 15 years from 1980 to 1995 in the "more developed countries" shows an increase of 47% in the absolute number of students, *i.e.* about 3% annually, of 34% in the number per 100 000 inhabitants and of 60% among young people in the typical age for study. The comparison clearly indicates an increase in the average duration of study among students in more developed countries. The figures do not allow for disentangling the growth due to an increase in the entry rate and that due to the increasing length of study.

The OECD employs entry rates as indicators of initial participation in tertiary education. For international comparisons and analysis of trends, this is certainly superior to the growth in the enrolment ratio, because the average length of study varies among countries and changes over time. For example, the relatively low gross enrolment rate in Japan in 2006 shown above is clearly due to the fact that the average number of years spent in tertiary study is lower in Japan than in most other highly developed countries.

Entry rates in European OECD members can be estimated to have increased from a country mean of less than 5% of the corresponding age group around 1950 (university education) to more than 20% around 1970 (higher education) and to more than 40% in the mid-1990s (tertiary education). Average annual growth of more than 5% was due in part to upgrading.

For western European OECD members for which data are available, we find a mean entry rate of:

- 38% in 1991, with 24% beginning study programmes of tertiary-type A education and 14% entering other tertiary education programmes;

- 64% in 2005, with 49% entering tertiary-type A education and 17% tertiary-type B education. In the new Central and Eastern European OECD member countries, the net entry rate was 63%.

Thus, the mean tertiary education entry rate among western European OECD members has increased since the early 1990s at an annual average rate of almost 4%. It exceeded the increase in overall absolute enrolment rates, primarily owing to an increasing share of students studying for a relatively short period.

Table 5.3 shows that the rise in entry rates varied significantly. It was higher on average in Central and Eastern European OECD members and lower in the other member countries covered. In western Europe, the average annual growth of entry rates over the 14-year period was less than 2% in Finland and Germany, between 2 and 4% in Belgium and the Netherlands, and 4.5% or more in Austria, France, Denmark, Spain, Ireland, Sweden and the United Kingdom.

Table 5.3. **Entry rates into tertiary education in selected OECD countries, 1991 and 2005**

Percentage of corresponding age groups

	1991			2005		
	Non-university tertiary	University	Total	Tertiary-type B	Tertiary-type A	Total
Western Europe						
Austria	5	23	28	9	37	46
Belgium	22	28	50	34	33	67
Denmark	14	24	38	23	57	80
Finland	29	33	62	m	73	73
France[2]	15	29	44	34	39	73
Germany	11	33	44	14	36	50
Ireland	16	17	34	14	45	59
Italy	m	36	36	m	56	56
Netherlands	25	13	38	m	59	59
Spain	m	40	40	22	43	65
Sweden	34	13	47	7	76	83
Turkey	2	12	15	19	27	46
United Kingdom	8	20	28	28	51	79
Central and eastern Europe						
Czech Republic[1]	1	15	16	8	41	49
Slovak Republic[1]	m	m	m	2	59	61
Hungary	9	7	16	11	68	79
Other countries						
Australia	16	36	52	m	82	m
Japan	29	24	53	30	41	71
United States	27	38	65	m	64	m

1. 1991: Czechoslovakia.
2. 2003 instead of 2005.
m = missing.
Source: OECD (1993, 2005 and 2007), *Education at a Glance: OECD Indicators.*

The differences in entry rates in some countries were clearly linked to upgrading; this upgrading also explains to some extent the increase in the proportion of students studying for a relatively short period. There was substantial upgrading from vocational training outside tertiary education to tertiary-type B education in Spain, Turkey and the United Kingdom.

Demographic developments

The impact of demographic changes on enrolment in education tends to become an issue at times of marked increases or decreases in the relevant age cohort. Since the 1990s, concerns have been voiced about the reduced size of the typical college-going age cohorts in most highly developed countries. According to OECD statistics (OECD, 2006, *Education at a Glance*, Table C.2.2), however, the mean number of students in European OECD member countries would have declined by 5% from 1995 to 2004, if changes in student enrolments were determined exclusively by demographic factors (an annual demographic decline of more than 0.5% on average). Demographic change affected overall absolute enrolment to a lesser extent than changes in entry rates or changes in the choice of long or short study programmes.

In contrast to western Europe, demographic changes played a major role in recent years in Japan. The 18-year-old population in Japan (Japan, Ministry of Education, Culture, Sports, Science and Technology, 2004) was about 2 million in 1960, declined to 1.4 million in 1964, increased dramatically to 2.5 million in 1966, declined to 1.6 million in 1975 and remained on that level until 1985. It then increased to more than 2 million in 1992, declined to 1.5 million in 2002, and is expected to decline moderately to 1.2 million in 2009 and to remain more or less constant until 2020.

In spite of the drop in the relevant population between 1992 and 2002, the number of new entrants to tertiary education in Japan only declined from 1.15 million to 1.05 million. As Table 5.3 shows, the entry rate increased over 14 years from 53% to 71%. Thus, potentially vacant places due to the demographic downturn were almost entirely filled by increased absorption of the relevant age group. However, this affected the various types of tertiary education institutions differently. The number of new entrants in colleges of technology and tertiary (type B) vocational programmes remained more or less constant. In contrast, the number of new entrants to junior colleges declined from about 250 000 to about 110 000. Experts estimate that more than half of the decline in enrolments in junior colleges is linked to the upgrading of many of these to universities. Altogether, the demographic downturn since 1992 led to a serious financial crisis in more than one-tenth of private universities, to more or less open access to more than one-third of universities, and to a less competitive mood among the larger proportion of young people potentially heading for universities (see Yonezawa and Kim, 2008).

In sum, the available data show that entry rates to tertiary education continued to increase in western Europe at different rates in recent years. The higher increase in mean entry rates than in overall enrolment figures is primarily due to increasing options for short study programmes, partly as a result of the upgrading of vocational training programmes to tertiary education programmes. In addition, a moderate demographic decline was not very relevant in recent years but is likely to play a more important role in the future.

5.3. The composition of the student body

Did the expansion of higher education come from or lead to a change in the composition of the student body? The question is difficult to answer on the basis of international statistics. While we know that the bulk of tertiary enrolments continue to be in general higher education and that female student enrolments have risen, there has been no systematic collection of data at the international level on students' age or socio-economic background. Although numbers of foreign students have increased significantly in recent years, this has clearly not been a driver of massification of higher education in OECD countries.

Institutional composition

In statistics on student enrolment, the OECD distinguished between "university tertiary education" and "non-university tertiary education" around 1990 and between "tertiary-type A education" and "tertiary-type B" education following the last ISCED classification in 1997. The definitions of the two categories are quite similar, but one major distinction is worth noting. Students at various bachelor-level programmes at non-university institutions of higher education, *e.g.* HBO in the Netherlands, *ammittikorkeakoulu* in Finland and university colleges in Sweden, were classified as "non-university tertiary education" in the early 1990s, but as "tertiary-type A" in recent years.

In addition, the OECD provides various categories for dividing "university education" or "tertiary-type A" education according to years of study and programme level. In statistics of student enrolments, entry rates and graduation rates, these categories have varied over the years and often in the same year.

The available data on entry rates, student enrolments and graduation rates show that the university and tertiary-type A sector is generally the largest one in western European countries and that it has grown more in recent years than the other tertiary education sector. However, this is largely due to the redefinition of the categories, notably the reallocation of non-university bachelor programmes in various European programmes.

A time-series analysis of the institutional composition of the student body is hampered by the continual upgrading of programmes. Currently, efforts are under way in Europe to introduce a bachelor-master structure in the context of the so-called "Bologna process" and to increase the quality of vocational education and training and possibilities for moving to tertiary education in the context of the "Copenhagen process". This calls for revision of the statistical classification of tertiary education and is likely to lead to further efforts to upgrade the vocational education and training currently registered as secondary education in available statistics to "tertiary-type B" or even to bachelor programmes.

Socio-biographic composition

Gender is the only information on the socio-biographic composition of the student body consistently published by international agencies that provide systematic information on education. Comparative data on educational background, socio-economic background, ethnic background, etc., are sometimes presented for a limited number of countries and are often taken from representative surveys. This reflects both the limits of general statistical datasets and the international diversity of data collection.

For many years, reference to gender meant information on the under-representation of women. This was generally true for the first few decades after World War II for OECD member countries and even longer worldwide. During the 1980s, however, entry of women to tertiary education surpassed that of men in western European OECD countries. In 1991, the mean entry rate was 36.0% for men and 39.1% for women and men accounted for 48% of all new entrants. Of the 15 western European countries for which information was available, the number of new female entrants was larger than that of new male entrants in nine countries. According to UNESCO statistics, in 2005 women accounted for 50% of all tertiary education students worldwide, although there were strong differences across countries.

In 2005, 56.9% of men and 71.2% of women in western Europe began tertiary education. Out of all new entrants, 46% – measured as the mean of all countries providing information – were men (47% for entry to tertiary-type A and 44% to tertiary-type B education). As Table 5.4 shows, more women than men began tertiary level study in 13 of the 15 western European countries for which data were available. The information provided in Table 5.4 suggests that other OECD countries also show a trend towards a higher percentage of women. Only in Switzerland and Turkey was the number of men still higher than that of women (Vincent-Lancrin, 2008).

Table 5.4. **Entry rates into tertiary education by gender in selected OECD countries, 1991 and 2005**

Percentage of corresponding age groups

	1991			2005		
	Men	Women	Total	Men	Women	Total
Western Europe						
Austria	27	28	28	41	51	46
Belgium	45	52	48	58	76	67
Denmark	33	43	38	68	92	80
Finland[2]	54	71	62	63	84	73
France[2]	40	49	44	56	90	73
Germany[1]	49	39	44	47	53	50
Ireland	34	33	34	54	64	58
Italy	35	36	36	49	64	56
Netherlands[2]	38	34	36	54	63	59
Norway[2]	32	42	37	64	89	76
Spain	39	43	41	57	74	65
Sweden	43	52	43	71	97	83
Switzerland	31	23	27	55	51	53
Turkey	19	11	15	51	40	46
United Kingdom	28	27	28	65	94	79
Central and Eastern Europe						
Hungary	16	16	16	65	91	78
Other countries						
Australia[2]	42	62	52	74	91	82
Japan	52	54	53	70	72	71
United States[2]	61	69	65	56	71	64

1. 1991 only Western Germany.
2. 2003 instead of 2005.

Source: OECD (1993, 2005 and 2007), *Education at a Glance: OECD Indicators.*

In recent years, the OECD has also provided information on the age of students at the time of entry to tertiary education. In 2005 in 18 European OECD members, the mean age at entry was 21.7 years for the 20th percentile, 23 years for the 50th percentile, and over 27.4 years for the 80th percentile. There are striking differences among countries. In Europe, the Nordic countries, Hungary and Switzerland reported 20% or more students aged over 25 years (see the data for the 80th percentile, OECD, 2007, *Education at a Glance*). Among members outside Europe, this is also true for Australia and New Zealand.

In sum, information provided in international statistics on the socio-biographic profile of tertiary education students is scarce. Improvement is unlikely because national data collection is likely to remain limited in this domain, and controversies about the most valuable categories are likely to persist. Therefore, national or internationally comparative surveys remain the most valuable sources.

Foreign and mobile students

Over the years, public attention has increasingly been paid to another category of the student body: the internationally mobile student. Unlike gender, age or educational background, this is not a sub-group of a student body of a given size in each country; instead, mobility affects the size of the student body in each country. If, for example, inward mobility surpasses outward mobility, the overall number of students rises.

The international bodies that collect educational statistics did not until recently collect data on student mobility, strictly speaking, but on nationality. The number of foreign students and the number of persons studying abroad were used as a proxy for mobility. However, some foreign students live in the country of study before entering tertiary education and thus are not mobile for the purpose of study and some students return to their home country to study and thus are mobile but not foreigners.

The number of foreign students reported in student statistics has more than doubled in OECD member countries from the early 1990s to 2005, a period during which international student mobility became a major issue in higher education policy. According to the available UNESCO statistics, the number of foreign students worldwide increased from about half a million around 1970 to almost 1 million in 1980, more than 1.5 million in the mid-1990s and almost 2.7 million in 2005. The share of students studying abroad, however, remained at roughly about 2% of all students worldwide. As most students studying abroad go to highly developed countries and as both the population and the relative growth rates of students in these countries were below world average, the percentage of foreign students in all students in these countries has increased substantially over time.

The number of foreign students reported in the official statistics of western European OECD member countries nearly doubled between the early 1990s and 2005. The average ratio of foreign students to all students enrolled increased from about 4% to more than 6%. In Central and Eastern Europe, the rate of increase was higher but started from a much lower level and remained lower. Among OECD members outside of Europe, the ratio of foreign students varies so widely that any generalisation would be misplaced. Altogether one might be inclined to consider study abroad as a major factor in changes in enrolment rates in highly developed countries. In fact, however, the increase in foreign students appears to explain on average at most one-tenth of the overall rise in enrolments.

Table 5.5 gives information on foreign students in selected OECD member countries from 1998 to 2005. It shows the percentage of foreign students among all students. It increased by about 8% points in Australia (from 12.6% to 20.6%) and by at least 3% points in the Czech Republic, Denmark, France, Germany, Sweden and the United Kingdom. The pace was slower in most countries and in Turkey, the percentage slightly declined.

From 1998 to 2005, the number of foreign students increased by more than 50% in Canada, New Zealand, the Czech Republic, Hungary, Iceland, Sweden, the Netherlands as well as in Japan and Korea. In Japan, for example, the number of foreign students increased from about 40 000 in 1990 to about 60 000 in 2000 and then dramatically to more than 125 000 in 2005.

Table 5.5. **Proportion of foreign students in total tertiary enrolment in selected OECD countries, 1998 and 2005**

Percentage

	1998	2005
Western Europe		
Austria	11.5	14.1
Denmark	6.0	11.7
Finland	1.7	2.8
France[1]	7.3	10.8
Germany	8.2	11.5
Ireland[1]	4.8	6.9
Italy	1.2	2.2
Norway	3.2	4.8
Spain	1.7	2.5
Sweden	4.5	9.2
Switzerland	15.9	18.4
Turkey	1.3	0.9
United Kingdom	10.8	17.3
Central and Eastern Europe		
Czech Republic	1.9	5.5
Hungary	2.6	3.1
Poland	0.5	0.5
Other countries		
Australia	12.6	20.6
Japan	1.4	3.1
United States[1]	3.2	3.4

1. International students in 2005.

Source: OECD (2007), *Education at a Glance – OECD Indicators*, Paris.

Most national governments, as well as UNESCO, the OECD and Eurostat, have traditionally collected data on foreign students, although they have recently been looking for new ways to track the frequency and flows of mobile students (since *Education at Glance 2006*). Until recently, the number of foreign students differed substantially from that of mobile students, notably in three respects (see Kelo, Teichler and Wächter, 2006):

- Many foreign students lived and learned in the country of study before they enrolled in tertiary education.
- Students studying abroad temporarily (*e.g.* "exchange students", ERASMUS students), mostly for half a year or one year, are only partially included or not included at all in many countries' statistics on foreign students.
- Students returning to their country of citizenship to study are treated in the statistics of most countries as home students, though they were in fact as "mobile" as the majority of foreign students.

A recent study of several European countries for which more refined data are available (Kelo, Teichler and Wächter, 2006) illustrates the differences resulting from these distinctions. Table 5.6 provides data on the United Kingdom, Germany and Switzerland. Depending on the definition used, figures on foreign and mobile students may vary by about one-third, and might be greater if all temporarily mobile students are taken into account.

Table 5.6. **Percentage of foreign and inward mobile students in Germany, Switzerland and the United Kingdom, 2003**

Citizenship and mobility status	Germany	Switzerland	United Kingdom
a. Foreign inward mobile	8.5	14.1	13.0
b. Home country citizens inward mobile	1.5	2.0	0.6
All mobile (a, b)	10.0	16.1	13.6
c. Foreign non-mobile	3.4	5.4	4.6
All foreign (a, c)	11.9	19.5	17.6

Source: Based on M. Kelo, U. Teichler and B. Wächter (2006).

Since 2005 the agencies that collect international statistics have encouraged all countries to collect mobility statistics in addition to statistics on foreign students (UNESCO-UIS, OECD and Eurostat, 2005). However, they exclude from the count all students enrolled in another country for the purpose of study for less than one semester.[1]

As regards total entry, enrolment and graduation ratios, available information suggests that the effect of mobility on overall enrolment figures is somewhat smaller than statistics on foreign students suggest. Mobility varies substantially by country, however it is most pronounced in countries where many foreigners live and learn prior to tertiary education without becoming citizens of that country and where the amount of temporary inward mobility is not very high.

5.4. The output of tertiary education

Data on student enrolments are often misleadingly referred to as an indication of a move towards a highly educated society. Entry rates often figure almost as projections of the output of tertiary education. However, according to the "rules of the game", students are usually viewed in Europe as having attained tertiary education only if they successfully complete a study programme and graduate from higher education. Western Europe has generally reached "universal tertiary education" according to Martin Trow's terminology, but this does not mean that western Europe has achieved "universal" graduation rates.

Success rates

The OECD calculates success rates, or "survival rates", by comparing the number of graduates in a given year with the number of new entries some years earlier. As these calculations have not been made regularly, it is not possible to carry out a trend analysis.

According to the OECD, the mean survival rate for all OECD member countries in 2004 was 71% in tertiary-type A education and 67% in tertiary-type B education. The rate varied substantially by country. In tertiary-type A education, the highest survival rates in Europe was reported for Ireland (83%); the survival rate was highest in Japan (91%).

Graduation rates

According to OECD statistics, the tertiary graduation rate increased from 35% in 1994 to 41% in 2005 in 13 western European member countries for which data are available. The annual rate of increase was almost 3% and corresponded to about 1% of the age group annually.

The decline from a mean non-university graduation rate of 17% in 1994 to an 11% tertiary-type B graduation rate is due to the upgrading of major areas of non-university higher education and thus to changes in category. While bachelor-equivalent programmes at non-university higher education institutions were classified by the OECD in 1994 as non-university tertiary education, they have recently been reported as tertiary-type A programmes.

According to Table 5.7, graduation rates in western European OECD members in 1994 ranged from 14% to 70%. They ranged from 28% to 62% in 2005. While the substantial decline in Norway is obviously due to changes in definitions and data collection, the data suggest that the gap between countries has in fact narrowed as a consequence of "catching up" by countries with previously low graduation rates.

Table 5.7. **Tertiary graduation rates in selected OECD countries, 1994 and 2005**

Percentage of corresponding age groups

	1994			2005		
	Non-university tertiary	University	Total	Tertiary-type B	Tertiary-type A	Total
Western Europe						
Austria	5	9	14	8	20	28
Denmark	9	26	35	10	46	56
Finland	25	21	46	0	47	48
France[1]	25	14	39	19	27	45
Germany	11	13	24	11	20	31
Ireland	14	23	37	24	38	62
Italy	9	11	20	m	41	m
Norway	47	23	70	2	41	42
Spain	1	21	22	17	33	50
Sweden	12	13	25	5	38	42
Switzerland	25	9	33	9	27	35
Turkey	2	7	9	m	11	m
United Kingdom	25	27	52	17	39	57
Central and Eastern Europe						
Czech Republic	5	14	19	6	25	31
Hungary	m	14	m	4	36	40
Other countries						
Japan	28	23	52	27	36	63
United States	22	32	54	10	34	44

1. 2003 instead of 2005.

m = missing.

Source: OECD (1996, 2005 and 2007), *Education at a Glance – OECD Indicators.*

Table 5.7 shows in addition that the graduation rate increased moderately in Japan during the period studied. The decline in the United States is primarily due to changes in calculation.

The average annual increase in the graduation rate obviously varied substantially among European countries, with almost no growth in some, in others annual growth of 2% or 3%, while in Austria, Denmark, Ireland, Sweden and Spain it was more than 5%.

In sum, it is no surprise that western European graduation rates have increased in parallel to the entry rates of a few years earlier. It is safe to predict that they will continue to increase in the near future. Again, there are noteworthy variations. Altogether, the available data on trends in graduation rates have to be viewed with more caution than data on entry rates, because substantial changes in graduation rates in some countries must be explained as changes in definitions and data collection rather than as valid information on trends.

Attainment of tertiary education

Annual graduation rates affect the educational attainment of the working age population over a period of about 40 years. At the beginning of the period under observation, *i.e.* in the early 1990s, persons who graduated from tertiary education during or shortly after World War II reached the typical retirement age. As tertiary education has grown substantially over the intervening years, the percentage of the adult population, defined in most overviews on educational attainment as the population aged 25-64 years old, graduating from tertiary education was substantially smaller than the percentage of recent graduates in that age group.

In 1992, an average of 16% of the adult population in western European OECD member countries for which information was available had graduated from tertiary education. In 2005 the share had increased to more than 24%. Thus, the annual growth rate was roughly 3.4% and the percentage of tertiary education graduates increased by more than 0.6% points annually.

Table 5.8 contains no trend data for Central and Eastern European OECD member countries but enrolment statistics suggest some growth and a likely increase in the near future. In contrast, some OECD members outside Europe have moved towards a flattening of the curve for the share of the adult population with tertiary education training.

In 2005, the percentage of tertiary education graduates in OECD countries was 19% in the age group 55-64 and 32% in the age group 25-34. The available data therefore suggest that the share of tertiary education graduates in the adult population will grow by about 0.4% in the next few decades, *i.e.* only moderately less than in previous decades. Canada, Japan and Korea are the first countries in which the percentage of tertiary education graduates in the age group 25-34 surpassed 50% (54%, 53% and 51% in 2005, respectively). If recent trends continue, 50% of age group 25-64 in OECD countries may have a tertiary education degree before 2020.

Table 5.8 shows enormous differences among countries. In western European OECD members, the percentage of tertiary education graduates in 1992 ranged between 5% and 25%. In 2005, it ranged between 10% and 34%. In the future, the differences are likely to be further reduced.

The moderate levelling-off in the attainment rates is due to the fact that graduation rates generally increase to a greater extent in countries that start off from relatively low levels. To a certain extent, this is a "catching-up" process. Overall, however, the differences in the share of tertiary education graduates in the population in western Europe have remained so striking that one wonders why the debate on the impact of expansion on graduate employment and work is so similar in these countries.

Table 5.8. **Rate of 25-64-years-old having attained tertiary education in selected OECD countries, 1992 and 2005**

Percentage

	1992			2005		
	Non-university tertiary	University	Total	Tertiary-type B	Tertiary-type A	Total
Western Europe						
Austria	7	7	7	9	9	18
Belgium	11	9	20	17	13	31
Denmark	6	13	19	8	26	33
Finland	8	10	18	17	17	34
France	6	10	16	10	14	24
Germany	10	12	22	10	14	23
Greece[1]	3	10	13	7	14	21
Ireland	9	8	17	11	18	29
Italy	m	6	6	1	12	12
Netherlands	m	21	21	2	28	29
Norway	13	12	25	2	30	32
Portugal[1]	2	5	7	x	12	12
Spain	3	10	13	8	19	28
Sweden	12	12	24	9	21	30
Switzerland	13	8	21	10	17	26
Turkey	m	5	5	x	10	10
United Kingdom	8	11	19	9	15	23
Central and Eastern Europe						
Czech Republic	m	m	m	x	13	13
Hungary	m	m	m	m	17	m
Poland	m	m	m	x	17	17
Slovak Republic	m	m	m	1	13	13
Other countries						
Australia	11	12	23	9	23	32
Canada	26	15	41	23	23	46
Japan	m	m	m	18	22	40
United States	7	24	31	9	28	38

1. 1991 instead of 1992.
m = missing.
x = included elsewhere.
Note: Category A includes tertiary-type B education for Portugal, Turkey, the Czech Republic and the Slovak Republic.
Source: OECD (1994, 2005 and 2007), *Education at a Glance – OECD Indicators.*

5.5. Beyond tertiary education: outcomes

The expansion of tertiary education is expected to have a substantial impact in many areas. It is indispensable for advancing knowledge in society, it plays a role in culture, it is hoped to help reduce inequality of opportunity. Moreover, policies in favour of expansion of higher education in the 1950s would certainly not have been enacted if there had not been the expectation that higher levels of education would, as a rule, be beneficial for individual graduates' employment and work and overall for economic growth.

From its foundation in the 1950s, the OECD underscored the links between educational expansion, graduate careers and economic growth. Consequently, in compiling data on education the OECD did not confine itself to educational statistics, but added employment and economic statistics to demonstrate the outcomes of education. Two indicators on the relationship between education and employment are often used: differences in unemployment and earnings according to level of educational attainment.

Unemployment rates

The mean unemployment rate in western European OECD member countries for non-university/tertiary-type B graduates was 4.7% in 1992 and 6.1% in 2005. For university/tertiary-type A graduates it was 4.1% in 1992 and 3.9% in 2005.

As Table 5.9 shows, across all member countries included, unemployment rates for university graduates (1992) and tertiary-type A graduates (2005) were lower in most countries than those for non-university tertiary education graduates or tertiary education type B graduates.

Table 5.9. **Unemployment rates of tertiary education graduates in selected OECD countries, 1992 and 2005**

Percentage

	1992			2005[1]		
	Non-university tertiary	University	Total	Tertiary-type B	Tertiary-type A	Total
Western Europe						
Austria	m	1.3	3.6	m	3.3	4.3
Belgium	2.3	2.2	7.8	3.5	4	7.1
Denmark	5.8	4.8	10.6	3.9	3.6	4.3
Finland	5.7	3.4	11.4	4.9	4	6.8
France	4.6	4.4	8.8	5.3	6.4	8.4
Germany	4.5	3.7	6.2	5.9	5.3	10.8
Ireland	5.8	3.3	13.5	2.2	1.8	3.6
Italy	m	6.0	7.4	8.5	5.6	6.3
Netherlands	m	3.9	5.6	2.2	2.9	4.1
Norway	2.8	1.8	4.6	0.7	2.3	3.5
Spain	12.5	9.9	14.7	6.5	6.1	7.8
Sweden	2.3	2.0	3.8	4.5	4.5	5.9
Switzerland	2.3	3.0	2.5	1.9	3.1	3.8
Turkey	m	4.1	5.2	x	6.9	8.5
United Kingdom	3.3	3.6	8.4	1.9	2.1	3.4
Central and Eastern Europe						
Czech Republic	m	m	m	x	2.0	6.9
Hungary	m	m	m	1.8	2.3	6.2
Poland	m	m	m	x	6.2	15.6
Slovak Republic	m	m	m	7.8	4.2	14.3
Other countries						
Australia	5.7	4.4	8.8	2.9	2.4	4.0
Canada	9.0	5.2	10.0	4.8	4.4	5.7
Japan	m	m	m	3.8	2.7	4.2
United States	4.6	2.9	6.6	3.6	2.3	4.4

1. Average of men and women.
m = missing.
x = included elsewhere.
Note: Category A includes tertiary-type B education for Turkey, the Czech Republic and Poland.
Source: OECD (2004, 2005 and 2007), *Education at a Glance – OECD Indicators.*

Also, the overall unemployment rate in western European countries was 7.6% in 1992 and 5.9% in 2005. Thus, on average, tertiary education graduates had an advantage in terms of the risk of unemployment, but this advantage has generally diminished. In 2005, the advantage was most pronounced in Central and Eastern Europe, but it was marginal for tertiary education graduates in Denmark and Switzerland.

Relative earnings

On average, the relative earnings of graduates of tertiary education (100 = upper secondary education) have not changed from the early 1990s until recently in the western European OECD members for which information is available:

- Men with non-university/tertiary-type B education earned 123% in 1992 and 122% in 2005 of the earnings of men whose highest level of education was upper secondary education; the earnings of women with non-university/tertiary-type B educational attainment were 129% in 1992 and 125% in 2005.
- Both men (157% in 1992 and 155% in 2005) and women (156% in 1992 and 153% in 2005) with university/tertiary-type A educational attainment earned on average about 50% more than persons with upper secondary education.

Table 5.10 shows that tertiary-type A graduates, compared both to non-tertiary graduates and tertiary-type B graduates, have substantially higher income advantages especially in Hungary and also in the United States where the advantage has markedly increased recently.

Table 5.10. **Relative earnings of graduates by gender in selected OECD countries, 1992 and 2005**

100 = upper secondary education and post-secondary non-tertiary education – 25-64-year-olds

	Men				Women			
	Non-university tertiary	Tertiary-type B	University	Tertiary-type A	Non-university tertiary	Tertiary-type B	University	Tertiary-type A
	1992	2005	1992	2005	1992	2005	1992	2005
Western Europe								
Belgium	115	117	149	153	137	127	164	155
Denmark	110	113	146	141	111	115	135	128
Finland	132	131	192	180	132	129	176	165
France	127	129	174	167	131	130	142	152
Germany	116	128	170	159	114	117	175	161
Italy	–	–	134	183	–	–	116	134
Netherlands[1]	–	–	132	143	–	–	147	155
Norway	131	143	165	139	131	148	157	141
Spain	–	107	138	144	–	97	149	156
Sweden	118	107	160	145	119	114	156	133
Switzerland	127	123	152	149	126	131	152	158
United Kingdom	121	117	171	152	156	141	206	200
Central and Eastern Europe								
Hungary	m	138	m	253	m	131	m	188
Other countries								
Australia	121	115	158	143	124	120	175	156
Canada	107	111	162	169	116	120	174	176
United States	120	117	164	194	130	122	170	173

1. Year 2003 used instead of 2005.
m = missing.
Source: OECD (1994, 2005 and 2007), *Education at a Glance – OECD Indicators.*

In sum, the two indicators do not suggest any recent major changes in the labour market outcomes of tertiary education. In the past, some observers predicted that they would decline as the natural result of the massification of tertiary education. However, two arguments as to why the labour market should continue to reward tertiary education gained popularity. First, the more tertiary education expands, the larger the share of those without tertiary education who risk being socially excluded and have "employability" deficits. Second, it is widely assumed that tertiary education has diversified substantially in the process of expansion and that the employment system rewards tertiary education attainment more unevenly than before so that students choose the most rewarded fields, programmes, institutions and sectors.

5.6. Concluding observations

Throughout the world, expansion has been a more or less regular feature of tertiary education in the last few decades. In western Europe and other highly developed countries, this trend was widely viewed as beneficial for economic growth in general, for labour market rewards of those participating, for reducing inequality of opportunity and for general cultural enrichment, but there were always voices indicating tensions and unfulfilled promises as well. There were concerns about "over-education" and, last but not least, there were expectations that expansion might cease. The OECD, however, pointed out in *Redefining Tertiary Education* (1998) that expansion of tertiary education had revived from the mid-1980s to the early 1990s and cited predictions that almost everyone might participate in tertiary education in the 21st century.

The aim of this chapter has been to shed some light on trends in student enrolments from the early 1990s to the beginning of the 21st century in western Europe and some other highly developed countries. It has drawn on statistical data compiled by the OECD and some other sources. As such data are often far from ideal, the sources of the data are commented on as well.

The increase in entry rates to tertiary education was generally high in western European and other OECD member countries from the end of World War II until about the mid-1970s. From then until the mid-1980s, the increase was small; it picked up somewhat after the mid-1980s but at a slower pace than before the mid-1970s. The analysis presented here shows that the trend of the late 1980s has continued up to the time of the most recent data. In fact, the mean entry rate in western European countries for which data are available increased from 38% to 62%. Altogether, the mean entry rate in OECD member countries surpassed 50% in the late 1990s and thus, according to Trow's well-known definition, moved towards "universal" tertiary education.

In recent years, the entry rate rose most sharply in countries that are "latecomers" to educational expansion. By and large, there has been a narrowing of differences in participation in tertiary education across OECD countries but they remain strong. In a substantial number of OECD countries, more than 70% of the traditionally relevant age group embark on some type of tertiary education, but the rate has remained below 50% in a substantial number of others.

A detailed analysis of various patterns and underlying factors shows that the increase in the mean entry rates to tertiary education in some western European countries is primarily the result of the upgrading of vocational education and training institutions to tertiary education institutions, while in others it is due to growth of established tertiary education institutions and programmes. Entry rates grew faster than enrolment figures, largely owing to a relative increase in students in short study programmes. In addition, the typical entry age cohorts declined only marginally in Western Europe – as the contrasting example of Japan underscores – and this marginal decline was clearly offset by increasing entry rates. Finally, the rise in student mobility explains only to a limited extent the recent expansion of tertiary education in western Europe.

Available statistical data on the institutional composition of student enrolments underscore the continuous trend towards upgrading. However, the percentage of students enrolled in relatively short programmes seems to have increased recently in western Europe. The definitions of institutional composition used in the statistics presented have often changed over time. Upgrading has often occurred: for example, enrolment in tertiary-type B in some countries declines as a consequence of upgrading to tertiary-type A or increases in other countries as a consequence of upgrading from vocational training to tertiary-type B. Unfortunately, the available statistics are not suitable to cast light on the impact of the Bologna process, *i.e.* changes in the number of students in Bachelor programmes and Master programmes.

As regards the socio-biographic composition of students, the available statistics give relatively limited information. They are most useful as regards gender, and increasing public interest in student mobility seems to be leading to a gradual methodological improvement in that domain.

Since the early 1990s, the proportion of foreign students rose from 4% to 7% on average in European OECD member countries. Yet, in most OECD countries, the net increase in foreign enrolments (*i.e.* foreign students outnumber those who study abroad) has remained a relatively small factor in the overall expansion. Ironically, the more mobility increases, the more statistics on foreign students become less valid as indicators of mobility. Available information suggests that valid statistics on student mobility, *i.e.* crossing borders for the purpose of study, would differ from statistics on foreign students in western Europe by one-third or more.

Data on output of tertiary education do not differ markedly from data on entry only because of a time lag in the process of expansion. Drop-out plays a far more prominent role. The mean "success rate" or "survival rate" in western Europe is around 70%.

In fact, graduation rates increased in western European OECD countries from somewhat more than 30% on average in the early 1990s to 45% in 2005, and the share of tertiary education graduates in the population rose from 16% in 1992 to more than 24% in 2005. These rates were lower in Central and Eastern European countries and higher on average in OECD members outside Europe. If current trends persist, it will take several decades to reach a level of 50% of tertiary education graduates in the adult population.

Data on the development of the labour market since the early 1990s suggest that tertiary education graduates have lost some of their advantages as far as low unemployment risk is concerned, but their earnings advantage has remained unchanged on average in western Europe. It is difficult to draw any conclusions about the future from these observations.

Data on enrolment trends, the institutional and socio-biographic composition of students, the output of tertiary education and labour market outcomes will certainly continue to provide an interesting basis of information for scholars analysing tertiary education and practitioners involved in tertiary education. The OECD's statistical overview *Education at a Glance* would certainly gain in quality if it included more systematically time-series data and if the international organisations that collect education data continue to work to persuade national agencies in charge to increase the range of data collection, the quality and validity of the data and their international compatibility.

While it is difficult to draw conclusions about the future development of tertiary education on the basis of information on the recent past, current tertiary education policies and trends in Europe suggest a further increase in entry rates and further upgrading and most likely a more or less common structure of study programmes and degrees which also call for new statistical categories.

More attention will certainly be paid to demographic developments as well as to the overall effects of student mobility. At the same time, increasing attention is paid in public debate to issues that are not covered well in public statistics. These include differences in the quality and reputation of individual institutions, departments and programmes and in institutional composition; and the relation between the expansion of tertiary education and social exclusion of the increasing share of persons who lack tertiary education. Nonetheless, official statistics will certainly continue to provide valuable information for understanding the dynamics of tertiary education.

Note

1. This definition has changed several times in recent years, and used to exclude from the count students enrolled in another country for the purpose of study for up to one year.

References

Japan, Ministry of Education, Culture, Sports, Science and Technology (2004), *2003 White Paper on Education, Culture Sport, Science and Technology*, Tokyo.

Kelo, M., U. Teichler and B. Wächter (eds.) (2006), *EURODATA: Student Mobility in European Higher Education*, Lemmens, Bonn.

OECD (1970/71), *Development of Higher Education 1950-67*, OECD Publishing, Paris.

OECD (1974), *Policies for Higher Education*, OECD Publishing, Paris.

OECD (1983), *Policies for Higher Education in the 1980s*, OECD Publishing, Paris.

OECD (1998), *Redefining Tertiary Education*, OECD Publishing, Paris.

OECD (various years), *Education at a Glance – OECD Indicators*, OECD Publishing, Paris.

OECD/CERI (2005), "Selected Post-secondary OECD Data and Indicators", OECD Publishing, Paris, mimeo.

Pellegrin, J.-P. (1974), "Quantitative Trends in Post-Secondary Education 1960-1970", *Towards Mass Higher Education: Issues and Dilemmas*, OECD, Paris, pp. 9-61.

Trow, M. (1974), "Problems in the Transition from Elite to Mass Higher Education", *Policies for Higher Education*, OECD, Paris, pp. 51-101.

UNESCO (1998), *World Statistical Outlook on Higher Education: 1980-1995*, Paris.

UNESCO Institute for Statistics (2006), *Global Education Digest 2006: Comparing Education Statistics Across the World*, Montreal.

UNESCO Institute for Statistics (2007), *Global Education Digest 2007: Comparing Education Statistics Across the World*, Montreal.

UNESCO-UIS, OECD and EUROSTAT (2005), "UOE Data Collection Manual – 2005 Data Collection on Educational Systems", OECD, Paris, mimeo.

Vincent-Lancrin, S. (2008), "The Reversal of Gender Inequalities in Tertiary Education: An On-going Trend", *Higher Education to 2030, Volume 1: Demography*, OECD Publishing, Paris.

Yonezawa, A. and T. Kim (2008), "The Future of Higher Education in a Context of a Shrinking Student Population: Policy Challenges for Japan and Korea", *Higher Education to 2030, Volume 1: Demography*, OECD Publishing, Paris.

ISBN 978-92-64-04065-6
Higher Education to 2030
Volume 1: Demography

Chapter 6

Access to Post-secondary Education in the United States: Past, Present, and Future Perspectives

by

Eugene Anderson and Bryan Cook*

This chapter discusses the past, present and future of enrolments in US post-secondary education by examining the institutional, economic, and public policy factors over the last 25 years that had a major impact on college enrolment in the United States. It uses the state of US higher education today and the current economic and political environment as the starting point for understanding the challenges and opportunities facing the future growth of higher education, especially among minorities and people from low income background.

* The American Council on Education. The OECD Secretariat thanks the US Census Bureau, particularly Frederick W. Hollmann and Carole Popoff, for providing population estimates and projections and consistent time series for the population by race and Hispanic origin.

6.1. Introduction

During the next decade, post-secondary education in the United States is likely to continue its growth and rapid diversification. Although significant challenges loom, the necessity of education in a technologically based and increasingly global economy will continue to increase in importance. As the United States continues to become more racially diverse, Americans of color will comprise an increasing share of post-secondary enrolments. The future growth of American higher education will depend on both old and new obstacles, such as the uncertainty of state funding and rising tuition, access dilemma of the poor, and accountability and outcomes assessment movements. In many ways, the United States will continue on a course set in the 1980s, as immigration increased, the economy shifted from manufacturing and production to knowledge and service. Technological advances and globalisation will only accelerate the pace of economic change.

During the past twenty-five years, post-secondary education in the United States experienced massive growth and change as the national population and economy were changing. Since 1980, higher education enrolments expanded and became more racially diverse despite significant declines in the size of the traditional college-age population. Sometimes the size and complexity of a system can limit its ability to change, but the variety of American higher education allowed for various institutions to adapt in differing ways to the changing society and economy. Growth occurred at most types of post-secondary institutions as the demand for access to higher education reached unprecedented levels.

6.2. The expansion of access to higher education: from past to present

The change in enrolment in post-secondary education in the United States over the last 25 years is a complex trend occurring within the context of changes in the racial and cultural make-up of the nation. Post-secondary education in the United States changed as the nation became more diverse. Enrolments in post-secondary education steadily increased while the college-age population was slightly declining, thanks to a rising participation rate and the intake of older students. This pattern was reflected in all racial/ ethnic groups of the US population and, with some differences, in all post-secondary institutions making. However, enrolment patterns differ significantly by income groups.

The impact of a changing US population on post-secondary education

Since 1980, the US population grew steadily by 26%, topping 293 million in 2004 (US Census Bureau). It reached 300 million in 2006. This population increase was driven by tremendous growth among Americans of color, primarily Hispanics, Black Americans, and Asian Americans.

From 1980 to 2004, the white population increased by less than 10%, compared to an increase of 100% among Americans of color (see Figure 6.1).[1] Because of the sheer number of whites in the United States, a 10% increase equaled 18.9 million more whites in 2004 than in 1980. The numerical growth among Hispanics during the last twenty-five years

Figure 6.1. **Percentage change in US population by race/ethnicity, 1980-2004**

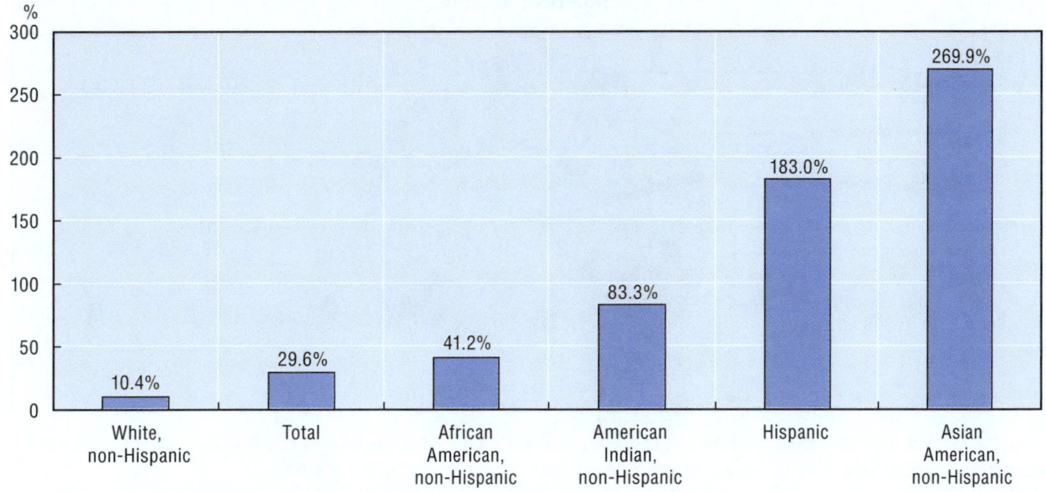

Source: US Census Bureau, Population Division: National Estimates; Quarterly Population Estimates, 1980 to 1990; National Center for Health Statistics, Bridged-Race Vintage 2005 Population Estimates.

easily dwarfed the growth among whites.[2] The Hispanic population in the United States increased by 183%, growing by nearly 27 million persons to surpass 41 million in 2004. The largest percentage growth during this period was among the Asian American population which increased by 269%, from 3.5 million to 13.2 million. The Black American population only increased by 41.2%, but because of the large size of this population in 1980, growth of this group was greater than that of Asian Americans, 10.8 million additional Black Americans compared to 9.6 million Asian Americans.

The differing rates of growth of the various racial/ethnic groups in the United States are a result of changes in fertility rates and immigration. During the first half of the 20th century the white population had a high fertility rate, but during the second half of the century, whites became a much older population, characterised by a low fertility rate. The extremely large rate of growth in the Hispanic and Asian American population is the result of high fertility rates and high immigration during the last twenty-five years. The Black American population grew because of high fertility rates, but was only minimally affected by immigration (Hobbs and Stoops, 2002).

While whites continued to be the majority racial/ethnic group in the United States, the growth of minorities significantly changed the overall composition of the nation. In 1980, 77% of Americans were white. Twenty-five years later the white share of the US population decreased by 10 percentage points to 68% (see Figure 6.2). These changes had an obvious effect on the school-age population in the United States. The school-age population became more diverse than the overall population because the median age of whites became older as the post-war "baby boom" generation aged, nearly 40 years old, while the median age of persons of color remained in the mid-20s.

As the overall population in the United States was growing, the opposite was occurring among 18 to 25-year-olds. From 1980 to 2004, the number of 18- to 25-year-olds declined by nearly 2.5%, a loss of almost 850 000 (see Table 6.1). The decline was due to a decrease in the number of whites in this age range, a loss of 5.7 million persons. A significant increase in Hispanics and Asian Americans in this age group helped reduce the overall decline, thereby causing greater diversity among this age group. The number of 18- to 25-year-old

Figure 6.2. **US population by racial/ethnic group, 2004**

Numbers in millions

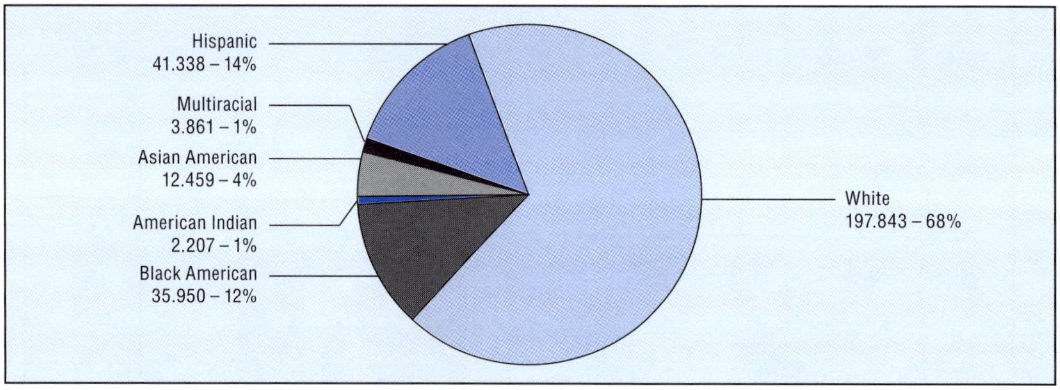

Source: US Census Bureau (2004), Population Division, Table 3: "Annual Estimates of the Population by Sex, Race and Hispanic or Latino Origin for the United States: 1 April 2000 to 1 July" (NC-EST2004-03).

Table 6.1. **US population of 18- to 25-year-olds by race/ethnicity, selected years: 1980 to 2004**

	1980	1990	2000	2004	% change from 1980 to 2004	Numeric change from 1980 to 2004
Total	**34 138 425**	**31 050 463**	**30 887 993**	**33 297 127**	**–2.5**	**–841 298**
White, non-Hispanic	26 487 557	21 949 964	19 330 153	20 745 941	–21.7	–5 741 616
Black, non-Hispanic	4 358 774	4 167 977	4 336 786	4 784 559	9.8	425 785
American Indian, Eskimo and Aleut, non-Hispanic	222 760	249 043	296 378	339 172	52.3	116 412
Asian American, non-Hispanic	529 331	990 198	1 485 476	1 560 172	194.7	1 030 841
Hispanic origin, any race	2 540 003	3 693 281	5 439 200	5 867 283	131.0	3 327 280

Note: The data follow a consistent race definition.

Source: US Census Bureau, Population Division: National Estimates; Quarterly Population Estimates, 1980 to 1990; National Center for Health Statistics, United States Census 2000 Population with Bridged Race Categories; National Center for Health Statistics, Bridged-Race Vintage 2005 Population Estimates.

Hispanics more than doubled, increasing by 3.3 million persons. The number of Asian Americans in this age range increased by 1 million persons.[3]

One could have expected the decline in the college-age population from 1980 to 2006 to cause a decline in enrolment in post-secondary education in the United States. However, the opposite occurred; enrolments jumped by 51% over this period, increasing from about 12 million students to more than 18 million students (Table 6.2). During this period when the size of the college-age population was declining in the United States, access was expanding to include more students than ever before. In 1980, less than a third of high school graduates aged 18- to 24-year-old were enrolled in post-secondary education. By 2006, the share of high school graduates aged 18 to 24 participating in post-secondary education was 45% (US Census Bureau, 2008). While the college-going rate differs for each racial/ethnic group, each group showed significant increases. The growth in enrolment was also spurred by an increase in the number of older Americans attending college. From 1980 to 2005, the number of persons over the age of 24 enrolled in post-secondary, degree-granting institutions increased by 34% (US Department of Education, 2008a).

Table 6.2. **Total fall enrolment in US post-secondary institutions by race/ethnicity: selected years, 1980 to 2006 and projections to 2015**

	1980	1984	1990	1995	2000	2006	2015[1]
ALL STUDENTS	**12 087 000**	**12 235 000**	**13 818 600**	**14 261 781**	**15 312 300**	**18 205 474**	**19 874 000**
White	9 833 000	9 815 000	10 722 500	10 311 243	10 462 100	10 896 819	12 113 000
Black American	1 107 000	1 076 000	1 247 000	1 473 672	1 730 300	2 207 271	2 755 000
Hispanic	472 000	535 000	782 400	1 093 839	1 461 800	1 897 258	2 569 000
Asian American/Pacific Islander	286 000	390 000	572 400	797 359	978 200	1 081 627	1 415 000
American Indian	84 000	84 000	102 800	131 304	151 200	174 936	229 000
Foreign students	305 000	335 000	391 500	454 364	528 700	600 715	793 000

1. Projections by NCES (analysis by authors).
Source: US Department of Education, National Center for Education Statistics, Integrated Post-secondary Education Data System (IPEDS), Fall Enrolment Survey, 1980 to 2006.

From 1980 to 2006, the largest growth in college enrolments occurred among students of color. The number of minorities enrolled in post-secondary institutions grew by nearly 3.5 million persons, an increase of 175%. The number of whites enrolled rose by only 1 million people, 11%. The large growth among minority students from 1980 to 2006 was due largely to increases in two populations: Hispanics and Black Americans. Hispanics and Black Americans were responsible for the largest numerical increases, 1.4 and 1.1 million respectively (see Table 6.2). This growth in minority enrolment dramatically changed the composition of American higher education. In 1980, only 16% of college students in the United States were persons of color. By 2004, their share significantly increased to 26%.

The diversity of (and within) US higher education

Through all the population changes the United States has developed into one of the largest and most diverse systems of post-secondary education in the world. Today there are 4 300 accredited, degree-granting post-secondary institutions in the United States. These institutions consist of a mixture of schools of varying size, unique missions, and scope. Using broad categories, there are four major types of institutions in the United States: private not-for-profit four-year schools (36% of institutions), public two-year schools (24% of institutions), private for-profit schools (23% of institutions), and public four-year schools (15% of institutions).[4] Public four-year institutions are the smallest sector however this sector consists of many large institutions. As a result public four-year schools enrolled 39% of college students in the United States in 2005.

In the fall of 2006, more than 18 million persons were enrolled in post-secondary institutions in the United States.[5] The majority of these persons were enrolled in undergraduate programmes and courses (15.6 million in 2006, full- and part-time). The majority of undergraduates in the United States are white (60%) while minority and foreign students make up 31% and 2% of enrolment respectively (in 2006, see Figure 6.3, US Department of Education, 2008b).[6] The increase in minority enrolment depicted above has occurred at all types of institutions. Both four-year institutions and two-year institutions grew by a similar number of minority students from 1980 to 2005, 2 million and 1.5 million respectively. Most of this growth occurred at public institutions (US Department of Education, 2008a).

Undergraduate students in the United States are not homogenous 18- to 24-year-olds attending in similar patterns. Women make up more than half of undergraduates (57%).

Figure 6.3. **Undergraduate enrolment in the United States by race/ethnicity and nationality, fall 2006**

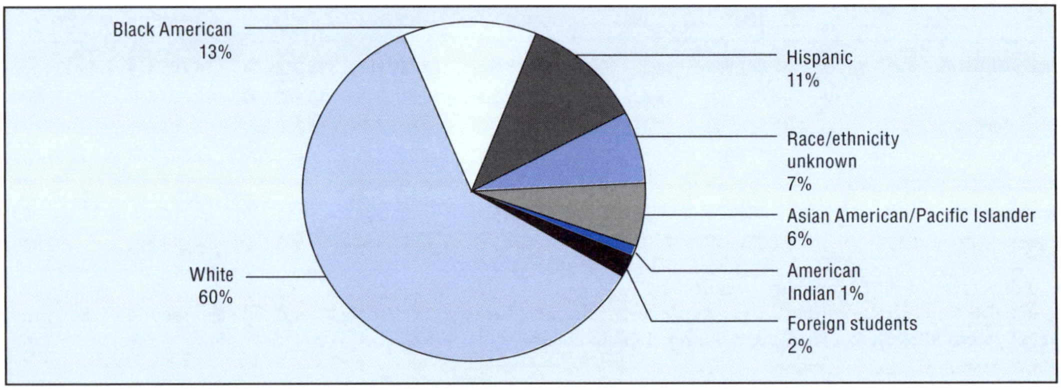

Source: US Department of Education, National Center for Education Statistics, Integrated Post-secondary Education Data System (IPEDS), Fall Enrolment Survey, 2006 (analysis by authors).

The majority of undergraduates are under the age of 25, but a large percentage – 31% – are aged 25 and older (US Department of Education, 2008a). Because so many undergraduates are older students, it is no surprise that 32% of all undergraduates are married and/or have children. The majority (54%) of undergraduate students attend on less than a full-time, full-year basis (American Council on Education, 2005).

Of the 2 600 four-year public and private institutions, only 151 focus on research and award a large number of doctorates in a variety of fields. These are commonly referred to as doctoral or research institutions.[7] Because of their long history and role in research and graduate education, many of these institutions are among the most recognised internationally, such as Harvard University, University of Michigan, and University of California at Berkeley. A finite amount of research funding from the federal government and business and industry limits the number of research institutions that can exist in the United States. The majority of four-year institutions have very little research focus and serve the primary goal of educating students.

Because post-secondary education institutions in the United States vary in selectivity, mission, and cost, it is not surprising that enrolment patterns vary by demographic characterisitics. Among the more than 15.6 million undergraduate students in 2006, more than half (51%) were enrolled at four-year institutions. However, the majority of Hispanic (52%) students attend public two-year post-secondary institutions (see Table 6.3). In addition to being the least likely to attend two-year institutions, white students are nearly twice as likely to attend doctoral/research institutions as African American and Hispanic students.

Enrolment patterns also differ significantly by income. Although there are many ways to categorise income, this chapter categorises persons into three income groups which adjust based on family size, especially number of dependent children: low-income (persons with family incomes twice the national poverty level or less), middle-income (persons with family income more than twice the national poverty level and less than five times the poverty level), and upper-income (persons with family incomes higher than five times the poverty level).[8] Low-income persons are the only income group with less than half of its students at four-year schools. Half of low-income students attend two-year

Table 6.3. **Total fall undergraduate enrolment in US post-secondary institutions by race/ethnicity and sector, 2006**

Full and part-time

	Total	Public, 4-year	Private not-for-profit, 4-year	Public, 2-year	Private for-profit[1]	Other[2]
All students	15 630 823	5 622 555	2 409 256	6 276 185	1 203 120	119 707
White	9 405 394	3 651 979	1 580 149	3 620 888	485 848	66 530
	100%	39%	17%	38%	5%	1%
Black American	1 965 454	625 412	265 073	813 124	244 220	17 625
	100%	32%	13%	41%	12%	1%
Hispanic	1 762 753	522 718	147 271	910 144	167 382	15 238
	100%	30%	8%	52%	9%	1%
Race/ethnicity unknown	1 076 176	265 924	205 207	367 155	229 927	7 963
	100%	25%	19%	34%	21%	1%
Asian American/Pacific Islander	934 987	368 845	119 916	399 147	40 957	6 122
	100%	39%	13%	43%	4%	1%
American Indian	159 777	57 306	15 361	73 666	9 745	3 699
	100%	36%	10%	46%	6%	2%
Foreign students	326 033	130 371	76 279	91 812	25 041	2 530
	100%	40%	23%	28%	8%	1%

1. Includes 4-year, 2-year and less-than-2-year programmes.
2. Includes private not-for-profit 2-year and less-than-2-year as well as public less-than-2-year programmes.

Source: US Department of Education, National Center for Education Statistics, Integrated Post-secondary Education Data System (IPEDS), Fall Enrolment Survey, 2006 (analysis by authors).

schools, compared to only 42% of their middle-income peers, and 35% of high-income students. Similar to all undergraduates, 58% of low-income undergraduates are female. There is no difference in the percentage of low-income students and all undergraduates aged 25 or older, 39% respectively. However low-income persons in higher education are twice as likely to be single parents as all undergraduates, 22% compared to 11% (American Council on Education, 2005). Cost and accessibility are probably the main reasons why more low-income persons are likely to enroll at two-year institutions.

The larger share of low-income students enrolled at two-year institutions is consistent across all racial/ethnic groups. The percentage of high-income whites, Black Americans, American Indians, and Asian Americans enrolled at two-year institutions ranged from 33% to 37%, compared to 47% to 58% of low-income students from each of these racial/ethnic groups (see Table 6.4). Although a large percentage of high-income Hispanics are enrolled at two-year post-secondary institutions, 47%, the percentage remains significantly lower than that percentage of middle- and low-income Hispanics.

The college participation rates for all racial/ethnic groups have increased since 1980, but there remains a 5.6 percentage point gap between the college participation rate of whites and African Americans. The college participation rate among Hispanics is 8.5 percentage points less than African Americans. Research has shown that what appears to be a black-white gap in college participation is really a difference by income (Adelman, 2004 and 2006). Adelman using socioeconomic status (SES), found that nearly all (93.8%) of high school graduates in the highest SES group entered college within eight years after graduating from high school (see Table 6.5). The college participation rate declines for each group down the SES ladder, bottoming out in a college participation rate of 53.6% among students from the lowest SES quintile.[9]

Table 6.4. **Undergraduate enrolment by institution level, income and race/ethnicity, 2003**

	Income level	Institution level		
		4-year (%)	2-year (%)	Less than 2-year (%)
Total	Low	46.2	50.4	3.4
	Middle	56.2	42.2	1.6
	High	64.4	34.5	1.1
White	Low	50.7	47.1	2.3
	Middle	58.5	40.2	1.4
	High	66.2	32.9	0.9
Black American	Low	41.5	53.9	4.7
	Middle	54.4	43.5	2.1
	High	61.7	36.0	2.4
Hispanic	Low	36.1	57.4	6.5
	Middle	43.2	54.0	2.8
	High	49.7	47.5	2.9
Asian American	Low	51.0	46.8	2.3
	Middle	54.1	44.2	1.7
	High	61.6	37.5	0.9
American Indian	Low	39.7	58.2	2.2
	Middle	53.8	45.1	1.1
	High	62.5	36.7	0.9

Source: US Department of Education (2005), National Center for Education Statistics, 2003-04 National Postsecondary Student Aid Study (analysis by authors).

Table 6.5. **Percentage of high school 12th graders who entered post-secondary education by end of cohort study, 1982 and 1992**

Socioeconomic status (SES) quintile	Class of 1982	Class of 1992	Increase in access
	1982-1993	1992-2000	Class of 1982 to class of 1992
81st-100th percentile (high)	87.7	93.8	6.1
61st-80th	72.6	86.7	14.1
41st-60th	64.4	77.0	12.6
21st-40th	54.0	65.3	11.3
1st-20th percentile (low)	43.0	53.6	10.6

Source: Adelman (2004), Table 2.4, p. 24.

6.3. The expansion of access to higher education beyond demography

The expansion of access to post-secondary education in the United States can be traced back to a variety of factors, but most notably, changes in the national economy and student financial aid. For minorities the increase in access has also been related to governmental and legal efforts to end racial discrimination in college admissions. Changes in the size and composition of the US population were not the only national changes affecting post-secondary enrolments during the last twenty-five years. Changes in post-secondary student enrolments in the United States occurred during a time of tremendous economic and institutional change that likely impacted minority and white students in differing ways. Despite several periods of decline, enrolment in US post-secondary, degree-granting institutions increased by 31% between 1980 and 2005 (US Department of Education, 2008a). This growth in enrolment is not likely the result of any one event but rather the result of a confluence of changes during this period. The ability and desire of students to pursue post-secondary education is typically related to a variety of institutional, economic, and national policies such as cost of attendance (tuition, fees, housing, and board), financial aid availability, local or national economic conditions, and rate of return on a college education. All of these factors, while not necessarily a direct correlation, set the context for changing post-secondary enrolments. Indeed, as Johnes (1993) put it, "the links between the labour market and the demand for education are complex. Signals are transferred from one market to the other imperfectly, and are subject to lags".

The US economy changes

There is evidence that the increase in post-secondary enrolment is partly due to significant gains in the economic returns to a college education that are the result of a changing US economy. The early 1980s was a period of multiple economic recessions and rising unemployment. Between 1981 and 1982, the United States lost 2.4 million jobs. The sectors most affected by the recession were those that did not require considerable formal education beyond high school: manufacturing, agriculture, transportation and construction.[10] However, even within a recession that pushed the unemployment rate in the United Stated to a post World War II high of 10.1%, there were several sectors experiencing significant growth ("slow unemployment", 1982). From 1983 to 1991, seven occupational fields in the United States saw job growth of more than 1 million jobs; three of these fields were higher paying managerial fields that typically require a college education. The other four fields were lower paying administrative support and service occupations that do not require a college education (US Census Bureau, 2004a). The pattern of job growth in the 1980s began the growth of high paying jobs in managerial and specialised skill fields and "low-skill, low-wage" jobs.

The 1990s brought about a drastic upswing in the US economy. The emergence of new technology and a renewed entrepreneurial spirit created a robust economy that added 20 million jobs since the recessions of the 1980s. Despite the record job growth of the 1990s, Americans continued to need some form of post-secondary education to be competitive in the US labour market. Even many low-skill, low-wage jobs required some level of specialised skills due to the increasing use of computers in the workforce (Levy and Murnane, 2004). According to the US Census Bureau, 24% of Americans used a computer at work in 1984. By 2001, nearly 60% of American workers used computers (US Census Bureau, 2004a). From 1983 to 2002, twelve occupations added more than 1 million jobs. With the exception of construction trades, six of these occupations were "high-skill, high-wage" jobs, such as managerial occupations and mathematical and computer scientists, and the other half were low-skill, low-wage jobs, like administrative support and sales.

Although there are numerous public and private returns on the investment in post-secondary education, typically people make a decision to pursue a post-secondary education because of private returns, especially economic ones. As the United States moved from an industrial to a knowledge-based economy with a large service sector, the difference in earnings between working Americans with a college degree and those without a college education began to increase. In 1980, the median salary of male and female college graduates was 19% and 34% higher, respectively, than the median salary of high school graduates. By 2002, male and female college graduates earned, on average, 65% and 70% more than male and female high school graduates (US Census Bureau, 2004b). Over the course of a 40-year-career, a college graduate will earn nearly USD1 million more than the typical high school graduate (Baum and Payea, 2004).

Affirmative action and access to elite institutions

The changes stated above increased desire for, and expanded access to, post-secondary education on a broad level over the past twenty-five years. However, the effort to increase minority access at selective public and private four-year institutions during this same period took critical steps with a legal ruling in 1978. In 1978 the US Supreme Court issued a ruling in Regents of the University of California v. Bakke that established a national policy for the practice of affirmative action (the use of race in the admissions process) at public and private institutions. Alan Bakke filed suit claiming the admission policy of the Medical School at the University of California, Davis (UC-Davis) discriminated against him because he was white. UC-Davis had an affirmative action policy for admissions that reserved sixteen of the hundred seats in the entering class for disadvantaged members of certain minority groups. The Supreme Court issued two historical rulings in this case: first, the Court ruled that the admission policy of UC-Davis medical school was not permissible under the law, and secondly, the Court ruled that the use of race was permissible under certain circumstances. The Court said that racial classifications must serve compelling governmental interests and the proposed policy must be closely related to the compelling interest (Anderson, 2001). The ruling in Bakke set a legal precedence and to some a mandate to expand access for non-white students to selective and elite public and private post-secondary institutions. Only a very small number of four-year institutions in the United States can be classified as elite but the importance of this small group of institutions is mostly due to their national and often international stature as pathways to local, national, and international leadership positions in business, politics, and legal and medical professions. Elite institutions are generally thought of as public flagship research universities and highly selective private research and liberal arts institutions.[11]

In 1976, prior to the ruling in Bakke, few Black Americans were attending selective institutions. Black Americans represented only 9% of college students, just over 1 million students. Forty per cent of these Black students were enrolled at public two-year institutions, which are not selective. Among the 600 000 Black students at four-year institutions, nearly 200 000 were enrolled at historically Black colleges and universities (Wilson, 1982). Historically Black colleges and universities were established to provide higher education to Black Americans when many post-secondary institutions were not integrated. In 1964, the United States Congress passed the Civil Rights Act. Title VI of this law was intended to provide equal educational opportunity to African Americans by forcing public post-secondary institutions to end racial segregation and discrimination. Many public post-secondary institutions maintained a legacy of discrimination against Black Americans. Previous laws and legal rulings allowed such unfair treatment if the state offered separate institutions for the discriminated group. The Civil Rights Act was the first major effort by the federal government to override state laws that discriminated against Black Americans.

After 1964, some progress was made and many public post-secondary institutions ended stated admissions policies that discriminated against Black Americans. However, many replaced explicit discriminatory policies, *de jure segregation,* with *de facto* discriminatory policies. *De facto* discriminatory policies appeared race-neutral, but in reality limited access of Black Americans. An example of *de jure* segregation is a written policy of not admitting Black students. A *de facto* segregation policy would replace the written policy of not admitting Black students with admissions criteria that were guaranteed to result in something similar, *e.g.*, requiring a minimum standardised test score on a test that is not meant to be used to determine student ability to succeed in college. In 1973, the United States District Court for the District of Columbia ruled in Adams v. Richardson that the Department of Health, Education, and Welfare order public post-secondary institutions in the ten southern states that continued to discriminate against Black Americans develop plans with affirmative action to remedy the vestiges of past discrimination (Adams v. Richardson, 1973).[12]

Following the Bakke ruling, affirmative action in college admissions remained unchallenged until 1995. In July 1995, after a year of debates, protest, and national media attention, the Board of Regents of the University of California System led by Governor Pete Wilson, voted to end affirmative action in the admissions process at its institutions. The attention Wilson brought to the issue of affirmative action helped generate financial support for a ballot initiative in California to end all affirmative action by government entities. In November 1996, 55% of California voters voted for Proposition 209, which banned the use of race as a factor in college admissions and state hiring (Pusser, 1999).

Also in 1996, the US Court of Appeals for the Fifth Circuit ruled in Hopwood v. Texas that the University of Texas could no longer use race in its admissions process. This ruling did not directly impact many other institutions because the Fifth Circuit only has jurisdiction in three states: Mississippi, Texas, and Louisiana. The greatest impact of the Hopwood decision was to encourage conservative groups, like the Center for Individual Rights, to file similar suits in other states. Soon after the Hopwood decision, the Center for Individual Rights filed suit against the University of Michigan and the University of Washington Law School. The case against the University of Michigan eventually reached the US Supreme Court in 2003.

In 2003, the Supreme Court issued its second ruling related to affirmative action in college admissions. The Court ruled on two cases involving the University of Michigan, Grutter v. Bollinger, which involved the law school, and Gratz v. Bollinger, which involved the undergraduate admissions policy. In Gratz v. Bollinger the Court ruled against the University of Michigan's undergraduate admissions policy because the Court thought the policy placed too much emphasis on race in the selection process. In Grutter v. Bollinger, the Court ruled in favor of the use of race in the admissions process at the university's law school. The two rulings made clear that within strict limitations the use of race in college admissions was permissible because racial diversity serves a compelling government interest (Schmidt, 2003). However, these recent developments reflect a backlash against affirmative action in many states, and it is not clear whether this will remain a major policy instrument for minority access in selective institutions in the coming decades. While affirmative action has recently been under attack for its potential undue discrimination against white students, it should be noted that it has also been criticised for its narrow focus on minority access to elite and selective institutions. Some argued that while helping minority students from advantaged socio-economic groups, it did not do enough to widen participation of the bulk of low income minority students.

While the impact of Hopwood was limited to three states, the impact on minority admissions at selective four-year institutions in these states was immediate. For example, at Texas Agricultural and Mechanical University, the admission rate for African American and Hispanic students dropped from 90% to 70% (Card and Krueger, 2004) and the enrolments for these groups of students declined dramatically by fall 1997 (Hurtado and Wathington, 2001). Similar trends followed the Gratz v. Bollinger decision. A year after the decision was rendered, the University of Michigan reported its smallest class of African American freshmen in 15 years (Dobbs, 2004). In addition to the University of Michigan, several other universities have reported significant declines in African American enrolment including the University of California system, the Pennsylvania State University, the University of Minnesota, the University of North Carolina at Chapel Hill, the University of Pennsylvania, the University of Georgia, the Ohio State University, and the University of Illinois (Dobbs, 2004).

The challenge of equal opportunity for low income students

Whereas minority access to post-secondary education has fairly progressed over the past decades in the United States, as noted above the picture is more mixed when one takes into account students' socio-economic background. Lower income persons attend post-secondary education institutions at a significantly lower rate than higher income persons for a myriad of reasons, many of which are interrelated to the reality of life for lower income persons in the United States. Many low-income families find themselves in this situation because of limited earnings potential due to low levels of education. The lack of experience in post-secondary education among most low income adults leaves a college information void for their children. Research shows parental education, involvement, and encouragement to be strong predictors of college attendance (Cabrera and La Nasa, 2000; King, 1996; McDonough, 1997; and Stage and Rushin, 1993; St. John, 2002). Parents who did not attend college do not have the experience or information to assist their child in preparing for post-secondary education. The lack of this experience may also lead to less encouragement because of a lack of understanding about all the benefits of a college education. In addition to parental encouragement and support, students also are impacted by support from peers and counselors (King, 1996). Family and friends, especially older persons can provide valuable information and encouragement to students. Because communities are concentrations of persons of similar financial standing, lower income students are likely to live around other low-income persons, therefore these students have peers that lack post-secondary experience and information. As stated previously, financial aid is a major factor. Lower rates of attendance among lower income persons is also partially due to college cost, concerns about forgone earnings, and the perception of limited financial resources available to pay for college (Kane, 1999).

Finally, lower income persons have less access to quality primary and secondary education that can lead to post-secondary enrolment. The poor quality of primary and secondary education that many low-income students receive in the United States does not adequately prepare them for post-secondary education (Adelman, 2006). Although public primary and secondary education in the United States is the domain of each state, with states providing 47% of school revenues in 2005, the federal government does influence primary and secondary education policy through funding requirements. Funding can vary greatly across schools, often (though not always) to the disadvantage of schools located in districts with higher percentages of lower income persons. Although the problems of schools hosting high percentages of low-income students are not always related to funding, school districts with lower amounts of funding suffer from various problems related to their limited economic resources: teachers with less experience, larger class sizes, and less library books and computers (US GAO, 2002).

The quality of public primary and secondary schools may be the result of funding differences, but the determination of quality is based on outcomes, not funding. Because school districts that serve lower income families are usually operating with less than adequate funding, the schools suffer from teacher shortages, classroom overcrowding, deteriorating classroom facilities, and limited course offerings. Many of the schools in school districts serving large numbers of lower income families fail to meet minimum state proficiency levels in core subjects like reading and math (Center on Education Policy, 2006). At the secondary level, many of these schools do not have the resources to offer higher level courses that can better prepare students for post-secondary education. The difference in access to important higher level courses is apparent by income; 72% of students in the highest income quintile attended high schools that offered calculus, compared to only 44% of students in the lowest income quintile (Adelman, 2006). The effects of these educational inequalities on enrolment in post-secondary education are important. That being said, preparation to college is only part of the explanation. Data from the US National Education Longitudinal Survey show that students from low income backgrounds have less chances to go to college than their richer peers *regardless* of their high school test scores: 72% of high income students with high school test scores in the *bottom* quartile of the test score distribution go to college, compared with 68% of low income students with test score in the *top* quartile (Carnevale, 2006).

Today in the United States more Americans have access to higher education than ever before. However, the reality of access to post-secondary education is that it is not partitioned equally. Significant gaps in access between whites and persons of color persist, however much of this disparity is related to income and social class. The fact that lower income students lack the preparation, resources, aspiration, and support to pursue post-secondary education at rates similar to more affluent students is an acknowledgment of a nation still struggling to fulfill the promise of equal opportunity.

6.4. The future of enrolment in American higher education

In the last 25 years post-secondary education in the United States has evolved into a diverse assortment of institutions educating an increasingly diverse nation as well as persons from around the globe. Today there are several factors that present the opportunity for post-secondary education enrolment in the United States to continue to grow: population growth among the young and the changing US economy under globalisation. The college-age population is projected to grow with a shift towards an increased share of minority students and the US economy will continue to provide students with strong incentives to have a post-secondary education.

Growth in the pipeline

As stated previously, post-secondary enrolment in the United States increased over the past twenty-five years despite a decline in the college-age population. The future potential for the growth of American higher education is extremely strong because the younger than 15 population has been growing since 1980. The number of American children increased by 19% from 1980 to 2004. In just the last fifteen years this age group increased by over 7 million persons.

Because of lower fertility rates among whites, all of the growth in persons younger than 15 occurred among persons of color. The number of whites in this group declined by nearly 6% from 1980 to 2004 (see Figure 6.4). The increase in the number of persons of color was led by Asian American and Hispanics, 182% and 157%, respectively. The number of Hispanic children increased by 7.4 million persons. The growth in the number of minorities

Figure 6.4. **Percentage change in US under 15 population by race/ethnicity, 1980-2004**

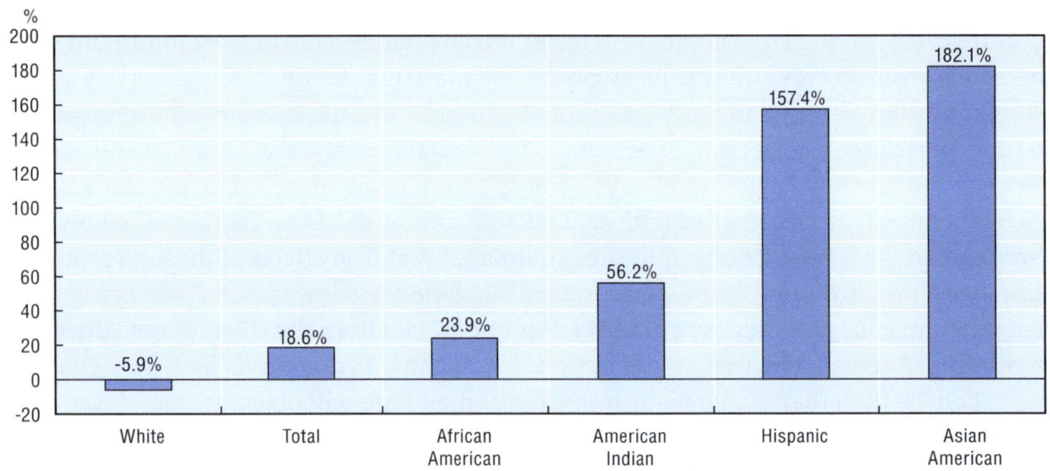

Source: US Census Bureau (2004), Population Division, Tables 1 and 4: "Annual Estimates of the Population by Sex and Five-Year Age Groups for the United States: April 1, 2000 to July 1" (NC-EST2004-01); 1980 Decennial Census.

in this age group is rapidly shifting the racial composition of the youth of America. In 1980, one out of four American children was a person of color. Twenty-five years later nearly one out of two young Americans are persons of color. From 2004 to 2025, the number of (non-Hispanic) whites in the 18-25-year-old population is projected to decrease by 9% (that is, 1.9 million persons) while the total 18-25-year-old cohort is projected to increase by 7% (5.7 million persons). While the Hispanic population (of any race) will grow by 48% in this age group, the non-Hispanic population will actually decrease by 2%. Projections between 2004 and 2035 show a more marked increase of the college-age Hispanic population by 73% against a 6% increase for the non-Hispanic population. By 2025, whites will make up 53% of the 18-25-year-old population, and become a minority (49.7%) by 2035 (see Figure 6.5).

Population projections from the US Census Bureau show the impact of these changes in the future make-up of the US population. The (non-Hispanic) white population is projected to decrease from 68% in 2004 (see Figure 6.2) to 59% by 2025, and 56% by 2035 (see Figure 6.6). While the total US population is projected to grow by 19.3% between 2004 and 2025, the (non-Hispanic) white population is forecast to increase by 5% against 27% for Blacks or African Americans, 62% for Hispanic whites, 67% for Asians and 60% for all other groups. Again, the growth of the Hispanic population (of any race) is the most significant change: it is projected to grow by 63% against 12% for the non-Hispanic population.

More importantly, post-secondary enrolment projections from the US Department of Education support the assertion that enrolments will continue to climb based on growth of young persons in the United States. According to the enrolment projections, over the next ten years post-secondary enrolment will increase by 16%, topping 20 million students in 2015 (Hussar, 2005). While all groups will continue to grow, recent projections forecast that white students will account for 61% of total enrolment in 2015 (against 66% in 2004), and that all other groups will increase their share, with Black Americans, Hispanics and Asian representing 14%, 13% and 7% of enrolments, respectively (against 13%, 10% and 6% in 2004) (see Table 6.2 and Figure 6.7). More detailed projections show that the absolute

Figure 6.5. **Population estimates and projections for 18-25-year-olds for the United States**

Number in millions and percentages

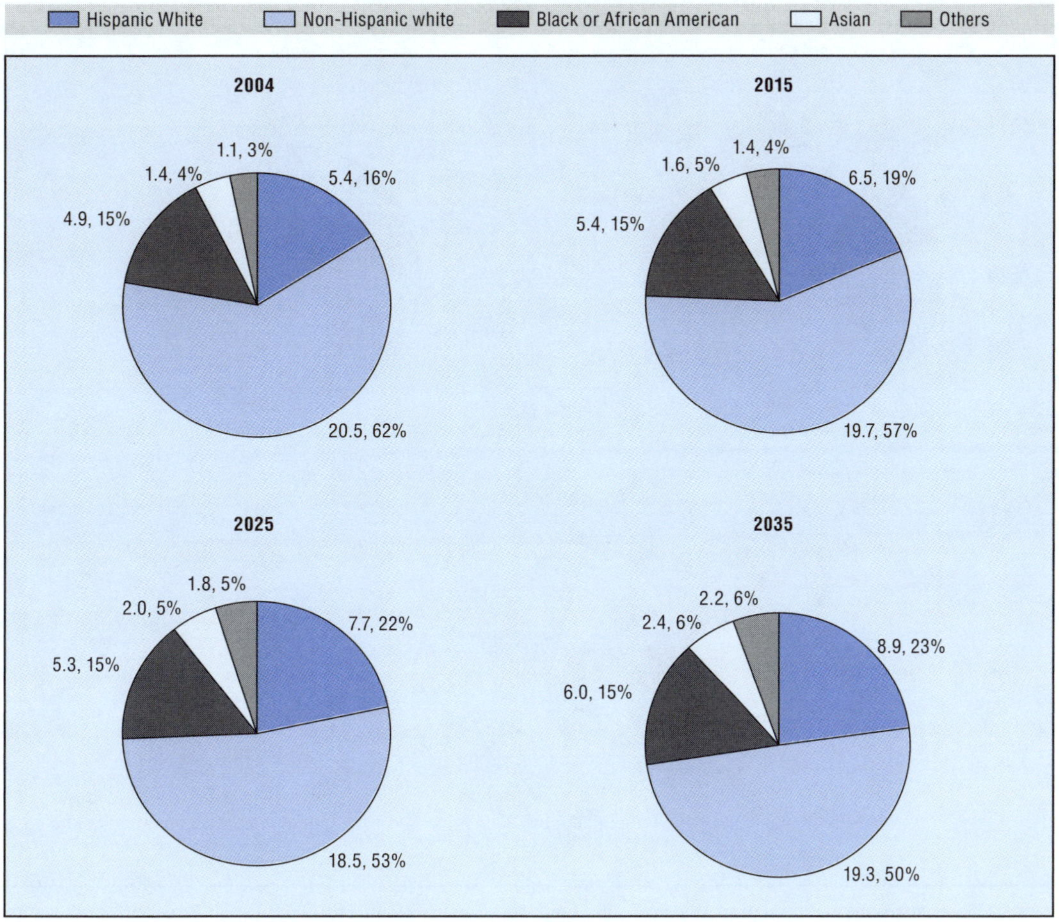

Note: The projections and 2004 estimates follow the 1997 guidelines for the coding of race issued by the US Office of Management and Budget (OMB), hence the differences in categories and numbers with the historical data presented in the first section of the chapter (Figures 6.1 and 6.2 and Table 6.1).

Source: US Census Bureau, Population Division, US Population Estimates; Interim Population Projections consistent with Census 2000.

number of white undergraduates will fall in ten states by 2015, and that minorities will become the majority on a growing number of campuses: minorities will become the majority in four states (Hawaii, District of Columbia, California and New Mexico) and will range between 40 and 50% in 8 other states (Texas, New York, Maryland, Florida, New Jersey, Louisiana, Mississippi and Georgia). The largest increase will come from Hispanic undergraduates, who were forecasted to outnumber African American undergraduates in the near future (Carnevale and Fry, 2000).

Globalisation and the US economy

Throughout much of the 20th century, the United States has perceived itself and was often considered abroad as the land of opportunity. As the largest industrial country in the world, the United States provided more employment opportunities for its citizens than any other country. However advances in software and computer technology alongside other factors have created a global knowledge based economy which has resulted in non-Western

Figure 6.6. **Population estimates and projections for the United States**

Numbers in millions and percentages

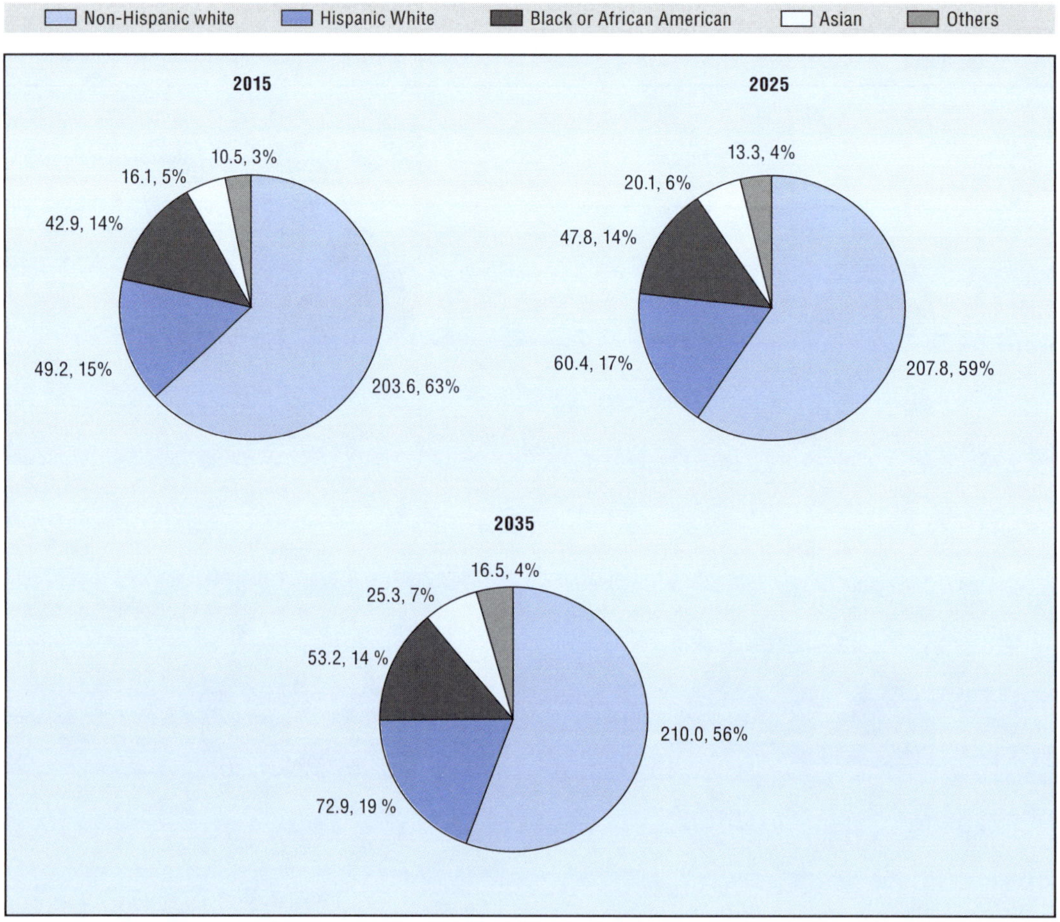

Source: US Census Bureau, Population Division, US Population Estimates; Interim Population Projections consistent with Census 2000.

Figure 6.7. **Actual and projected distribution of US total enrolments in post-secondary education by race/ethnic groups (1984-2015)**

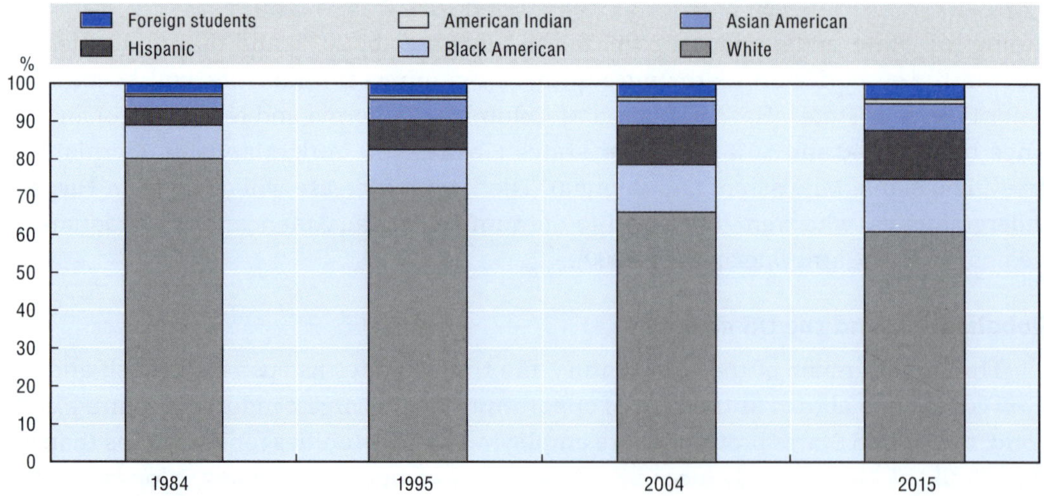

Source: US Department of Education, NCES.

countries being able to compete for jobs in industries that have no geographic boundaries, like computer software development (Friedman, 2005). Technology has expanded the potential for many industries in the United States to utilise highly skilled labour in other parts of the world. Indian accounting firms are increasingly doing American income tax returns and increasingly more US hospitals are having their CAT scans read by Indian or Australian radiologists (Friedman, 2005). Professions such as these, which tend to be populated by the American middle class, are increasingly being outsourced to other countries that can do these jobs cheaper and more efficiently.

As a result, the US economy is fast becoming a dichotomous labour market with, as noted above, a division of labour increasingly consisting of so-called "low skilled, low wage" and "high skilled, high wage" jobs. The result of this dichotomy is that the path to professional and financial security, that is high skill, high wage jobs, requires a post-secondary education (Friedman, 2005). If the United States is to remain competitive in the global economy, it is widely believed that the level of education among all Americans must increase significantly. Just as an earlier shift in the economy played a part in the increase in Americans pursuing a college degree, globalisation will likely have the same impact on young people in the United States.

The continuing dichotomous nature of the US job market is apparent when analysing the occupations with the largest projected job growth in the next decade. Twelve of the thirty occupations listed have a median earnings (in 2004) above USD 28 000. Most of these twelve occupations require some form of post-secondary education:[13] registered nurse, post-secondary teacher, general and operations manager, elementary school teacher, accountants and auditors, truck drivers, computer software engineers, maintenance and repair workers, executive secretaries, sales representatives, carpenters, and computer systems analysts. The remaining occupations are mostly low-skill, low-wage jobs (Hecker, 2005).

6.5. Challenges for the future

The challenges facing American higher education are complex and both unpredictable and uncontrollable. Much success can be gleamed from the rising college participation rates of all racial/ethnic groups, however numerous challenges exist: unpredictability of state funding, access and equity issues, and the spread of accountability and assessment of student learning.

Uncertainty of state support for public higher education and the rising cost of going to college

American post-secondary institutions are facing a funding crisis from one of their largest sources of funding. Public post-secondary institutions receive the majority of their funding from the federal and state governments. The federal government contributes 40% of total revenue at public four-year institutions and state governments contribute about 36%. The percentage of revenue from states has declined significantly since 1980 when states contributed 45.6% of total revenue (US Department of Education, 2005). Another way to understand the decline in state support for higher education is to look at state post-secondary educational appropriations per full-time equivalent students (FTE).[14] In 2007, state governments appropriated slightly more money to post-secondary education per FTE than in 1982, despite the rising cost of educational equipment and facilities such as computers and laboratories (see Figure 6.8). State support for public higher education is not

Figure 6.8. **Constant-dollar[1] educational appropriations[2] per FTE (US), fiscal years 1982-2007**

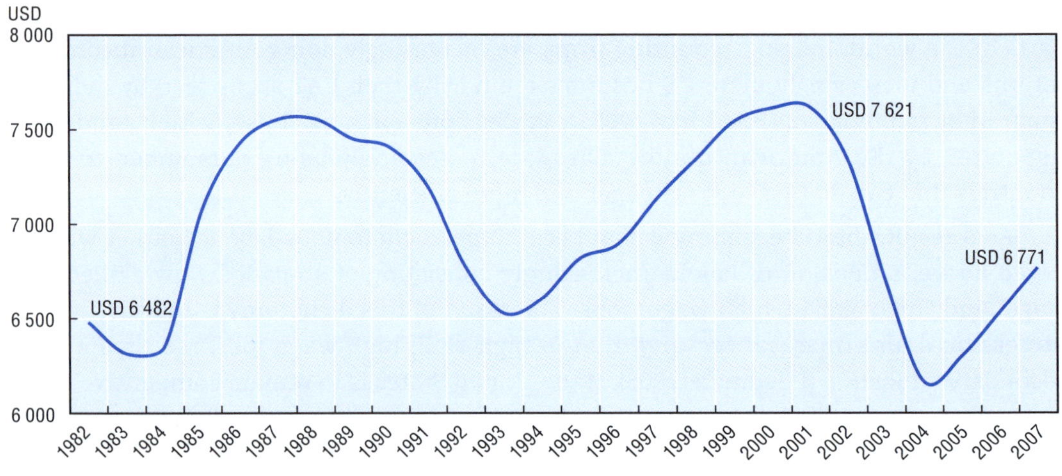

1. Constant 2007 dollars adjusted by SHEEO Higher Education Cost Adjustment (HECA).
2. Educational appropriations (state and local funds available for public higher education operating expenses, excluding spending for research, agriculture, and medical education and support to independent institutions and students).

Source: State Higher Education Executive Officers (2008).

capricious and arbitrary but usually the result of state economic conditions that limit fiscal resources (State Higher Education Executive Officers, 2005): it follows business cycles.

The decrease in state funding per full-time-equivalent (FTE) is correlated with an increase in tuition over the last twenty-five years. As Figure 6.9 shows, in most years there is an inverse relationship between annual percentage changes in tuition and fees and state

Figure 6.9. **Annual percentage change (constant-dollars[1]) in educational appropriations per FTE and tuition and fee charges at public 4-year institutions (US), 1982-2007**

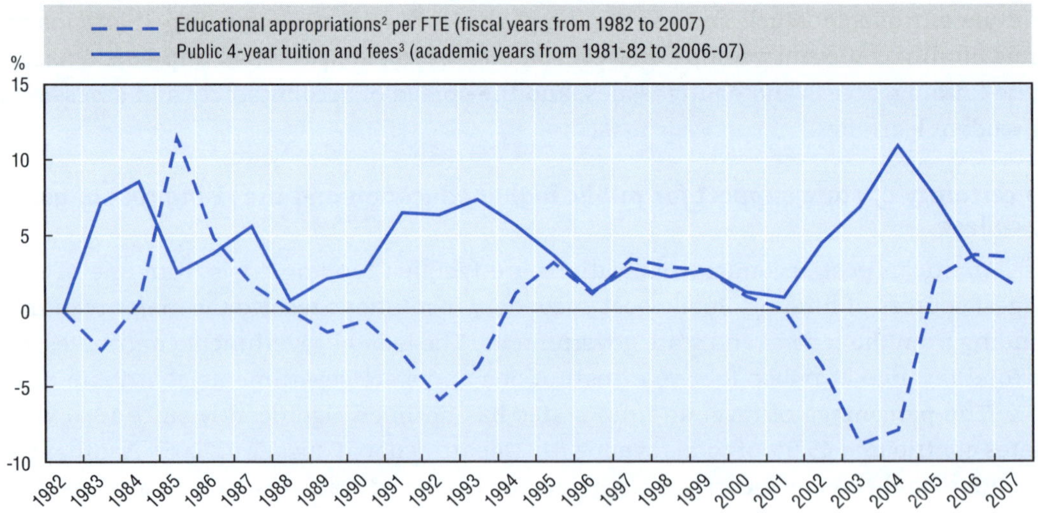

1. Constant 2007 dollars adjusted by SHEEO Higher Education Cost Adjustment (HECA).
2. Educational appropriations (see Figure 6.8).
3. Tuition and fees are enrolment-weighted.

Source: State Higher Education Executive Officers (2008), College Board (2007).

educational appropriations per FTE students. When the state appropriation per FTE decreased, tuition and fees increased. The cost of attending a post-secondary institution has increased significantly since 1980. From 1982 to 2007 (in constant 2007 dollars) the average tuition and fees at a public two-year institution as well as the cost of attendance at public or private four-year institutions more than doubled, increasing by 137%, 195% and 152%, respectively.[15] Despite these increases, the tuition and fees for one year at a public post-secondary institution remained relatively low, about USD 6 000 at public four-year schools and USD 3 200 at public two-year schools (College Board, 2007).

As tuitions increased to account for declines in state funding, student financial aid became increasingly important. In the first half of the 1980s, student loan programmes saw considerable growth, while federal grant programmes, such as the Pell Grant, declined in real value (McPhearson and Schapiro, 1998).[16] From 1987 to 2007, average federal loans per FTE increased by more than USD 2 500 (in constant 2006 dollars), from USD 1 826 to USD 4 337. During this same period, average grant aid per FTE also saw considerable growth, from USD 3 967 to USD 9 499. Despite funding increases, the largest federal grant programme, the Pell grant, actually lost buying power (College Board, 2005 and 2007). Student financial aid from non-federal sources also increased during the 1980s. According to McPhearson and Schapiro (1991), "from 1975 to 1989, state programmes grew by 53%, while institution-based aid...grew by 78% in real terms from 1981 to 1989 (p. 29)".

Research on the effect of rising tuition and changes in student financial aid suggest that the impact was hardest on lower income students, but did not adversely affect the enrolment patterns of the majority of Americans above the lowest income category. Investments in student financial aid for lower income students softened the negative impact of rising cost of attendance; however, the gap in the college going rate between low-income students and high-income students widened in states with higher public tuitions (McPhearson and Schapiro, 1998; Kane, 1999). Any such college going rate gap between low-income and high-income students is going to have a greater impact on persons of color, because Black Americans, Hispanics, and American Indians are more likely to be low-income than whites. Although recent improvement in economic conditions in many states has led to increases in funding, it is impossible to predict the impact of future economic conditions on state funding for higher education.

The access dilemma of the poor

Despite rising enrolment numbers, US higher education is becoming less affordable for some US students, especially low-income students. As stated previously, more than 86% of high school graduates from the two highest socioeconomic status quintiles enrolled in post-secondary education, compared to only 54% of students in the lowest quintile (see Table 6.5).

Low-income students rely on the Pell Grant programme as a major tool in accessing college. Between 1973 and 1990, 42 million low-income students utilised the Pell Grant programme to access college. Since 1990, 52 million low-income students have benefited from Pell Grants. While the number of students utilising the Pell Grant has increased significantly, the value of the Pell Grant has dropped sharply over the past 20 years. The cost of attending college increased 80% at public institutions and 66% at private institutions between 1995 and 2004, and the maximum Pell Grant award increased only 43%. From 1980 to 2003, the percentage of the cost of attendance that the maximum Pell Grant award covered at public two-year post-secondary institutions declined from 99% to 68%.[17] At four-year public institutions the buying power of the maximum Pell Grant dropped by 39 percentage points to cover only 38% of the cost of attendance. Over the same period of time the value of the maximum Pell Grant award at four-year private institutions declined from 36% of cost of attendance to a mere 16%.[18] Since the mid-seventies, the real cost of higher education (understood as total price minus all aid) has risen only slightly for students from advantaged socio-economic backgrounds but has doubled for low income students. For students (or families) in the bottom quartile of the US family income distribution, college costs have increased from 42 to 63% of total family income, while they have remained stable for the top 40% of the family income distribution (Carnevale, 2006).

Access to post-secondary education among low-income persons is also affected by lack of information about the availability of financial aid. Nearly 60% of low-income students and their parents reported not having enough information about how to pay for college (Sallie Mae Fund, 2003).

A lack of access to post-secondary education among low-income persons will have an impact that reverberates beyond poor communities in the United States. Overall, the continued growth in post-secondary enrolment will likely not be negatively affected by limited access among low-income persons. The majority of students in US post-secondary education are from middle- and high-income families. Low-income students represent a small segment of the post-secondary population.

However, the benefits this groups receives from advanced education are substantial because a college education has the ability to change their socioeconomic status. Research shows that Americans with less than a college degree are more likely to be incarcerated, unemployed, require welfare assistance and report being in less than good health (Baum and Payea, 2004). While these traits diminish the quality of life for these Americans, they also require a significant amount of support from local, state, and federal governments. With health care and prison cost rising and the number of Americans living in poverty increasing annually, the plight of Americans with low educational attainment extends beyond just an individual issue. All working Americans will bear the burden of the unemployed.

The new minority challenges

Because of the racial shifts occurring among the college-age population, the future growth of US higher education will greatly depend on the ability to maintain and increase access among Black Americans and Hispanics from all income levels. Given that Black American and Hispanic students are more likely to come from a low-income background, the challenge is really correlated to the increased access of the poor discussed above.

While participation in and access to post-secondary education has increased among all racial and ethnic groups of students, there has been less progress made in terms of graduation. Bailey (2005) shows that the gaps between Black Americans, Hispanics and Whites grew in actual percentage point if one considers who earned 10 credits in post-secondary education: Black Americans and Hispanics still achieve rates equivalent or inferior to what whites had achieved 20 years ago. In 2000, about 32% of the white 25-34-year-old population has a Bachelor degree, against 16% of the corresponding African American and 11% of the Hispanic population – and the share of tertiary educated Hispanic males actually fell between 1990 and 2000. With Black Americans and Hispanics representing over 30% of the US population in 2020, it will be important to raise their post-enrolment success to meet the demands of the US economy, which is predicted to require more workers with skills learned in college (Bailey, 2005).

Other challenges associated to this demographic shift will be cultural and possibly linguistic ones. With Hispanic students becoming a majority in a few states of the United States, the higher education sector will have to adapt to new cultural demands, possibly including a changing language of instruction. While historically Black colleges and universities were a response to segregation, Hispanic-Serving Institutions (HSI) have become a *de facto* reality in places where the population was mainly Spanish-speaking. To date, their language of instruction has primarily been English, but more states and institutions will have to adapt their curricula and teaching to the traditions and distinctive experience of Hispanic Americans in the coming decades.

This may also mean that minority issues will become more diversified than they have been in the past, where affirmative action has dominated the US policy agenda in this respect. Minority education will no longer be synonymous with affirmative action, but instead shaped by a much wider range of concerns (for example new questions like completion) and a much more varied group of "minorities" – which, again, in the next generation, will be the new majority in some states.

The spread of accountability and assessment of student learning

Although accountability in US higher education is nothing new, over the past 20 years there has been a significant change in the concept and practice of accountability. While earlier notions of accountability focused on regulating the flow of campus resources and the decisions of campus officials, the new accountability movement is outcome driven with policy makers seeking to influence institutional behavior for the purpose of improving institutional performance and student learning (McLendon, Hearn and Deaton, 2006). While much of the push for accountability has come from policy makers, concern has also been expressed by business leaders concerned about the preparedness of the US workforce and parents looking to get the most for their tuition dollars.

Accountability in higher education is gaining in popularity, particularly at the state level (McLendon, Hearn and Deaton, 2006). Between 1979 and 1990, only four states adopted either a performance funding or performance budgeting policy.[19] Between 1990 and 2002, 38 states adopted one of these policies (McLendon, Hearn and Deaton, 2006). In addition to state level policies, the federal government is exploring ways to make post-secondary institutions more accountable for student outcomes (Kerkstra, 2006; US Department of Education, 2006).

Accountability policies that fail to recognise the uniqueness of each post-secondary institution could lead schools to limit access. One concern for state and federal officials is the low graduation rate of students in US post-secondary institutions, 58% for full-time students beginning at a four-year institution seeking at least a bachelor's or equivalent degree (cohort years 2000 and 2003, US Department of Education, 2008b). As stated previously, only a small number of post-secondary institutions in the US are selective, the majority of four-year institutions are not selective and offer the opportunity for students from a variety of backgrounds to attend a four-year post-secondary institution. The low graduation rate among US students can partially be attributed to this policy that encourages all types of students to attempt to earn a college degree regardless of their academic preparation. State and federal accountability efforts that seek to measure institutions by graduation rates and evaluate a standard set of knowledge ignore the uniqueness of post-secondary institutions and may actually stymie the growth of many post-secondary institutions by forcing less selective institutions to become more selective. This shift in admission policy would shut the door of four-year institutions on many lower-income Americans.

6.6. Conclusion

The future of post-secondary education in the United States will continue to be affected by internal and external pressures in the next decade. Population growth among young Americans will likely lead to expanding enrolments at all types of post-secondary institutions. In the coming decade post-secondary education will reflect the increasing racial/ethnic diversity of the nation. As selective elite institutions adjust their recruitment of minority students, the number of students of color at elite institutions should begin to increase. National and local efforts to raise the quality of primary and secondary education provided to low-income students if successful should increase the percentage of low-income students attending post-secondary education.

However, if government support for post-secondary education institutions and its students does not increase, access for low-income students will decline significantly. Access for low-income students will become even more of a pressing issue in the next decade because most of the population growth among potential college students will be among minority students who are more likely than whites to be from low-income families.

The challenge of globalisation may serve as a positive force on post-secondary educational opportunity for Americans from all racial and economic backgrounds. Today governmental and business leaders in the United States realise the importance of post-secondary education, especially in science, technology, engineering, and math fields, in order for the nation to maintain its place in the global economy. The US government recently passed legislation aimed at increasing the number of students majoring in science and technology fields (Frist, 2006). According to a survey of 100 top science and technology companies in the United States, most of the leaders of these companies fear that a shortage of Americans trained in science and technology will jeopardise the nation's standing in the global economy (Bayer Corporation, 2006). This heightened awareness has already resulted to special funding (both governmental and corporate) targeted at increasing the production of scientists, engineers, computer programmers, and mathematicians.

The past twenty-four years in American higher education proved that enrolments can grow even when the college age population declines. The expansion of college access beyond the most affluent students benefited post-secondary education by preventing enrolment declines. More importantly, the expansion of college access in the United States benefited the nation and allowed for more people from diverse backgrounds to obtain a higher education and succeed in the changing US economy at the end of the 20th century. Future developments in US higher education will once again depend heavily on the expansion of access, the changing nature of the economy and the global marketplace.

Notes

1. In this chapter "white" refers only to white, non-Hispanic persons.
2. It should be noted that the term *Hispanic* refers to all people of Spanish heritage from Mexico, Central and South America and the Caribbean, no matter their race. For the purposes of this chapter, however, the Hispanic population is included in discussions of minority populations.
3. There was a major change in the guidelines for the coding of race in the United States in 1997, which took effect in Census 2000. The new guidelines allow the coding of two or more racial categories, whereas the earlier practice required respondents to choose a single race. Provided by the US Census Bureau, the data in this paragraph and in Table 6.1 do however reflect the old definition through 2004. Because race and Hispanic origin are reported subjectively in decennial censuses, occasional trends, even if consistent in definition, need to be interpreted with caution. For example, the 52% increase in the American Indian population from 1980 to 2004 (Table 6.1) is not plausible as population growth and is most likely influenced by an increasing tendency of people to report this category in census enumerations.
4. In this chapter the term "four-year" refers to institutions that grant at least a bachelor's degree, but may also grant master's, professional, and doctoral degrees. The term "two-year" refers to associate's degree granting institutions.
5. The US Department of Education collects enrolment data for the fall semester/quarter of each year. An enrolment estimate for the entire 12-month academic year includes persons who were not enrolled for the fall semester/quarter count, but enrolled some time during the academic year. This estimate is called an unduplicated 12-month headcount. For academic year 2003-04 the unduplicated 12-month headcount was 23.5 million students.
6. The remaining share of enrolment consists of persons of unclassified race/ethnicity.
7. The 2000 Carnegie Classification definition of Doctoral/Research Universities-Extensive: these institutions typically offer a wide range of baccalaureate programmes, and they are committed to graduate education through the doctorate. They award 50 or more doctoral degrees per year across at least 15 disciplines.
8. The national poverty level is a sliding income scale based on family size. For example, in 2002, the poverty level for a family of four (including two children under the age of 18) was USD 18 244. So, for this size family low-income equals USD 36 388, middle-income equals USD 36 389 to USD 91 220, and upper-income equals more than USD 91 220. For a single-headed household with only one child under the age of 18, the income ranges would adjust downward.
9. These college participation rates are significantly higher than the overall rate of 45% mentioned above because the 93-53 percentage rates are based on enrolment within 8 years after high school (for students who completed high school). The 45 percentage rate is a one-time snapshot of persons aged 18- to 24-years old.
10. It is important to distinguish between formal education, such as a course at a college or university and work-related training. Many manufacturing jobs require considerable training for example, but do not require formal education.
11. The term "elite institution" does not refer to specific definition of institution type or notion of quality, but refers to the perception of certain institutions based on selectivity and rank in various publications that rank institutions.
12. States listed in the Adams ruling: Louisiana, Mississippi, Oklahoma, North Carolina, Florida, Arkansas, Pennsylvania, Georgia, Maryland, and Virginia.
13. This refers to the provision of formal instructional programmes with a curriculum designed primarily for students who have completed the requirements for a high school diploma or equivalent. This includes programmes of an academic, vocational, and continuing professional education purpose, and excludes avocational and adult basic education programmes (US Department of Education).
14. When discussing funding for post-secondary education it is important to connect funding to student enrolment. In pure dollars state funding for post-secondary education has increased significantly over time. However, because of rising enrolment, the funding increases are actually declines.
15. Tuition data are based on tuition and mandatory fee charges. Data are enrolment weighted and in 2007 dollars.

16. The Pell Grant programme is a federally funded need-based grant. It is the largest single grant programme in the United States.

17. Cost of attendance includes tuition and necessary fees at all institutions and room and board at four-year institutions.

18. "Students at lower-priced institutions could only receive grants equivalent to no more than a fixed percentage of college prices...After 1985, when the cap was raised from 50% to 60%, only students at public two-year institutions (and other similarly low-priced institutions) were affected. The 1992 reauthorisation of the Higher Education Act revoked this limitation (King, 2003, p. 5)."

19. *Performance funding* is an approach where an institution receives a designated share of state funding if it reaches a specified performance target. Under *performance budgeting*, state policy makers use campus achievement on performance indicators as one of several factors that determine state funding.

References

Adams v. Richardson (356 F. Supp. 92) (D.C. 1973).

Adelman, C. (2004), "Principal Indicators of Student Academic Histories in Post-secondary Education, 1972-2000", US Department of Education, Washington DC.

Adelman, C. (2006), "The Toolbox Revisited: Paths to Degree Completion From High School Through College", US Department of Education, Washington DC.

American Council on Education (2005), *College Students Today: A National Portrait*, Washington DC.

Anderson, E.L. (2001), "Johnson v. Board of Regents: The Controversy Over Standards and Meritocracy in American Higher Education", unpublished doctoral dissertation, University of Virginia, Charlottesville, VA.

Bailey, T. (2005), "Implications of Educational Inequality for the Future Workforce", unpublished paper presented at the Symposium on "The social costs of inadequate education", Columbia University, New York.

Baum, S. and K. Payea (2004), "Education Pays 2004: The Benefits of Higher Education for Individuals and Society", College Board, Washington DC.

Bayer Corporation (2006), "Bayer Facts of Science Education XII", *www.bayerus.com/msms/news/facts.cfm?mode=detail&id=summary06*.

Cabrera, A.F. and S.M. La Nasa (2000), "Understanding the College Choice Process", *Understanding the College Choice of Disadvantaged Students: New Directions for Institutional Research*, Jossey-Bass, San Francisco, No. 107, pp. 5-22.

Card, D. and A. Kruger (2004), "Would the Elimination of Affirmative Action Affect Highly Qualified Minority Applicants? Evidence from California and Texas", unpublished paper.

Carnevale, A. (2006), "The Great Sorting", unpublished paper.

Carnevale, A. and R. Fry (2000), *Crossing the Great Divide. Can we Achieve Equity when Generation Y Goes to College?*, Educational Testing Service, Washington DC.

Center on Education Policy (2006), "From the Capital to the Classroom: Year 4 of the No Child Left Behind Act", *www.cep-dc.org/_data/global/nidocs/CEP-NCLB-Report-4.pdf*.

College Board (2003), *Trends in College Pricing 2003*, Washington DC.

College Board (2004), *Trends in Student Aid 2004*, Washington DC.

College Board (2005), *Trends in Student Aid 2005*, Washington DC.

College Board (2007), *Trends in College Pricing 2007*, Washington DC.

Dobbs, M. (2004, November 22), "Universities Record Drop in Black Admissions", *The Washington Post*, p. A01.

Friedman, T. (2005), *The World is Flat: A Brief History of the Twenty-First Century*, Farrar, Straus and Giroux, New York.

Frist, B. (2006, January 26), "Why We Need the SMART Program [Editorial]", *Inside Higher Education*, *http://insidehighered.com/views/2006/01/26/frist*.

Hecker, D.E. (2005, November), "Occupational Employment Projections to 2014", *Monthly Labor Review Online*, Vol. 128, US Department of Labor, Bureau of Labor Statistics, *www.bls.gov/opub/mlr/2005/11/contents.htm*.

Hobbs, F. and N. Stoops (2002), *Demographic Trends in the 20th Century*, US Census Bureau, Census 2000 Special Reports, Series CENSR-4, US Government Printing Office, Washington DC.

Hurtado, S. and H.C. Wathington (2001), "Time for Retreat or Renewal? Perspectives on the Effects of *Hopwood* on Campus", in D. Heller (ed.), *The States and Public Higher Education Policy: Affordability, Access, and Accountability*, The Johns Hopkins University Press, Baltimore, MD.

Hussar, W.J. (2005), *Projections of Education Statistics to 2014* (NCES 2005-074), US Department of Education, National Center for Education Statistics, US Government Printing Office, Washington DC.

Johnes, G. (1993), *The Economics of Education*, Macmillan Press, London.

Kane, T. (1999), *The Price of Admission: Rethinking How Americans Pay for College*, Brookings Institution/ Russell Sage Foundation, Washington DC.

Kerkstra, P. (28 March 2006), "Standardized Testing at the University Level? Colleges Pushed to Prove Worth", *Philadelphia Inquirer*, p. A01.

King, J. (1996), "The Decision to Go to College: Attitudes and Experiences Associated with College Attendance Among Low-Income Students", College Board, Washington DC.

King, J. (2003), *2003 Status Report on the Pell Grant Program*, American Council on Education,Washington DC.

Levy, F. and R.J. Murnane (2004), *The New Division of Labor: How Computers are Creating the Next Job Market*, Princeton University Press, Princeton, NJ.

McDonough, P. (1997), *Choosing Colleges: How Social Class and Schools Structure Opportunity*, State University of New York Press, Albany, NY.

McLendon, M.K., J.C. Hearn and R. Deaton (2006, Spring), "Called to Account: Analysing the Origins and Spread of State Performance-Accountability Policies for Higher Education", *Educational Evaluation and Policy Analysis*, Vol. 28, pp. 1-24.

McPhearson, M.S. and M.O. Schapiro (1991), *Keeping College Affordable: Government and Educational Opportunity*, Brookings Institution, Washington DC.

McPhearson, M.S. and M.O. Schapiro (1998), *The Student Aid Game: Meeting Need and Rewarding Talent in American Higher Education*, Princeton University Press, Princeton NJ.

New York Times (1982, October 17), *Slow Unemployment Decline Foreseen by Job Experts*, p. 1.

Pusser, B. (1999), "The Contest Over Affirmative Action at the University of California: Theory and Politics of Contemporary Higher Education Policy", unpublished doctoral dissertation, Stanford University, Palo Alto, CA.

Sallie Mae Fund (2003), "Strengthening our Commitment to Access: National Consumer Study of Parent and Student Financial Aid Awareness", unpublished study, Reston, VA.

Schmidt, P. (2003, July 4), "Affirmative Action Survives, and so Does the Debate", *The Chronicle of Higher Education. Special Report*, Vol. 49, Issue 43, p. S1.

Stage, F.K. and P.W. Rushin (1993, July), "A Combined Model of Student Predisposition to College and Persistence in College", *Journal of College Student Development*, Vol. 34, pp. 276-281.

State Higher Education Executive Officers (2005), *State Higher Education Finance FY 2005*, Denver, CO.

State Higher Education Executive Officers (2008), *State Higher Education Finance FY 2007*, *www.sheeo.org/finance/shef/Early%20Release%20FY2007%20REVISED%203-12.pdf*.

St. John, E.P. (2002), "The Access Challenge: Rethinking the Causes of the New Inequality" (available from EDRS, ED 467 615).

US Census Bureau (2004a), Current Population Survey, Annual Average Total Employment Data 1983-2003 (analysis by author).

US Census Bureau (2004b), Current Population Survey, Table PINC-04, March Supplement 1981 to 2002, and 2003 Annual Social and Economic Supplement (analysis by author).

US Census Bureau (2005), Current Population Survey, School Enrolment – Social and Economic Characteristics of Students. Table 1: Enrolment Status of the Population 3 Years Old and Over, by Sex, Age, Race, Hispanic Origin, Foreign Born, and Foreign-Born Parentage: October 2004 (analysis by author), *www.census.gov/population/www/socdemo/school/cps2004.html*.

US Census Bureau (2008), Current Population Survey, School Enrolment – Social and Economic Characteristics of Students, Table 2 "Single Grade of Enrollment and High School Graduation Status for People 3 Years Old and Over, by Sex, Age (Single Years for 3 to 24 Years), Race, and Hispanic Origin – October 2006" (analysis by author), *www.census.gov/population/www/socdemo/school/cps2006.html*.

US Department of Education, National Center for Education Statistics (2004), *Digest of Education Statistics*, NCES Number: 2006005 (Table 332. Current-fund revenue of public degree-granting institutions, by source of funds: Selected years, 1980-81 to 2000-01; Table 173. Total fall enrolment in degree-granting institutions, by attendance status, age, and sex: Selected years, 1970 to 2014), *http://nces.ed.gov/programs/digest/d04/*.

US Department of Education (2005): 2003-04 National Postsecondary Student Aid Study, National Center for Education Statistics, Washington D.C, *http://nces.ed.gov/pubs2005/2005163.pdf*.

US Department of Education (2006), "A Test of Leadership. Charting the Future of US Higher Education", *www.ed.gov/about/bdscomm/list/hiedfuture/about.html*.

US Department of Education (2008a), *Digest of Education Statistics: 2007*, National Center for Education Statistics (2008-022), *http://nces.ed.gov/programs/digest/d07/*.

US Department of Education (2008b), *Enrollment in Postsecondary Institutions, Fall 2006; Graduation Rates, 2000 and 2003 Cohorts; and Financial Statistics, Fiscal Year 2006. First Look*, National Center for Education Statistics (2008-173), *http://nces.ed.gov/pubs2008/2008173.pdf*.

US General Accounting Office (GAO) (2002), "School Finance: Per-Pupil Spending Differences between Selected Inner City and Suburban Schools Varied by Metropolitan Area" (GAO Publication GAO-03-234), *www.gao.gov/new.items/d03234.pdf*.

Wilson, R. (1982), *First Annual Status Report on Minorities in Higher Education, 1982-1983*, American Council on Education, Washington DC.

ISBN 978-92-64-04065-6
Higher Education to 2030
Volume 1: Demography

Chapter 7

The Future of Higher Education in the Context of a Shrinking Student Population: Policy Challenges for Japan and Korea

by

Akiyoshi Yonezawa* and Terri Kim**

This chapter looks at the future of higher education policy in Japan and Korea in light of the rapid demographic changes, characterised by ageing populations, low birth rates, and the saturation of the higher education markets following the completion of universal higher education in the two countries. This comparative analysis of Japan and Korea provides useful information for other OECD countries that will have to face similar long-term demographic challenges when developing their higher education policy agendas.

* Center for the Advancement of Higher Education (CAHE), Tohoku University, Japan.
** Brunel University and Centre for Higher Education Research and Innovation (CHERI), Open University, United Kingdom.

7.1. Introduction

Korea and Japan have achieved very high participation in initial tertiary education. In Korea in 2005, 97% of 18-year-olds graduated from high school, and 78.9% of the age cohort went on to higher education institutions.[1] In Japan in that year, 97.5% of 15-year-olds entered senior secondary education, and 76.2% of 18-year-olds went on to higher or post-secondary education institutions (MEXT, 2006).

Declining fertility and an ageing population are common in most OECD countries, and Japan and Korea are no exception. Indeed, Japan's birth rate has been declining continuously since the mid-1970s and reached 1.29 in 2004, the lowest on record for the nation. Korea's total fertility rate fell from 1.19 in 2004 to 1.08 in 2005, the lowest level on record for the nation and among the world's lowest.

Japan and Korea are thus in the lead in terms of experiencing the effects of universalisation of higher education and population ageing simultaneously. Both countries face the challenge of developing appropriate higher education policies in a context of considerable demographic change. The number of the traditional age cohort enrolling in higher education started to decrease in 1992 in Japan and in 2000 in Korea, and an increasing number of universities and colleges in both countries are having difficulty recruiting enough students to meet higher education enrolment quotas. The student population is decreasing as a consequence of continuing low fertility, while the adult population participating in lifelong learning in Japan and Korea is still at a relatively low level.

In spite of the many similarities between higher education in Japan and Korea, a comparison of their experience has rarely been undertaken. This chapter considers the future of higher education policy in Japan and Korea in light of their rapid demographic change, characterised by ageing populations and low birth rates, and the saturation of their higher education markets following their successful realisation of universal higher education. It recalls the history of higher education in both countries and describes the current situation, with particular attention to the labour market for graduates of higher education, before turning to the future impact of demographic change on higher education policies and practices in Japan and Korea and comparing the future direction of their higher education policies. This comparative analysis of Japan and Korea can also provide some useful information for other OECD countries that will have to address similar long-term demographic challenges when developing their higher education policy agendas.

7.2. The path to universal access to higher education

Before World War II, Japan had already diversified its higher education institutions, which ranged from research-intensive, nationally funded "imperial" universities to private universities, colleges and polytechnics that relied almost entirely on income from tuition fees. In 1920, the participation rate was only 2.2% (CCE, 2005a). In the period 1910-45, Korea's higher education system was organised and administered to meet the Japanese

 HIGHER EDUCATION TO 2030 – VOLUME 1: DEMOGRAPHY – ISBN 978-92-64-04065-6 – © OECD 2008

colonial government agenda, with public higher education mainly restricted to Japanese residents in Korea. The Japanese colonial higher education policies strictly limited the number of Koreans with access to higher education; less than 1% of college-aged youth received any form of higher education (Henderson, 1968; Kim, 2001).

After 1945, when Korea had recovered political independence from Japan, democratic education initiated by the US military government (between 1945-48 in Korea and 1945-52 in Japan) eventually afforded the populace greater opportunities to access higher education. In both countries, higher education soon came to be regarded as a crucial means of upward social mobility and national development, although access to higher education was still elitist. However, the introduction of four-year bachelor's and other short-term programmes provided wider access to higher education in both countries. Private colleges established by American missionaries and Korean nationalists in the late 19th and early 20th centuries also gained four-year university degree-granting status, and in both Japan and Korea, many new private universities and colleges were established.

In Japan, public universities and other higher education institutions have maintained fixed enrolment quotas since their establishment in the late 19th century as a way to maintain the quality of university education, and demand for public higher education has always exceeded supply. While the government has controlled student numbers by authorising fixed quotas in both public and private universities, control of student numbers in private universities and colleges has varied from time to time.

In Korea, the Ministry of Education has also regulated the establishment and expansion of private universities as well as national universities. Especially during the 1970s, it exerted strong control over new faculty appointments, curricula and tuition fees, as well as student enrolment quotas set for each university at the departmental level (see Box 7.1). This strong central management by the government in Japan and Korea has contributed to the notion of the East Asian model of a "developmental state".

From 1947 to 1949, Japan experienced a baby boom, after which both the birth rate and the mortality rate decreased strongly owing to the implementation of the Eugenic Protection Act of 1948 which allowed easy access to induced abortion, to public and private family planning efforts and to improvements in public health (JICA, 2003). In 2005, the first instance of a population decrease in modern history, Japan's total population was close to 128 million, of which over 62 million were male and over 65 million female. Japan's birth rate has been declining continuously since the mid-1970s.

After the armistice following the Korean War in 1953, Korea also experienced a baby boom. Then, in 1961, the Korean government devised an explicit population control policy, and in the following year, a national family planning programme was established as a component of the government's first Five-Year Economic Development Plan. Under governmental control, which continued up until the early 1980s, the Korean population increased steadily in accordance with the needs of rapid economic development. The government's programme and the compliance of the population quickly reduced the average number of children per family in Korea from nearly six in 1960 to less than two in 1990 (Tedesco, 1996)[2] and the fertility rate has stayed below replacement level in the most recent decade. In 2004, Korea's population was estimated at close to 48 million, evenly divided between male and female (JICA, 2003, p. 6). At 1.08 in 2005, Korea's birth rate is much lower than the average 1.6 to 1.7 for OECD member countries and significantly lower than the 2.1 needed to maintain a country's current population level. Korea's total

Box 7.1. **The Korean higher education system**

The Korean higher education system was reorganised and developed under American influence after political independence but still reflected many aspects of the former Japanese style of governance. The Ministry of Education's direct control over public and private higher education is a good example. During the rapid expansion and massification of higher education, the government (three consecutive military regimes from 1961 to 1992) tried to prevent university students from protesting against the right-wing autocratic government policies. The Korean government tried not only to curb the expansion of higher education but also to reduce demand. During that period, the government's higher education policy focused on the practical function of university education for economic development. Along with the Five-Year Economic Plans started from 1962, the Ministry of Education established ten junior technical colleges in 1963 to produce technicians for industry. Overall, the aim of the government's intervention was both political and economic and reflected the continuing Japanese (colonial) pattern of governance. Regardless of the differences among institutions, uniformity was imposed in both public and private higher education. For instance, today, with the exception of Seoul National University, which has its own Ordinance, all national universities are placed under the Education Act, supervised by the Ministry of Education. This means each national institution does not have its own "charter". Private institutions of higher education are under the control of the Private School Law, which emphasises restrictions and rules rather than autonomy as in the colonial period.

Source: Kim (2001, pp. 147-149).

fertility rate (TFR) is lower than that of Japan (1.288) and far lower than that of the United States (2.04). If this trend continues, the Korean population will decrease from 48.17 million in 2005 to 39.48 million by 2050 (*The Korea Herald*, 2005; *Chosun Ilbo*, 2006).[3]

Overall, the success of both governments' population control policies along with strong family support for and investment in education and cost-effective management of education contributed to the early realisation of universal (higher) education and to both countries' rapid economic development.

The post-war population increase, accompanied by rapid economic development and the expansion of education led to wide-reaching social demand for higher education. Both governments continued to maintain strong control over the establishment and expansion of private universities as well as national and local public universities and to regulate student numbers in both the public and private higher education sectors. However, rapid economic development and increasing demand for highly skilled labour led them to loosen their control over higher education enrolment quotas and allow private higher education institutions to absorb market demand for higher education, from the 1960s to the mid-1970s in Japan and during the 1980s in Korea.

In Korea, the Ministry of Education adopted a so-called "graduation quotas" policy which obliged the university to drop a certain portion of students before graduation. The policy resulted in 100% growth in the number of university students between 1980 and 1983. Many two-year national teacher colleges and technical colleges were also upgraded to four-year universities in that period. However, the policy was very unpopular among university students, academics and administrators alike, and a few years later, the policy was rescinded in response to public pressure.

Increasing demand for higher education was mainly met by the private sector, with tuition paid by students and their families, although the number of teachers, facilities and equipment lagged the increase in student numbers. The quality of the learning environment, such as the student-teacher ratio, deteriorated in many universities and was one of the sources of political activism among students in the late 1960s in Japan. In 1970, the Japanese government started to give financial support to private universities and colleges for operational expenditures, and again exerted stronger control over enrolment quotas, from the mid-1970s through the mid-1980s. It also established non-university short-term post-secondary education system in the form of professional training colleges. Then, from the mid-1980s, to meet the demand by the second wave of baby boomers for access to higher education in an era of economic prosperity, the government started to loosen its control over enrolment quotas. Even after the population of 18 year olds peaked in 1992, the government continued to allow the establishment of new universities and colleges as part of a transition from a planning policy to a market-oriented policy in higher education enrolment (Amano, 1997).

During the 1990s, global trends towards neo-liberal policies, such as labour market flexibility, privatisation and a "lean" state co-ordinating market competition began to be felt in Japan and Korea, leading to a shift in their higher education policies. In Korea, up until 1995, the government maintained strict regulations for university governance, the establishment of new higher education institutions, admission criteria and the number of students for each institution. Nevertheless, by 1995 the rate of enrolment in higher education had reached 55.1%, which means, according to Martin Trow's definition (Trow, 2000), that Korea had passed the phase of mass higher education and reached the level of universal higher education. In 1995, the Korean government implemented a deregulation policy and abolished enrolment quotas. Many new small private universities were established in regions outside of metropolitan Seoul.

Between 1945 and 2000, Korean higher education expanded from 19 establishments and almost 8 000 students to 352 establishments and well over 3 million students.[4] In 2005, Japan had 1 194 universities and junior colleges enrolling over 3 million students, and in addition, close to 700 000 students enrolled in 2 973 professional training colleges (MEXT, 2006). In absolute numbers, there are today enough places available in universities and colleges to admit all applicants who want to receive higher education, although competition to enter elite higher education institutions continues to be severe. However, higher education is now encountering a decline in demand owing to demographic changes in both countries.

7.3. A declining and ageing population and the saturation of traditional student markets

According to the UN *World Population Prospects: The 2004 Revisions*, the countries with the most rapid drop in fertility are largely in Asia (United Nations, 2004). Japan is far in the lead with a rapidly ageing population and a stagnating low birth rate, and Korea seems to be following this model (Table 7.1).

However, the longer-term prospects for demographic change look more dramatic for Korea than for Japan (Table 7.2). Although the average annual rate of change seems insignificant over 20 years, by 2045-50 it is likely to be –0.65 for Korea and –0.49 for Japan.

Table 7.1. **Demographic trends in Korea and Japan**

	Population (thousands)				
	1950	2005	2015	2025	2050
Japan	83 625	128 085	127 993	124 819	112 198
Korea	18 859	47 817	49 092	49 457	44 629

Source: World Population Prospects: The 2004 Revisions, United Nations, pp. 36-37.

Table 7.2. **Average annual rate of demographic change, Korea and Japan**

	Average annual rate of change (%)				
	1995-2000	2000-2005	2010-2015	2020-2025	2045-2050
Japan	0.25	0.17	–0.07	–0.30	–0.49
Korea	0.77	0.44	0.22	0.03	–0.65

Source: World Population Prospects: The 2004 Revisions, United Nations, pp. 61-62.

Qualitative changes in the age structure of both populations are even more significant. Table 7.3 indicates the changing proportion of each age group over time. By 2050, more than 50% of the population is expected to be over 60 years old in both Japan and Korea.

Table 7.3. **Changes in the age structure of population, Korea and Japan**

	2005				2050			
	Age groups				Age groups			
	0-14	15-59	60+	80+	0-14	15-59	60+	80+
Japan	14.0	59.7	26.3	4.8	13.4	44.9	41.7	15.3
Korea	18.6	67.7	13.7	1.4	12.0	46.8	41.2	13.0

Source: World Population Prospects: The 2004 Revisions, United Nations, pp. 69-70.

These demographic changes in age cohorts will have a significant impact on the traditional student market and thus on the future of higher education systems. Figure 7.1 indicates that Japan, Korea and China are the countries that will experience the most notable, continuous long-term decrease of the 18-23 year old population. Japan and Korea saw their population of 18-year-olds begin to decline in 1993 and 2003, respectively, and have continued to see a decline in their young population and an increase in their elderly population.

Given the changing demographic profile described above, it is now anticipated that 30% of Korea's primary schools will disappear in ten years. As a result of the decrease in the birth rate, by 2020 there will be 360 000 fewer enrolments in Korea's higher education institutions; accordingly, about 100 higher education institutions are expected to cease operations by then (*Chosun Ilbo*, 2003).[5]

The Japanese Ministry of Education, Culture, Sports, Science and Technology (MEXT) has also warned that all needs for four-year and two-year higher education will be met by government student quotas in 2007. In Japan by 2005, more than ten national universities had merged, and the government has set guidelines for the closure of private universities.

Overall, the saturation of the traditional student markets and the crises in private higher education institutions are expected to intensify in both countries. In Korea, the

Figure 7.1. **Estimated trends for the population 18-23 years old**

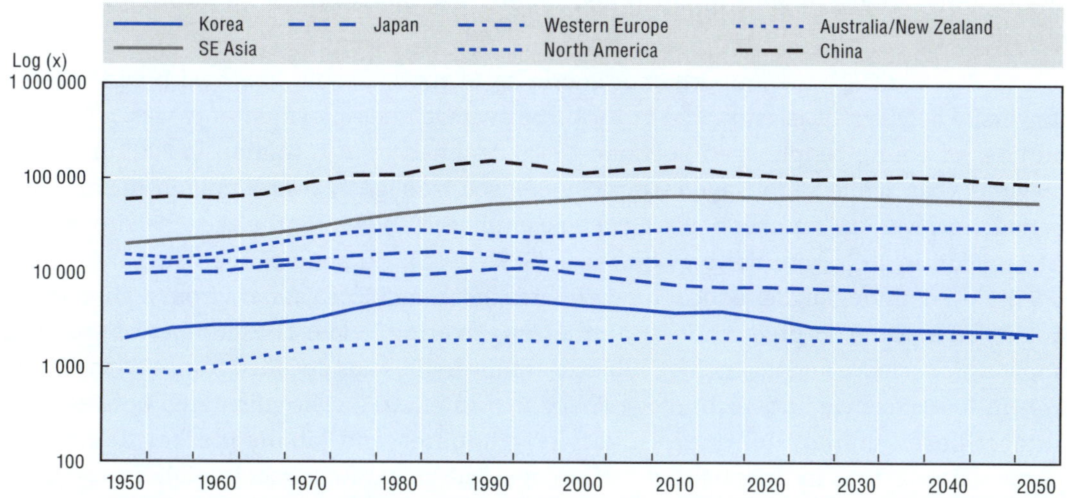

Source: Population Division of the Department of Economic and Social Affairs of the United Nations Secretariat, *World Population Prospects: The 2004 Revision* and *World Urbanization Prospects: The 2003 Revision, http://esa.un.org/unpp.*

supply of higher education has started to exceed demand. Korea currently has over 200 four-year universities and about 160 junior colleges; in 2003, there was a shortage of 85 000 new students, resulting in the lowest rate of admissions ever. Japanese private higher education is also now faced with a serious oversupply. In 2005, 160 out of 542 (29.5%) four-year universities and 158 out of 383 (41.3%) junior colleges did not fill their governmentally allocated enrolment quotas (Promotion and Mutual Aid Corporation for Private Schools of Japan, 2006).

7.4. Linking higher education supply and labour market demand

There are challenges for linking the supply of higher education with the demands of the labour market. There are also challenges arising from economic globalisation, the internationalisation of higher education and the changing infrastructures of society and national economies in general. In Korea, the reform of higher education has not kept up with the structural changes in the national economy which have created strong demand for highly skilled knowledge workers. Korea now faces the challenge of upgrading the quality of higher education and the development of human resources to meet the demands of a global knowledge economy and to supply the competencies required on the transnational corporate labour market.

In Japan, MEXT has tried to promote structural changes within higher education by expanding postgraduate programmes, especially in professional education. Japan still has a small number of postgraduate students (1.62 per 1 000 population in 2000, compared to 3.86 in the United States, 2.72 in the United Kingdom and 3.70 in France [CCE, 2005b]). Yet, there is already excess supply of postgraduate education, which has not made use of its potential for fulfilling industry's need for the development of human resources. Total enrolments represent 91.3% of the government quota for postgraduate programmes. Enrolments in law schools – newly established in 2004 as a new type of professional postgraduate education – only filled 92.7% of the government quota (PMACPSJ, 2006).

Given the oversupply of higher education and an increasing unemployment rate among university graduates in Japan and Korea, the value of higher education has been questioned.

In Korea in 2004, the proportion of unemployed young people – both with and without university degrees – was estimated at 7.9% (the average unemployment rate was 3.5%). The number of young people aged between 15-29 declined by 1.95 million in 2005 from the previous year, while people aged over 65 increased by slightly over 2 million in the same period. However, the number of young people employed and below the age of 30 dropped by 1.88 million in 2005 from the previous year (SERI, 2005).[6] In spite of the rising number of unemployed among higher education graduates, however, Korea suffers from a shortage of quality manpower in production and other engineering fields. The number of students applying for science and technology subjects at universities has declined from 43% in 1997 to 27% in 2001 (Science and Technology Policy Institute, 2003). The mismatch between the subject-based employability of university graduates and labour market demand is particularly serious in science and technology. The mismatch was as high as 41.1% for university graduates with natural science degrees in 2004, and the unemployment rate of university graduates with engineering degrees was 23.2% (KEDI, 2004). Overall, the rapid expansion of higher education has led business leaders to express concern about the quality of university graduates.[7] At the same time, the number of those employed who are over age 50 increased dramatically to account for 26.2% of total employment in 2005, the largest figure on record, a sign that Korea is becoming a rapidly ageing society, and it is feared that the young workforce alone cannot meet changing economic demands (SERI, 2005).

In Japan, the recent economic recovery has reduced the problem of employment of higher education graduates (as of March 2006 the unemployment rate of 15-24-year-olds is 10.9% among males and 8.6% among females, and that of 25-34-year-olds is 5.5% among males, and 5.6% among females (the average unemployment rate is 4.1%),[8] although the value of higher education degrees has been questioned for a long time, especially because of the retention rate in Japanese higher education (the world's highest at 94% in 2000 [OECD, 2002]).

At the same time, there is increasing pressure to enhance the quality of postgraduate and lifelong education in both countries. As shown in Table 7.4, however, the higher education enrolment rate for the 30-39 year-old age cohort is very low in Korea compared with other OECD countries. Indeed, among the 30-39-year-olds, the OECD average for tertiary education is 5%, and the United Kingdom leads with 16%. For those over 40 years old, the OECD average is 2%, and the United Kingdom again leads with 8%.

Furthermore, at 7.8%, the participation rate of Korean adults in vocational training is much lower than in other OECD countries, *e.g.* 40% in the United Kingdom, 35% in the

Table 7.4. **Higher education enrolment rate by age, Korea**

	Colleges and universities			Graduate schools	
	16-19	20-29	30-39	20-29	30-39
1998	22.8	21.8	1.7	1.2	0.7
2000	27.4	24.3	2.3	1.5	0.9
2002	31.0	26.2	2.8	1.6	1.0
2004	32.9	27.0	2.6	1.7	1.1

Source: MOEHRD; *Statistical Yearbook of Education* (each year).

United States and 30% in Germany. In Japan, because of the long tradition of in-house training, lifelong learning is underdeveloped (Yonezawa and Kosugi, 2006).

The contribution of human resources to economic growth in Korea has decreased, owing to a changing economic structure and rapidly increasing female participation in "low-wage, low-skill" service industries, especially over the last ten years. Moreover, unlike other rapidly developing East Asian economies, the contribution of education to economic growth in Korea in the period 1984-94 actually decreased, although overall economic productivity increased (Collins and Bosworth, 1996). Economists have suggested that massive input of labour was the key contributor to Korea's rapid economic growth. Over the period 1963-2000, labour's contribution was recorded as 33.4%, while that of education was as low as 4.0%. In the United States the contribution of education to economic growth was 13.2% in the same period (Kim *et al.*, 2002).

In both countries, one challenge for the future will lie in how the economies manage to effectively use female graduates and, more generally, the female human capital. While female participation and graduation in higher education have significantly increased over the past decades, the Japanese and Korean economies still have difficulties reaping all the benefits from this trained human capital.

In Korea, the participation of women in higher education has continued to increase. According to the National Statistical Office record, as of 2006, 25.4% of Korean women have university degrees and 80.8% of the female age cohort enrolled in higher education institutions (NSO, 2006). Korean women also have relatively high participation rates in first university Natural Science and Engineering degrees. The ratio of women-earned degrees in these fields to the female 24-year-old population was 4.9 per 100 in 1998, which is higher than the participation rate of women in other Asian countries, Germany, or the United States (NSF, 2002).

But overall, in spite of equal participation by females in higher education in Korea, there is lack of equal opportunity for women in employment. Korean women in general have structural difficulty developing long-term sustained professional careers.

The female participation rate in economic activities has gradually increased since 1965 (37.2%). In 2006, one in two women over the age of 15 participated in economic activities (50.9%). The proportion of women in employment is estimated at 42%; and the number of women working in professions and senior management positions is estimated at 183 600 in 2006, an increase of 15 700 from the previous year. Nevertheless gender inequality still persists in the overall pattern of employment in Korea – *e.g.* only 13.2% of university academics and 19.2% of medical doctors are female (National Statistical Office, 2006). Most Korean women in employment work in low-skill service industries under short-term or temporary contracts. Women are more likely to work in small or medium-sized companies, often without social security and welfare benefits. Full-time employment is interrupted more often among women than among men, owing to pregnancy, birth and child care. It is noteworthy that the duration of full-time employment of women with higher education degrees tends to be shorter than that of women with secondary education certificates (SERI, 2003a). Also a policy providing for equality of career opportunities for university-educated women who are over their mid-30s and return to labour market after an interruption is lacking. The average labour market participation rate of university-educated women was 55.8% as of 2004, much below the OECD average of 78.4%, and one of the lowest among OECD member countries (Korean Women's

Development Institute, 2005). There is also a *de facto* income discrepancy between men and women in employment and promotion opportunities are unequal.[9]

In Japan, the junior college system has significantly influenced female participation in higher education. In 1955, male students accounted for 43% of junior college enrolments. During the period of rapid increase in higher education in the 1960s and early 1970s, however, female students gradually outnumbered males in the junior college system, and the share of male students dropped to 11.9% in 1975 (Figure 7.2).[10] One of the reasons was the unequal treatment of female and male higher education graduates in the Japanese labour market. In general, companies had a policy to employ male graduates of four-year universities for careers as future executives and female high school or junior college graduates for support staff. However, the Equal Employment Opportunity Law, enacted in 1986, prohibited unequal treatment by gender. With the opening up of job opportunities for female graduates of four-year universities, female students shifted their preference from junior colleges to four-year universities. Even during the economic recession of the 1990s, they maintained this preference, and there has been a considerable drop in female enrolment in the junior colleges system, aggravated by the decline in the 18-year-old population.

Figure 7.2. **Enrolment in four-year universities and junior colleges by gender, Japan, 1955-2004**

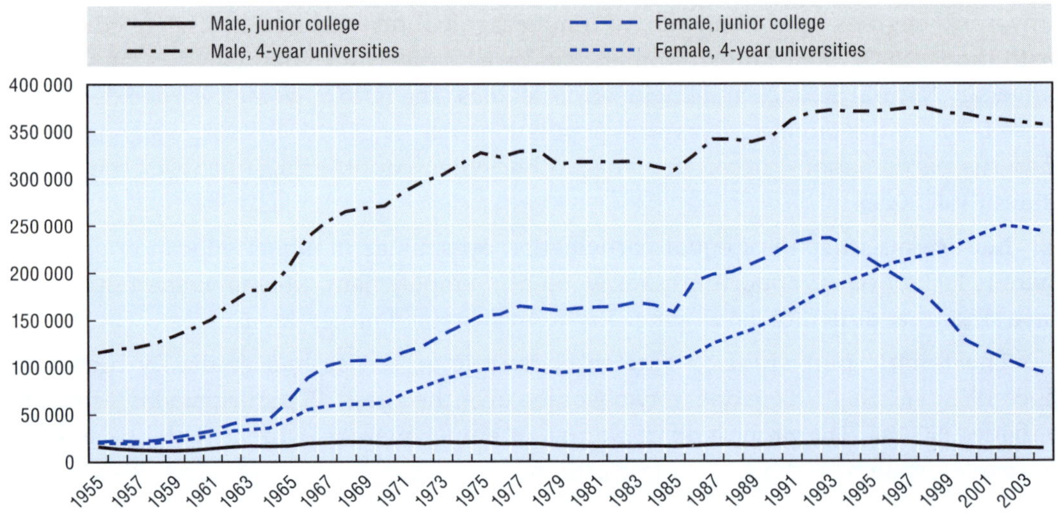

Source: Japanese Ministry of Education, Culture, Sports, Science and Technology (MEXT).

However, these tendencies do not mean that female workers are equally treated with male workers in the Japanese labour market. Tachibanaki pointed out that Japanese female workers are still disadvantaged in almost every aspects, namely, in recruitment, job-offering, training opportunity, promotion, and earning. Especially, the life-time employment and career promotion system typically applied to university graduates in Japanese enterprises is still discourageing female university graduates to re-enter the full-time regular job market after child-raising (Tachibanaki, 2005).

A future challenge for Japan and Korea over the next decades will thus be, on one hand, to better link higher education supply to the labour market demand and, on the other hand, to make a better use of its highly skilled female human capital – a challenge for social policies and employment practices rather than for higher education.

7.5. Structural policy strategies and challenges for the future of higher education

Given the declining number of the age-cohort enrolling in higher education and the simultaneous rapid increase in the ageing of the population, the governments of Korea and Japan have adopted policy strategies to induce structural reform and downsize both the public and private sectors. They aim to combine their initiatives, deregulation and guiding functions in a similar way, and resource allocation and quality assurance are becoming more crucial policy issues (see below).

While Japan's and Korea's structural policy strategies are not explicitly or directly meant to address the downsizing of the higher education sector, they are in some ways a response in that they try to encourage more diversified demand and supply. While the demographic situation can facilitate the implementation of structural reform and lead institutions to differentiate themselves more clearly by their mission, policy strategies encourage institutions to look for new audiences (international students, local communities, e-learners, lifelong learners) and help set up the infrastructure that will allow this new demand to emerge. Should the goals of these policies effectively be achieved, this "non-traditional" demand would help alleviate the decline of student enrolments in both countries. The following discussion compares the Japanese and Korean policy directions.

Diversification

The Japanese government officially welcomes the realisation of universal access in higher education. MEXT stresses the importance of providing various levels of educational programmes in various fields to meet individual needs for higher education at any time and on demand. The report of the Central Council for Education (2005a) advocates the transformation of higher education policy from "planned provision and regulation" to "provision of future images and policy guidance". Although the functions of higher education are diversifying, students tend to find it difficult to perceive differences in the characteristics of universities and other higher education institutions mainly because many universities try to fill all possible functions (MEXT, 2006). The report also recommends increasing the distinctiveness of higher education institutions to respond to diverse and focused demands for higher education, such as world excellence in research or lifelong learning.

In Korea, there is still strong conformity and a lack of strategic diversification among higher education institutions. About 75% of the four-year general universities produce postgraduate degrees, far more than in the United States (61%) or Japan (48.5%). In this context, the Korean government's higher education reform strategies focus on how to achieve the necessary diversification. In December 2004, the Ministry of Education and Human Resources Development (MOEHRD) announced a University Restructuring Plan in a bid to raise the competitive edge of Korean universities. In May 2005, it put forth a detailed strategy for reforming both public and private universities which involves, among other things, reducing annual undergraduate intake by about 15% by 2009. This is expected to enhance quality but it will increase pressure on institutions to merge.

World-class excellence in research

There is greater concentration of the allocation of government research funding to selected research universities. In Korea, the BK21 (Brain Korea 21) project ran for seven years (1999-2005) with a research budget of USD 1.2 billion. The second phase of BK21 (2006-13), will see more "selection and concentration" of research on a few key areas with a greater number of university-industry partnerships. In Japan, MEXT started its 21st Century COE [Center of Excellence] Programme in 2002. This programme supports the formation of global research and education centres by introducing competition with third-party peer evaluation. In 2002-04, 274 projects were selected, mostly from top universities (Yonezawa, 2003). Based on the positive social acceptance of the COE21 scheme, MEXT revealed a proposal to set up a Post 21st Century COE scheme from 2007, aimed at further concentration of research investment into around 150 research units (Central Council for Education, 2006).

Internationalisation

Given the demographic and economic challenges, the Korean government promotes internationalisation to increase the competitiveness and diversity of Korean higher education. The government provides scholarships (and this incentive) for foreign students to come to Korea for degree programmes.[11] Similarly, it has introduced a Brain Pool Scheme to recruit more distinguished foreign academics in the fields of information technology, biotechnology and basic sciences. English is increasingly used as a medium of instruction in Korea's higher education institutions. For example, Yonsei University's new Underwood College runs undergraduate education programmes entirely in English for first-class international students recruited from the Asian region and elsewhere.

Owing to increasing demand for international education at all levels, pressure and increased awareness owing to the WTO/GATS negotiations, and lobbying from national governments such as the United States, Japan, Australia and China, the Korean government in 2003 removed restrictions on direct provision of educational services by foreign institutions. The government seeks to attract more foreign direct investment and economic activities in Special Economic Zones, with tax incentives, fast-track permit processing, etc., made available in 2002. The details of new regulations for foreign educational institutions have yet to be finalised. The Korean government is also considering new free trade agreement negotiations in educational services with the United States. It is expected that such an agreement will not only liberalise the education market, but may also help to curb the increasing trend for Koreans to go abroad for education.[12]

The Japanese government is also trying to internationalise its higher education, basically through institutional initiatives. The government started the Strategic Fund for Establishing International Headquarters in Universities among 20 public and private universities in 2005 (*www.u-kokusen.jp/index_e.html*). In 2004 it also set up an official system for designating foreign universities' Japanese campuses for programmes officially authorised by their home countries. The government also supports the idea of Japanese universities delivering their educational programmes outside Japan, but such initiatives basically emerge from the higher education institutions.[13] Overall, both Japan and Korea are undertaking strong international networking and long-term strategic development to recruit international students and academic staff; international graduate and professional schools newly established in these countries are becoming competitive in the region.

Nevertheless, there is no clear strategic policy link in Japan and Korea between internationalisation of higher education and internationalisation of labour market. This is partly due to the absence of a tradition of immigration in these countries: in 2003, foreign nationals accounted for 1.5% of the population in Japan, and 0.9% in Korea (*OECD Factbook*,

2006). In contrast, many OECD member countries have developed immigration and employment policies. For instance, the UK government now more actively promotes the employment of international students after their graduation from UK universities. The existing Science and Engineering Graduates Scheme is being extended to international postgraduate students who successfully complete and obtain a UK recognised Master's degree or PhD in any subject.[14]

Setting up a new learning space in local communities

The Korean government is trying to induce balanced national development through the NURI (New University for Regional Innovation) project. NURI is the Korean version of the "triple helix" model of university-industry-regional-government partnerships aimed at nurturing the development of excellent local manpower and boosting the employment rate of regional university graduates through specialised education programmes. On a per capita basis, Korea has a large number of higher education institutions, many of which are small and private and run similar programmes. Overall, the government's aim is to restructure the higher education system for concentration, specialisation and diversification in each region through the NURI project.[15]

The Japanese government also supports the idea of regional consortia and linkage among various higher education institutions, triple helix activities, and so on. These networks may support to some extent the small private universities and colleges that will face difficulties in a shrinking student market. However, in most cases, initiatives come mainly from higher education institutions and local municipal governments. A representative example is the Consortium of Universities in Kyoto (*www.consortium.or.jp/english/index.html*), which allows the students of 35 universities and colleges to access classes, internships and other activities across universities and colleges within Kyoto City. In 2006, the Consortium published a proposal for attracting students to Kyoto City, where the capacity of higher education institutions far exceeds the number of 18-year-olds in the local population.

Supporting innovation in teaching and learning

ICT-based teaching-learning and research networks have developed rapidly in Korea since the first comprehensive education information service, EDUNET, was launched in 1996. In 2002, the National Digital Library Support System was launched, and by 2003 all universities and research institutes in Korea had joined the Research Information Service System (RISS) (*www.keris.or.kr*). With this ICT-based education and research infrastructure, the Korean government's plan is to create the world's largest "ubiquitous city" in New Songdo, which is considered the largest private real-estate development in the world. The ubiquitous city will be a free enterprise zone with English as the lingua franca. In the ubiquitous city, computers will link home life and life outside the home, will provide space for branches of world-class international education institutions and will attract international business investments. When completed in 2014, it is estimated that the ubiquitous city will be home to 65 000 people and that 300 000 will work there and benefit from the new U-environment.[16] In addition to the New Songdo ubiquitous city project, the Korean government has also announced its new Nationwide Ubiquitous City project, a plan to cover whole regions with wireless Internet access, connecting each and every household to the network. So far, six regions have announced plans to invest in their own U-City projects while also participating in the central government's plan.[17] Private higher education institutions have also joined; for instance, Yonsei University has announced that it will open a new campus in the ubiquitous city.

In Japan, MEXT promotes trials of innovative teaching and learning through various project-based incentive funds, such as the Support Programme for Distinctive University Education[18] and the Support Programme for Contemporary Education Needs.[19] Higher education institutions apply for those incentive fund programmes, and the Japan University Accreditation Association (JUAA) and other third-party organisations carry out the selection process on behalf of the government.

Lifelong learning

The Korean government started the lifelong learning city project in 2001. In the following year, the government announced a Comprehensive Plan for Lifelong Education Promotion to support lifelong education programmes operated on a local basis, to incorporate lifelong education as a part of daily routines and to offer adults more opportunities and diverse routes to higher education at various stages in their lives. Since then, it has contributed considerably to helping local governments initiate lifelong learning programmes. With increasing funds allocated to the project to build the new infrastructure and networks for regional city-based lifelong education, the government has announced that it will select 25 lifelong learning cities in addition to the 33 currently involved. The lifelong learning city project will expand to 100 lifelong learning cities across the nation by 2008. Although lifelong learning city programmes have so far focused mainly on culture and leisure content, local governments are now expected to develop programmes that reflect the unique characteristics of their cities and produce more labour opportunities so as to generate sustainable links between learning and employment for the local adult population (MOEHRD, 2006).

In Japanese higher education policy, learning opportunities related to career development, including lifelong learning, postgraduate professional education, and vocationally-oriented university education, are promoted, but the government's role is basically to set frameworks. In 2004, the government established a legal framework for professional postgraduate education, such as law schools and business schools, separate from the existing, more "academic" postgraduate programmes. In addition, the Cabinet set up a framework for Special Districts for Administrative Reform, allowing for a new pilot project for deregulation. Should this project prove successful, deregulation will be applied nationwide. Osaka City and Chiyoda District of Tokyo have embarked on special districts for career development, where vocational, profit-oriented universities are allowed to establish. Deregulation of online programmes is also ongoing, with some full-scale universities now beginning operations in addition to the publicly supported University of the Air, which broadcasts programmes and lessons.

Overall, both governments have recognised the need to develop lifelong learning and have started various policy trials to encourage it. However, whether these efforts in both countries lead to the increase in adult participation in higher education will depend on the demands of the labour market.

7.6. Co-ordinating the shrinking higher education market

In spite of the higher education reform strategies outlined above, it seems almost inevitable that the higher education market will shrink in both Japan and Korea. Ironically, the sustained low birth rate in both nations is often attributed to the high cost of education which parents are expected to bear. In these circumstances, financial issues in higher education require special attention not only to maintain universal access but also to prevent further demographic decline. This section describes some key higher education reform programmes that illustrate the overall direction of higher education policy in Japan and Korea and how these countries try to address the downsizing of their higher education system.

Incorporation of public universities

The management capacity of higher education institutions is becoming a crucial factor for providing higher education flexibly enough to meet the various needs of stakeholders and face the decline in student enrolments. In 2004, all Japanese national universities, junior colleges and colleges of technology were incorporated. Some local public higher education institutions are doing the same. These incorporated institutions have to publish six-year, medium-term goals and plans, and have to accept and report third-party evaluation of the achievement of these goals and plans. In Korea, the government's plan is to complete the incorporation of public universities by 2010 in the course of structural reforms of higher education management.

Quality assurance, mergers and closures

The saturation of higher education is increasing the need for appropriate co-ordination of quality higher education provision. The Japanese government is approaching this issue by strengthening quality assurance policies. From 2004, all four-year universities, junior colleges and colleges of technology are required to submit institutional level certified evaluations, a third-party, accreditation-type process implemented by certified evaluation organisations authorised by the government within every seven years. In addition, certified evaluation for professional postgraduate programmes was introduced, and follow-up monitoring after governmental authorisation of newly established programmes was strengthened. In May 2005, the government published guidelines for the monitoring and advisory process for universities and colleges facing financial and management difficulties, which focuses on establishing a safety net to ensure that students will be able to transfer to nearby universities (MEXT, 2005). In June 2006, the Private School Law was amended to ensure greater transparency in their activities, including financial conditions. In July 2006, the Promotion and Mutual Aid Corporation for Private Schools of Japan (PMACPSJ), the public grant council for private education institutions, released an interim report on the management difficulties and bankruptcy of private education institutions, suggesting that PMACPSJ should strengthen its monitoring and merger-arrangement function with respect to school corporations[20] that operate universities and colleges facing financial and management difficulties (Table 7.5) (PMACPSJ, 2006).

In Korea, the government has developed merger and acquisition standards and plans for both national and private universities to be implemented by 2009. The number of universities will be reduced primarily through mergers and restructuring, and they will be provided with financial incentives. The government gives subsidies to both private and public universities and both have to follow the same rules. As of 2007, 27 national universities had merged. The government has also announced its plan to reduce the total number of private universities by a quarter to 271 by 2009 (MOEHRD, 2005).

Table 7.5. **Number and share of Japanese private school corporations unable to cover operating costs with annual income**

	School corporations operating four-year universities		School corporations operating junior colleges	
	Number/total	%	Number/total	%
1998	31/409	7.6	66/227	29.1
1999	37/418	8.9	72/219	32.9
2000	69/435	15.9	81/204	39.7
2001	109/456	23.9	85/189	45.0
2002	122/469	26.0	79/178	44.4
2003	120/482	24.9	57/164	34.8

Source: Promotion and Mutual Aid Corporation for Private School of Japan (PMACPSJ), 2006.

These policies are very important for responding to a shrinking higher education market, not least to protect students and make sure they can transfer to another institution if theirs has to close.

Financial support for educational expenditure

Last but not least, an increase in public financial support for educational expenditure has become crucial in both countries. There is a link between family expenditure on education and low birth rates in the two countries. In 2005, the Japanese Cabinet Office implemented an international survey of people's attitudes on the birth rate in Japan, Korea, the United States, France and Sweden (*http://www8.cao.go.jp/shoushi/cyousa/cyousa17/kokusai/ishiki.pdf*). These results show that Japanese and Korean respondents tend to limit the number of children more than other countries, the primary reason being the high costs of raising a child and education (Japan, 56.3%; Korea, 68.2%; United States, 30.8%; France, 13.3%; Sweden: not included in the five primary reasons). Korean and Japanese respondents regard support for educational expenditure as the basic aspect of raising children (Korea, 58%; Japan, 42.8%; France, 39.4%, United States and Sweden, not included in the five primary answers). In June 2006, the Japanese Cabinet Office issued a policy plan, A New Deal for Low Fertility (Cabinet Office, 2006), arguing that national and local governments, industry, local communities and society in general should support families that raise children. Financial support for raising children was proposed as was an increase in the student loan scheme for higher education. In July 2006, the Council on Economic and Fiscal Policy, a core advisory board for the Japanese Prime Minister, issued the Basic Policy 2006, which clarified the Cabinet's plan to promote a comprehensive policy relating to low fertility (Council on Economic and Fiscal Policy, 2006).

As Table 7.6 shows, the share of household expenditure that goes towards higher education is extremely high in Japan and Korea.[21] This is mainly due to heavy reliance on tuition fees, notably in the private sector.

Both Japan and Korea fall well behind the OECD average for public expenditure on tertiary education as a percentage of GDP (at 0.5% compared to the OECD mean of 1%) (OECD, 2007). Even including private contributions, higher education expenditure per student as a share of GDP is below the OECD average. The incorporation of national and local public universities may accelerate this trend in Japan, because the government is planning to cut the financial budget of the national universities by 1% a year from 2005. Most national universities have tried to compensate for this by increasing tuition fees.

Table 7.6. **Expenditure on tertiary education institutions as percentage of GDP and share of household expenditure on tertiary education in OECD countries (2004)**

	Share of household expenditure %	Percentage of GDP %
Australia	35.6	1.6
Austria	4.8	1.2
Belgium	5.1	1.4
Canada[1]	22.9	2.5
Czech Republic	9.2	1.1
Denmark	3.3	1.8
France	9.8	1.3
Greece	0.4	1.1
Hungary	6.6	1.1
Iceland	9.1	1.2
Ireland	15.6	1.2
Italy	18.4	0.9
Japan[1]	**56.9**	**1.1**
Korea	**55.6**	**2.3**
Mexico	30.6	1.3
Netherlands	12.0	1.3
New Zealand	39.2	1.4
Poland	27.1	1.5
Portugal	14.0	1.0
Slovak Republic	9.7	1.1
Spain	20.8	1.2
Turkey	10.0	1.0
United Kingdom	19.4	1.1
United States	35.1	2.9

1. 2001 instead of 2004

Source: OECD (2004 and 2007), *Education at a Glance: OECD Indicators.*

In Korea, however, government financial support for the higher education sector has continued to increase over the last 15 years. The higher education endowment market has also continued to grow, although it is concentrated in a few private elite institutions.[22] However, the financial resources of Korean higher education institutions still very much depend on tuition fees (over 60%); and the overall size of the higher education market is likely to shrink along with the decreasing numbers of 18-year-olds.[23]

High tuition fees for higher education put significant pressure on households in both Japan and Korea. Moreover, in these countries it is very common for parents, despite the heavy financial burden, to send their children to private lessons to prepare them for university entrance examinations. According to a survey of Korean parents by KEDI in 2003, 73% of primary and secondary students received private tutoring after school hours, for a total expenditure estimated at KRW 13.6 trillion (USD 13.6 billion, EUR 10.6 billion), which represents 2.3% of GDP (Choi *et al.*, 2003). Meanwhile, according to a 2004 survey by the Korean government on household expenditure, spending on private tutoring exceeded private expenditure on educational institutions by 30%, a larger amount than that found in the KEDI survey (NSO, 2004). Overall, private tutoring expenditure in Korea appear to have risen significantly over the past few decades (Baek and Jones, 2005). Japan also has a long tradition of *juku* (cramming schools) and private tutoring, and family expenditure on this is recognised as an accelerator of socioeconomic diversification as well as a financial hardship. According to a MEXT survey, the average annual expenditure on education and training activities outside of formal schooling for public junior high school students was estimated at JPY 299 469 in 2004 (EUR 2 018, USD 2 600) (MEXT, 2004).

7.7. Conclusion and implications for other OECD countries

Japan's and Korea's higher education policies and practices show a tendency towards neo-liberal, market-framed higher education reform while simultaneously promoting the principle of social cohesion. Both countries face a policy dilemma between the global trend towards a neo-liberal policy agenda and the increasing national popularity (in the case of Korea) of social democratic policy ideas. In both countries, there is strong support for the idea of small government, efficiency, market-framed reforms of the public sector and internationalisation. At the same time, recent Korean public policy tends to put more emphasis on social cohesion based on egalitarianism, given public criticism of the widening gap between rich and poor and the increasing pressure from demographic changes that combine low fertility and an ageing population. Japan, whose population is already declining, is now experiencing a fierce policy debate on income inequality and social cohesion.

This comparative review suggests that higher education policies and practices in Japan and Korea are the result of achieving universal access to higher education with limited public resources and high levels of private expenditure on education. The heavy financial burden on families raising children in the absence of significant public support for completing post-secondary education has contributed to sustained low fertility rates in both countries, and in turn has accelerated the process of population ageing and decline. Social cohesion is becoming a key issue in both countries, and policy debate over how to break this vicious circle – high cost of education, low birth rates to limit the number of children to be raised, and further private expenditure on education leading to higher cost per child as part of the family investment strategy – is ongoing.

On the other hand, a shrinking student population seems unlikely to have a major impact immediately on the stratification and organisation of higher education in Japan and Korea. Given their very hierarchical systems of higher education, elite institutions are likely to strive to become more competitive and selective, whereas non-elite, local private institutions of higher education are likely to merge or close down as a result of demographic change and pressures from strong competition in a more open market.

The Japanese and Korean governments have adopted strategies to respond to the coming impact of demographic change on higher education, by downsizing the higher education system, establishing new lifelong learning infrastructure, promoting balanced regional economic development and the internationalisation of higher education. However, the governments have just started to address publicly long-term strategies to deal with the shrinking labour market due to ongoing demographic change in the very foreseeable future.

In view of the pattern of demographic change across OECD member countries, national governments urgently need to adopt new definitions of ageing and fresh approaches to policies on ageing (*e.g.* the OECD's Active Ageing strategy) and lifelong learning programmes. State pension and welfare systems have already started to be challenged by demographic projections: by 2050, the dependency ratios of people over 60 to those between 15 and 59 are likely to double (United Nations, 2004). Given these prospects, it has become more urgent for Japan and Korea to enable the ageing population to remain engaged in economically and socially productive activities and to combine this with lifelong learning. It is especially important to increase adult participation in lifelong learning to resolve the problems of the shortage of highly skilled knowledge workers. It would also be desirable to internationalise the national education system to recruit more foreign students and staff. At the same time, it would be well worth considering opening the labour market more widely to foreign workers. In addition to financial support for educational expenditure, the working environment should be fundamentally reconsidered, so that both male and female workers as well as education institutions and local communities can be actively engaged in lifelong learning and more committed to the well-being of the next generation. At the same time, the question of how to ensure that current and future young generations have stable and productive career prospects through higher education needs careful consideration.

Notes

1. According to the *Yearbook of Educational Statistics in Korea 2005* (KEDI, 2005), 569 272 completed upper secondary education and 467 508 of them enrolled in higher education institutions in Korea as of 2005.
2. Women were especially co-operative in the national family planning movement in Korea, as was seen in the increasing participation of women in higher education and greater participation of young females in the labour market (Tedesco, 1996).
3. *The Korea Herald*, 25 August 2005; *Chosun Ilbo*, 8 May 2006.
4. Korean National Statistical Office (*www.nso.go.kr*). The total number of higher education institutions in Korea is 352, among which are 156 four-year universities (26 national/public, 130 private), 158 junior colleges [*jeonmun daehack*] (of which 6 are national, 9 public, and 143 private), 11 universities of education (11 national/public), 18 universities of industry/technology (8 national/public, 10 private), and an open university (1 public) as of 2004 (*www.moe.gov.kr*).
5. *Chosun Ilbo*, April 18, 2003, *http://english.chosun.com/w21data/html/news/200304/200304180031.html*.
6. According to the National Statistical Office, May 2005. For details, see Samsung Economic Research Institute (SERI) Annual Report 2005, pp. 15-16.
7. About 77.7% of corporate personnel managers in Korea think the quality of Korean university education is a serious problem. Corporate CEOs also expressed strong dissatisfaction with the quality of Korean university graduates. The estimated average time spent on in-house education/on-the-job training after recruitment is 20.3 months and the costs of retraining at business firms have increased – *e.g.* Hyundai Motor Co. (USD 6 million), Samsung Electronics (USD 6.4 million) (Federation of Korean Industries Report, 2005).
8. See *Labour Force Survey* by Statistic Bureau, Ministry of Internal Affairs and Communication (*www.stat.go.jp/english/index.htm*). The Recruit Works Institute conducts an annual survey on job supply and demand for four-year university graduates (undergraduate and master's programmes) and reports continuing recovery in demand since 2001 (*www.works-i.com/pdf/bairitsu_2007.pdf*).
9. Women are paid 35% less than men in Korea even if they have the same level of educational qualification. At 28.8%, the level of female participation in management in Korea is low compared with other OECD countries – *e.g.* Japan (36.9%), Germany (33.7%), the United States (49.7%). For details, see SERI (2003a).
10. The share of male student enrolment was 12.4% in 2004.
11. The flow of students to Korea is small with approximately 12 000 international students reported by the end of 2003, just under 8% of the number of Koreans going abroad. However, the number of foreign students coming to Korea has increased annually by around 20% since 2001 (The Observatory on Borderless Higher Education: *www.obhe.ac.uk/cgi-bin/news/article.pl?id=310&mode=month*).
12. According to the OECD, Korea has the third largest absolute number of students (after China and India) studying abroad in the world, followed by Japan. The increasing number of Korean students going abroad for education at all levels indicates strong demand for quality international

education in Korea. Some 7 000 primary and secondary school students in Seoul went abroad to study between March 2005 and February 2006, an increase of 15% (Seoul Metropolitan Office of Education; *Donga Ilbo*, 11 May 2006). The financial implications are significant. According to the Korean International Trade Association, Koreans studying abroad spent USD 4.6 billion in 2002 on tuition fees and living expenses, while foreigners studying in South Korea spent only USD 20 million (The Observatory on Borderless Higher Education: *www.obhe.ac.uk/cgi-bin/news/article.pl?id=310&mode=month*).

13. For example, a new MOT programme of Waseda University (a top private university in Japan) operated in Singapore, and a joint master's programme between the Tokyo Institute of Technology and Tsinghua University.

14. See the UK Home Office Immigration and Nationality Directorate: *www.ind.homeoffice.gov.uk/lawandpolicy/immigrationrules/changecm6339*.

15. Currently 109 out of 241 regional universities are participating in the project (for a total of 123 project teams comprising 170 000 students). An estimated KRW 1.4 trillion (USD 1.4 billion) is to be invested over the period 2004-09.

16. *The New York Times*, October 5, 2005 (*www.nytimes.com/2005/10/05/technology/techspecial/05oconnell.html?ei=5088&en=4a368c49e8f30bd2&ex=1286164800&adxnnl=1&pagewanted=1&adxnnlx=1145786647-esM5EP2r7n9xFQQ6LSUikg*).

17. *The Korea Times*, November 21, 2005 (*www.asiamedia.ucla.edu/article.asp?parentid=33986*).

18. In operation from 2003, it supports the efforts of universities to achieve distinctive and outstanding education and provides information to society by holding forums, publishing collections of case studies, etc. Projects: FY2003: 80; FY2004: 58.

19. In operation from 2004, it supports outstanding efforts of universities to respond to recommendations of the various councils and policy issues with strong social demands. Projects: FY2004: 86.

20. In Japan, private universities and colleges (except for newly admitted, for-profit ones) are operated by non-profit legal entities called school corporations.

21. Korea is one of the countries that spend the most on tertiary education as a percentage of GDP (2.3%) among OECD countries (an average of 1.4% in 2004). However, around 79% of funding for tertiary education comes from private sources.

22. For instance, Yonsei, Korea, POSTECH, Sung Kyun Kwan Universities have more than 30% of the total higher education endowment market created mainly by corporations and alumni (MOEHRD, 2005; Ryu *et al.*, 2006, pp. 45-46).

23. In 2003 the supply of higher education already started to exceed the demand (MOEHRD, 2005; Ryu *et al.*, 2006, p. 43).

References

Amano, I. (1997), "Structural Changes in Japan's Higher Education System – From a Planning to a Market Model", *Higher Education*, Vol. 34(2), pp. 125-139.

Baek, Y. and R. Jones (2005), "Sustaining High Growth and Innovation: Reforming the R&D and Education Systems in Korea", OECD Working Paper No. 470, pp. 29-30.

Cabinet Office (Japan) (2006), *Atarashii Shoushika Taisaku ni Tsuite* ("A New Deal for Low Fertility"), 20 June (*www8.cao.go.jp/shoushi/taisaku.pdf*).

Central Council for Education (CCE) (2005a), *A Vision for the Future of Higher Education in Japan*, Tokyo.

Central Council for Education (CCE) (2005b), "Graduate School Education in the New Age: Towards Development of Internationally Attractive Graduate School Education" (Report).

Central Council for Education (CCE) (2006), "On Post 21st Century COE Programme" (Proposal), a document distributed at 55th meeting of university subdivision.

Choi, S.-K. *et al.* (2003), "A Study on the Reality and Volume of Private Tutoring Expenditure", Korean Educational Development Institute Research Paper No. CR 2003-19, Seoul (in Korean).

Collins, S. and B.P. Bosworth (1996), "Economic Growth in East Asia: Accumulation *versus* Assimilation", Brookings Papers on Economic Activity 2.

Council on Economic and Fiscal Policy (Japan) (2006), *Keizai Zaisei Unei to Kozo Kaikaku ni Kansuru Kihon Hoshin 2006* ("Basic Policy 2006 for Economic and Financial Operation and Structural Reform"), 7 July (*www.keizai-shimon.go.jp/cabinet/2006/decision0707.html*).

Federation of Korean Industries (2005), *Enterprises' Tasks to Activate Development of Overseas Resources*, FKI Research.

Henderson, G. (1968), *Korea: The Politics of the Vortex*, Harvard University Press, Cambridge, Mass., p. 89.

JICA (2003), *Second Study on International Cooperation for Population and Development New Insights from the Japanese Experience*, Japan International Cooperation Agency.

Kim, T. (2001), *Forming the Academic Profession in East Asia: A Comparative Analysis*, Routledge, New York and London.

Kim, D.S. *et al.* (2002), "Korea Development Institute (KDI) Report: The Analysis of the Factors of Korean Economic Growth", requited from Samsung Economic Research Institute (SERI) (2003) "Report on Human Capital and Growth Potential in Korea", November 2003, p. 16.

Korean Education Development Institute (KEDI) (2004), Report on the employment trends of university graduates, Seoul.

Korean Education Development Institute (KEDI) (2005), *Yearbook of Educational Statistics in Korea 2005*.

Korean Women's Development Institute (KWDI) (2005), "The Trends of Human Resource Development for Women Aged over 30s and Policy Recommendations in Korea" (Research Report 16), p. *iii*.

Ministry of Education, Culture, Sports, Science and Technology (Japan) (MEXT) (2004), *Survey on Learning Expenditure of Children*, Tokyo, Japan.

MEXT (2005), Higher Education Bureau, *Keiei Konnan na Gakko Hojin heno Taio Hoshin ni tsuite* ("Principle for Dealing with School Corporations Facing Management Difficulty"), *www.mext.go.jp/b_menu/houdou/17/05/05051901/all.pdf*.

MEXT (2006), *OECD Thematic Review of Tertiary Education: Country Background Report of Japan*.

Ministry of Education and Human Resource Development (MOEHRD) (2005), "Plans to induce M&A", Policy Document, 7 December, *www.moe.gov.kr*.

Ministry of Education and Human Resource Development (MOEHRD) (2006), Lifelong Learning Policy Division, *Press release*, 14 April.

National Science Foundation (2002), Division of Science Resources Statistics: Science and Engineering Indicators, *www.nsf.gov/statistics/seind93/chap2/doc/2c293.htm*).

National Statistical Office (NSO) (2006), *Social Indicators in Korea*, ISSN 1599-0907, Seoul (in Korean).

OECD (2002), *Education at a Glance: OECD Indicators 2002*, OECD Publishing, Paris.

OECD (2004), *Education at a Glance: OECD Indicators 2004*, OECD Publishing, Paris.

OECD (2007), *Education at a Glance: OECD Indicators 2007*, OECD Publishing, Paris.

Promotion and Mutual Aid Corporation for Private Schools of Japan (PMACPSJ) (2006), *Shiritsu Gakko no Keiei Kakushin to Keiei Konnan Hatan heno Taio* ("Coping with Management Innovation and Management Difficulty/Failure"), Interim Report, July.

Ryu, J.-S. *et al.* (2006), *Seven Strategies for University Reform*, Samsung Economic Research Institute, Seoul (published in Korean).

Samsung Economic Research Institute (SERI) (2003a), *Annual Report*.

Samsung Economic Research Institute (SERI) (2003b), "Research Report: Human Capital and Growth Potential", SERI, November.

Samsung Economic Research Institute (SERI) (2005), *Annual Report 2005*, pp. 15-16.

Science and Technology Policy Institute (STEPI), *Report 2003-21*.

Tachibanaki, T. (2005), *Gendai Josei no Rodo, Kekkon, Kosodate* ("Current Issues Surrounding Women at Work and in the Family: Proposals Going Beyond this Age of Decreasing Population"), Research Institute of Economy, Trade and Industry (RIETI), Minerva Press, Tokyo.

Tedesco, F.M. (1996), "Rites for the Unborn Dead: Abortion and Buddhism in Contemporary Korea", *Korea Journal*, Vol. 36, No. 2, pp. 61-74.

Trow, M. (2000), "From Mass Higher Education to Universal Access: the American Advantage", *Minerva* 37, Spring, pp. 1-26.

United Nations (2004), *World Population Prospects: The 2004 Revision.*

Yonezawa, A. (2003), "Making 'World-class Universities': Japan's Experiment", *Higher Education Management and Policy*, Vol. 5(2), pp. 9-23.

Yonezawa, A. and R. Kosugi (2006), *Education, Training, and Human Resources: Meeting Skill Requirements in Japan as Knowledge Economy – Assessment and Lessons*, edited by L. Meissner, World Bank Institute, Washington DC.

ISBN 978-92-64-04065-6
Higher Education to 2030
Volume 1: Demography

Chapter 8

Adapting Higher Education to the Needs of Disabled Students: Developments, Challenges and Prospects

by

Serge Ebersold*

This chapter seeks to identify the transformations and types of adaptation which have favoured the enrolment of disabled students and helped higher education open up to diversity. To this end, it will make use of research conducted in 2001 and 2002 by the OECD into the situation of disabled students in higher education in Ontario (Canada), the United Kingdom, France, Germany and Switzerland.

* OECD Directorate for Education.

It may seem surprising to be concerned about the access of disabled students to higher education given the apparent paradox between the terms higher education and disability. Indeed, little work has been done on this topic. Such work as does exist dates from the late 1980s and reflects individual concerns (Hurst, 1998; van Acker, 1999) or those of international bodies (OECD, 1997; European Commission, 1996). There are many possible explanations for this relative lack of interest: public policies had first to be restructured around measures to combat discrimination before the inequalities in this field were realised (OECD, 1999); it is only over the last two decades that steps have been taken to end the marginalisation of disabled pupils in the school system, an important barrier to access to higher education; since higher education is optional and, historically, concerns elite sections of the population in particular, the presence of disabled students for long seemed exceptional or even "incongruous". Lastly, the independence of higher education institutions often means that access to higher education is subject to the strategies adopted by these institutions, making it uncertain and difficult to measure (OECD, 2003). This relative lack of interest must not, however, conceal a reality which is set to grow over the coming decades.

The issue of access to higher education by disabled students can no longer be ignored in view of the significant rise in the number of students with disabilities or special needs in many OECD countries. In the United Kingdom, 31 395 students with a known disability were enrolled in higher education in 1994-95, representing 2% of the student population. In 2006-07, this number had grown to 57 750, or 6.5% of the student population. In France, 695 students with disabilities were registered in 1981, a number which grew to 8 763, or 0.4% of the population in the year 2006-07. In Sweden, the number of students with disabilities grew by 125% between 1993 and 1999, and in Ontario, their number increased more than fourfold during the 1980s. The reason for this increase is no doubt the gradual spread over the last two decades of inclusive policies facilitating access for pupils with special needs or disabilities to the normal school system (OECD, 1999). But beyond this aspect, the increase in the number of disabled students reflects a move towards a huge diversification of student profiles: the democratisation of higher education has helped to ensure a growing, though still minority, enrolment of students from modest backgrounds (Selz and Vallet, 2006), less comfortable with educational and occupational choices, at higher risk of failure and more inclined to give up in case of failure (Galland and Rouault, 1996). The internationalisation of trade and career paths has increased the proportion of foreigners in higher educational institutions: in OECD countries, the number of foreign students has grown on average by 8.3% a year since 1998 (OECD, 2005 and 2007). The spread of vocational training and lifelong learning has also increased the number of older students returning to higher education to follow courses based on their professional activity or a professional activity compatible with their existing qualifications: in the United States, between 1970 and 2000, the most rapid increase in enrolment was among part-time students aged over 30 (Douglass, 2004).

Thus, the increase in the number of disabled students in higher education cannot be attributed to inclusive education policies alone. It reflects the trend towards a diversification of student profiles which in turn has an influence on expectations *vis-à-vis* the university system in terms of education, support and access to employment. The increase in the number of disabled students thus goes hand-in-hand with a redefinition of the roles and tasks of higher education which of course has its origin in the role played by education and training in the development of human capital as well as in economic development (OECD, 2005), and in the preference expressed by industry for graduate labour. A final reason is the principle of equity. We expect higher education to reduce the economic and social impact of the many sources of inequality by being more attentive to the needs and special characteristics of students, by being concerned for their future.

To show no interest in the mechanisms at work in higher education institutions would amount to forgetting that access to education (like access to health care) determines individual well-being and the opportunities for personal development and fulfilment. To exclude persons with disabilities from higher education would be to ignore their chances of international exchanges or of combining courses with a professional activity or traineeship. Students with disabilities would be made more fragile; the tendency for those who do not fit the mould to become socially invisible would be reinforced, as would discrimination. Any such lack of interest would also mask certain challenges to higher education imposed by the diversification of career paths generated by the Bologna process, the generalisation of lifelong learning, and the strengthening of links with the business world. It would also conceal certain conditions for its adaptation to the challenges and issues facing a society which has built its wealth and dynamism on the bedrock of individual participation.

This article will endeavour to identify the transformations and types of adaptation which have favoured the enrolment of disabled students and helped higher education open up to diversity. To this end, it will make use of the most available data and build on a research conducted in 2001 and 2002 by the OECD into the situation of disabled students in higher education in Ontario (Canada), the United Kingdom, France, Germany and Switzerland (OECD, 2003). It will also use elements of information taken from research into the transition opportunities for disabled persons after higher education, including in particular information from studies in the United States.[1]

8.1. Becoming a learning organisation by opening up to disability

Opening up to diversity in order to become receptive to disability

Whatever the country and whatever the institution, the way in which disabled students are admitted depends on the attitude of the institution to diversity. There are different ways of adapting to handicaps depending on how disability is perceived. A defectological approach focusing on the impairment and its implications, makes it more difficult for disabled students to enrol than an ecological approach, which concentrates on the capacity of institutions to be accessible and to adapt to the rhythms and needs of those concerned. The chances of French or Swiss students with disabilities attending higher education are thus lower than those of disabled students following the same curriculum in other countries. In 2006, students with disabilities represented some 0.4% of the student population in France, whereas they accounted for 8.9% in Ontario. In 2003, in the United Kingdom, 5.3% of British students enrolled in the first year of higher education declared a disability. Unlike France (at least until the Act of 11 February 2005), the other countries studied think of "disability" first and foremost as a need to be met in relation to the curriculum chosen by the student rather than as a special condition caused by a pathology. Thus in Ontario, an individual requiring no special support for his/her studies is not registered as a "disabled" student even if he has a disability. However, a student who, in light of tests conducted by approved psychologists, shows signs of disturbance or has special characteristics meaning that he/she has learning difficulties may be listed as a "special needs" student. This approach is different from that used in France where disability is described in terms of the degree of incapacity caused by the disability as certified by an advisory board (COTOREP):[2] even though the situation can vary widely across universities, the special arrangements and technical and/or human support provided for in law depend on the degree of handicap as determined, a priori, by the incapacity rate and condition of the disabled worker recognised by the COTOREP rather than being related to the design of a curriculum or the practical implementation of a career path.

This leads to radical differences in the level of receptivity to diversity. In countries where disability is perceived in terms of accessibility to institutions, universities and colleges are legally obliged to take the special needs of disabled persons into account in their building plans and to provide, in conditions that are more or less clearly defined, human, technical and financial resources to ensure their accessibility from the physical, psychological and pedagogical viewpoints. In Sweden, universities must allocate 0.15% of the funds they receive from the State to support disabled students studying for their first degree (Danermark, 1998). In the United States, the Americans with Disabilities Act (ADA) requires universities and colleges to make the necessary arrangements to ensure their accessibility at no cost to the student (Gagliano, 1998). The Special Needs and Disability Act promulgated in the United Kingdom in 2001 makes universities and colleges liable for any discrimination suffered by disabled students. Far from being an exception, openness to diversity appears in these circumstances as one of the aspects on which the legitimacy of higher education institutions is based: in some countries, they are asked to provide an annual accessibility plan detailing measures taken and conditions of implementation; in others, as is the case in Ontario (Canada), special integrated services exist in which disabled students and professionals identify the needs and the accommodations and human, technical and pedagogical support required and, in some cases, prepare a document detailing these accommodations and support as well as the responsibilities of the different stakeholders, whether students, teachers or administrators. Diversity is here reflecting the commitment of the university community to its environment and its desire to contribute to the development of all by involving everyone concerned.

As for the defectological approach, it tends to place the equality of opportunity to which disabled students can claim in the context of their "educability", *i.e.* their ability to satisfy the requirements of the university. Specific needs in terms of learning are concealed by the incapacities suggested by the fact of having another and different type of body. Before involving the mobilisation of the university community, access to higher education depends on the motivation of the disabled person and his/her capacity to adapt to the educational and social environment. In some countries, such as Switzerland, institutions have no accessibility obligations; in others, like France, implementation of the legal obligation on institutions to ensure accessibility depends largely on the initiative and dynamism of the persons in charge and on the ability of students to overcome the various obstacles they may encounter. Instead of being assessed by experts in transition and guidance, needs may be assessed by doctors, social workers and administrative staff specialised in assisting students in difficulty. Assistance and support are aimed at resolving problems and difficulties rather than concentrating on the implementation of educational pathways. They may in certain cases take the form of psychological support, medical consultations on request, financial support or assistance given as and when the need arises. Opening up to diversity is an exception made for exceptional beings and curriculum adaptation depends on individuals' goodwill. Openness to diversity is not seen as a matter of rights and responsibility that has to be assumed by higher education institutions, but as a constraint which can hinder the smooth functioning of the institution or the regular implementation of the curriculum.

Disabled student enrolment reflects the relationship to diversity countries and, more particularly, higher education institutions may have. Accessibility to higher education is easier if policy makers understand diversity as a source of economic and social enrichment, and the development of human capital as a condition of the development of a knowledge-based society. This standpoint does not consider disability as a type of deviance but as a factor of diversity amongst others which must be taken into account to foster economic and social well-being towards social cohesion by making HEI's physically, socially and pedagogically accessible. Enrolling disabled students is for example more or less an integral part of the tasks of British universities created after 1992 in order to increase participation in higher education and some universities, like that of Leeds, offer classes to young people on assistance schemes in order to fight against exclusion. Similarly, awareness campaigns promoting access to higher education for young people on assistance schemes are being developed in French universities as part of the fight against exclusion. Those numerous universities which conduct awareness campaigns targeting the university community to remove the prejudices relating to disabled persons and highlight the diversity of students profile and needs, come to see all students as having special needs.

Openness to disability, a source of effectiveness

The attitude to diversity also reflects an education system's predisposition to ensure that students develop their full potential as a guarantor of social and professional integration. Thus, disabled students have widely varying profiles across countries. In 1996 and 1997, the disabled students accepted for enrolment in post-secondary education in the United States were made up of students with learning difficulties (45.7%), students with a motor or orthopaedic deficiency (13.9%), students with a sensory deficiency (9.9%) and students with health problems (11.5%) or psychological problems (7.7%). In Ontario (Canada), in 2000-01, nearly half such students had "learning difficulties" (47.9%) while a fifth (21.7%) suffered from a chronic organic illness. Persons with a sensory (6.3%) or motor (8.7%) deficiency accounted for only 15% of disabled students. In the United Kingdom, dyslexic students (43%) and those with pathologies such as diabetes, asthma or epilepsy (16%) accounted for nearly two-thirds (59%) of disabled students registered in 2006 while students with motor or sensory deficiency accounted for only 11.8% of disabled students. Such a distribution is radically different from that seen in France or Germany. In France, 44.5% of disabled students enrolled in higher education presented a sensory or motor deficiency in 2006. There are many fewer persons with health (20.6%) and psychological (11.2%) problems than in the United Kingdom or Ontario. Students with learning difficulties are not counted as "disabled" or if they are, they are classified under the heading "miscellaneous". In Germany, 73.5% of the students identified as disabled in 2006 had a chronic illness such as an allergy or lung condition. Of these, 59.5% suffered from an allergy or a respiratory problem and 16% had a skin problem. Students with some sort of impairment represented only 29% of disabled students, and those having a psychological problem, 11%.

A reflection of the attitude to diversity of education systems, this disparity also illustrates (despite all the caution the interpretation of these data requires) the degree to which higher education institutions think about how to promote student success. For example, the financial incentives and methodological support given by the United Kingdom government have no doubt helped institutions to include more openly as one of their concerns, the future of students who previously had not only had difficulty accessing higher education but who were also confronted with particularly damaging failure from a social and professional point of view. The increase in disabled student enrolment in the United Kingdom can thus be explained by the development of procedures for identifying special and/or specific needs. This has helped reduce the proportion of students *suspected* of having a disability (and for whom learning difficulties are possible), which fell from 33.9% of enrolled students in 1995 to 2.2% in 2004. The increased consideration now given to these issues has also led institutions to take account in their educational strategies of persons with special learning difficulties such as dyslexia, dyscalculia, limited attention span and language problems, persons who as a result were for a long time at an educational, social and professional disadvantage. The proportion of students with dyslexia all but trebled between 1994 and 2006: representing only 15.5% of clearly identified disabled students in 1994, more than ten years later they accounted for almost half (43%).[3] Lastly, it may be observed that in the United Kingdom, once again, the success rate of disabled students increased by leaps and bounds in the space of ten years: the proportion of disabled students attaining a first class honours degree grew from 5.4% in 1994 to 9.2% in 2003; 35.6% achieved upper second class honours in 1994, the figure for 2003-04 being 43.4%.[4] At the same time, the proportion of students obtaining lower second class honours fell from 35.6% to 33.7% over the same period, and that of disabled students getting third class honours, fell from 12.6% to 7.6%. The proportion of postgraduate students has increased over the last ten years: in 1994, they represented only 10.5%, a figure which reached 17.2% in 2003-04.

This reflexivity requirement applies in most OECD member countries as is shown by the growing importance given to the success rate and future of students. It can, however, take different forms depending on the underlying concept. Thus, in France, the survey showed that the reflexivity requirement tends to be based on a relatively limited concept of accessibility: that students, especially those with reduced mobility, should be able to access institutions as easily as possible and move around them and find their way as freely as possible; technical and human resources to support them pedagogically should also be provided, giving them the same chance of passing exams and allowing them, possibly, to benefit from certain arrangements in the organisation of their studies. The idea, no doubt, is to give disabled students the same opportunities as the others. This equality of opportunity, however, sometimes seems to apply less to the various aspects involved in ensuring student success than to the multiple factors involved in compensating for a disadvantage resulting from a handicap: while successful schooling for pupils with a disability is a clearly affirmed objective in texts relating to elementary and secondary education,[5] higher education institutions have the sole obligation to make themselves accessible to disabled students by accepting them for enrolment and organising their courses having regard to the student's situation. Thus, the assessment of needs only very rarely determines the definition and implementation of support measures: according to the higher education accessibility guide, in 2006, only 7% of French universities specifying the support and arrangements which can be envisaged for disabled students expressly indicate that the definition and implementation of support measures are subject to a formal assessment of student needs.

The success opportunities and future of disabled students are only very vaguely and partially taken into account as is suggested for example by the absence, in certain countries, of data on degrees obtained by disabled students and their social and professional inclusion. As a result, the diversification of practices relates to the disability alone, neglecting the multiple factors involved in determining student success (competence of staff, effectiveness of support, quality of teaching, etc.) and referring to the educational strategies adopted. Matching the organisation of courses, teaching styles and forms of support with the diversity of student needs and expectations becomes difficult and may seem impossibly complex. This may call into question the access of persons with a handicap to higher education as is suggested, amongst other things, by the decreasing proportion of disabled students having an impairment compared with the increasing proportion of students with health or psychological problems, categories which were not registered as such before the end of the 1990s in France.[6] This makes it more difficult to access the upper and graduate levels of higher education: disabled students are proportionally fewer in number to succeed at these levels than the average student, in particular when their problem is essentially psychological, a health problem or temporary incapacity (Ebersold, 2007).

The presence of disabled students does not only show the attitude of higher education institutions to diversity. It also reflects a certain tendency not to define the quality of education solely in terms of the learning and knowledge transmitted to students, but to include also their future prospects as regards not only obtaining a degree and finding work but, more generally, their integration into society. Accessibility stops being defined in physical terms only, and includes pedagogical, psychological and social aspects. From this perspective, the requirement for individualisation and diversification no longer relates first and foremost to a specific characteristic but becomes an essential vector for the motivation and success of all students. The quality of education thus becomes linked to the quality of support offered to students so that they can learn how to learn, how to make progress having regard to their expectations and needs, and how to acquire the knowledge and skills required for their social and professional integration. The curriculum of students is thus rooted in a project dynamic based on active and interactive pedagogical methods which imply active and reactive learning. The institution becomes a learning organisation finding the sources for its development within itself. Thus, certain establishments in Ontario (Canada) regularly check with their students about their degree of pedagogical, physical and psychological accessibility. They consider this to be a factor which should be taken into account in order to match the organisation of education as closely as possible with the expectations and pace of students, to make efficiency gains and optimise the chances of success for all students. This is why post-secondary institutions in the United States which welcome disabled students are more inclined than those which do not to have structured their practice around formal transition plans (NCES, 1999).

Openness to disability, a source of dynamism and innovation

Disability is not only an indicator, it is also a source of innovation. Implementing a personalised plan often depends on the capacity of those involved to provide coherent and effective support to the students' learning process. It therefore requires the joint mobilisation of all stakeholders concerned, at one level or another, by the future of the student. It thus modifies the relationship between institutions and their environment.

The quality of the support and pathways proposed to students will be all the better if close links are maintained with secondary education institutions (OECD, 2003). Through such links, students are informed about their choice opportunities and the consequences thereof. Links of this type also provide a continuity which may mean that students do not have to make a claim based on their problem or special needs in order to benefit from support, and they also make it possible to identify sufficiently in advance the resources and skills needed and the conditions for employing them. The level of accessibility of premises depends to a large extent on the possibilities offered to disabled students to move around and gain access to the buildings. Thus for example, in Grenoble (France), certain institutions make a point of anticipating accessibility at municipal level and of working in close collaboration with local authorities so that public transport is accessible, recreational premises enabling students to integrate into local life are accessible, etc. Others HEIs work in close collaboration with the different stakeholders concerned or who might be concerned to consider the best accessibility possible, and also to prepare information documents (CDs, videos, etc.) and resources destined for all those living in the commune and not only for students. In some cases, measures may be introduced in liaison with associations representing disabled persons and their families, or with bodies specialised in monitoring students and providing them with the technical and human support necessary. Thus in the United States, post-secondary education institutions enrolling disabled students work more closely with vocational rehabilitation bodies than those which do not (NCES, 1999). Lastly, the success of a curriculum depends often on access to employment or traineeships, and certain institutions have therefore established and/or strengthened links with employers.

The admission of disabled students encourages higher education institutions to look at their activity in the context of their environment and to open up to the latter by creating links among the different local stakeholders, whether economic, political, associative, etc. They thus become resource centres for students (disabled or not) and for the different local stakeholders concerned by the future of students. A space for learning and research, institutions also become spaces for innovation, and their activity contributes to the development of the whole community: for example, the University of Toronto works with the business world, associations and parents to ensure the availability of computer tools; similarly, the University of Grenoble takes measures to increase awareness of the fact that its initiatives can affect the city as a whole and not just the university community. In the United Kingdom, the Higher Education Funding Council for England (HEFCE) has encouraged universities to work closely with schools, further education colleges, employers and regional associations (Newby, 2003).

The implementation of personalised plans also helps modify the relationships which the different categories of stakeholders may have amongst themselves. By focusing on the quality of practices and support, those involved in supporting disabled students are encouraged to work towards common objectives. It is not rare for teachers, those in charge of admitting students and those responsible for following the progress of disabled students to try to work in close collaboration in order to elaborate information documents, to define how to implement the supports and accommodations required by disabled students. Just as often, the traditional divisions between academic work and administrative or technical work, between teaching and non-teaching staff, may be broken down. In addition to welcoming disabled students, those working in an integrated service for disabled persons at university level often also make arrangements for note-taking, identify sources of funding which students may use to pursue their studies, and possibly take the necessary steps to adapt timetables, workstations and exams as required. Teaching staff may be involved in the identification of needs: in Ontario, for example, they are invited to point out any difficulties students might be experiencing to the support/contact service for disabled students, which service then checks whether the difficulties arise from problems requiring particular support measures. By breaking down the barriers between academic and non-academic work, admission of disabled students leads the different stakeholders to discuss what measures should be taken at the level of the institution rather than taking a formal and legalistic approach. University activity is thus rendered more complex and, as suggested notably by Pickersgill (Pickersgill *et al.*, 1998), this means that we tend no longer, as we did in the past, to think of university activity in terms solely of research and teaching by the academic staff. It means that academic work has to be seen in the context of the large number of activities engaging institutions with their environment and the various aspects requiring joint mobilisation of all staff to work towards the success and future of the students.

Lastly, the implementation of personalised projects requires a greater variety of pedagogical means and resources, making use, notably, of the possibilities offered by new technologies. In this respect, distance learning is a source of accessibility which is particularly suited to disabled students: it allows them to follow their courses from home, hospital bed or rehabilitation centre, giving them access opportunities which did not previously exist or were very rare. It is also an essential pedagogical tool for the continuity of the education of such students and their success, especially when the evolution of certain pathologies (mental illness, for example) may require them to interrupt temporarily their curriculum or to spread it out over time. It also constitutes a social anchor enabling disabled students to pursue their education from their region of residence and no longer be deprived of the support of family and friends, thus helping them overcome the many obstacles they encounter on a daily basis (French *et al.*, 2000).

No doubt, in some countries, taking account of diversity can cost higher education institutions up to 35% more than the normal financing required per student (Newby, 2003). However, these extra costs aside, disability seems to be a vector for dynamism and a source of innovation. The presence of disabled students makes higher education institutions redefine themselves as learning organisations, the degree of openness and accessibility of which helps all students to succeed, be they disabled or not; it invites them to think about how to favour the continuity of courses, whether through diversifying learning methods, ways of dividing up tasks and distributing roles among the different categories of personnel or the different kinds of resources which could be mobilised. All these elements suggest that inclusive education policies do not only encourage disabled students to enrol in growing numbers. By placing diversity at the heart of an institution's concerns, such policies encourage awareness of the challenges imposed by a knowledge-based society which makes the development of human capital a vector of economic and social well-being for all. In so doing, they help modernise higher education.

Combining equity, effectiveness and innovation to consider the diversity of profiles and pathways

The receptivity of higher education to disabled students depends on the adoption by higher education institutions of an ecological approach of disability within comprehensive strategies linking in a coherent manner dimensions related to equity, effectiveness and innovation. The absence of any comprehensive approach tends to reduce the admission of disabled students to a philanthropic act in favour of students in need rather than as an integral part of the institution's mission. It tends to reduce equity to access, neglecting the conditions for student success and the underlying dynamic innovation. The quality and coherence of the admission process as well as the support given to vulnerable students tend to depend on the goodwill of stakeholders, the quality of their interpersonal relationship instead of resulting from a collective dynamic involving students, teachers, researchers, administrative staff, etc. Openness to difference may become a constant struggle which, although a potential source of success, can also be exhausting for the different stakeholders involved.

Institutions focusing only on efficiency restrict somewhat their degree of openness. With such an approach, equity tends to be linked to results alone, and openness to diversity with a concern for selectivity at the expense of the social issues bound up with higher education. This concern for selectivity tends to relate the quality of the curriculum to the talents of the student (whether disabled or not) independently of any support and resources which could be mobilised to enhance his/her chances of success, of the links which could be forged with secondary education. A student's success depends on his/her ability to obtain information, to identify his/her needs and to mobilise the support and resources necessary. His/her professional and social inclusion depend to a large extent on the social resources he/she will have at his/her disposal in order to maintain links with the world of work and develop the conditions for his/her integration. When it exists, support is usually the responsibility of the administrative staff, and provision often depends on their sense of commitment and conviction. The quality of support and the coherence of courses have to overcome the statutory differences separating administrative and teaching staff, and this can make them more uncertain and fragile depending on the power relationships within the institution and the types of support the student can mobilise himself/herself. The admission of vulnerable students, while not impossible, is exceptional in nature since openness to difference depends in many ways on the capacity of those involved to make it possible and acceptable by transforming their resource environment. Access to higher education can then become easier for those with resources (social capital, cultural capital, etc.) at their disposal, allowing them to legitimise and protect themselves at the expense of those who are not in this position (Ebersold, 2005; Nakhili, 2005; Bourdieu, 1979).[7]

Finally, strategies based primarily on managerial considerations also make institutions less receptive to diversity. Separating management from effectiveness and equity tends to promote procedural approach of innovation and to judge the quality of courses by means of assessment procedures, the implementation of projects and transition plans, project management techniques and consultation procedures independently of their impact in terms of the motivation, participation and success of students. This procedural approach tends to view dynamism and innovation in terms of compliance with the technical and administrative aspects underlying the procedures, detrimental to the factors which determine students' success, their social and professional inclusion as well as their well-being. There is a tendency to reduce procedures for determining and evaluating needs to normative tools used to identify students with problems rather than as vectors for dynamism and support for successful educational paths. The admission and quality of support is correlated with the ability of students to know their needs and to contribute actively in defining support and assistance, as well as monitoring their quality. In some universities, for example, students are asked, before any enrolment, to specify clearly their university and professional objectives, to reveal any special characteristics, describe the resources at their disposal and the support they enjoyed in secondary education and those they may now require. Students whose disability and/or particularity are not visible may hesitate to state their needs (and thereby their rights), fearing a risk of being stigmatised and disadvantaged for no purpose. Such a procedural approach favours a technical approach of accessibility which may lead higher education institutions to adopt a minimalist approach, concentrating on the physical accessibility of premises at the expense of all the other aspects promoting their dynamism and the success of students. Any special arrangements may be seen as unreasonable, with regard to the cost involved, but also to the low number of students likely to benefit from them. While it is not formally discouraged, access to higher education can constitute a risk for students since the real conditions for providing support may be uncertain and courses may be discontinuous or become excessively complex. Such discontinuity exposes students to disturbances of rhythm which can lead to failure and vulnerability.

Combining in a coherent fashion the aspects relating to equity, effectiveness and innovation within comprehensive strategies thus seems to be another factor for adapting higher education to disability. Furthermore, the formal consideration of such aspects in the plans of institutions incites them to better measure the impact of openness to diversity in terms of the success of students, whether disabled or not.

8.2. Openness to diversity subject to various models of inclusion

The reforms carried out in recent years by several OECD countries reflect their growing interest in diversity issues and their desire to find constructive solutions. The reform of higher education undertaken in the United Kingdom is intended, amongst other things, to make higher education accessible to all those eligible for it by offering them curriculum and courses taking account of their expectations, and offering qualifications recognised on the labour market.[8] The Equal Rights and Opportunities, Participation and Citizenship of Disabled Persons Act of 11 February 2005, promulgated in France, postulates an ecological concept of disability. Its purpose is to facilitate the access of disabled students to higher education and promote their success by asking institutions to make the accommodations required for a personalised education plan specifying the pedagogical, educational, social, medical and paramedical measures needed.[9] For some years now, the United States has been conducting longitudinal studies of the evolution of disabled persons' profiles, endeavouring to identify the conditions needed for the access and success of disabled students in post-secondary education (Wagner *et al.*, 2005b).

Although widespread, this approach is not adopted everywhere, and the ways in which higher education might adapt to disability in the future may be based on different concepts and rationales. Three future approaches may thus be identified depending on the concept underlying inclusion, the dominant representations of disability and disabled persons, modes of financing, the tools and resources mobilised by policy makers, and the roles and missions of higher education. Naturally, these rationales are model ideals. They are in no way intended to reflect or reduce the complexity of the real situations, since institutions may use aspects belonging to one or other of these rationales depending on the issues and challenges facing them. They highlight a number of general principles likely to influence, in the future, the inclusion of disabled persons and their access to higher education. While they may be observed in some countries more than others, it is nevertheless difficult to match a given country to a given approach. Given the autonomy enjoyed by higher education institutions, they may make strategic choices based on different rationales: it is not impossible to imagine that the rationale specified by a country with regard to its legislative framework and modes of financing is modified by strategic choices made by higher education institutions to adapt themselves to the changing profiles of students and to enhance their attractiveness.

An educational model of inclusion

The first form of adaptation reflects an educational approach of inclusion wishing to enhance the opportunities for participation of the most disadvantaged and/or vulnerable. It links the presence of disabled students in higher education to the requirements imposed by the knowledge-based society. Under this approach, inclusion must contribute to the development of the human capital of all members of society (even the disabled) and allow everyone to contribute actively to the development of society. Diversity is seen as a source of collective enrichment and a vector of excellence, and it is promoted at all levels of education. An ecological approach of disability predominates which relates personal handicaps essentially to the impossibility for the individuals concerned to fulfil themselves and to participate to the development of society: rather than being the consequence of impairment, disability arises from the lack of accessibility of public places, discriminatory attitudes and institutions incapable of adapting to the needs, rhythms and expectations of individuals (UNESCO, 1997). In other words, disability and the compensation systems which may be linked thereto, depend on the ability of institutions to adapt their curriculum, on the methods of pedagogical organisation used and on the existence of human and material resources to stimulate the students. Far from being defined only in terms of persons with a handicap, disability concern all those individuals who, in one form of another, require support in order to complete their courses and to be socially and professionally included.

The legislative framework is used to develop the accountability of the stakeholders involved, whether disabled persons, institutions or those working in them. Anti-discrimination legislation encourages institutions to assume social responsibility with regard to their environment and the persons they admit, and makes them legally liable for any discriminatory act or practice which restricts the access of disabled persons or burdens their chances of success with debt. In addition to this type of development of accountability, another may arise from the personalisation of forms of financing: the financial means allocated to students are not so much referred to the impairment but to the resources required for the completion of a plan identified by an assessment of needs and expectations and to active student participation throughout the process; the financing allocated to institutions focuses on a wider concept of accessibility, including physical aspects as well as pedagogical and social ones. To this end, institutions must make their policy with regard to disability explicit, specify the objectives pursued to facilitate the enrolment of disabled students, and define the conditions required for implementation. Institutions can also benefit from funding to make themselves technically and pedagogically accessible, conduct training programmes for the university community and open up to their environment. Institutions which are not able to meet physical accessibility requirements are invited to solve the problem through the use of new technologies, pedagogical alternatives and the mobilisation of human and/or technical support.

This rationale requires also a statistical tool providing precise details of the profile of disabled students, their needs, expectations, success and, more generally, their situation. This statistical tool identifies the conditions of access of the persons concerned to their rights and the possibilities of social and professional inclusion offered to them, and thus provides information about the capacity of educational systems to be equitable and effective. It also gives the public and private stakeholders the information needed to formulate and implement public policies in favour of the practical application of individual rights, the development of human capital and economic and social dynamism. Lastly, this statistical device provides institutions with the tools needed to guide the processes and changes having regard both to the needs and expectations of students and to environmental obligations as well as specific local characteristics.

The coherence of this approach can be found lastly in the social involvement of institutions *vis-à-vis* students and the territories in which they are located, and in the social responsibility they accept. Institutions are invited not to think of their attractiveness in economic and managerial terms alone, but to consider quality as a source of success and, thus, of protection for all students: an indicator of an institution's effectiveness, the quality of teaching and support also demonstrates its ability to offer equal opportunities from the personal, professional and social viewpoints, to all students, whether disabled or not; beyond the economic aspects, an institution being anchored in the local community creates links with the local stakeholders who are vital for the continuity of the students' pathways and their professional and social inclusion. Using new technologies is seen as an important vector for development and openness to diversity. Over and above the dynamics involved in and around admission procedures, a student's success is linked to his/her integration into the university community: institution projects include campaigns to raise awareness about disability, arrangements for assistance and support by peers capable of mobilising all students around the question of diversity, training for teachers and administrative personnel in how to deal with the diversification of profiles and pathways.

This rationale considers inclusion as a vector for social justice enabling all citizens to participate actively in the development of society. By focusing on educational needs instead of any categorical approach, it helps identify and take into consideration difficulties ignored in the past. It opens the door of higher education to populations who had until then been excluded: in the United Kingdom, for example, the proportion of students with dyslexia or learning difficulties applying for places in higher education increased from 16.2% of disabled students in 1994 to 42.9% in 2006.[10] By encouraging institutions to diversify their practices and focus on student success, this rationale leads certainly to increased numbers of disabled students, and of others. Disabled students could, depending on needs arising from the disability, be admitted to different forms of courses and education, and be enrolled either in institutions offering long courses or in ones offering shorter and/or more professional oriented ones (Wagner, 2005a; Dyson *et al.*, 2004).

This approach also includes some risks. It can, for instance, result in openness to diversity focussing on learning difficulties rather than physical ones. Persons with a motor or sensory deficiency, for example, could continue to have problems accessing higher education if institutions reduce the question of accessibility to its pedagogical dimension to the detriment of its physical and technical aspects. As happened in the first half of the 20th century for primary education (Ebersold, 1992), the openness of higher education to disability could give priority to conditions originating in the distance separating students from the institution's educational standards to the detriment of persons whose condition originates in an impairment that may sometimes require more varied and numerous types of support. Openness to diversity risks being only partial since openness to the difference resulting from an impairment would remain restricted.

A socio-educational model of inclusion

The adaptation of higher education can also take the form of a socio-educational approach to inclusion. This approach looks at inclusion in terms of economic and social costs for society of educating disabled persons within a specialised environment. Unlike the previous one, this rationale is based on a within-person approach of disability, linking the difficulties encountered by disabled persons to the incapacities inherent in the disability or to learning difficulties. Before being considered in terms of the support needed, the disability is looked at in terms of individual impossibilities and difficulties in satisfying the requirements of the education system. Diversity continues to be a synonym of difficulties and does not appear as an essential issue for society in terms of economic and social development. Thus, while not impossible or discouraged, the enrolment of disabled students in higher education is supported only in terms of access, the success of students being considered, in a certain fashion, as their business.

Thus, the public authorities and higher education institutions work much less closely together. The legislation is aimed at encouraging institutions to be more accessible physically rather than inciting them to see diversity as a challenge. Anti-discrimination legislation does not oblige schools and universities to enrol disabled pupils or students, and if they do so, their responsibility is not directly engaged. Financing is essentially allocated to a specialised sector. The financial, technical and human support provided for students is intended first and foremost to compensate for an incapacity. This latter having already been identified independently of needs and their evolution, support is not personalised. When given, resources allocated to institutions are almost exclusively in response to requests from students and institutions. The statistical device on which inclusion is based is designed less to enable stakeholders to guide processes as to provide information on the profiles of disabled students with regard to their difficulties, impairments, administrative situations, etc.

This means that the admission and guidance of disabled students tend to be delegated to the social and/or medical services that are responsible for checking the eligibility of the students and gathering together, on a case-by-case basis and after negotiations with the stakeholders, the conditions necessary to enable the student to pursue his/her education. The student's success depends often on the ingenuity and inventiveness shown by university staff, the persons concerned, their families and, in some cases, associations of disabled persons. They are also responsible for adapting examination conditions, finding among the students (or their families) persons willing to assist the student (translation into sign language, note-taking, accompaniment during breaks), and finding the resources and means needed to mobilise the technical support required. Planning the future and success of the students and guiding the processes which determine these become particularly complex and uncertain; the student's curriculum can resemble an out-of-control adventure and his/her success may seem to be due to hazard and chance rather than the result of high-quality teaching and support.

Conversely to the previous rationale, the socio-educational approach shows only a very limited openness of higher education to disability. This type of adaptation to disability reflects a perception of diversity rooted in a problem-solving approach rather than being based on innovation. The presence of disabled students is seen as a constraint: the need to take account of the health problems of some students if they are to be able to pursue their education. This type of approach tends to give priority to those students with chronic problems rather than those with cognitive difficulties or an impairment as can be observed in some countries. It is true that little encouragement is given by the modes of financing: these, based on the compensation of an incapacity, linked to the existence of difficulties, can lead universities to perceive enrolling disabled students as a risk to their attractiveness and dynamism, and as potentially penalising (Danermark, 1998). Equally, the lack of training and absence of support at institutional level can mean that those responsible for admitting and providing assistance to disabled students feel they have insufficient resources to cope with the huge and complex tasks confronting them.

Lastly, this socio-educational approach is no doubt discouraging also for those concerned: the lack of information, the relative lack of support, and the many interruptions they experience when applying for higher education or in the course of their curriculum all appear as ordeals highlighting their disability. The presence of disabled students in higher education remains a paradox and their admission to it tends to seem impossible and/or unrealistic to all concerned: the making of institutions pedagogically, physically and socially accessible may then be seen directly in terms of cost which may always seem unreasonable given the number of students likely to benefit. The socio-educational approach would thus doubtless help to exclude most persons with health problems from higher education (whether long-term illness, cognitive problems or a disability) and to reinforce their social and professional marginalisation. The openness to diversity and disability which can be observed in most OECD countries could as a result be gradually called into question. Mainstream education may seem just as incapable as education in special schools, of reducing the costs caused by disability and giving the persons concerned and their families opportunities for social and professional inclusion which respect to their special needs as well as their dignity, guaranteeing their economic and social well-being.

A socio-economic model of inclusion

A third, more socio-economic, approach is also possible. This places the legitimacy of inclusive education in the satisfaction felt by disabled students in accessing training and education suited to their needs. Diversity is seen as a vector for economic and social dynamism for institutions, which may view this as a source of legitimacy and a vector for economic viability. The ecological approach of disability underlying this rationale sees disability first and foremost as a specific need and the difficulties of disabled persons as the inability of institutions to meet this need effectively. Defined in this way, a disabled person is anyone coming up against the ineffectiveness of institutions and thus finding himself/herself prevented in one way or another from participating actively in the economic development of society.

Under this approach, the responsibility of stakeholders *vis-à-vis* disabled persons is anchored in the use of market mechanisms. This may operate through anti-discrimination legislation aimed primarily at guaranteeing effective educational services for disabled students. It may also focus on ensuring that students are solvent by personalising modes of financing. Such financing may come from public authorities or grants and enable them to choose the university which seems best suited to their needs and to access the various forms of support and assistance available to help them succeed. Modes of financing designed to encourage institutions to invest time and money with regard to accessibility is another possible approach. Allocated by bodies created for the purpose, such funds may be given first and foremost to those institutions able to show their capacity to achieve the expected results. In this context, statistical tools focus on the various aspects of the effectiveness of institutions with regard to the costs incurred, objectives pursued, the professional future of students and their degree of satisfaction. In a second stage, consideration would be given to the various aspects making up the effectiveness of institutions and those relating to social and professional integration.

Such an approach can make disability a factor differentiating institutions. It invites institutions to turn accessibility into a way of attracting students likely to have difficulties in accessing higher education. It leads some institutions to make adaptation to disability a major strategic objective and source of funding. It encourages them to develop distance learning, to use new technologies and to see a comprehensive accessibility strategy as a competitive advantage. It can encourage them to view staff training, measures to increase the awareness of the university community, research into the social conditions underlying disability, etc., as an investment they can make to improve their quality and as a vector for development. By closely linking effectiveness and social justice, this approach is no doubt conducive to the adaptation of higher education to disabled students: it makes disability an economic and social challenge for some institutions and encourages them to give greater consideration than they do today to the situation and circumstances of disabled persons. It also no doubt helps enhance the quality of the support offered to students and, hence, their chances of success.

It is not, however, certain that by reducing the entrepreneurial spirit to a financial and organisational dimension, this form of adaptation will achieve the objectives pursued. Its financial aspect can increase the unequal opportunities faced by disabled students rather than reducing them: if funding is linked to results and investments, those institutions best able to show their effectiveness and with most money may be privileged to the point of discouraging the others from making the necessary changes (Gagliano, 1998). Nor is it certain that the financial support given to students is a guarantee of success: budgetary constraints may mean that the amounts paid are insufficient to pay for the most appropriate technical and human resources. Once again, disabled students become dependent on the goodwill and availability of their friends and relations, and may be penalised in terms of access and success (OECD, 2003; Ebersold, 2005). Furthermore, by being linked to success within a given timeframe, funding may ignore the special rhythm of students with a developing problem or those constrained to particular rhythms by their handicap. Their chances of access to higher education may be fragmented, the continuity of their courses difficult, and their chances of success more limited than those of other students.

By inviting institutions to concentrate on their strengths, this rationale may transform the dynamic of differentiation into one of specialisation. It may also encourage the emergence of universities specialised in disability either with respect to a specific impairment or to a particularity requiring specific services. Students, whether disabled or not, would no doubt have a greater chance of accessing higher education. Creating institutions specialised in disability may however help reinforce inequalities of professional and social opportunities between disabled students and non disabled students. Institutions wishing to link attractiveness with selectivity might be encouraged to see any student likely to need support as a student at risk. Even without having a disability or any particular problem, these students may be relegated to "specialised" institutions and appear, also, as disabled students. This can already be seen in the sector of specialised education: the fact of being specialised means that institutions become an indicator of student disability. The risk of this model would therefore be that pedagogical and organisational accessibility are finally linked to student incapacity rather than being a synonym of quality and success, and that the investments made by institutions become penalising rather than status-enhancing. The value of the degrees given by such institutions would be diminished, and they would be less likely to provide access to employment.

8.3. Conclusion

The opening of higher education to disability is a reality, as is shown by the increase in the number of disabled students in a number of OECD member countries. The adoption of public policies aimed at encouraging the participation and involvement of every citizen in the development of society has been a strong contributory factor. Another reason for the increase is the adoption of anti-discrimination policies which consider social inequalities and injustices as obstacles to individual participation resulting from the inaccessibility and autarky of institutions, obliging them to a greater or lesser degree to open their doors to disabled persons and ensure that these latter have the same rights and opportunities as any other student. The redefinition of disability contained, for example, in the new international classification adopted in 2001 by the World Health Organization (WHO) has also played an important role. By defining disability in terms of the interaction between an individual, the constraints and possibilities imposed by his/her impairment and the forms of support offered by the "environment", WHO has made disability a universal issue. Disability is less a matter of maladjustment or incapacity related to an impairment than of difficulties which have their origin, amongst other things, in the quality of the pedagogical practices and support provided to individuals. The idea has thus gained acceptance that anyone not enjoying the appropriate support enabling him/her to learn and develop is in a way "disabled"; this has helped the development of forms of support for disabled students and for higher education institutions so as to make them more accessible to all students. Disability has thus been transformed into an indicator of the degree of openness of institutions and their propensity to be innovative, fair and focused on the success of all students. This shift in perspective has of course taken different forms across countries and it is no doubt more accurate to decline the concept of inclusion in the plural rather than in the singular, as is generally done. But whatever the reason behind it, this shift in perspective often seems to have been a source of effectiveness, equity and innovation for institutions, of professional enrichment for university staff (whether teachers or not) and of personal enrichment for "valid" students.

This openness to diversity is not, however, necessarily synonymous with equality of opportunity. In the United States, less than a third of students with special needs continue to post-mandatory education after high school (Wagner *et al.*, 2005a). Of those that do, proportionately fewer enrol in the two-year courses offered by Community Colleges; as for students without any handicap, they are proportionately more numerous in long courses, notably at university (Wagner *et al.*, 2005b). In France, disabled students enrolled in higher education are proportionately more numerous in the arts, *i.e.* no doubt the least selective curricula, but also, a priori, less likely than others to have links with the world of work. They are also proportionately fewer in postgraduate education and, *a fortiori*, at PhD level. Thus, the adaptation of higher education to disability is of major importance from an economic, political and social viewpoint. It enhances the employability of disabled persons and helps support public policies focusing on the promotion of work, income security, poverty prevention and social exclusion, thus reducing the costs linked to inactivity. It reinforces the attractiveness of institutions by leading them to consider the difficulties which students may have (as they are invited to do by the Bologna process), to design their courses in a coherent and effective manner and thus to enhance the chances of success of all students, in particular the most disadvantaged. It thus contributes to making the development of human capital a source of economic growth guaranteeing individuals the possibility of personal and professional development throughout their life as well as income security. Such adaptation to disability will only, however, meet these challenges if it leads institutions to look at themselves as learning organisations which see a diversification of student profiles, practices, courses, rhythms and social times as an opportunity for consolidating their attractiveness by satisfying at the same time the requirements of excellence, effectiveness and equity.

Notes

1. As this article is based on the OECD research conducted in 2001 and 2002 (OECD, 2003), little account is taken of the most recent developments in certain countries. For example, although aware of them, it does not go into detail about the practical implications of the Act of 11 February 2005 for the equality of rights and opportunities, participation and citizenship of disabled persons promulgated by France. Not all the implementing Decrees have been published and their application is still too recent for precise conclusions to be drawn.
2. The *Commission Technique de Reclassement et d'Orientation Professionnelle* was a technical board for occupational reclassification and guidance. The Act of 11 February 2005 replaced it by the Commission for the Rights and Autonomy of Disabled Persons (*Commission des droits et de l'autonomie des personnes handicapées* – CDAPH). The pace of implementation of the Act does not allow for any detailed information about what changes have been made in practice.
3. The proportion of disabled students suffering from an intellectual handicap almost doubled over the same period as did that of students with multiple handicaps.
4. In addition to a basic pass, there are four levels of degree in the British system, depending on the marks obtained in the exams: *first class honours* is the most prestigious, given to about 10% of students at national level; *second class honours* is the intermediate degree, divided into two sub-categories, *lower* and *upper*, and given to most graduates; and *third class honours*, the lowest degree. Candidates for postgraduate studies normally require to obtain at least *second class honours*, and preferably *upper second class*.
5. Circular No. 2006-051 of 27 March 2006, elementary and secondary education, preparation for the start of the school year 2006, *Official Gazette* of 31 March 2006.
6. In France, the proportion of students with a sensory deficiency fell from 34.8% in 1996 to 24.7% in 2006, and that of persons with a motor deficiency fell by nearly 10%, from 31.5% in 1996 to 20.3% in 2006.

7. At the moment, in France, children from working-class families are 7 times more likely to be sent to a special institution than those from middle-class families. These inequalities become more marked in adulthood since those from the working class are 12 or 13 times more likely to be institutionalised than the rest of the population (see Mormiche, 1999).
8. DFES, *Widening Participation in Higher Education*, 2003.
9. Ordinary Act 2005-102 of 11 February 2005 for the Equal Rights and Opportunities, Participation and Citizenship of Disabled Persons.
10. Higher education statistics agency 2008.

References

van Acker, M. (1999), "Supporting Students with Disabilities in Belgium", *Higher Education and Disabilities: International Approaches*.

Bourdieu, P. (1979), *La Distinction. Critique sociale du jugement*, Les Éditions de Minuit, Paris.

Danermark, B. (1998), "Including Students in Higher Education – A Vice-Chancellor's Perspective", presentation made at the conference on disabled students in higher education, Grenoble, 24-26 March.

Danermark, B. (1999), "Disabled Students in Higher Education: Management for Inclusion", *Higher Education Management*, Vol. 11, No. 3, OECD Publishing, Paris.

Douglass, J.A. (2004), "The Dynamics of Massification and Differentiation: A Comparative Look at Higher Education Systems in the United Kingdom and California", *Higher Education Management and Policy*, Vol. 16, No. 3, OECD Publishing, Paris.

Dyson, A. *et al.* (2004), "Post 16 Transitions: A Longitudinal Study of Young People with Special Educational Needs: Wave 2", Institute for Employment Studies, University of Manchester.

Ebersold, S. (1992), "*L'invention du handicap*", CTNERHI, Paris.

Ebsersold, S. (2005), *Le temps des servitudes, la famille à l'épreuve du handicap*, PUR, Rennes.

Ebersold, S. (2006), *La participation à l'aune de l'affiliation*, University of Strasbourg.

Ebersold, S. (2007), "Être étudiant et présenter une déficience", *Quelles trajectoires d'insertion pour les personnes handicapées ?*, Collection Échanges santé social, ENSP, Rennes.

European Commission (1996), *Higher Education and Disabled Students*, European commission, Brussels.

French *et al.* (2000), "Disability and Social Inclusion for the E-university", P. Bacsich and F. Bristow (eds.), *The E-university Compendium*.

Gagliano, G. (1998), "Funding the Curb-cuts into Higher Education: Laws-Policies and Logistics of Financing Students with Disabilities", presentation made at the conference on disabled students in higher education, Grenoble, 24-26 March.

Galland, O. and P. Rouault (1996), "Des études supérieures inégalement rentables selon les milieux sociaux", *INSEE première*, No. 469, July.

Hurst, A. (1998), "Staff Training, Continuing Professional Development and Students with Disabilities in Higher Education", presentation made at the conference on disabled students in higher education, Grenoble, 24-26 March.

Mormiche, P. (1999), "Les personnes dépendantes en institution", *Insee première*, No. 669.

Nakhili, N. (2005), "Impact du contexte scolaire dans l'élaboration des choix d'études supérieures des élèves de terminale", *Éducation et formation*, No. 72.

National Center for Education Statistics (NCES) (1999), *Students with Disabilities in Post Secondary Education: A Profile of Preparation, Participation and Outcomes,* US Department of Education, Office of Educational Research and Improvement.

Newby, H. (2003), "The Management of Change in Higher Education", *Higher Education Management and Policy*, Vol. 15, No. 1, OECD Publishing, Paris.

OECD (1997), *Post-compulsory Education for Disabled People*, OECD Publishing, Paris.

OECD (1999), *Inclusive Education at Work – Students with Disabilities in Mainstream Schools*, OECD Publishing, Paris.

OECD (2003), *Disability in Higher Education*, OECD Publishing, Paris.

OECD (2004), *Internationalisation and Trade in Higher Education: Opportunities and Challenges*, OECD Publishing, Paris.

OECD (2005), *The Well-being of Nations: The Role of Human and Social Capital*, OECD Publishing, Paris.

OECD (2007), *Education at a Glance: OECD Indicators 2007*, OECD Publishing, Paris.

Pickersgill, R., K. Van Berneveld and S. Bearfild (1998), "General and Academic Work, Are they Different?", Department of Employment, Education, Training and Youth Affairs, Evaluations and Investigations Programme.

Selz, M. and L.A. Vallet (2006), "La démocratisation de l'enseignement et son paradoxe apparent", *Données sociales*, INSEE.

UNESCO (1997), *International Standard Classification of Education*, UNESCO, Paris.

Wagner, M. *et al.* (2005a), "After High School: A First Look at the Post-school Experiences of Youth with Disabilities", a report from the National Longitudinal Transition Study (NLTS2), US Office of special education programmes SRI International, Menlo Park, CA.

Wagner, M. *et al.* (2005b), "Changes over Time in the Early Post-school Outcomes of Youth with Disabilities – A Report of Findings from the NTLS and the NLTS-2", US Office of special education programmes, SRI International, Menlo Park, CA.

ISBN 978-92-64-04065-6
Higher Education to 2030
Volume 1: Demography

Chapter 9

Immigration and Access to Tertiary Education: Integration or Marginalisation?

by

Francisco Marmolejo*, Sean Manley-Casimir* and Stéphan Vincent-Lancrin**

This chapter includes a review of trends and issues on immigration and higher education, using the United States and France as cases in point. It highlights the importance of widening access to higher education to immigrants and their children in the coming decades. It does not cover international (or foreign) students, i.e. migrants coming to their host country for the purpose of studying.

* Consortium for North American Higher Education Collaboration (CONAHEC).
** OECD Centre for Educational Research and Innovation (CERI).

9.1. Introduction

Regional integration efforts and globalisation trends are making national boundaries more porous, causing substantial shifts in the locations and methods of producing and distributing products. The intensity and patterns of migration are also being affected. Migratory flows due in part to these phenomena are having increasingly important economic and social ramifications in many regions of the world, including in higher education.

The transition towards knowledge-based societies and economies in developed countries as well as equity issues require that their national higher education systems adapt faster to changing social demographics to ensure that they provide more ample and sustained opportunities for those seeking access to higher education. However, for migrant communities living in those societies it is often not an easy road. (Box 9.1 defines the migration vocabulary used in this chapter.)

Access to higher education is critical for migrants so that they can adapt and integrate into the societies to which they have relocated. Since economies and societies are changing rapidly and knowledge and information are becoming commodities crucial to economic competitiveness, those who do not have access to lifelong learning opportunities, including higher education, are left behind. The resulting risks are socio-economic marginalisation and other integration problems. Not only does this contribute to the creation of enclaves within society but also to the severity of inequality and in some extreme cases, instability. The current and expected scale of the problem requires deliberate action since migration rates and levels are likely to continue to increase despite restrictive migratory policies in developed countries.

The central argument of this chapter is that changes must be made in order to ensure that access to higher education for migrants is equitable – and merely possible for undocumented migrants, as it is generally the case for schooling. Migrant populations must not be relegated to a social underclass where they are sometimes located. The competitiveness and social cohesion of their newfound societies is at stake.

The chapter begins with an overview of migration trends and educational attainment of migrants. It then discusses the context and developments in the area of migrant access to higher education in the United States and France. Future implications of national actions for the provision of access to higher education for migrants are examined in conclusion.

International students – that is migrants going abroad to study at tertiary education level – are not covered by this analysis. Indeed, they do not present the same kinds of challenges and opportunities for countries (OECD, 2004a, 2006b).

Box 9.1. **A few definitions**

Migration: The term "migration" refers to a population movement, encompassing any kind of movement of people, whatever its length, composition and causes as defined by International Organisation for Migration (IOM) (2004). This generic definition is inclusive of the terms "immigration" (a process by which non-nationals move into a country for the purpose of settlement) and "emigration" (the act of departing or exiting from one country with a view to settle in another).

Migrants: At the international level, no universally accepted definition of migrant exists. The term migrant applies to persons, and family members, moving to another country or region to better their material or social conditions and improve the prospect for themselves or their family (IOM, 2004).

Immigrants: There are major differences in how immigrants are defined. Some countries have traditionally focused on producing data on foreign residents (European countries, Japan and Korea) whilst others refer to the foreign-born (settlement countries, *i.e.* Australia, Canada, New Zealand and the United States). In this paper, they refer to the foreign-born population, that is, born abroad with a foreign citizenship at birth; they can be viewed as first-generation migrants. They may consist of both foreign and national citizens (they may have acquired their host country's citizenship).

Foreigners and *natives:* The term foreigner applies to people with a foreign citizenship. Foreigners who were born in their host country are not immigrants (as they are not foreign-born). Natives are those who had the country's citizenship at birth. They may be born abroad.

Second-generation immigrants, people with *immigrant background* or from *immigrant descent:* these terms refer to native-born people whose parents are immigrants. A further distinction can be made depending on whether they have one or two immigrant parents. Immigrant families are families with immigrant family householders.

Undocumented migrants: Also referred as unauthorised or illegal migrants, these terms refer to persons who reside in a country, but who are not citizens of that country, have not been admitted for permanent residence, and are not in a set of specific authorised temporary statuses permitting longer-term residence and work (Passel *et al.*, 2006).

9.2. Migratory patterns and educational attainment

The growing migrant population

According to the International Organisation for Migration (2008), around 193 million people, or approximately 3% of the world's total population, reside in a country other than where they were born. The number of migrants has more than doubled since 1975, and while between 1965 and 1990 this represented an annual growth rate of about 2.1%, the current rate has increased to 2.9%.

Approximately 60% of the world's migrants reside in the more developed regions, representing nearly 10% of the population there, and 40% in the less developed regions where they represent only 1.4% of the total population. Most of the world's migrants live in Europe (64 million), Asia (53 million) and North America (44 million). The United States is by far the country with the largest overall number of migrants at 38 million. They represent 12.9% of the country's total population (see Figures 9.1 and 9.2). Qatar ranks first in relative terms, with a population of migrants accounting for 78.3% of its total population (Population Division of the United Nations Secretariat, 2006). Thirteen OECD countries host

Figure 9.1. **Countries with largest international migrant stock, in thousands (2005)**

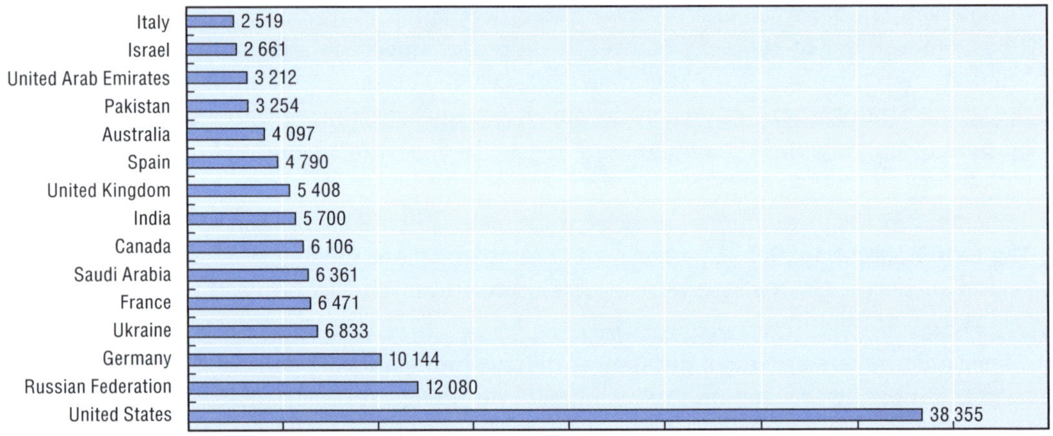

Source: United Nations (2006).

Figure 9.2. **Immigrant population: foreign-born as a percentage of total population, 2005**

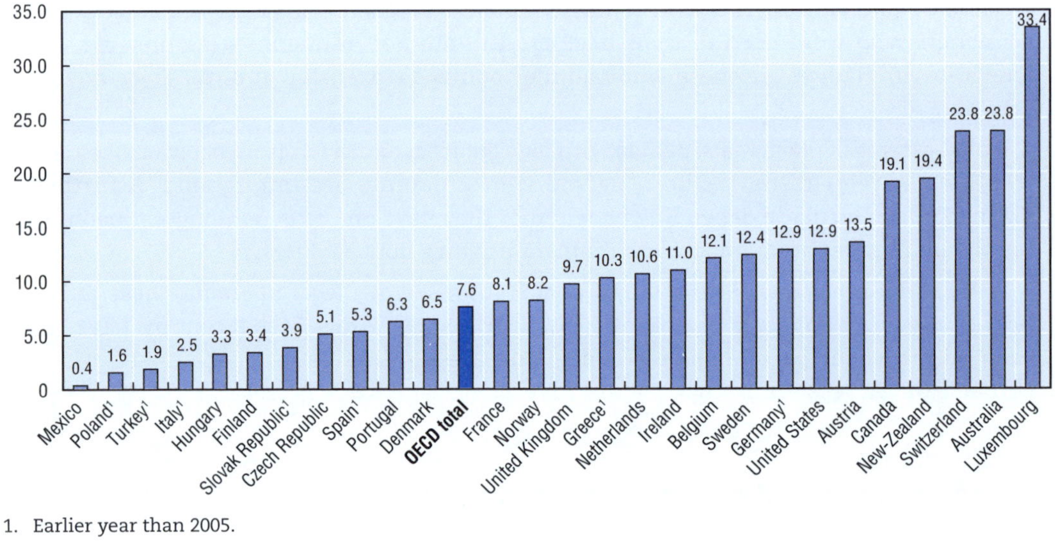

1. Earlier year than 2005.

Source: OECD (2007c).

more than 10% immigrants in their total population, the OECD average for the immigrant population being at 7.6% (Figure 9.2). In light of the growing concerns in public opinion about the economic, political and social consequences of migration, 44% of developed countries have implemented stricter policies aimed at lowering immigration levels, as have 39% of developing countries (United Nations, 2002; OECD, 2006a).

For an increasing number of countries, estimates of unauthorised migration are now available. Unauthorised or undocumented migrants may have entered the country illegally or may have become unauthorised after entering legally the country, for a variety of reasons. In some countries, like Greece and the United States, this population represents a significant share of the immigrant population, and of the overall population (Table 9.1).

Table 9.1. **Estimates of the unauthorised immigrant population in selected OECD countries**

	Number	% of total population	Year	Method of estimation
Australia	50 000	0.2	2005	Double card system
Japan	210 000	0.2	2005	Double card system
United States	10300 000	3.6	2004 (18)	Residual method
Netherlands	125 000 – 230 000	0.8-1.4	2004	Capture/recapture
Switzerland	80 000 –100 000	1.1-1.5	2005	Delphi method
Spain	690 000	1.6	2005 (4)	Regularisation
Italy	700 000	1.2	2002 (4)	Regularisation
Portugal	185 000	1.8	2001 (6)	Regularisation
Greece	370 000	3.4	2001 (3)	Regularisation

Note: The number in parentheses indicates the number of years since the previous major regularisation. The regularisation numbers cover only persons applying and thus are a lower bound for the number of unauthorised immigrants. The methods of estimation are detailed in OECD (2006a).
Source: OECD (2006a).

Costs and benefits of migration

Most concerns regarding migration are social and economic. The perceived costs and benefits associated with migrants generally relate to the social and economic impact that they have on their sending and receiving countries. There are a variety of arguments in favour of and against migration, as well as perceived incentives and disincentives for governments in developed and developing nations to regulating migrant movement.

A major driving force in contemporary migration is economic. Migrants often go abroad in the hope of brighter economic prospects in their receiving country, where their expected income will generally be higher than in their sending country (notwithstanding the relative cost of living in both countries). For example, according to Freeman (2006) a Mexican with five to eight years of schooling earned six times more in the United States than in Mexico in 2000 (USD 11.20 an hour in the United States against USD 1.82 in Mexico). At the same time, societies in countries experiencing a substantial influx of migrants enjoy the benefits of their relatively inexpensive labour and products as immigrants generally earn less than the native-born overall and less than the native-born with the same years of schooling in many cases (Freeman, 2006). Since many developed country societies are ageing and reproduction rates are not adequate to fully replace the labour force, migrants also assume many of the economic functions for which there might otherwise be serious labour shortages, not only in a variety of low-skill low-pay jobs (such as agriculture, construction and services), but also in high-skill higher pay jobs, such as health professionals. Shortages of labour workforce are projected in some sectors. For instance, in Canada the shortage of nurses is expected to reach 78 000 by 2011 and 113 000 by 2016 (Dawson, 2006). In Spain, in 2005, one of each three new doctors entering into the labour market were foreign-born and foreign-trained (Benito, 2006). Migration can also follow some labour market shortages related to economic cycles (*e.g.* the massive influx of engineers in the United States during the dotcom boom) or sometimes to migration pattern themselves (*e.g.* the shortage of bilingual teachers in elementary schools located in high migrant-receiving cities in the United States).

Concerns about the economic cost of migration in receiving countries include the views 1) that migrant labour increases the competition for those naturally born citizens who would work in the same capacities given the opportunity; 2) that migrants use similar (or higher) levels of publicly funded services as non-migrants; and 3) that in the case of unauthorised migrants labour is frequently not taxed or "under-the-table" and that migrants do not pay taxes. While migrants can in principle have a lowering effect on wages in some sectors, this has to be balanced with the welfare increase they offer their receiving society; moreover, empirical evidence shows differing impacts according to the receiving countries (Freeman, 2006). In countries like the United States, recent research shows that the two last arguments are unfounded. Undocumented workers do pay taxes, including unrecoverable payments to social security and sales taxes; the majority are concentrated into labour market niches which are principally constituted by migrants; and they use public services at a lesser rate than non-migrant users. For instance, migrants in the United States use less than half the dollar amount of health care on average than do US citizens, and only about 25% of migrant health care expenditure are reimbursed by government programmes (NILC, 2006a). Actually, migrants spend a large share of their income in their host country and thus contribute to its economic activity and public income. In the United States, Latin American immigrants are estimated to have over USD 500 billion of purchasing power, more than 90% of which is spent in the states and towns where they live as a direct contribution to their local economies (IADB, 2006). Migration presents clear economic benefits for receiving countries and economies.

In developing countries which are net exporters of migrants, governments sometimes implement measures to moderate the exodus of their population in order to appease receiving countries. Migration can also be viewed as a cause of social disruption since it leads to the disintegration of families who are separated as a result of family members going abroad in search of work. Finally, the issue of "brain-drain" has gained notoriety in recent years. Highly skilled migration (that is, the migration of tertiary-educated people) can be viewed as a loss of human capital, although highly skilled migrants still represent a minority of expatriates in most cases (OECD, 2005). However, migration also presents important economic benefits for sending countries. Governments of sending countries have little incentives for limiting emigration because remittances sent back by those who have moved abroad to family members or friends who remain behind are an important source of income for many developing nations. In the case of Mexico, for instance, while remittances represent only about 10% of Mexican immigrants in the United States, they represent the second largest source of external income, exceeded only by oil revenues. In some other countries, remittances are by far the largest source of international revenue: in Tonga, Moldova, Lesotho, Haiti and Bosnia and Herzegovina they represented from 22% to 31% of GDP in 2004 (Figure 9.3). Remittances now overtake official development aid and are regarded as a major lever of development in the developing world (World Bank, 2006; OECD, 2006a). While highly skilled workers tend to remit less than workers, they contribute to the development of their country of origin by facilitating investment and business between their host country and their country of origin. Recent research shows that highly skilled migration can benefit both "exporters" and "importers", especially in the case of scientists (Hudson, 2005; OECD, 2007a) – although this is not always necessarily the case in practice. In conclusion, the benefits of migration reaped in both the host and home countries are significant.

Educational attainment of migrants, integration and (higher) education challenges

Migrants do present different challenges for their host country depending on their level of educational attainment.

Figure 9.3. **Top 30 countries with the highest total remittances received, in billion USD and as a percentage of GDP, 2004**

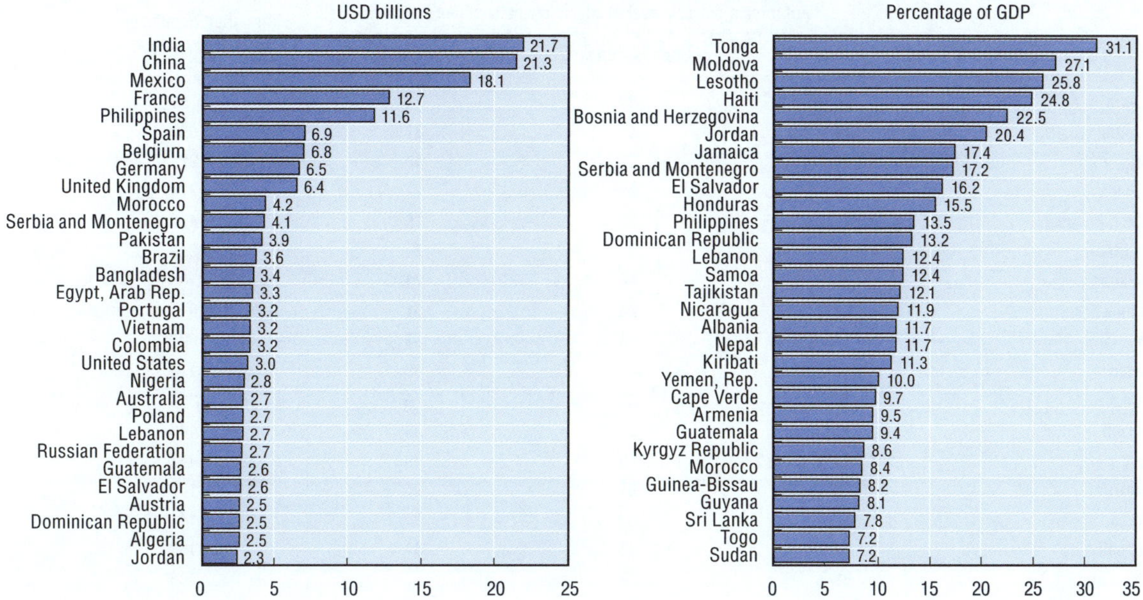

Note: "Remittances" refer to the sum of the "compensation of employees", "worker's remittances", and "other current transfers in other sectors".

Source: Based on World Bank (2006).

Highly-skilled migrants (that is, foreign-born tertiary education graduates) are generally welcomed by receiving countries. Recent migration policies have tended to facilitate this type of migration (OECD, 2004, 2005, 2006a). On average, highly skilled immigrants accounted for about 12% of the tertiary educated residents in the OECD area around 2000 (OECD, 2006a, 2007a) and represented the largest group of migrants in Canada, Ireland and Mexico (Table 9.2). On average, they represent more than one quarter of the migrant population in the OECD area. When they migrate after their studies, destination countries benefit from the investment in education which has been assumed by the country of origin as well as from their skills. As highly skilled migrants tend to be "middle class", well paid and relatively "invisible" (Salt, 1997). However, as noted above, they generally earn less and participate less in the labour market than native-born with the same level of education (Freeman, 2006; OECD, 2006a). Some highly-skilled migrants can encounter difficulties in having the qualifications they received abroad recognised in their destination country and can end up working in jobs requiring lower skills than one would expect given their educational qualification: immigrants are more often overqualified than their native-born workers (OECD, 2006a, 2007a). Finally, unauthorised migrants are frequently forced to work in "low-paid low-skill" jobs, despite any formal preparation they might have.

Whereas according to recent research (Hinojosa-Ojeda *et al.*, 2000; NILC, 2006b) migrants with limited formal training represent for the most part a net gain to the receiving country, frequently this view is not shared by all citizens, political groups and policy makers in the host country. At the global level, a majority of migrants fall into the low-skilled category (United Nations, 2002; Solimano, 2001). Within the OECD area, low and medium skilled migrants accounted on average for 69% of the migrant population

Table 9.2. **Size and composition of the foreign born population in OECD countries by level of educational attainment, 2003-04**

	% of foreign born by level of educational attainment			Immigrant population (thousands), 2004
	Tertiary	Upper secondary	Secondary and under	
Australia	**36**	40	24	4 751
Austria	**19**	45	**37**	1 059
Belgium	25	27	**48**	1 220
Canada[1]	**46**	32	22	5 774
Czech Republic	**16**	55	**29**	499
Denmark	**38**	38	**24**	343
Finland	28	**48**	**24**	166
France[1]	21	28	**51**	4 811
Germany	17	44	**37**	10 620[1]
Greece	19	**42**	38	1 123
Hungary	**28**	56	16	319
Ireland	**45**	31	24	443
Italy	**11**	**40**	49	1 447
Japan[1]	30	**44**	26	1 157
Korea[1]	32	**44**	24	141
Luxembourg	**23**	41	**37**	150
Mexico[1]	**38**	26	37	406
Netherlands[1]	24	32	**44**	1 736
New Zealand[1]	**38**	**47**	16	764
Norway	**36**	47	**17**	361
Poland	**23**	**50**	27	776
Portugal	**22**	**26**	52	714
Slovak Republic	**17**	62	**21**	207
Spain	**30**	**29**	41	2 172
Sweden	**20**	49	**22**	1 100
Switzerland	28	43	**30**	1 738
Turkey[1]	17	34	**49**	973
United Kingdom	**34**	44	**22**	5 552
United States	35	35	**30**	37 592
OECD	30	37	32	88 114
Country mean	27	41	31	

1. Earlier year than 2003-04.

Note: Migrants with unknown educational attainment were assumed to follow the known distribution across the three groups. Bold figures indicate an overrepresentation of foreign-born at that level of education compared to natives. Data refer to the population aged 15-64 for Australia. Figures for upper secondary education include post-secondary non-tertiary education.

Source: OECD (2007c).

in 2003-04. About 32% of the migrant population had at most secondary educational attainment. Like for the native population, the higher the level of educational attainment of migrants, the lower their unemployment rates and the higher their employment rates. But with the same level of qualification, migrants are more likely to be unemployed and not to participate in the labour force than natives with the same educational attainment. Actually, the disadvantage of migrants relative to their native counterparts increases with their level of educational attainment when measured by unemployment and employment rates. While the picture varies according to countries (Table 9.3), low skilled migrants in an OECD country will typically have an unemployment rate one third higher than natives, while it will be twice as high for highly skilled migrants.

Table 9.3. **Ratio of foreign-born unemployment and employment rates to native ones, by level of education, 2003-04**

	Unemployment			Employment		
	Level of education			Level of education		
	Low	Medium	High	Low	Medium	High
Australia	0.84	1.05	1.98	0.86	0.86	0.91
Austria	1.47	2.50	2.35	1.24	0.94	0.92
Belgium	2.25	2.35	3.15	0.81	0.81	0.88
Canada	0.96	1.40	2.35	0.96	0.91	0.90
Czech Republic	1.13	1.41	0.61	1.61	0.87	1.01
Denmark	2.29	2.58	2.80	0.73	0.70	0.73
Finland	1.68	1.83	3.54	0.82	0.89	0.82
France	1.51	1.84	2.05	1.01	0.88	0.90
Germany	1.31	1.42	2.82	1.12	0.90	0.81
Greece	1.04	0.98	1.89	1.31	1.08	0.84
Hungary	0.56	0.76	1.15	0.93	1.01	1.00
Ireland	1.43	1.73	1.94	0.93	0.89	0.88
Italy	0.94	1.08	0.97	1.31	1.02	0.97
Luxembourg	0.70	2.38	3.19	1.89	1.04	0.95
Netherlands	1.99	4.05	2.13	0.79	0.86	0.89
Norway	1.87	2.45	1.91	0.83	0.87	0.91
Poland	0.51	1.44	0.41	0.48	0.44	0.64
Portugal	1.68	1.17	1.64	1.02	1.12	0.95
Slovak Republic	0.88	1.46	1.11	2.17	0.80	1.01
Spain	1.21	1.17	1.50	1.15	1.15	0.92
Sweden	2.29	2.20	3.03	0.80	0.83	0.87
Switzerland	2.17	2.64	2.94	1.11	0.92	0.89
United Kingdom	1.39	1.69	1.88	0.75	0.86	0.93
United States	0.59	0.85	1.33	1.63	0.99	0.93
Country mean	**1.36**	**1.77**	**2.03**	**1.09**	**0.90**	**0.89**

Note: Data refer to 2002 for the Netherlands, 2003 for Canada and to 2004 for Australia, Denmark and the United States. Read that in Australia the unemployment rate of low skilled foreign-born populations is 84% the unemployment rate level of low skilled natives.

Source: Based on OECD (2006a), Table I.10. European countries: European Community Labour Force Survey (data provided by Eurostat) except Denmark (Population Register); United States: Current Population Survey March Supplement; Australia: Survey of Education and Work; Canada: Survey of Labour and Income Dynamics.

Given current demographic trends and because the immigrant population, especially recent arrivals, tend to be younger than the native population, its share in the labour force and in populations is expected to continue to grow in the coming decades. If current patterns continue, this implies that countries' labour force will increasingly be composed of foreign-born workers, so that the challenge of building a knowledge economy will increasingly depend on their skills. This also means that the percentage of foreign-born in the unemployed population will continue to grow relative to natives, with the risk that this group becomes increasingly marginalised and that social cohesion becomes at risk. Facilitating the contribution of migrants and their children to the knowledge society and economy will thus increasingly become a major stake for education policies.

While a variety of employment and migration policies and measures can help integrate immigrants in the labour market and society (OECD, 2006a), education (and especially tertiary education) plays a key role as it is often a critical means of social and economic mobility for migrants and their families, especially when they are low-skilled migrants. This might partly explain why immigrants and their children have on average higher (and, compared with their measured performance at school, unrealistic) expectations about their future educational attainment than natives (OECD, 2006e): they know education will be their main resource for upward social mobility. Economic, linguistic, cultural, educational, and sometimes legal, barriers limit their participation and success in the mainstream education available to non-migrants, especially in higher education. Results from the OECD Programme for International Student Assessment (PISA) of 2003 show that 15-year-old first-generation immigrants (foreign-born) and second-generation immigrant students (whose both parents are foreign born) perform less well in maths, science and reading than their native counterparts, except in Canada (OECD, 2006e).[1] In general, second-generation immigrant students tend to outperform first-generation immigrant students but in Germany, Denmark, Belgium (Flemish Community) and New Zealand second-generation students lag behind native and first-generation students. Factors such as socio-economic status, knowledge of the language of instruction and the age at migration explain some part of immigrant students' outcomes from education in most OECD countries (OECD, 2006b). Whatever the reasons, this underperformance slows or prevents the progress of migrants in integrating into society and enjoying higher levels of economic and social welfare – especially the low-skilled. One challenge for the future will be to improve the participation and graduation levels of migrants and their children in tertiary education – which will first require a stronger graduation rate from upper secondary school, but not only.

Another, generally unknown, issue lies in the accessibility of higher education for unauthorised migrants. In many countries access to the primary and secondary education, and sometimes appropriate remedial services, is mandatory and guaranteed regardless of the migratory or legal status of students. However, access to higher education is much more limited, costly, selective, and in some cases legally forbidden in the case of unauthorised migrants. If unauthorised immigrants have received their primary and secondary education in their host country (as is sometimes the case) it is a potential waste of human capital if their legal status prevents them from accessing tertiary education. In some cases, they might be regularised and become legal residents in their host country, especially as some of them cannot be deported under the law of their host country. Were they to go back to their home country, their tertiary education qualification would not be a loss to their host country either, as is widely recognised for foreign students when they go back home (OECD, 2004, 2006b): they would indeed probably continue to have social and business links with their host country. Their tertiary education degree could actually facilitate their departure. Limits on access to tertiary education exacerbate the stratification of the societies in which migrants live, which affects the whole society. While the issue is still minor in most OECD countries, depending on the magnitude of the issue countries should consider the pragmatic choice of removing legal and financial barriers that sometimes prevent undocumented migrants from gaining access to higher education. While allowing undocumented migrants into tertiary education may be at odds with firm policies against unauthorised migration, excluding these groups may prove counterproductive in the long term.

The magnitude of the educational problem for migrants is such that national and international bodies such as the United Nations (UN) are taking steps to ensure the protection of the rights of migrants, including in education. The UN has enacted the *United Nations International Convention on the Protection of the Rights of all Migrant Workers and Members of their Families* which entered into force on 1 July 2003. This Convention has been signed by 49 countries (UNESCO, 2006) most of which are net exporters of migrants but is not signed by any of the net importers of migrants such as the United States and Canada. Actually, Mexico and Turkey are the only OECD countries which have signed the Convention. This agreement has specific provisions guaranteeing for migrants and their families "equality of treatment with nationals of the host country in relation to access to educational institutions and services subject to the admission requirements and other regulations of the institutions and services concerned".

9.3. Access of migrants to higher education: the cases of the United States and of France

This section focuses on two large migrant-receiving countries with different types of immigration, different policies of integration for immigrants and different types of education and tertiary education systems. Both countries face challenges of access to tertiary education for documented and undocumented immigrants or their children – and are increasingly addressing them. While the access of undocumented migrants to tertiary education is a relatively well-known issue in the United States, it is still largely unknown in France, partly because the problem has a very small scale. However, beyond their differences, the two countries face similar problems of access of migrant students or their children to higher education.

Migrants in higher education in the United States

Regarded as a migrant-receiving or settlement country, the United States has experienced historically significant waves of migrants which have changed in demographic composition in recent years. In 2005 there were approximately 27.3 million foreign born inhabitants in the United States, of which it was estimated that 16.8 million were legal residents, and 10.5 million were undocumented migrants and 1.2 million are temporary migrant workers (US Census Bureau, 2006). Among the immigrants, 53.5% were born in Latin America (37.7% in Central America, mainly Mexico, 9.7% in the Caribbean, and 6% in South America), 25.4% in Asia, 13.6% in Europe, and the remaining 7.5% in the rest of the world. Immigration flows in the 1990s exceeded those in any decade in the history of the United States, with flows from 700 000 to 1 million a year, and this high pace has continued between 2000 and 2004 with an immigrant population increasing by over 1 million a year (US Census Bureau). The immigrant population more than doubled from less than 5% for the total US population in 1970 to 12% in 2004, and is expected to reach 42-43 million or 13% of the total US population by 2010 (Capps *et al.*, 2005).

The share of children of immigrants among the school age population has also increased quickly from 6% in 1970 to 19% in 2000, that is, 11 million children. About three quarters of them are native-born, while foreign-born children represented 5% of the school age population (up from 2% in 1970). This growth is also noticeable in tertiary education. For example, the number of foreign-born students has increased from one third in 1990 to almost one half in 2000 at the City University of New York (CUNY), a public higher education institution in the city that has historically played a central role in the education of minority and immigrant New Yorkers (Leinbach and Bailey, 2006). In terms of educational attainment, foreign-born people have on average similar characteristics to the native-born population, one in four holding a bachelor degree or more (27.3% for foreign born over 25 against 27.7% for native-born over 25 in 2004). However, immigrants' (and children of immigrants') characteristics vary greatly by country and region of origin. While only 11.1% of immigrants over 25 from Latin America held a bachelor degree or more in 2004, the percentage was 49.7% for immigrants from Asia, 36.4% for those from Europe, and 37.7% for those from the rest of the world. Foreign-born who were born in Latin America represent 51% of all immigrants but only 21% of immigrant tertiary graduates. Immigrants from Central America (mainly Mexico) have the lowest educational attainment with only 6.1% of tertiary graduates among them: they represent 7.8% of all foreign-born tertiary education graduates (against 35% of the foreign-born population over 25).

Given that since the second half of the 20th century, most migrants to the United States have arrived from Latin American countries, principally Mexico, and that access to higher education is more of an issue for them, this section will primarily focus on Mexican-born immigrants and their children. There are now more than 11 million Mexican born individuals living in the United States, equivalent to almost 10% of the total population in Mexico, and representing 3.6% of the total population living in the United States. It is estimated that over 6 million of them are undocumented, of which 40% arrived between 2000 and 2004 and at least 40% are younger than 18 years of age. Among immigrants below 19, 45.4% were born in Central America (mainly Mexico). In addition, over 14 million US inhabitants are of Mexican descent. According to the US Census Bureau the Hispanic population increased by 58% from 1990 to 2000, now totalling more than 40 million, most of whom are Mexican American or Mexican born. In fewer than 50 years, the Hispanic population in the United States is forecast to exceed 100 million. Among the 2 million foreign-born children enrolled in high school, 37% were born in Mexico.

Most migration from Mexico to the United States is motivated by economic conditions on either side of the border. In Mexico, as mentioned above, remittances represent an important source of revenue, helping to alleviate what are often conditions of extreme poverty in the migrant sending communities. On the US side migrants fill labour market needs that would be difficult to satisfy if the country were relying solely on the existing non-immigrant labour pool. Migrants represent 23% of production workers and 20% of service workers (Bureau of Labour Statistics, 2004).

Especially true for undocumented migrants, work in low-salary low-skill jobs is the norm. According to a study by the Pew Hispanic Center (2006b), undocumented migrants in the United States represent almost 25% of domestic workers, a half of agricultural workers and 9% of restaurant workers. Also, approximately 43% of immigrants work in jobs offering less than the minimum wage, in comparison with 28% of the total labour market (Fix *et al.*, 2001; Marmolejo, 2004a).

This migratory pattern is a historic reality, strongly interlinked with the economic, social and political dynamics of both the United States and Mexico. In the United States, federal legal regulations have established strong restrictions on the use of public benefits by migrants and even more stringent rules relating to the public benefits usage of undocumented migrants.[2] Implications for education, and more specifically higher education, are largely ignored or minimised. Not being able to further their education, migrants – especially the younger ones – are more likely to experience unemployment or to work in low-skill, low-paid jobs.

Why does this matter? In general, as mentioned earlier, migrants have limited economic and educational opportunities. This keeps migrants trapped in a circle of poverty. The children of migrants are more likely to be disadvantaged than those of non-migrants. On one side, they are more likely to be poor (24% vs. 16%), uninsured (22%

vs. 10%), etc. (Capps, 2001), while on the other side, given that parental levels of educational attainment have strong positive correlations with those of their children (Swail *et al.*, 2005a and b), they are also more likely to have low educational attainment. This educational vicious circle is a real problem as for migrants, education, if available, is generally the principal means of social and economic mobility.

Ultimately this problem goes beyond migrants themselves to become a social liability. For example, studies conducted in the state of California show that economic and social inequality has increased substantially, a fact that can be partially explained by the high number of immigrants in the state whose low education levels contribute to their low earnings. The growth in inequality is due in part to the rising education *premia*. These factors suggest that one way to reduce income inequality would be to raise the earnings of workers at the bottom of the income distribution by improving their education (Reed, 1999).

How big is the problem? Accurate figures are difficult to obtain since data on migration, especially with regards to undocumented migration, are usually based on estimates. However, a compilation from a variety of sources shows that between 65 000 and 80 000 undocumented students graduate from US high schools each year; in 2000 there were as many as 79 000 undocumented aliens under 21 who had graduated from US high schools but who had not enrolled in college, and in the same year as many as 607 000 undocumented aliens age 12 to 20 were enrolled in US schools and about 25 000 undocumented students were enrolled in public higher education (Marmolejo, 2004b).

The challenges faced by the migrant population, both regular and undocumented, have a powerful effect on their weaker than average educational performance. In this context, the questions of whether or not to make tertiary education more accessible to migrants, and furthermore, whether or not to allow access to tertiary education for undocumented migrants, and under what conditions, become paramount.

A specific example is related to financial barriers. In the United States, residents of a state can enrol in public higher education institutions where they pay "in-state" tuition. In general, this amounts to approximately one third of the cost of "out-of-state" tuition. In addition, they have access to state and federal financial aid programmes which subsidise the cost of attendance. Within the current legal framework, recent legal migrants have to pay out-of-state tuition and are not always eligible for federal financial aid.

In the case of undocumented migrants, there is frequently not even the possibility to enrol since they often cannot properly document their residence and in some cases even their legal identity,[3] and they are obviously not eligible to apply for federal financial aid. Higher education for this group is out of reach. Moreover, in 1996 the US federal government enacted ambiguous legislation discouraging state governments from offering in-state tuition to undocumented immigrants.[4] Given the law's vague language, and the decentralised nature of the educational system in the United States, the needs to address the issue of access led a number of US state governments to enact legislation permitting in-state tuition to undocumented students, under certain eligibility conditions in any case. On the contrary, other states have considered, and eventually approved, stricter regulations to impede the possibility of paying in-state tuition but also to simply deny access to undocumented students even if they are academically eligible and are willing to pay full tuition. Just in a few states no action in either direction has been taken. In a parallel development, attempts by a bipartisan group of federal legislators to further amend the

Immigration and Naturalisation Act to allow undocumented students access to in-state tuition in public higher education institutions have failed several times. This proposal, known as the DREAM Act, was last submitted for vote in the US Congress in 2007.

Ten out of the 50 US states, including the most populated Texas, California, and New York, are the ones which have implemented measures to provide access to higher education for undocumented migrants making them eligible for "in-state" tuition in public institutions, and, in some cases, even providing state financial assistance.[5] Each has enacted laws which permit in-state tuition to students regardless of immigration status, as long as they have attended school for a certain minimum number of years in the state, completed high school or passed a national equivalency exam known as the General Equivalency Diploma (GED), and sign an *affidavit* promising to apply for permanent residency once eligible to do so. However, this pattern is not followed in all the states, and even in some cases, sporadically, some proposed laws are intending to forbid undocumented migrants and their dependents access to higher education.

Even those able to attend an educational establishment face big challenges. First, fewer immigrant students are eligible for college. The findings of many studies demonstrate that, for instance, Hispanics in the United States, most of them Mexican-American or Mexican-born, are the demographic group performing among the weakest in elementary education and have the highest drop-out rate in secondary schools. Some estimates show that in 2000 school drop-out rates of 15-to-17-year-old foreign-born youths were much higher (11.3%) than native-born (3.3%) (Fry, 2005). This figure is much higher in recently arrived migrants. As an example, in the same period, Mexican-born migrants registered a high school drop-out rate of 32.6% in comparison to 8.1% of early childhood arrivals. As shown in Table 9.4, there are significant differences between migrants of different geographic origin: Hispanic foreign-born students are more likely to drop-out than other migrant groups, some of whom can perform better than natives.

Second, some migrant groups, especially Hispanics, have among the lowest participation and success rates in higher education. Less than one quarter (23.2%) of Hispanic students graduate with a four-year degree within 10 years of leaving high school, in comparison with 47.3% of white students (Swail *et al.*, 2005b). Moreover, migrants more often rely on 2-year community colleges for their studies. According to Vernez and Abrahamse (1996), migrants who had some exposure to US high school were 10% more likely than native-born to begin and complete their higher education at community colleges. Among Hispanics, immigrants were more likely than native-born to then transfer to a 4-year institution, possibly illustrating the stronger democratising effect community colleges can have for them. Overall, Hispanics, and especially Hispanic immigrants rely disproportionately on community colleges. While they are under-represented in higher education, they are over-represented in community colleges where the majority of them (53%) enrol. However, they tend to experience to a lesser extent the disadvantages of community colleges than other groups (Leinbach and Bailey, 2006).

Finally, in the case of students of Mexican descent, lower educational achievement continues over time, as shown by De la Garza *et al.* (1994) (see Table 9.5). While second-generation migrants have higher educational attainment than first-generation migrants, fourth generation migrants – or students of Mexican descent – continue to have much lower educational attainment than average in the United States, which illustrates the existence of a persistent vicious circle between low educational attainment and

Table 9.4. **United States: school drop-out rates of 15-to-17-year-old foreign-born youths, 2000**

Percentage

Place of birth	Early childhood arrival	Recent arrival	Total
Canada	2.8	4.7	3.8
Mexico	8.1	32.6	22.8
El Salvador	5.3	24.0	16.1
Guatemala	6.5	26.8	18.9
Honduras	9.1	20.3	16.8
Nicaragua	3.7	7.9	5.2
Other Central America	4.2	7.2	5.8
Cuba	11.0	4.9	6.0
Dominican Republic	4.7	5.5	5.2
Puerto Rico	6.4	13.2	9.2
Haiti	2.8	6.8	5.5
Jamaica	1.7	3.8	2.9
Trinidad &Tobago	5.1	0.9	3.0
Other Caribbean	0.8	2.9	1.4
Brazil	0.7	5.4	4.2
Colombia	2.2	4.4	3.6
Ecuador	4.8	15.2	11.6
Guyana/British Guyana	0.5	0.0	0.3
Peru	4.1	4.7	4.5
Venezuela	1.4	1.3	1.4
Other South America	2.6	4.8	3.7
England	5.1	1.9	3.5
Other United Kingdom	0.0	2.0	1.1
Germany	6.1	3.1	4.2
Poland	0.9	2.5	2.0
Russia	3.2	2.9	3.0
Ukraine	2.1	2.3	2.2
Other former USSR	1.1	3.8	2.6
Other Europe	4.3	5.4	5.0
China	2.5	5.3	4.4
Hong Kong (China)	2.5	0.0	1.1
Taiwan	1.0	1.7	1.4
Japan	0.4	2.0	1.4
Korea	0.8	3.2	1.9
Philippines	1.2	2.9	2.2
Thailand	5.3	4.7	5.2
Vietnam	4.2	2.6	3.2
Other Indochina	2.1	2.5	2.2
India	1.2	0.8	1.0
Pakistan	1.5	2.4	2.1
Iran	1.2	4.1	2.4
Other Asian	0.9	5.3	3.6
Africa	1.4	3.5	2.9
Australia, New Zealand and other countries	2.2	2.5	2.4
Residual other[1]	15.4	8.0	11.4

1. "Residual other" includes youths born in Bermuda and Cape Verde.

Source: Fix *et al.* (2001).

Table 9.5. **Inter-generational analysis of educational attainment of Mexican Americans in the United States (1989-90)**

Percentage

Educational level	**First generation**	2nd generation	3rd generation	4th generation	**Average USA**
Less than high school	**69.9**	51.5	33	41	**23.5**
High school	**24.7**	39.2	58.5	49.4	**30.4**
More than high school	**5.4**	9.3	8.5	9.6	**45.1**

Source: De la Garza *et al.* (1994).

disenabling socio-economic background. A recent study of access and achievement of Hispanics and Hispanic immigrants at the City University of New York shows that in 2000 Hispanics tended to have lower rates of bachelor's degree attainment when compared with other racial/ethnic populations, and that Hispanic immigrants have very low rates of achievement compared to other native- and foreign-born populations (Leinbach and Bailey, 2006).

Mitigating barriers to access to higher education for migrants in the United States, and especially Hispanic migrants, will and should become a higher priority for political decision makers, as the implications in the long run are cause for concern. Although the scale of the challenge is quite different, some similar patterns as well as dissimilarities are present in other countries.

Migrants in higher education in France

Although it is not regarded as a migrant-receiving country, France has long been a country of migration. It hosts the third largest population of immigrants in Europe, after Germany and Russian Federation (Figure 9.1). Although France is a country of many immigrants from a variety of origins, the French conception of the state is secular and republican and its related conception of migrant integration is assimilationist rather than pluralist or multiculturalist. French citizens are expected to be and become first and foremost French as individuals rather than French as members of a particularistic group or community (van Zanten, 1997; Jennings, 2000). One practical implication of this philosophy is that educational statistics by "minority" or "community" background are not collected whereas statistics by parental occupation abound. Most information on the educational participation and achievement of immigrants and their descendants comes from census data or specific surveys rather than educational statistics collections.

Substantial immigration to France started in the 18th century, when it began to industrialise and to experience a decline of its fertility rate. At the turn of the 20th century, it hosted over 1 million immigrants, that is 3% of its population. France has encouraged immigration through labour migration programmes from 1919 until 1974 in order to fill gaps in the labour pool and to rectify demographic deficits after the two world wars. Migration brought substantial waves of Europeans, mainly from Southern Europe and Poland, and also, after World War II, from its former colonies in Africa, especially from Maghreb countries (Vaillant, 2006; INSEE, 2005). From 1974, the French government officially ended its labour migration programmes and instituted provisions against the hiring of undocumented immigrants, and most of the subsequent migration was family migration.

According to the 2004 and 2005 census, there were 4.9 million immigrants in (metropolitan) France in 2004, representing 8.1% of the population. About 40% of them are of French citizenship. The immigrant population has increased by 18% since 1990 against 7% for the rest of the population. This growth is partly due to recent migration as 960 000 new migrants, that is one in five immigrants, have entered France between 1999 and 2004, with 25% coming from Europe (EU25). While most immigrants come from Europe (40%), the share of European immigrants has steadily decreased since 1975; conversely, the shares of immigrants from the Maghreb countries (31%) and from other parts of the world (29%) have increased. The number of migrants from (mainly francophone) sub-Saharan Africa has increased by 45% since 1999 to reach 570 000. Immigrants born in Algeria were the largest single group of migrants in France in 2004 and represented 11% of immigrants, followed by Morocco (10%), Portugal (10%), Italy (6%), Spain (5%), Turkey (4%), Tunisia (4%), Germany (2%) and the United Kingdom (2%) (Borrel, 2006; INSEE, 2005). Immigrant and second-generation immigrants represented 22.4% of the French population in 1999, and 19% of families in France (INSEE, 2005). In Europe, France has the largest number of migrants or descendants of migrants coming from Islamic countries: people from Muslim culture are estimated to be 4 million (HCI, 2000).

Undocumented migrants ("*sans-papiers*") have become a high profile recurring political and sensitive issue in France. In 1993, legislation aimed at reducing immigration and eliminating illegal immigration was met with protests in the streets by the "*sans-papiers*" (undocumented migrants) and their supporters, which gave them a new public profile. While subsequent legislation, including the latest from 2003, has continued to deter undocumented immigration, France has recently implemented two regularisation programmes in 1997-98 (79 500 regularisations out of 144 000 applications) and in 2006 (targeting undocumented migrants whose children are schooled in France, which led to 7 000 regularisations out of 30 000 applications). According to several official estimates, there are currently 200 000 to 400 000 undocumented migrants in France (Cour des Comptes, 2004). These estimates are extrapolated from a variety of sources: the number of applications to the regularisation programmes, the growth of asylum demands, and the number of users of a special public health care programme for undocumented foreigners unable to benefit from regular social security, called *Aide médicale d'État* (AME). As for flows, 30 000 to 100 000 undocumented migrants are estimated to settle in France annually, though sometimes only on a temporary basis (Cour des Comptes, 2004; Vaillant, 2006). While undocumented migrants are estimated to account for almost one in three US immigrants, they represent thus at most one in fifteen immigrants in France.

Like in the United States, the immigrant population in France has a different, younger, age structure than the total French population, but school age immigrants are relatively few. According to the 2004 and 2005 census results, about 8% of the immigrant population was under 18 (374 000 persons), representing 3% of the total population in that age group. Young immigrants represented 3% of the total French compulsory school age cohort (6-15) and 8% of the total 20-29 age cohort (the typical age cohort for participation in higher education). In 2004, 39 100 non-francophone students entered French schools (18 400 in primary school, 18 200 in middle high school, and 2 500 in upper high school): 70% of them had a foreign citizenship (and were thus probably immigrants). The French Ministry of Education estimates enrolments of foreign students in French schools at about 5% of total enrolments in 2000. However, immigrants are not equally distributed within France and within schools and are highly concentrated in some regions and schools: 40% of immigrants live in Ile-de-France (Paris and its surroundings). Moreover, given the age of arrival of immigrants, most of their children are generally not immigrants but natives.

The percentage of tertiary education graduates in the immigrant population has quadrupled between 1982 and 2005, from 6% to 24%, and is now close to the share of tertiary education graduates in the native French population (which increased from 12% to 29% in the same period). Several studies of immigrants' educational achievement within the French education system consistently show a decreasing gap between foreign and French students, and between students with no, one or two immigrant parents. But given that most immigrants arrive after school age, this increase is probably due to a great extent to the change in the qualification of recently arrived migrants. Tertiary education in France still focuses on initial training and further training of older students in higher education is probably as low for immigrants as for natives. Thirty-three per cent of the migrants who arrived in France between 1995 and 2004 had a tertiary education degree, against 27% for those arrived between 1985 and 1994. Recent migrants are thus more educated than older ones (although there has been a slight decline of tertiary education graduates in immigrants arrived in the past 5 years) (Borrel, 2006). This increase probably reflects the overall increase of educational attainment in sending countries (Teichler and Bürger, 2008), but also the recent shift in French immigration policy. In 1997, legislation was passed to provide highly skilled workers, scholars and scientists with special immigration status. Subsequent laws eased admission requirements even further for highly skilled employees and university graduates.

The access of immigrants to higher education in France is more limited than the access of the total population because immigrants have lower performance at school level and fewer immigrant students are eligible to enter higher education. According to a longitudinal cohort survey of pupils who entered middle high school in 1989 (and who were thus typically expected to enter higher education around 1997 or 1998), 46.9% of foreign pupils[6] against 63.7% of French pupils hold a *baccalauréat* (the degree granting access to tertiary education in France) (Cour des Comptes, 2004). The percentage was 62.3% for the full cohort, which reminds us of the modest number of foreigners in the schooling system. All indicators converge with the results of PISA 2003 (OECD, 2006e) showing that immigrant students under-perform compared to the overall and native populations, and that the gap is reduced for second-generation immigrants (that is, native French students with two immigrant parents). The difference in performance can be observed at all educational levels between immigrants, second-generation immigrants and natives, although the gap has been closed over the past decades. It can also be observed at the level of students' study paths, which are significantly different according to students' migrant characteristics (students from immigrant descent are more likely to be enrolled in vocational high school programmes, less likely to lead to higher education). The probability of leaving school without any degree is almost twice as high for a grade 6 (*sixième*) foreign student than for a French student (15.1% against 8%).

In the 1998 cohort who transited from tertiary education to work, there were 9% of students from an immigrant background (probably including some immigrant students) (Frickey, Murdoch and Primon, 2004). By comparison, about 16% of the cohort entering middle high school in 1995 had an immigrant background: 10% of the students had two immigrant parents (and may be immigrant themselves), 3.4% had an immigrant father (only) and 3.1% an immigrant mother (only) (Cour des Comptes, 2004). Students from immigrant background who managed to access tertiary education had higher drop-out rates than the overall student cohort, but with significant variations between students of different immigrant backgrounds: while 25% of all tertiary education students dropped out without any degree, the percentage was 29% for students from southern European immigrant background against 46% for students with immigrant backgrounds from the Maghreb countries. Female students with immigrant background from Maghreb countries are the only group with more participation than their male counterparts in all tertiary education levels, including the highest tertiary education level ("advanced studies"). Tertiary education graduates with immigrant background from Maghreb countries also have more difficulty finding a job and getting a permanent job than their peers of French and southern European descent, which can be explained by discrimination in the labour market but also by a comparative lack of social capital and by their more disadvantaged family backgrounds (Frickey, Murdoch and Primon, 2004).

Most studies on educational achievement show that socio-economic background is a greater determinant of success than immigration status and that most of the difference in educational attainment can be explained by socio-economic status (Schnapper, 1991; van Zanten, 1997; Tavan, 2005; Cour des Comptes, 2004; Education et formation, 1996; Brinbaum and Kieffer, 2007). In PISA 2003, the gap between first generation, second generation immigrant and native students is also reduced for France after controlling for the socio-economic background of students, though not totally. The most significant reduction is observed for second generation immigrants (OECD, 2006e). But immigrant families are on average of lower socio-economic means, and even more so for immigrant families from Maghreb countries compared to those from southern European countries: they are more likely to be workers (40.5% against 24.7% for non-immigrants in 2002), to have lower income, to be poor (18% against 5.1% for non-immigrants), to live in over-crowded housing (28.4% against 5% for non-immigrants in 2002) (INSEE, 2005). There is also an increasing tendency to urban segregation of migrant populations within France (Fitoussy, Laurent and Maurice, 2004): using census data, Maurin (2004) finds that adolescents who have foreign-born parents generally live in a neighbourhood where the percentage of foreigners is 4 to 5 times higher than those with native-born parents – the same result holding true when they have one or two foreign-born parents. The ratio is twice as high as in the United States. Finally, all these factors result in lower access to effective social networks, in less information and understanding of the system, and contribute to less access and success of migrants in education in relation to non-migrant peers (van Zanten, 1997). While second-generation migrants do much better than immigrants in terms of access to higher education and experience upward social mobility, deliberate measures to maintain and improve the proportional representation and equality of opportunity for migrant in higher educational attainment, including in the most selective institutions, are increasingly discussed and considered as a crucial factor of social cohesion in France.

Like in the United States, undocumented migrants have more difficulties than French citizens or legal migrants to gain access to higher education. The barriers do not relate as much to the level of tuition fees though, as French citizens and foreign citizens pay the same level of highly subsidised fee. However, while nationality is not a criterion for eligibility for public maintenance grants, only documented foreigners can apply for them. Access to the first level of higher education is not totally closed to undocumented immigrants holding a French *baccalauréat*, a case that is not explicitly considered in French law. This depends instead on the admission requirements set by higher education institutions. The legal admission procedure to gain access to universities does not include a mandatory check of the legal status of immigrant students in France, but many institutions do include one.[7] French universities have the autonomy to set their own admission requirements. But the anxiety associated with the possibility of being deported if their documentation status is revealed during their application process does probably discourage many from applying. Undocumented immigrants holding a foreign secondary school degree cannot gain access to university at the undergraduate level at all, as the pre-admission procedure is open only to foreigners who can produce a one-year residence document. However, this procedure does only apply to the university sector, and not to other (generally selective) higher education institutions (general or vocational). At the master's level, it all depends again on the admissions requirements of the higher education institution, including for universities. In the case of France, the admission of possibly eligible undocumented immigrant students is hindered by administrative requirements set by institutions rather than by legal barriers.

9.4. Conclusion

There is accumulating evidence that the foreign-born and their children are significantly worse off than the native-born in terms of educational attainment, access to and success in tertiary education. In the context of the ageing of societies in many OECD countries, of population changes in others (with *e.g.* the white population ageing in the United States while this is not true for the overall population), and of migration growth in the past and coming decades, it is likely that immigrants will represent a higher share in OECD countries labour forces and populations in the coming decades. Migrants who relocate to developed countries constitute, in general, the demographic group which is growing at the fastest rate. According to a recent study, immigrant workers will likely account for between one-third and one-half of the total national labour force growth through 2030 in the United States (Lowell, Gelatt and Batalova, 2006). Economies will thus increasingly rely on the skills of migrants and their children.

Many experts believe that a transition towards knowledge economies is taking place and that OECD countries will increasingly need a highly skilled, tertiary educated workforce. They concur that desirable characteristics for inhabitants are that they reach high levels of education and develop their capacities to become economic and social "agents of change" within a rapidly changing, highly competitive, technology based, and most importantly, knowledge-based global environment. These requirements cannot be met merely by facilitating the migration of highly skilled people but will also require more participation in and graduation from tertiary education among migrants and their children.

The vicious circle of immigrants and their children having less access to tertiary education than natives might also raise other problems for the societies where they live. Beyond the loss of some positive social outcomes of learning for society (see *e.g.* OECD, 2006d; OECD, 2007b), one important adverse effect lies in the risk of marginalisation of this group. Education, and particularly tertiary education, is often a necessary (though not sufficient) condition for migrants and their children to experience upward social mobility as they typically lack the social capital that could help them to experience it by other means. Given that educational attainment and socio-economic background of parents are important for the success of their children, children of migrants are generally not in a good position to significantly better their social position. While not all individuals can experience the same upward mobility, it is important for social cohesion in meritocratic democracies that there is not too much imbalance between different groups of society in terms of their access to the different positions in the society. An identifiable link between specific immigrant groups and low social positions can generate negative prejudices and stereotypes about the concerned groups in the population and make their integration more difficult over time, as these prejudices become pervasive, including in the labour market.

According to PISA 2003, immigrant students tend to be motivated learners, have positive attitudes towards school, and have high expectations about their educational attainment (OECD, 2006e). This might also be true for their parents, as a study shows in the case of France (Education et formation, 1996; Brinbaum and Kieffer, 2007). These favourable dispositions towards learning can help facilitate immigrant students' educational performance. On the other hand, the discrepancy between their expectations and the reality of underperformance might lead to some disappointment and frustration, and become a challenge to the equity principles of their society.

Governments face the difficult issue of improving the socio-economic condition of immigrants and their children and of providing access to better education for them and their children. Continued globalisation will probably lead to a continued growth of migration in the coming decades, which in turn will change the demographic composition of the population in OECD countries. Equity issues will be increasingly related to migration.

As a consequence, proactively addressing the need to increase the general level of education among the demographic segment of immigrants and their children should be considered a top priority for the future of higher education in OECD countries. First, this should rely on policies helping them to be eligible for higher education. In addition, not only should their participation in higher education be encouraged, including within the most selective of higher education institutions, but the ultimate goal of programme completion should be supported. Finally, this involves a closer statistical monitoring of the study paths and educational achievement of immigrants and their children.

Notes

1. In PISA 2003, "natives" refer to students with one or two native parents.
2. Undocumented immigrants are not eligible for federal public benefits, such as income supplements, health care, and food stamps. Federal law also imposes harsh restrictions on lawfully present immigrants' eligibility for public benefits. Most documented immigrants cannot receive some federal benefits during their first five years or longer in the United States, regardless of how much they have worked or paid in taxes (National Immigration Law Center, 2006a).
3. In the United States, there is not a national identity card like in some other countries. Instead, a number assigned to citizens and legal residents, known as Social Security Number, is commonly used as identifier. Undocumented individuals cannot obtain this number.
4. The Illegal Immigration Reform and Immigrant Responsibility Act in Title V, Section 505 states that: "...an alien who is not lawfully present in the United States shall not be eligible on the basis of residence within a State (or a political subdivision) for any postsecondary education benefit unless a citizen or national of the United States is eligible for such a benefit (in no less an amount, duration, and scope) without regard to whether the citizen or national is such a resident.". Source: 104th Congress (1996), *Illegal Immigration Reform and Immigrant Responsibility Act of 1996*, Government of the United States of America, Washington, DC.
5. California, Illinois, New York, Utah, Washington, Kansas and Nebraska allow undocumented students to enrol in public higher education by paying "in-state" tuition. In addition, Texas, Oklahoma and New Mexico also make available financial assistance for eligible undocumented students. An updated list can be consulted at *http://educamexus.org*.
6. Foreigners are not necessarily immigrants (foreign-born with a foreign citizenship), but this will be true for a majority of them, so that this is an acceptable indicator.

7. According to a *circulaire* from March 20th 2002 the Ministry of Education need not know whether immigrants have a residence permit until their legal majority (18). As for admissions of foreign students into higher education, an inter-ministerial *circulaire* (15 October 2002) by the Ministries in charge of education, migration and foreign affairs says that "all applications should be examined substantially on an individual basis, regardless of the legal status in France of the applicant", but asks institutions to inform foreign applicants of the entry conditions governing student visas and residence permits in France.

References

Benito, E. de (2006), "Uno de cada tres nuevos médicos en España ya es extranjero", *El País*, 2 December 2006, Madrid.

Borrel, C. (2006), "Enquêtes annuelles de recensement 2004 et 2005. Près de 5 millions d'immigrés à la mi-2004", *Insee Première*, No.1098, Insee, Paris.

Brinbaum Y. and Kieffer A. (2007), "Aspirations et parcours scolaires des jeunes issus de l'immigration: réussites et désillusions, transmission et rupture entre générations", 3e Rencontres Jeunes et Sociétés en Europe et autour de la Méditerranée, Marseille.

Bureau of Labour Statistics (2004), *Labour Force Characteristics of Foreign-Born Workers in 2003, Economic News Release*, December 1, BLS, Washington.

Capps, R. (2001), *Hardship among Children of Immigrants: Findings from the 1999 National Survey of America's Families*, Urban Institute.

Capps, R., M. Fix, J. Murray, J. Ost, J. Passel and S. Herwantoro (2005), *The New Demography of America's Schools. Immigration and the No Child Left Behind Act*, Urban Institute, Washington, DC, *www.urban.org/UploadedPDF/311230_new_demography.pdf*.

Cour des Comptes (France) (2004), "L'accueil des immigrants et l'intégration des populations issues de l'immigration", Paris, *www.ccomptes.fr/CC/documents/RPT/Immigration.pdf*.

Dawson, L. (2006), *A Managed Temporary Movement Program for Nurses from the Caribbean to Canada: The Short (but Interesting) Life of a Policy Advocacy Proposal*, FOCAL, Ottawa.

De la Garza, R. *et al.* (1994), "Mexican Immigrants, Mexican Americans and American Political Culture", in B. Edmonston and J. S. Passell (eds.), *Immigration and Ethnicity: The Integration of American's Newest Arrivals*, Urban Institute, Washington.

Education et formation (1996), "Les élèves étrangers ou issus de l'immigration dans l'école et le collège français. Une étude d'ensemble", French Ministry of Education, Direction de l'Evaluation et de la Prospective, Paris.

Fitoussy, J.-P., E. Laurent and J. Maurice (2004), *Ségrégation urbaine et intégration sociale*, Conseil d'analyse économique, Report No. 45, La Documentation française, Paris.

Fix, M. (2001), "Urban Institute Tabulation of Current Population Survey", Urban Institute, Washington.

Fix, M. *et al.* (2001), *The Integration of Immigrant Families in the United States*, Urban Institute, Washington.

Freeman, R. (2006), "People Flows in Globalization", *Journal of Economic Perspectives*, No. 20(2), pp. 145-170.

Frickey, A., J. Murdoch and J.-L. Primon (2004), "Les jeunes issues de l'immigration. De l'enseignement supérieur au marché du travail", CEREQ, Bref No. 205, Marseille.

Fry, R. (2005), *The Higher Dropout Rates of Foreign-Born Teens: The Role of Schooling Abroad*, Pew Hispanic Center, Washington.

Haut Conseil à l'intégration (HCI) (France) (2000), *L'islam dans la République*, La Documentation française, Paris.

Hinojosa-Ojeda, R. *et al.* (2000), "The US Employment Impacts of North American Integration After NAFTA: A Partial Equilibrium Approach", unpublished manuscript, North American Integration and Development Center, School of Public Policy and Social Research, UCLA, Los Angeles, *http://naid.sppsr.ucla.edu/pubs&news/public/wp_012_01/migrationpolicyreport.PDF*.

Hudson, R. (2005), "Scientific Migration: A Drain, or a Gain ... or Something Else?", *Science Business*, 24 November.

INSEE (2004), *La France en faits et chiffres: Immigrés selon le pays d'origine*, INSEE, Paris.

INSEE (2005), *Les immigrés en France – Édition 2005*, Paris, *www.insee.fr/fr/ppp/publications/fiche_ref.asp?ref_id=IMMFRA05*.

Inter American Development Bank (IADB) (2006), *Sending Money Home: Leveraging the Development Impact of Remittances*, IADB, Washington.

International Organisation for Migration (IOM) (2004), *International Migration Law: Glossary on Migration*, IOM, Geneva.

Jennings, J. (2000), "Citizenship, Republicanism and Multiculturalism in Contemporary France", *British Journal of Political Science*, Vol. 30, No. 4, pp. 575-597, Cambridge University Press, Cambridge.

Leclerc, J. (2006), *Histoire de la langue française*, Université Laval, Québec, *www.tlfq.ulaval.ca/axl/francophonie/histlngfrn.htm*.

Leinbach, D.T. and T.R. Bailey (2006), "Access and Achievement of Hispanics and Hispanic Immigrants in the Colleges of the City University of New York", CCRC, Columbia University.

Lowell, B.L., J. Gelatt and J. Batalova, (2006), "Immigrants and Labor Force Trends: The Future, Past, and Present", Migration Policy Institute, Washington.

Marmolejo, F. (2004a), "La educación de nuestra comunidad: urgente y prioritaria", *MX Sin Fronteras*, No. 7, July, Chicago.

Marmolejo, F. (2004b), "La educación de mexicanos en el extranjero: oportunidades para las instituciones de educación superior de México", *Educación Global*, No. 8, Asociación Mexicana para la Educación Internacional, Guadalajara.

Maurin, E. (2004), *Le ghetto français*, Seuil, Paris.

MRI (Migrant Rights International) (2003), "MRI Notes on the 59th Session of the Commission on Human Rights", MRI, Geneva.

NILC (National Immigration Law Center) (2006a), "Facts About Immigrants' Low Use of Health Services and Public Benefits", NILC, Los Angeles.

NILC (2006b), "Paying Their Way and Then Some: Facts about the Contributions of Immigrants to Economic Growth and Public Investment", NILC, Los Angeles.

OECD (2002), *International Mobility of the Highly Skilled*, OECD Publishing, Paris.

OECD (2004), *Internationalisation and Trade in Higher Education. Opportunities and Challenges*, OECD Publishing, Paris.

OECD (2005), *Trends in International Migration: SOPEMI 2004*, OECD Publishing, Paris.

OECD (2006a), *International Migration Outlook: SOPEMI 2006*, OECD Publishing, Paris.

OECD (2006b), "The Internationalisation of Higher Education. Towards an Explicit Policy", *Education Policy Analysis 2005-2006*, OECD Publishing, Paris.

OECD (2006c), *Education at a Glance 2006 – OECD Indicators*, OECD Publishing, Paris.

OECD (2006d), *Measuring the Effects of Education on Health and Civic Engagement*, OECD, Paris, web publication.

OECD (2006e), *Where Immigrant Students Succeed: A Comparative Review of Performance and Engagement in PISA 2003*, OECD Publishing, Paris.

OECD (2007a), *Cross border Tertiary Education: A Way towards Capacity Development*, OECD Publishing, Paris.

OECD (2007b), *Understanding the Social Outcomes of Learning*, OECD Publishing, Paris.

OECD (2007c), *International Migration Outlook: SOPEMI 2007*, OECD Publishing, Paris.

Paral, R. (2005), *Essential Workers: Immigrants Are a Needed Supplement to the Native-Born Labor Force*, Immigration Policy Center, American Immigration Law Foundation, Washington, *www.ailf.org/ipc/essentialworkersprint.asp*.

Passel, J.S. *et al.* (2006), *Narrative Profile with Adjoining Tables of Unauthorized Migrants and Other Immigrants, Based on Census 2000: Characteristics and Methods*, Sabre Systems, Alexandria.

Pew Hispanic Center (2006a), *Estimado del tamaño y características demográficas de la población indocumentada*, Pew Hispanic Center, Washington.

Pew Hispanic Center (2006b), *Estimates of the Unauthorized Migrant Population for States based on the March 2005 CPS*, Pew Hispanic Center, Washington, *http://pewhispanic.org/files/factsheets/17.pdf*.

Reed, D. (1999), *California Rising Income Inequality: Causes and Concerns*, Public Policy Institute of California, San Francisco.

Salt, J. (1997), "International Movements of the Highly Skilled", Directorate for Education, Employment and Social Affairs, International Migration Unit, Occasional papers No. 3, OECD Publishing, Paris.

Schnapper, D. (1991), *La France de l'intégration: Sociologie de la nation en 1990*, Éditions Gallimard, Paris.

Solimano, A. (2001), "International Migration and the Global Economic Order: An Overview", World Bank Policy Research Working Paper No. 2720, November, World Bank, Washington DC.

Swail, W.S. *et al.* (2005a), *Latino Students and the Educational Pipeline Part II: Latino High School and Baccalaureate Graduates: A Comparison*, Education Policy Institute, Washington, *www.educationalpolicy.org/pdf/LatinoII.pdf*.

Swail, W.S. *et al.* (2005b), *Latino Students and the Educational Pipeline Part III: Latino High School and Baccalaureate Graduates: Pathways for the Bachelor's Degree for Latino Students*, Education Policy Institute, Washington.

Teichler, U. and S. Bürger (2008), "Student Enrolments and Graduation Trends in the OECD Area: What can We Learn from International Statistics?", *Higher Education to 2030, Volume 1: Demography*, OECD Publishing, Paris.

Tavan, C. (2005), *Les immigrés en France: une situation qui évolue*, INSEE, Paris.

UNESCO (2006), *Present State of Ratifications and Signatures of the UN Migration Convention*, UNESCO, Paris.

United Nations (2002), *International Migration Report 2002*, United Nations Department of Economic and Social Affairs Population Division, New York.

United Nations (2006), *International Migration 2006 Wall Chart*, United Nations Department of Economic and Social Affairs Population Division, New York.

Vaillant, E. (2006), *L'immigration*, Éditions Milan, Toulouse.

Vernez, G. and A. Abrahamse (1996), *How Immigrants Fare in US Education*, Rand, Santa Monica.

Weil, P. (2005), *La République et sa diversité : Immigration, intégration, discriminations*, Éditions du Seuil et La République des Idées, Paris.

World Bank (2006), *Global Economic Prospects. Economic Implications of Remittances and Migration*, World Bank, Washington.

van Zanten, A. (1997), *Schooling Immigrants in France in the 1990s: Success or Failure of the Republican Model of Integration?*, American Anthropological Association, Arlington, Virginia.

ISBN 978-92-64-04065-6
Higher Education to 2030
Volume 1: Demography

Chapter 10

The Reversal of Gender Inequalities in Higher Education: An On-going Trend

by

Stéphan Vincent-Lancrin*

This chapter analyses gender inequalities in participation in higher education and degree awards in OECD member countries. After documenting these inequalities, in both quantitative and qualitative terms, and presenting the main possible explanations for their reversal, we show that this new trend is more than likely to persist in coming decades. While it should probably continue to help reduce the wage inequalities which disadvantage women, its other possible social consequences have yet to be studied. However, in terms of educational inequalities, it would seem that in promoting equal opportunities for men and women the focus can no longer be solely on women.

* OECD Centre for Educational Research and Innovation (CERI). The author is grateful to Francesca Borgonovi, Tom Schuller and William Thorn for their helpful comments.

For many years men have received a better education than women. In OECD member countries, more men than women went on to higher education and obtained more degrees. Since the mid-1990s, however, the gender gap has mainly been to the disadvantage of men. To the extent that girls and boys share the same homes and the same social environments, it might be thought that greater egalitarianism between the sexes would have led to educational equality of the sexes rather than to inequalities to the detriment of men. Is this reversal of gender inequalities a temporary or permanent phenomenon? Will its social consequences be as great as the impact that gender inequalities had on women? These are the two questions that this chapter proposes to explore. The first section analyses the gender differences in participation in higher education and degree awards in OECD member countries and extrapolates these differences to 2025. It also underlines the marked gender differences in choice of study options. The second section outlines the main explanations for the reversal of gender inequalities, while the third and final section discusses whether they will last and their potential social implications.

10.1. Gender inequalities in higher education: international trends

International trends in gender inequalities in higher education can be determined by examining the changes in the composition of the student population in higher education, the relative share of degrees awarded to women each year, the levels of education attained by men and women and, lastly, the differences between the subjects studied by men and women.

Participation in higher education: trends in the gender gap

Until the 1990s, there were on average more male than female students in OECD member countries. Women were disadvantaged by inequalities in access to higher education. Since then, inequalities to the detriment of men have emerged in almost all countries. Table 10.1 shows that women accounted for 46% of students in higher education in 1985 (1.2 men for every woman). However, the faster increase in female participation in higher education has reversed the trend in OECD member countries (but not in most of the rest of the world). Of the 18 countries for which data were available in 1985 and 2005, women students were in the majority in 5 countries in 1985 compared with 16 in 2005. In 2005, the average share of the student population accounted for by women amounted to 55% in the OECD area (1.2 women to every man) (Figure 10.1). If past trends were to continue, the inequalities to the detriment of men would be well entrenched at the aggregate level in 2025, with some 1.4 female students for every male. In some countries (Austria, Canada, Iceland, Norway, the United Kingdom) there could be almost twice as many female students as male. A linear projection of recent trends shows that only four countries would fail to achieve at least parity between men and women by 2015: Korea, Turkey, Japan and Switzerland (even though the last two would be very close, with a female student population of 47% and 49% respectively in 2015). The probability ratios of women and men entering into higher education are rising in all countries, indicating a narrowing

Table 10.1. **Percentage of women students in higher education: past twenty years and projections**

	1985	1990	1995	2000	2005	2015	2020	2025
Australia	m	m	50	54	54	55	55	56
Austria	44	45	48	51	54	61	66	72
Belgium	47	49	49	52	54	58	59	60
Canada	49	54	53	56	58	60	62	64
Czech Republic	m	m	48	50	53	53	54	54
Denmark	48	50	52	57	57	59	59	60
Finland	49	52	53	54	54	54	53	53
France	52	53	55	54	55	56	57	57
Germany	m	m	43	48	50	54	56	58
Greece	m	m	49	50	51	53	53	53
Hungary	m	m	52	54	58	59	60	60
Iceland	m	m	58	62	65	67	67	68
Ireland	43	45	49	54	55	58	58	59
Italy	45	48	52	56	57	57	57	57
Japan	m	41	44	45	46	47	47	48
Korea	m	m	35	36	37	38	39	40
Luxembourg	m	m	m	m	m	M	m	m
Mexico	m	m	47	49	50	52	52	52
Netherlands	41	44	47	50	51	53	54	54
New Zealand	46	52	55	59	59	59	60	60
Norway	50	53	55	58	60	63	64	65
Poland	m	m	m	58	58	58	58	58
Portugal	53	m	57	57	56	56	56	56
Slovak Republic	m	m	m	50	55	58	59	59
Spain	48	51	53	53	54	55	55	55
Sweden	52	53	55	58	60	62	63	63
Switzerland	32	34	37	43	46	49	51	52
Turkey	31	34	38	40	42	43	43	43
United Kingdom	45	48	51	54	57	65	68	71
United States	52	54	55	56	57	60	61	62
Average	**46**	**48**	**50**	**52**	**54**	**56**	**57**	**58**
Comparable average	**46**	**48**	**51**	**53**	**55**	**57**	**58**	**59**

m = missing.

Note: The gross enrolment rates by gender were derived by linear regression from the changes between 1998 and 2005 and applied to the corresponding age cohorts according to UN projections.

of the gender gap in the four countries mentioned above and a widening of the gender gap to the detriment of men in all the others. However, this strengthening of inequalities is primarily attributable to stronger growth in female participation compared with that of males. With the exception of Austria, Canada and the United Kingdom, where male participation (measured in terms of gross enrolment rates) has fallen slightly over the last decade, the number of men entering into higher education continues to grow. Thus a young man still has more chance of receiving higher education in 2005 than in previous decades and, if recent trends continue, he will have a greater chance of entering into higher education in 2025 than he did in 2005.

To the extent that, in some countries, more women resume their studies or follow vocational rather than general higher education programmes, it is possible that these averages conceal trends less favourable to women within the system.

Figure 10.1. **Share of females in tertiary education enrolments (1995, 2005 and projections)**

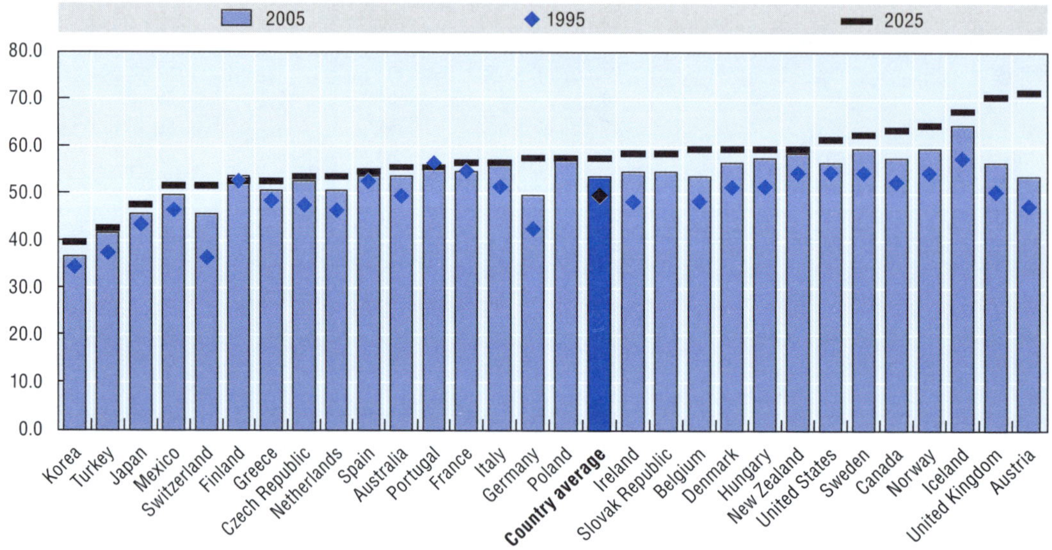

Does the trend reflect age-related participation models?

The international data do not permit analysis by age cohort. Nevertheless, data on the sex and age of students over the past decade are available for a great many countries. In the OECD area, women were on average in the majority or at parity with men in all the age cohorts for which data were collected in 2005.[1] In one OECD country, for example, 54% of students under the age of 24 years were women. In most OECD member countries, the share of women in the youngest student population is either close to or above the average share, except in Iceland (59% of women among students under 24), New Zealand (55%), Sweden (56%) and, to a lesser extent, the United Kingdom (54%) and the United States (55%). Between 1998 and 2005, the share of women increased in all age groups for which data were collected. For students aged over 40, the 23 OECD member countries for which information was available had, on average, a similar proportion of women in 1998 and 2005 (52% and 54% respectively). On the other hand, the typical gender gap across countries is three times greater for students over 40 than it is for other age groups. In 2005, the percentage share of students over 40 accounted for by women exceeded the percentage share of women in the under-24 population by 10% or more in some countries (Hungary, Iceland, New Zealand, Norway, the Slovak Republic, Sweden, the United Kingdom, while the reverse was true in Turkey). However, insofar as students over 40 represent on average only 8% of the student population in OECD countries, compared with 61% of the under 24 population, the sex of the older students has little impact on the overall gender composition of student populations.

Are there significant differences according to the type of higher education followed by men and women?

The international data do not allow an in-depth response to this question firstly because the historical series pre-1998 are not sufficiently detailed, and secondly because the International Standard Classification of Education (ISCED) does not distinguish between types of institutions but rather between types of education: general higher education (ISCED 5) can therefore be provided by different types of institution in terms of status and perception at national level. In Japan, *junior colleges* (*tanki daigaku*) are institutions where women students are very much in the majority, while men still remain in the majority in the universities. In the Netherlands, women far outnumber men in the HBOs (higher vocational colleges) while men are more numerous in the universities. In the United States, the share of women in *community colleges* is higher than in universities, even if women are also over-represented in the elite universities, which in some cases have introduced admission criteria that favour men (Long, 2007; Bailey and Smith-Morest, 2006). In Israel, women are relatively more numerous in *colleges* than in universities, where they are also in the majority, among other things because *colleges* train students for teaching, which is an essentially female profession (Shavit *et al.*, 2007). However, this trend is by no means systematic: in Germany, the *Fachhochschulen* admit a majority of men, which is no longer the case of the universities whose status is more prestigious (BMBF, 2005).

The international data do, however, allow the composition of the student population to be broken down by type of higher education since 1998. In 2005, there was virtually no difference in the gender composition of the student population in technical higher education (ISCED 5B) and that in general higher education (ISCED 5A), although there were slightly more women in higher technical education than general higher education.[2] Table 10.2 shows that between 1998 and 2005 the two sectors converged: the percentage of women in general higher education increased and declined in higher technical education. It should be noted, however, that the averages hide a greater difference across countries for vocational higher education than for the other two levels. In Austria, the Czech Republic, Germany, Japan and the United Kingdom, the share of women in vocational higher education is over 10% higher than in general higher education, the reverse being true in Denmark. (Poland, Finland, Iceland and Sweden also have contrasting models, but technical higher education is not quantitatively significant in those countries.)

The situation remains slightly different for doctoral students since at this level (ISCED 6) the average share of the student population accounted for by women in one OECD country amounted to 45%, while in 7 of the 28 countries women were in the majority. A catching-up effect is nonetheless visible, even over a relatively short period of time (Table 10.2 and Figure 10.2). In the 24 countries for which data were available in 1998 and 2005, a rise of 7% and an average share of 46% can be observed (the weighted average for the OECD area being 47% or 1.1 men for every woman). The trend is therefore no different at this level, even if the catching-up has been slower. The same situation can sometimes be observed in the most elitist higher education institutions. In France, women are still in the minority in the *Grandes Ecoles d'Ingénierie* (Engineering Schools) but not in the *Grandes Ecoles de Commerce* (Business Schools). Moreover, some of these schools did not admit women until the 1970s (Givord and Goux, 2007). Even though a PhD can provide access to certain prestigious professions, students enrolled at this level in one OECD country accounted on average to only 3% of the student population in 2005 (and 2% of all students enrolled in the OECD area).

Conclusion

The last few decades have been marked by greater growth in the participation of women than men in higher education, which initially led to a reduction in gender inequalities and their subsequent reversal. On average there are more women than men,

Table 10.2. **Percentage share of women in the different sectors of higher education and size of sector (1998, 2005)**

	1998						2005					
	Theoretical higher (ISCED 5A)		Practical higher (ISCED 5B)		Advanced research (ISCED 6)		Theoretical higher (ISCED 5A)		Practical higher (ISCED 5B)		Advanced research (ISCED 6)	
	% total students	% women	% total students	% women	% total students	% women	% total students	% women	% total students	% women	% total students	% women
Australia	72	55	26	52	3	44	80	55	16	53	4	50
Austria	81	49	10	61	9	40	83	53	10	68	6	45
Belgium	m	m	m	m	m	m	46	51	52	58	2	40
Canada	72	57	26	52	2	43	97	58	m	m	3	46
Czech Republic	72	46	22	61	6	32	83	52	10	68	7	37
Denmark	54	50	43	63	2	40	84	59	14	47	2	45
Finland	77	52	16	63	7	45	93	54	0	32	7	51
France	72	56	24	53	5	47	72	55	24	56	4	48
Germany	85	44	15	63	m	m	85	48	15	60	m	m
Greece	71	51	28	49	1	35	61	53	35	49	3	43
Hungary	98	54	m	m	2	40	93	58	5	64	2	45
Iceland	82	60	18	59	0	36	95	66	4	49	1	59
Ireland	m	m	m	m	m	m	67	58	30	49	3	48
Italy	98	55	2	56	1	52	97	57	1	60	2	51
Japan	69	36	29	67	1	22	74	41	24	62	2	29
Korea	59	35	40	36	1	23	61	37	38	37	1	33
Luxembourg	24	50	76	52	a	a	m	m	m	m	m	m
Mexico	94	48	x	x	6	42	96	51	3	42	1	40
Netherlands	99	49	1	53	n	m	99	51	a	a	1	m
New Zealand	72	57	26	62	2	44	73	59	25	58	2	52
Norway	91	58	7	48	2	34	97	60	1	57	2	43
Poland	97	57	1	84	1	42	97	57	1	81	2	48
Portugal	77	57	22	54	1	49	94	56	1	56	5	56
Slovak Republic	m	m	m	m	m	m	92	56	3	64	6	41
Spain	91	53	5	49	4	50	82	54	14	51	4	51
Sweden	94	57	x	x	6	40	91	61	4	50	5	48
Switzerland	68	42	24	40	8	33	73	48	18	41	8	39
Turkey	71	37	27	45	1	35	69	43	29	39	1	40
United Kingdom	66	52	30	56	4	39	73	55	23	66	4	44
United States	77	56	21	56	2	42	77	57	21	60	2	51
Country average	**77**	**51**	**22**	**56**	**3**	**40**	**82**	**54**	**16**	**55**	**3**	**45**
Comparable average (24)	**77**	**51**	**20**	**56**	**3**	**39**	**82**	**53**	**16**	**54**	**3**	**46**
OECD	**77**	**51**	**20**	**54**	**2**	**41**	**79**	**53**	**19**	**55**	**2**	**47**

m = missing; x = included in another column; a = not applicable; n = negligible.

irrespective of age, in both general higher education and higher technical education in OECD member countries. It is only at the doctoral level that men remain, on average, in the majority, although women are visibly catching up and parity has almost been achieved.

Degree awards: trends in gender inequalities

Is the higher propensity of women to study reflected in a higher propensity to obtain degrees in higher education? The answer is yes. The trends in this area are the same. During the last decade, the gap in favour of women in the award of degrees widened. As shown in Table 10.3 and Figure 10.3, it is wider than the gap in participation (Table 10.1). In 2005, OECD countries awarded 57% of their degrees on average to women (1.3 female graduates for each

Figure 10.2. **Share of female students in advanced research programmes (ISCED 6) (1998, 2005)**

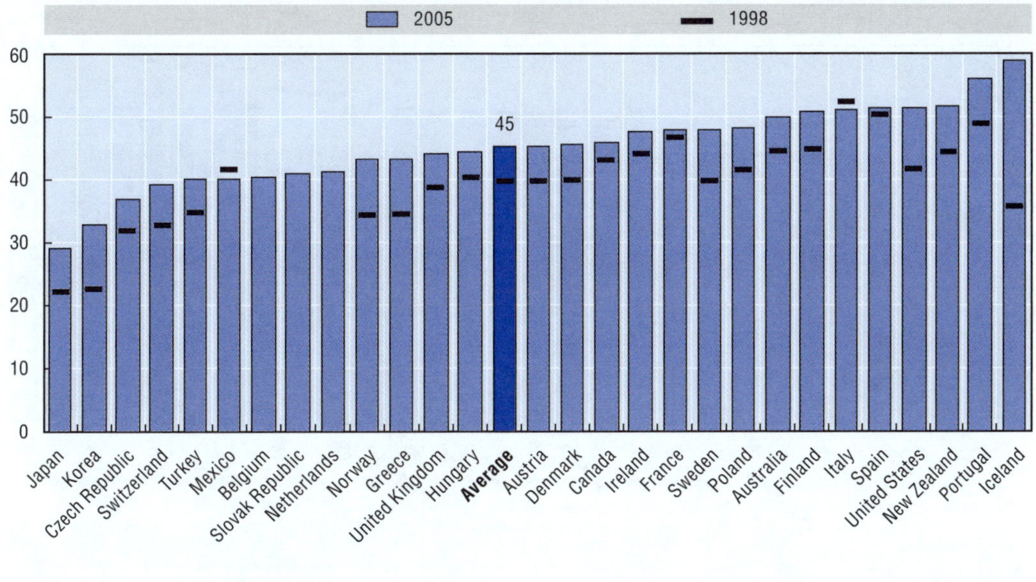

Table 10.3. **Percentage of women graduates in 1998, 2005 and projections**

	1998	2005	2015	2020	2025
Australia	57	56	62	62	62
Austria	46	52	62	60	57
Belgium	m	58	67	67	66
Canada	57	59	m	m	m
Czech Republic	50	57	55	61	66
Denmark	m	59	66	68	67
Finland	61	62	65	63	60
France	55	56	65	66	66
Germany	48	53	65	61	55
Greece	m	61	m	m	m
Hungary	57	64	66	73	77
Iceland	57	68	74	74	75
Ireland	52	56	59	59	62
Italy	57	59	68	70	70
Japan	50	49	49	54	55
Korea	47	49	54	56	57
Luxembourg	58	m	m	m	m
Mexico	55	55	46	51	55
Netherlands	51	56	70	70	68
New Zealand	60	61	74	74	76
Norway	61	62	65	65	63
Poland	53	66	63	62	65
Portugal	m	65	m	m	m
Slovak Republic	m	57	54	55	59
Spain	58	58	64	68	70
Sweden	59	63	74	76	76
Switzerland	40	43	49	48	44
Turkey	44	44	35	37	39
United Kingdom	53	58	72	72	71
United States	56	58	61	57	56
Country average	**54**	**57**	**62**	**63**	**63**
Comparable average	**54**	**57**	**63**	**64**	**63**

m = missing

Note: The projections are based on a linear regression of rates of award of degrees by gender observed between 1998 and 2005, then applied to the UN population projections by gender.

Figure 10.3. **Percentage of women graduates in 1998, 2005 and projections**

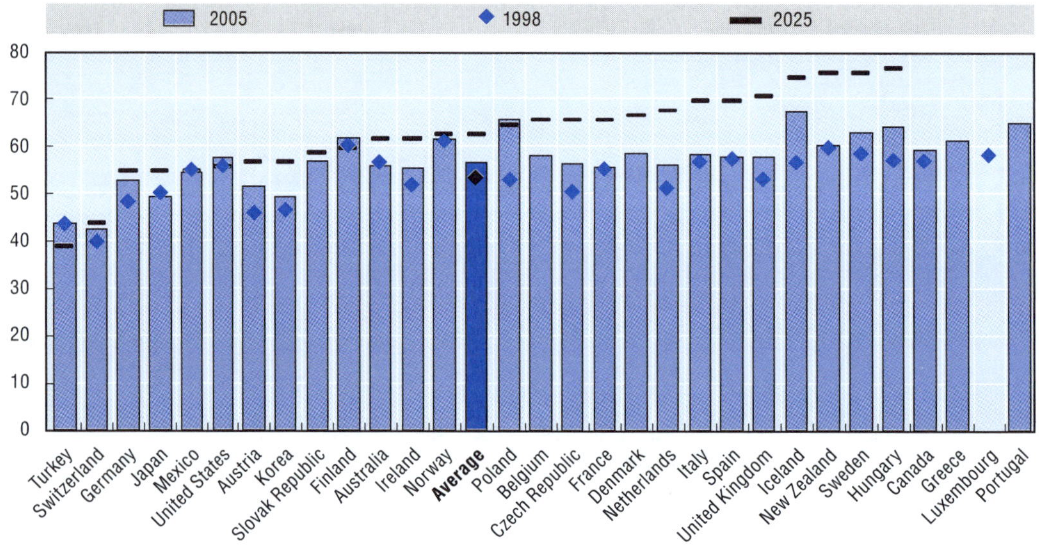

male graduate). If recent trends were to be maintained, the percentage could reach 63% by 2025 (1.8 female graduates for each male graduate). Here too, the widening of the gap between men and women does not reflect a decline in the number of degrees awarded to men so much as the higher rate of growth in the percentage of women graduates.

Studying levels of education in the population by gender allows this question to be viewed in terms of generations. On average (not weighted), the male and female populations aged from 25 to 64 years have the same level of education. OECD countries had an average of 26% of men and women graduates (on average 8% type B or vocational degrees and 19% type A or general).

Table 10.4 and Figure 10.4 show that there are nonetheless differences between countries and types of higher education. In 2005, the female population aged 25 to 64 years had a higher level of education in 16 OECD countries, the reverse being true in 12 others. However, the weight of the oldest cohorts weighs heavily on the analysis: women outnumber men in 25 out of 30 countries in the 24-35 year-old age bracket, and in only two in the 55-64 year-old bracket (2 other countries have parity). Men born between 1941 and 1960 are therefore, on average, better educated than women of their age, the reverse being true for subsequent age groups. The reversal of gender inequalities occurred later in general higher education and can be seen only in the youngest age group (whereas there was parity for the age cohort in vocational higher education). While the numerical superiority of women is still primarily on higher technical diplomas (type B), that is no longer the case for the youngest students, among whom the gender gap is more marked in general education than in technical education. For the age group born between 1971 and 1980, the gap between the proportion of women and men graduates is 6% on average. In terms of growth, women have gained 12 points compared with men between the oldest and the youngest age groups, *i.e.* in thirty years. While their advance will probably start to slow (otherwise there would be an 18-point gap between men and women in the lower age groups in 30 years time), the difference between the rates of men and women graduating could well exceed 10% on average between now and 2025.

 HIGHER EDUCATION TO 2030 – VOLUME 1: DEMOGRAPHY – ISBN 978-92-64-04065-6 –

Table 10.4. **Difference between the percentage of the female and male population with a tertiary degree by age group (2005)**

	Tertiary education type B (F-M)					Tertiary-type A and advanced research (F-M)					Total tertiary education (F-M)				
Age	25-64	25-34	35-44	45-54	55-64	25-64	25-34	35-44	45-54	55-64	25-64	25-34	35-44	45-54	55-64
	(1)	(2)	(3)	(4)	(5)	(6)	(7)	(8)	(9)	(10)	(11)	(12)	(13)	(14)	(15)
Australia	2	4	2	3	0	0	5	1	–1	–5	3	9	3	2	–4
Austria	–2	1	–2	–3	–6	–3	1	–2	–3	–6	–5	2	–5	–7	–12
Belgium	7	10	8	5	4	–4	0	–4	–7	–8	2	10	5	–1	–5
Canada	7	6	8	7	6	0	7	1	–2	–7	7	13	9	5	0
Czech Republic	x(11)	x(12)	x(13)	x(14)	x(15)	–3	1	–3	–4	–5	–3	1	–3	–4	–5
Denmark	–2	–1	–3	–3	–3	8	11	9	9	2	5	9	6	7	–1
Finland	8	8	13	9	3	1	11	1	–1	–4	9	19	14	7	–1
France	2	3	2	2	0	0	5	0	0	–3	2	8	2	2	–3
Germany	–4	0	–3	–5	–7	–5	0	–4	–5	–9	–8	–1	–7	–10	–16
Greece	–1	0	–1	–2	–2	–1	5	0	–6	–7	–3	5	–1	–8	–9
Hungary	0	0	0	0	0	2	6	4	2	–4	2	6	4	2	–4
Iceland	4	3	5	7	0	3	10	6	–3	–6	7	12	11	5	–6
Ireland	3	4	3	2	3	0	5	–2	–2	–4	3	9	1	0	–1
Italy	0	0	0	0	0	1	6	2	–1	–3	1	6	2	–1	–3
Japan	16	21	21	17	6	–19	–15	–22	–23	–16	–3	7	–1	–6	–10
Korea	0	3	–2	–2	–1	–10	–3	–15	–13	–10	–11	0	–17	–15	–10
Luxembourg	1	6	2	–1	–2	–6	–2	–7	–6	–11	–5	3	–5	–7	–13
Mexico	0	0	0	0	0	–6	–3	–7	–10	–8	–6	–3	–6	–10	–8
Netherlands	0	0	0	–1	–1	–5	2	–4	–8	–10	–5	2	–4	–9	–12
New Zealand	7	3	5	10	11	–1	4	0	–3	–5	6	7	4	7	6
Norway	–2	0	0	–3	–4	7	15	9	5	–1	5	15	9	2	–5
Poland	x(11)	x(12)	x(13)	x(14)	x(15)	4	11	5	2	–2	4	11	5	2	–2
Portugal	x(11)	x(12)	x(13)	x(14)	x(15)	4	10	4	2	0	4	10	4	2	0
Slovak Republic	1	1	1	1	0	–2	0	–3	–2	–5	–2	1	–2	–1	–5
Spain	–2	0	–2	–3	–3	3	10	4	–2	–6	0	10	2	–5	–9
Sweden	5	1	6	9	6	4	9	6	1	0	9	10	12	10	5
Switzerland	–8	–5	–9	–8	–8	–10	–7	–10	–11	–12	–17	–12	–19	–18	–20
Turkey	x(11)	x(12)	x(13)	x(14)	x(15)	–4	–3	–4	–4	–5	–4	–3	–4	–4	–5
United Kingdom	1	1	2	1	0	–1	1	–4	–3	–3	0	2	–2	–2	–3
United States	2	1	3	3	2	0	6	2	–2	–8	2	7	5	1	–6
OECD average	**2**	**3**	**2**	**2**	**0**	**–1**	**4**	**–1**	**–3**	**–6**	**0**	**6**	**1**	**–2**	**–6**

Note: x(a) included in column a; the totals are not always exact due to rounding up or down.

Figure 10.4. **Gap between female and male tertiary educational attainment by age group (2005)**

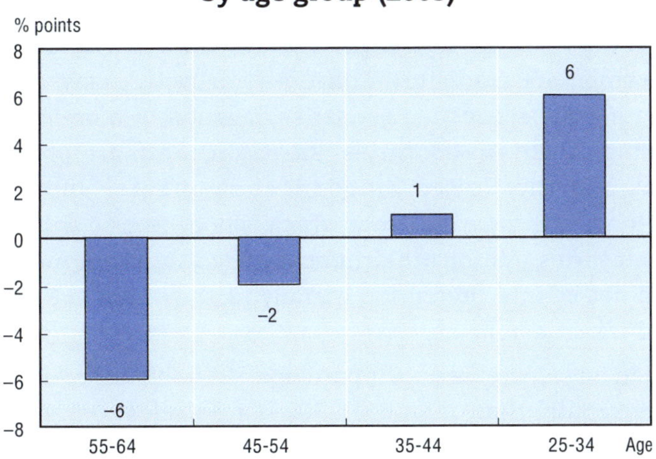

Choice of studies: significant differences between men and women

The reversal of gender inequalities, both in participation and degree awards, does not mean that the choice of studies has not remained highly gender-based. This is an important point in that gender wage differences are partly attributable to the subjects that men and women choose to study. Women, for example, are far more likely than men to study subjects relating to education, teaching, health and the social sector (and are subsequently over-represented in these professions). Men, for their part, are more likely to choose science or engineering which, in addition, lead to higher salaries in the labour market. Table 10.5 shows the differences in subject choices between men and women and trends from 1998 to 2005. 17% of women graduated in an education-related subject compared with 7% of men in 2005. Conversely, 21% of men compared with 5% of women graduated in engineering. Table 10.6 shows how this gender-based subject split is reflected in terms of percentage shares of degrees awarded to women and men in each subject. In 2005, 76% of education sciences degrees were awarded to women, but only 26% in engineering. International data allow more detailed comparisons than those shown in these tables, with each major subject group being broken down into several sub-groups. It will be noted that, among the sciences, there are two with a highly gender-oriented profile: 63% of natural science degrees are obtained by women (almost 2 women graduates for every man), but only 24% of information technology degrees (3 men for every woman). The gender imbalances in mathematics and physics favour men, but not to such a pronounced extent. Both tables show that, on average, all subjects increased their female share between 1998 and 2005. However, those with the greatest increase in women were the health, agronomy and services sectors, while science is increasing its share of women more slowly.

Gender segregation by subject, therefore, is still high and overall remained stable between 1998 and 2005. One simple way of measuring such segregation is to calculate an index which measures the number of people, men or women, who would need to obtain a degree in another subject to attain perfect equality between the sexes in each discipline.[3] Based on the major subject groups presented in Tables 10.5 and 10.6, OECD member countries had an average segregation index of 27 in 2005, compared with 28 in 1998. Thus, 27% of people on average would have to change subject to achieve perfect equality in the award of degrees. Figure 10.5 shows that this average hides contrasting trends across countries. Figure 10.6 shows the same index calculated more precisely on the basis of a more detailed classification (23 subject groups rather than 8) for those countries for which such data are available. In both cases, Turkey is the country with the lowest subject-related gender segregation: men and women are distributed evenly across the various subjects, although more men than women are graduates. Conversely, in both cases, the Nordic countries generally reveal strong subject-related gender segregation. A more detailed classification changes the ranking of certain countries. Based on the more precise measurement, Canada, Australia and the United Kingdom show greater subject-related gender segregation than Hungary, France and Italy, which is not the case with the index based on broader subject categories. As for other indicators (*e.g.* gross domestic product), small differences should not be interpreted too literally as they may not be significant. Major differences in level are more reliable.

In short, women have increased their participation in higher education and their level of education more rapidly than men over the last decades. Gender inequalities were therefore first narrowed and then reversed. This reversal of gender inequalities in the

Table 10.5. **Breakdown of male and female graduates by subject and subject-related gender segregation index (1998, 2005)**

Field of study		Education		Arts, and humanities		Social sciences, business and law		Sciences		Engineering		Agronomy		Health and social sector		Services		Total		Segregation index
		% F	% M	% F	% M	% F	% M	% F	% M	% F	% M	% F	% M	% F	% M	% F	% M	% F	% M	2005
Australia	2005	14.4	6.8	12.8	8.4	39.2	42.6	9.1	19.6	3.1	12.6	0.8	0.9	17.9	7.2	2.7	1.9	100	100	23
	1998	18.3	8.4	17.0	10.8	28.3	37.1	8.4	15.7	2.9	14.5	1.1	1.8	21.7	8.8	2.4	2.9	100	100	29
Austria	2005	13.4	4.2	13.0	8.3	43.4	34.7	9.4	18.1	5.6	24.1	2.2	1.4	10.6	6.7	2.4	2.4	100	100	27
	1998	6.5	2.2	21.8	10.3	42.7	36.7	9.4	17.5	5.0	22.9	4.4	4.2	10.2	6.3	0.0	0.0	100	100	26
Belgium	2005	11.3	4.9	18.8	12.8	36.7	33.6	8.3	15.5	5.5	17.4	3.0	3.7	15.0	10.9	1.3	1.2	100	100	20
	2000	10.2	4.3	19.3	11.7	37.8	34.8	7.5	12.4	5.3	19.8	2.9	4.2	15.7	10.9	1.4	1.8	100	100	21
Canada	2005	17.0	8.3	16.3	12.4	36.8	38.8	8.5	16.0	3.7	15.9	1.0	1.1	14.2	5.0	2.6	2.4	100	100	22
	1998	19.2	9.7	16.5	13.1	37.9	37.3	9.1	15.8	3.2	14.9	1.0	1.6	10.3	5.3	2.7	2.3	100	100	19
Czech Republic	2005	26.4	12.0	10.7	6.9	35.4	27.4	5.7	11.2	6.6	29.6	3.9	3.7	9.2	4.0	2.1	5.2	100	100	32
	1998	27.1	9.3	9.6	5.8	33.3	28.0	3.2	8.2	9.9	33.2	4.9	6.4	10.6	6.6	1.5	2.6	100	100	31
Denmark	2005	12.5	7.0	16.3	13.2	21.5	32.8	4.9	13.9	4.8	17.7	1.0	1.2	38.5	11.9	0.5	2.5	100	100	35
	2000	1.2	0.8	33.2	14.3	39.9	49.4	10.7	14.5	4.7	13.0	3.2	3.2	6.7	4.5	0.4	0.3	100	100	22
Finland	2005	9.5	3.3	15.2	8.6	26.0	17.9	7.0	11.7	7.4	44.0	1.8	3.0	26.0	7.6	7.0	3.9	100	100	43
	1998	15.7	4.7	16.9	8.4	26.2	20.1	6.5	9.9	7.9	44.3	2.4	3.9	21.7	7.0	2.6	1.7	100	100	41
France	2005	3.6	1.3	21.7	9.8	46.4	35.6	10.9	20.4	5.6	19.6	0.8	0.9	8.2	8.0	2.9	4.4	100	100	25
	1998	10.3	6.1	26.9	12.1	40.1	33.9	14.1	19.3	5.1	23.9	0.4	0.5	2.2	2.4	0.9	1.8	100	100	25
Germany	2005	11.4	4.3	20.5	8.8	28.9	30.0	11.2	19.4	7.0	24.5	2.2	1.8	16.6	9.7	2.2	1.4	100	100	27
	1998	11.7	3.0	21.2	8.1	24.0	25.9	10.6	17.7	7.6	29.3	3.0	2.5	18.7	11.5	3.2	2.1	100	100	31
Greece	2005	18.0	7.6	23.7	7.7	30.5	26.3	13.2	27.0	6.5	16.1	1.8	3.8	4.0	6.2	2.2	5.3	100	100	31
Hungary	2005	23.6	12.5	7.9	6.6	45.6	37.6	2.1	6.0	2.6	13.6	2.2	3.7	9.4	5.2	6.5	14.7	100	100	25
	1998	31.6	11.8	11.7	8.5	33.4	31.7	3.6	5.8	5.5	24.3	2.7	5.5	7.8	3.5	3.8	8.9	100	100	29
Iceland	2005	32.1	12.6	11.1	11.2	31.3	40.6	5.3	16.8	3.1	12.5	0.4	1.4	15.2	4.6	1.5	0.3	100	100	31
	1998	21.0	6.2	16.8	11.1	28.5	45.6	8.1	20.0	2.3	10.9	0.0	0.0	23.4	6.2	0.0	0.0	100	100	38
Ireland	2005	10.9	4.1	27.7	20.0	26.2	29.3	12.3	22.6	3.3	16.5	0.5	1.0	18.2	5.5	0.9	1.0	100	100	27
	1998	12.2	5.6	25.9	18.3	30.5	31.4	14.9	19.3	3.9	17.2	1.4	1.9	9.5	5.4	1.6	0.8	100	100	19
Italy	2005	14.1	3.8	17.8	7.1	35.0	37.5	6.5	7.9	7.6	25.9	1.4	2.5	15.8	12.4	1.7	2.9	100	100	24
	1998	4.0	0.7	19.3	5.8	34.3	37.5	11.6	10.5	7.6	25.3	1.5	3.0	21.4	16.9	0.2	0.3	100	100	22
Japan	2005	9.0	3.8	32.3	9.5	31.9	41.2	3.2	6.0	5.8	31.1	3.3	3.3	9.6	4.8	4.9	0.2	100	100	37
	1998	12.6	4.2	40.2	8.5	27.7	44.1	3.3	5.2	5.3	30.4	3.7	3.5	7.3	4.0	0.0	0.0	100	100	43
Korea	2005	7.8	2.9	31.0	11.2	22.3	23.0	10.1	11.4	14.0	38.9	1.6	2.1	10.7	6.4	2.5	4.2	100	100	29
	1998	10.8	2.9	32.5	11.7	17.7	25.3	11.6	10.6	14.4	37.4	3.5	4.1	6.9	5.4	2.7	2.6	100	100	31
Mexico	2005	18.6	4.1	4.4	3.9	47.4	41.7	8.8	14.5	7.1	23.6	1.2	3.1	9.8	6.9	2.8	2.1	100	100	24
	1998	21.9	11.4	0.0	0.0	47.7	48.4	2.8	2.8	14.5	27.7	1.4	3.2	11.7	6.5	0.0	0.0	100	100	16

Table 10.5. **Breakdown of male and female graduates by subject and subject-related gender segregation index (1998, 2005)** *(cont.)*

Field of study		Education		Arts, and humanities		Social sciences, business and law		Sciences		Engineering		Agronomy		Health and social sector		Services		Total		Segregation index
		% F	% M	% F	% M	% F	% M	% F	% M	% F	% M	% F	% M	% F	% M	% F	% M	% F	% M	2005
Netherlands	2005	23.7	7.9	8.6	7.2	35.1	41.3	3.3	12.9	2.4	16.2	1.8	2.7	22.6	9.5	2.5	2.4	100	100	30
	1998	23.5	9.7	9.2	5.8	32.3	37.7	3.0	8.6	2.8	21.9	1.8	3.5	25.2	9.9	2.3	2.8	100	100	32
New Zealand	2005	14.4	4.4	16.8	13.6	36.2	42.0	9.3	20.4	2.6	9.4	0.7	1.5	18.8	7.4	1.3	1.3	100	100	24
	1998	10.9	3.8	26.5	20.6	25.5	34.2	10.4	18.2	3.7	11.7	1.3	2.8	20.0	6.7	1.7	2.0	100	100	26
Norway	2005	23.6	13.3	6.9	7.6	21.4	28.6	3.9	15.2	2.9	15.9	1.1	1.5	36.0	11.5	4.2	6.4	100	100	35
	1998	42.0	21.8	4.8	5.3	15.0	24.7	2.0	7.4	3.9	19.1	1.0	1.9	29.9	11.1	1.4	8.6	100	100	39
Poland	2005	20.1	10.8	8.8	4.9	49.3	42.4	4.5	11.1	3.3	15.1	1.5	1.9	7.6	6.4	5.0	7.4	100	100	21
	1998	58.3	18.6	9.3	11.2	27.3	42.7	0.6	2.3	1.5	16.4	2.9	3.4	0.0	3.9	0.1	1.4	100	100	40
Portugal	2005	24.2	9.5	8.9	7.3	24.7	26.2	8.2	15.5	6.1	21.5	1.7	2.1	21.4	10.8	4.7	7.1	100	100	27
	2000	24.1	9.0	8.9	7.8	38.9	38.1	4.1	8.6	6.6	22.9	1.6	2.1	12.6	6.9	3.3	4.5	100	100	23
Slovak Republic	2005	21.4	8.8	5.7	5.7	33.4	26.1	7.1	12.6	10.2	27.1	2.8	4.9	14.7	5.9	4.8	9.1	100	100	29
	2000	30.2	10.9	5.9	5.1	32.5	27.5	4.0	10.0	8.8	22.6	2.7	6.2	11.3	5.4	4.6	12.3	100	100	31
Spain	2005	17.9	6.9	10.3	8.2	31.6	29.6	7.1	14.1	7.3	24.9	2.2	3.7	18.9	8.2	4.7	4.4	100	100	26
	1998	16.8	7.5	11.4	7.9	38.8	38.0	7.3	12.4	4.9	20.0	2.2	3.8	15.3	6.8	3.3	3.6	100	100	22
Sweden	2005	23.3	8.9	5.3	5.5	22.4	25.1	5.7	11.3	8.3	35.0	0.6	0.9	33.4	11.9	0.8	1.3	100	100	36
	1998	26.6	9.9	6.9	6.2	24.8	25.9	5.4	14.2	6.2	30.7	1.0	1.2	28.9	11.5	0.2	0.4	100	100	35
Switzerland	2005	16.9	4.6	15.2	7.7	40.3	42.7	9.1	15.5	4.9	21.0	1.5	1.2	10.9	6.2	1.0	1.1	100	100	25
	1998	15.4	7.5	20.0	10.3	29.5	29.4	8.2	13.6	5.2	24.8	1.6	1.6	16.9	9.5	3.2	3.2	100	100	25
Turkey	2005	35.1	27.7	10.6	7.3	22.3	24.5	9.9	10.5	6.1	16.9	2.6	4.3	12.5	6.9	0.9	1.9	100	100	16
	1998	22.4	20.0	11.3	7.8	30.2	32.3	12.2	9.4	6.6	14.1	4.6	5.1	10.5	6.9	2.2	4.2	100	100	12
United Kingdom	2005	14.1	6.4	19.3	14.1	34.7	34.1	10.3	21.6	3.3	15.7	1.0	0.7	16.5	6.8	0.9	0.5	100	100	24
	1998	16.2	7.2	22.5	15.1	28.0	27.5	11.4	17.8	4.3	21.2	1.1	1.3	14.9	8.2	1.6	1.7	100	100	24
United States	2005	17.5	7.0	16.3	14.7	38.5	43.1	6.9	12.6	2.5	11.6	0.9	1.3	12.6	4.7	4.8	5.0	100	100	20
	1998	17.9	7.1	15.2	12.7	40.1	43.7	7.2	11.8	2.4	12.7	1.7	2.5	13.8	5.8	1.7	3.6	100	100	21
OECD average	**2005**	**17.4**	**7.6**	**15.0**	**9.3**	**33.6**	**33.7**	**7.6**	**14.9**	**5.5**	**21.2**	**1.6**	**2.3**	**16.4**	**7.6**	**2.8**	**3.6**	**100**	**100**	**27**
	1998	**17.5**	**7.0**	**16.3**	**14.7**	**38.5**	**43.1**	**6.9**	**12.6**	**2.5**	**11.6**	**0.9**	**1.3**	**12.6**	**4.7**	**4.8**	**5.0**	**100**	**100**	**28**
Average change (1998-2005) (%)		–0.1	0.6	–1.3	–5.4	–4.9	–9.4	0.8	2.3	3.0	9.6	0.7	1.0	3.7	2.8	–2.0	–1.4			–0.3

Table 10.6. **Percentage of degrees awarded to women by subject in 2005 (% F) and percentage point trends between 1998 and 2005 (% Δ)**

	Education		Arts, and humanities		Social sciences, business and law		Sciences		Engineering		Agronomy		Health and social sector		Services		Total	
	% F	% Δ	% F	% Δ	% F	% Δ	% F	% Δ	% F	% Δ	% F	% Δ	% F	% Δ	% F	% Δ	% F	% Δ
Australia	73.2	–0.9	66.1	–1.3	54.3	4.3	37.5	–3.7	24.2	3.6	53.4	9.8	76.1	–0.2	65.1	12.4	56.4	–0.4
Austria	77.5	5.9	63.0	–0.8	57.7	8.4	36.3	5.5	20.2	4.8	62.5	15.7	63.3	6.0	52.4	52.4	52.2	6.7
Belgium	73.3	3.1	63.8	1.4	56.6	4.5	38.9	1.2	27.3	6.3	49.3	9.0	62.1	3.0	56.4	12.8	54.4	4.3
Canada	75.1	2.8	65.9	3.7	58.1	1.0	43.7	0.7	25.2	3.2	55.3	8.9	80.6	8.9	61.6	0.7	59.5	2.8
Czech Republic	73.6	1.8	66.2	7.0	62.0	11.0	39.1	13.8	21.9	1.2	57.0	16.9	74.1	15.6	33.5	–0.8	55.8	9.1
Denmark	74.1	14.8	66.3	–2.9	51.1	7.2	36.0	–5.7	30.2	4.4	57.3	7.4	83.8	24.8	25.3	–28.6	61.4	12.2
Finland	82.8	2.4	74.4	2.9	70.5	8.8	49.4	4.5	21.6	3.5	49.9	6.8	84.8	5.5	74.5	8.5	62.1	6.8
France	77.6	8.9	73.0	–1.1	61.5	1.1	39.6	–8.8	26.1	4.6	52.0	–0.5	55.7	1.7	45.1	6.7	55.1	–1.2
Germany	72.2	–1.7	69.4	3.8	48.3	7.9	35.9	5.7	21.8	5.9	54.7	8.0	62.3	8.0	60.3	7.1	49.3	7.1
Greece	79.3	m	83.3	m	65.3	m	44.2	m	39.7	M	43.9	m	51.2	m	39.9	m	61.9	M
Hungary	77.4	–0.9	68.6	3.7	68.8	10.2	38.7	–6.5	26.0	2.6	51.7	12.1	76.5	1.9	44.3	7.8	64.4	7.1
Iceland	84.5	2.2	67.9	0.3	62.2	15.8	40.3	4.6	34.5	12.3	40.0	m	87.4	3.6	90.3	m	68.1	10.1
Ireland	79.2	7.1	66.6	3.8	56.2	2.6	43.8	–4.1	22.3	0.9	44.1	–2.9	82.6	15.0	56.6	–12.6	59.0	4.6
Italy	84.1	–4.0	78.0	–3.5	56.9	2.1	53.8	–5.8	29.4	0.9	44.7	5.2	64.4	1.7	45.7	–6.3	58.6	1.6
Japan	61.3	2.8	69.5	0.6	34.1	11.3	26.0	3.3	11.1	3.5	40.0	6.4	57.1	11.2	m	m	40.1	8.0
Korea	71.0	–0.1	71.5	6.9	46.8	15.2	44.5	2.6	24.6	4.4	40.7	4.9	60.2	14.7	35.4	–4.7	47.5	7.8
Mexico	84.9	13.8	57.9	m	58.4	m	42.8	m	27.0	M	32.3	m	63.7	m	62.2	m	55.3	m
Netherlands	79.6	7.9	60.8	–1.4	52.4	5.3	25.2	–1.4	15.9	4.2	46.6	11.9	75.5	2.9	58.3	12.5	56.5	5.4
New Zealand	83.7	3.8	65.8	1.7	57.5	6.7	41.7	–2.5	30.0	–0.7	43.8	5.2	79.8	–0.7	59.8	5.6	61.0	2.9
Norway	74.4	–2.0	59.9	–0.1	54.9	4.5	29.3	–2.2	23.0	–2.6	55.3	8.3	83.6	1.7	51.6	30.1	62.0	–0.7
Poland	78.1	m	77.3	m	69.0	m	43.6	m	29.6	M	59.8	m	69.4	m	56.2	m	65.7	m
Portugal	83.2	0.2	70.5	3.2	64.7	–0.2	50.8	4.7	35.7	1.2	61.4	3.7	79.4	2.7	56.0	–0.6	66.0	1.6
Slovak Republic	75.5	0.3	55.3	–0.5	61.7	5.3	41.6	11.4	32.1	2.2	41.5	9.0	75.9	6.4	39.9	11.1	55.7	3.5
Spain	79.6	3.8	65.3	–1.5	61.7	3.0	43.3	–1.5	30.6	5.1	47.4	2.7	77.5	1.6	61.8	6.1	60.1	1.9
Sweden	82.3	2.8	63.4	1.8	61.3	3.3	47.4	12.0	29.7	6.9	54.1	–0.3	83.3	4.8	51.8	13.9	64.0	4.8
Switzerland	73.8	16.5	59.9	4.0	41.8	2.3	30.8	2.6	15.2	3.2	48.6	9.7	57.2	3.6	42.6	3.1	43.2	3.7
Turkey	52.2	9.8	55.8	7.1	44.0	6.0	44.8	–1.2	23.6	0.2	34.2	–3.1	61.1	11.3	28.8	3.1	46.3	6.6
United Kingdom	73.3	2.4	63.1	1.3	56.1	3.6	37.4	–3.6	20.8	2.8	62.3	12.8	75.1	8.7	67.6	16.5	55.6	3.6
United States	77.2	1.8	59.9	0.5	54.6	1.8	42.4	–0.3	22.2	3.3	49.3	3.9	78.2	3.9	56.4	19.6	57.4	2.4
Average	**76.3**	**3.9**	**66.5**	**1.6**	**56.8**	**5.9**	**40.3**	**1.0**	**25.6**	**3.4**	**49.4**	**6.9**	**71.8**	**6.5**	**52.8**	**7.1**	**57.0**	**4.7**

lower age groups led to equality of education levels between the two sexes for the entire population aged 25 to 64 years. For purely demographic reasons, these inequalities will persist over the next few decades even if men manage to catch up their lag in the years to come. Given that adult education does not change much after a certain age, the increased participation of men in younger generations will be unable to have any impact on the overall population for several decades to come. However, the choice of studies by gender remains highly differentiated. While this segregation has probably declined over the last decades, there was very little change between 1998 and 2005. With the exception of agronomic subjects, the feminisation of higher education has in effect exacerbated the gender segregation of already highly feminised disciplines, namely health, services and education.

Figure 10.5. **Index of subject-related gender segregation (8 subject categories)**

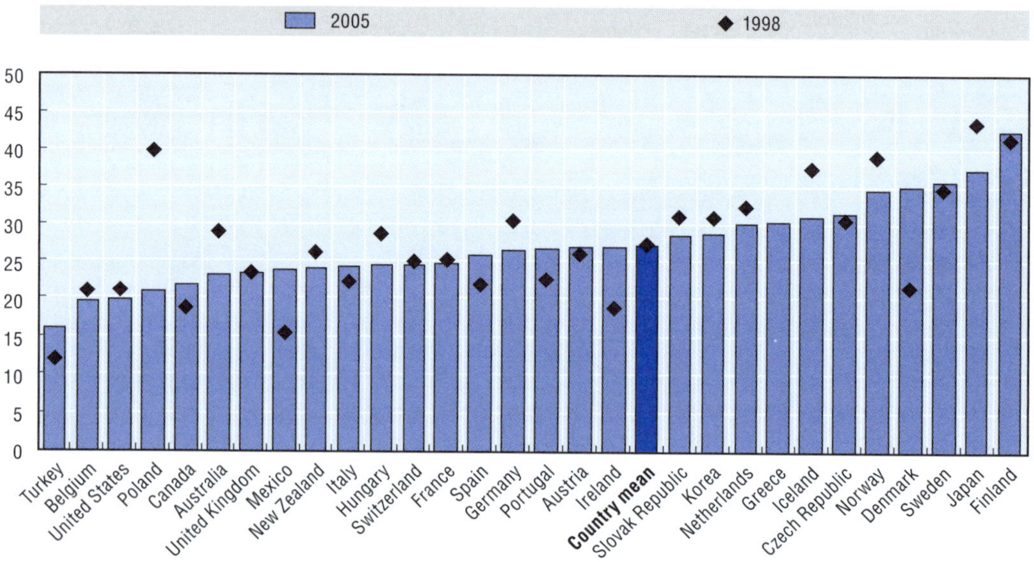

Figure 10.6. **Index of subject-related gender segregation (23 subject categories)**

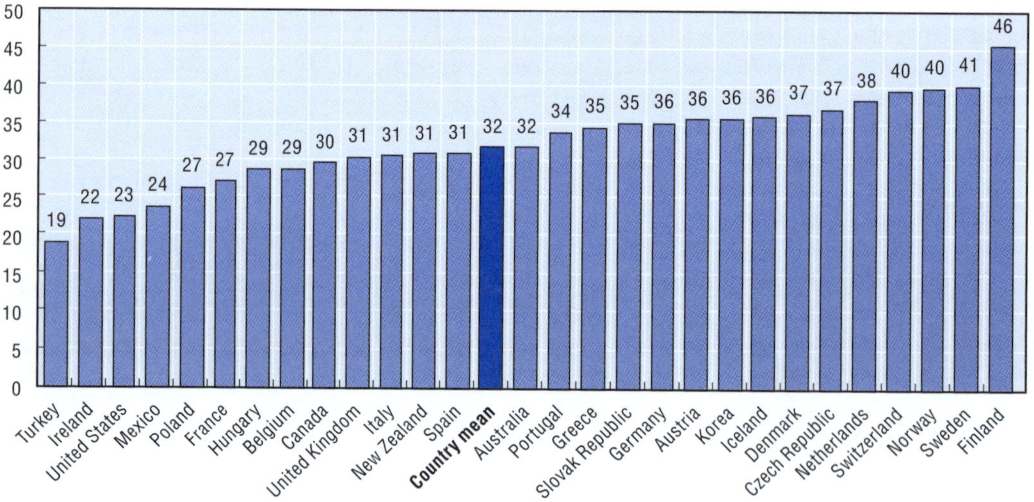

10.2. What is the reason for gender inequalities?

How can this reversal of gender inequalities in favour of women be explained? It was to be expected that the removal of material and psychological barriers to the participation of women should enable them to catch up with men, but it was by no means self-evident that it would be replaced by a reversal of the inequalities to the detriment of men. To explain this outcome, answers must be found to two distinct questions. Why did inequalities to the detriment of women disappear and why did inequalities to the detriment of men arise? It is easier to answer the first question than the second. The explanation for these changes is based on complementary and often interrelated analyses of an economic, demographic, sociological and educational nature.

 HIGHER EDUCATION TO 2030 – VOLUME 1: DEMOGRAPHY – ISBN 978-92-64-04065-6 – © OECD 2008

Demographic factors

Fecundity management and women choosing to marry and to have their first child at a later age are *demographic* factors which have allowed greater participation of women in higher education and a reduction in drop-out rates. They have also contributed to the greater participation of women in the labour market and to better career planning. The downsizing in families of OECD countries has also contributed to the greater participation of women in higher education.

The changes in demographic behaviour and policies of legalised contraception help to explain the rise in female participation in higher education in the last century. In the United States, studies show that the introduction of oral contraception in 1960 is one of the demographic factors which can explain the growing participation of women in higher education (Goldin and Katz, 2002) and the labour market (Bailey, 2006). Women were thus able to delay the age at which they married and had their first child, thereby enabling a greater number of women to start and complete their studies. However, these explanatory mechanisms vary according to culture and do not apply uniformly to all countries. In Japan, for example, the decision to marry and have a first child later probably explains in part the growing participation of women in higher education, but is not related to the introduction of oral contraception which was only legalised in 1999.

Family size is also an important demographic factor which can affect women and men differently regarding their access to higher education. In the United States, in past decades, the larger the family, and the more masculine the family, the less chance women had of participating in higher education (Averett and Burton, 1996). In Japan and Turkey the same thing has been seen (Ono, 2004; Tansel, 2002). The downsizing of families in OECD countries has thus contributed to greater participation in higher education, especially for women.

Sociological factors

Another series of explanations has more to do with *sociological* factors. These relate to the end or decline of discrimination in the labour market, changes in the behaviour of women in a more egalitarian society, changes in parents' decisions whether or not to invest in their sons' and daughters' education, in a social environment in which parents are better educated with greater equality between the sexes, or to the growth in the number of single parent families. What is required here, therefore, is an analysis of the mechanisms driving the reduction in discrimination and gender stereotypes in the labour market and families, and also the formation of individual identity.

Reduction in discrimination in the labour market

When the value of a degree cannot be readily realised in the labour market, there is less incentive to obtain one. All OECD member countries have experienced a rise, at varying rates, in female participation in the labour market and, more generally, greater social egalitarianism between the two sexes. The gradual disappearance of legal or tacit discrimination has encouraged women to study more. In the United States, over 50% of jobs were barred to married women between 1900 and 1950, forcing them to give up their job when they married. The abolition of this form of discrimination gave an added incentive to women to enter into higher education (Goldin, Katz and Kuziemko, 2006). In Japan, the law of 1985 on equal opportunities in employment (for men and women) led to a rise in female students' aspirations and increased participation by women in universities to the detriment of the *junior colleges*, whose qualifications were practically worthless in the labour market (Edwards and Pasquale, 2003; Yonezawa and Kim, 2008). This type of social change can explain the reduction in inequalities to the detriment of women, but not their reversal.

Combining having a family with professional life

The life choices available to individuals relate specifically to a given generation and to the social environment in which that generation evolves. Women graduates therefore had to base their decisions on whether or not it was possible to reconcile a career with having a family. Goldin (2004) examined five cohorts of women graduates in the United States to track the long road they had to follow. According to his study, the generation of women who graduated between 1900 and 1920 seem to have chosen *de facto* between having a job or a family. The next generation (1920-1945) had a job then a family, the following generation (1946 to the late 1960s) a family first then a job, and only in subsequent generations (late 1960s to 1980, and the following cohort graduating between 1980 and 1990) did the majority combine work and family before the age of 40. In other words, while women graduates in earlier generations were often forced to give up a family or a job, the fact that the younger generations of women can more easily combine having a family and a career probably encourages them to study (because their social environment allows them to do so). The first countries to achieve this family-career balance were the Nordic Countries in Europe, and these are also the countries where the inequalities to the detriment of men are now the most pronounced.

Declining discrimination within families

The decline in discrimination against girls within families is another important sociological change which explains the rise in female participation. Feminism and the decline in gender stereotypes in society (Scott, 2006), and in education in particular, have changed the attitude of parents towards the education of their daughters (and perhaps their sons too). In Japan, for example, families have traditionally favoured their eldest son, and girls therefore had easier access to higher education if they had few or no brothers (Ono, 2004). In Turkey, too, it seems that family income has more impact on the educational fate of girls than boys (Tansel, 2002). In the majority of OECD countries, such differences in behaviour have declined considerably if not disappeared altogether.

Generally, as shown by studies in Europe (Alwin, Braun and Scott, 1992; Dryler, 1998), in the United States (Buchmann and DiPrete, 2006), or in Japan (Edwards and Pasquale, 2003), the higher the parents' level of education, the more open minded they are to women in the workplace and the greater the chances of their sons and daughters of participating on an equal footing in higher education. The general increase in the level of education of populations has thus led to a decline in gender inequalities. This factor alone can explain the elimination of inequalities in favour of men, but not their reversal. However, the gap in favour of women is to be found in all social environments in countries such as France, the United States or the United Kingdom and, in the first two instances, is more pronounced in the least advantaged social groups or minorities (Brinbaum and Kieffer, 2007; Buchmann and DiPrete, 2006; Burgess *et al.*, 2004; Machin and McNally, 2006; Gorard, Rees and Salisbury, 2001). In Japan, the social class of the family has more impact on the educational fate of boys than girls (Ishida, 2007). As the reversal is found in all social environments, it cannot easily be attributed to changes in the social structure of OECD member countries.

One rarely studied hypothetical explanation for this reversal is that families now favour girls, especially in disadvantaged areas. In France, for example, parents' aspirations are often higher for their daughters than their sons and in working class backgrounds (blue-collar workers and lower grades of white-collar workers) more markedly in immigrant than French families (Brinbaum and Kieffer, 2007).

Gender-oriented parental model and changes in the composition of families

Imitation plays an important role in the development of individuals and societies (Tarde, 1890). Parents are a model for their children. According to certain models of socialising through imitative behaviour, children develop by taking the parent of the same sex as their principal reference. Brought up in a single parent home (generally headed by a woman), boys would therefore suffer more than girls. The increase in divorce rates and single parent families may therefore have affected boys and girls in different ways. Likewise, if the mother's influence on studies was more important than the father's, as seems to be shown by the greater importance of the mother's social characteristics than the father's in many analyses of social inequalities, girls would also be favoured. Taking data for the United States, Buchmann and DiPrete (2006) show a change between the groups born between 1938 and 1965 and those born between 1966 and 1977. For the older groups, girls and boys born in highly educated families studied more or less in the same proportions, while less educated parents seemed to favour their sons. The study of more recent generations shows that families with the best educated parents continue to have an egalitarian attitude, but that those where the father is not a graduate or where the father is absent give marked advantage to girls (whereas it was in favour of the boys in the preceding groups). This might be explained by the unequal distribution of such parental situations by social environment, but a study of this rules out this hypothesis. Furthermore, boys from minorities are much less successful than girls in cases where their father is poorly educated or absent. Other studies stress the importance of brothers and sisters and not just the parents as role models for girls and boys (Loury, 2004).

Differences in the role of peer groups

Another factor which might explain the difference in the rate of participation and award of degrees between boys and girls lies in the different roles played by peer groups for girls and boys during adolescence. It is not only parents or siblings who influence young people but also their peers, *i.e.* their friends and *potential* friends (Coleman, 1961; Dornbusch, 1989; Akerlof and Kranton, 2002). Frank *et al.* (forthcoming publication) show that peer influence is much higher for girls than boys in the choice of whether or not to study mathematics in high school, although there was little difference between girls and boys with regard to other impacts. Their study confirms other research showing that girls are more responsive to their social milieu than boys (Eccles, Adler and Meece, 1984; Gilligan, 1982), even if this is not always the case (Ridgeway and Correll, 2004). Apparently, the girls' response is even stronger if the milieu has pronounced gender stereotypes (Correll, 2001). In the case of reversal of gender inequalities, this differentiated impact of peer groups could explain why a change in attitudes toward higher studies spreads more quickly among girls than boys, and accordingly why the increase in participation and degree awards has been more rapid for women. Even if there is no proof that this can be extrapolated at this level, it would also mean that the gap would continue to grow if higher studies or the study of certain subjects became socially perceived as a feminine activity.

Economic factors

Economic factors or arguments can also explain the reversal of gender inequalities in higher education. According to human capital theory, individuals make their decisions to study (or not) in terms of the economic return expected from their studies. This may have developed differently over the past few decades with regard to men and women. Analysts have also addressed the economic and non-economic alternatives to studying which may give rise to differentiated strategies of participation or non-participation in higher education.

Higher return on studies in higher education and degrees for women

The decline in inequalities could be explained by the increase in the period of return on degrees for women. The reversal in inequalities, for its part, would derive from a higher return on degrees for women than for men. Thus, higher incentives for one sex could be reflected in higher rates of participation in higher education. It should be noted, however, that the higher return on degrees for women is not incompatible with higher salaries for men in the labour market. Only the difference with the holders of secondary school certificates of the same sex matters.

International data on personal internal rates of return on a degree show that in 2003, the rate of return on a degree[4] was higher for women than for men in 5 countries (Belgium, Korea, New Zealand, Norway and the United Kingdom), more or less equivalent in 5 others (Denmark, Finland, Sweden, Switzerland and, to a lesser extent, in the United States, with a difference of 1%) and markedly lower in one country (Hungary) (OECD, 2007b, Table A9.6). Historical series would be necessary, however, to evaluate the soundness of this hypothesis at the international level.

Numerous empirical studies have studied the reversal of the gender gap in the United States. With regard to wages alone, the increase in the wage premium related to higher education is not significantly higher for women than for men, even though that is not the case according to some estimates (Dougherty, 2005; Jacob, 2002; Murphy and Welch, 1992). Moreover, according to Averett and Burton (1996), women respond less strongly than men to the wage premium on their degrees, thus the growth in the premium attached to degrees does not necessarily explain the growth in their participation. On the whole, the wage return on degrees does not provide a particularly convincing explanation for the situation in the United States (Cho, 2007). In Japan, too, the return on degrees is not a major factor in female participation in higher education (Edwards and Pasquale, 2003). Nevertheless, it may perhaps provide an explanation for trends in other OECD member countries.

Other derived approaches are also interesting. Charles and Luoh (2003) attribute the difference in the responses of men and women to the greater spread of the premium for men. As they are less sure than women of a positive wage premium, risk aversion prompts them to study less. This argument is only valid, however, if there is a significant overlap between the wage distribution for graduates and that for secondary-school leavers, such that young men have the impression that having a degree will not significantly enhance their chances of earning a better wage than a secondary-school leaver. By broadening the measurement of the return on degrees, by including measurements such as the wealth of the home, the probability of getting and staying married and avoiding poverty, DiPrete and Buchmann (2006) show that in the United States the return on degrees has increased more strongly for women than men over the past few decades and can therefore explain the difference in the growth in participation in higher education. It would be interesting to test these different possible explanations in a systematic manner across OECD member countries.

Alternative choices and structure of economies

The alternatives to higher education for men and women with secondary school certificates can make higher studies less interesting or less accessible and, in certain circumstances, be a reason for the lower male participation in higher education. In France, for example, the abolition of compulsory military service for men in 1997 was associated with the decline in male participation in education and the probability of men obtaining a degree, especially those from a disadvantaged social background (Maurin and Xenogiani, 2007). In the United States, 4% to 6% of male participation in higher education could be attributed to draft-dodging (Card and Lemieux, 2001), such that women would have caught up more quickly without the secondary effect of the war. Also in the United States, the rise in the number of incarcerations is also cited to explain part of the decline in the ratio of male to female students (the number of prisoners rose fivefold between 1997 and 2004, with a prison population which was 93% male in 2004) (Long, 2007). Other alternatives are of a more economic nature. Low unemployment rates or high wages for activities which do not require higher qualifications can be an incentive not to study and to enter the labour market immediately, and *vice versa*. For example, Long (2007) shows that the differentiated growth in the gender gap in the different States of the United States has traditionally been associated with the structure of their economies: high wages in the finance, insurance and real estate sectors, which employ many more men, were linked to a higher proportion of women students, while high wages in services were linked to higher proportions of men.

Educational factors

A final series of explanations is based on *educational* factors. These relate to the difference in the academic preparation of men and women, which have changed over time, behavioural (or "non-cognitive") factors and developments in the provision of higher education, especially the introduction of new types of establishment or short courses more often pursued by women.

Changes in the academic preparation of girls and non-cognitive characteristics

The catching up and then overtaking of men by women could simply be attributable to improvements in their academic preparation compared with boys. As shown by the 2006 PISA study, a well-established international trend is that, at 15 years of age, girls score much higher in reading (+38 points on average in tests), obtain comparable results to boys in science (–2 points on average) and score slightly lower than boys in mathematics (–11 points on average). In the case of mathematics, the relative superiority of boys can be explained in many countries by a small number of boys who do very well in the subject: the majority of them have worse results than girls (OECD, 2007a). The changes in results by sex are not significant between the three editions of PISA (the first was in 2000). Some national longitudinal studies, however, indicate a trend in favour of girls over the past few decades, as in the case of the United States (see Box 10.1). In Germany, 57% of *Abitur*[5] were obtained by women in 2002 (BMBF, 2005). In France, girls have clearly made better progress than boys. In 2006, 53% of baccalaureates were obtained by girls and, in the age group which entered secondary school in 1989, 7 out of 10 girls obtained the baccalaureate compared with 6 out of 10 boys (Rosenwald, 2006). The same trend is also apparent in the United Kingdom. In England, for

Box 10.1. **Changes in academic preparation and non-cognitive skills of girls in the United States**

In the United States, an abundant empirical literature covers the changes in the academic preparation of girls using different types of panel data (Goldin, Katz and Kuziemko, 2006; Cho, 2007; Jacob, 2002; Buchmann and DiPrete, 2006).

The advantage of girls over boys in terms of school marks is not new since it dates back at least to the 1950s. It has, however, declined over the last three decades, as girls have increasingly chosen to study "difficult" subjects. The research into inequalities disadvantaging women has for many years been specifically aimed at resolving this paradox. However, the gap in terms of marks obtained at school did not correspond to girls' and boys' results in examinations, skills or IQ tests. In 1957, boys were well ahead of girls in mathematics and lagged slightly behind girls in reading. Between 1972 and 1992, girls considerably reduced their disadvantage in mathematics and increased their advantage in reading and foreign languages. During that period, the choice of courses chosen by girls converged with that of boys. Their study of mathematics and science became almost as intensive as boys (in terms of the number of units or classroom hours taken in these subjects). The changes in their academic preparation (class marks, test results and nature of courses) could explain, according to the methodologies used, from 30 to 60% approximately of the changes in obtaining degrees in higher education (Goldin, Katz and Kuziemko, 2006; Cho, 2007). These changes occurred simultaneously at all levels of cognitive skills and in all socio-economic environments. Indeed, the girls' advantage was greater in the most disadvantaged socio-economic environments.

In a study of four age cohorts, Jacob (2002) suggests that behavioural or non-cognitive skills might explain participation in higher education as much as social environment or cognitive skills. Although he finds the same cognitive differences between boys and girls in reading and mathematics as the previous studies, his composite index of cognitive skills is similar for boys and girls, as are the characteristics of their family background. The principal difference observable between boys and girls lies in their attitudes at school and towards school, also measured by a composite index (based, in particular, on the number of behavioural incidents, class marks, number of hours spent on homework and previous classes repeated). Combined with progress in their academic preparation, this behavioural advantage could be a determining factor in the differences in academic success between the sexes. Some authors, moreover, have interpreted the ease with which girls learn in an academic environment in terms of cost-benefit. The lesser effort by girls would increase the return on their degrees and encourage them to study more than boys (the benefits would be obtained at less subjective cost).

example, between 1974 and 2003, the gap in academic levels between boys and girls aged 16 widened in favour of girls, at the aggregate level (*i.e.* all disciplines together), in mathematics (with the girls catching up) and in English (where the gap widened). It could be attributed to the change in the form of examinations at the end of secondary school (again favouring girls) (Machin and McNally, 2006). This gap is found at all levels of pupils' academic performance, in all types of schools and for all social milieus, including the most disadvantaged. The gap appears to emerge in adolescence, between the ages of 11 and 16 years (Burgess *et al.*, 2004; Gorard, Rees and Salisbury, 2001; Machin and McNally, 2006).

Rise in educational and professional expectations of girls compared with boys

Another factor which explains the greater success of women may lie in the greater academic and professional aspirations of girls compared with boys. The 2003 PISA study shows that girls aged 15 years have more aspirations than boys to obtain a general degree in higher education and to exercise a highly qualified intellectual profession by the age of thirty in all OECD member countries for which data are available (and where the differences are statistically significant) with the exception of Japan (Tables 10.7 and 10.8). Based on a comparison between FISS 1970, SISS 1983, TIMSS 1995[6] and PISA 2003, McDaniel (2007) shows that girls' academic expectations have risen faster than boys internationally. The rise in these aspirations reflects the reduction in social discrimination against women (Goldin, 2004). Having high expectations does not necessarily mean that these expectations will be realised, but an abundant sociological literature shows that they influence the actual careers of individuals.

Table 10.7. **Percentage of pupils expecting to obtain an ISCED 5A or 6 degree by sex (2003)**

	All pupils		Boys		Girls		Statistically significant difference
	%	S.E.	%	S. Er	%	S. Er	
Australia	62.8	(0.8)	56.6	(1.3)	69.1	(0.9)	F > G
Austria	24.3	(1.3)	22.8	(1.4)	25.7	(2.0)	
Belgium	35.3	(1.0)	32.4	(1.4)	38.5	(1.4)	F > G
Canada	62.5	(0.8)	56.1	(1.0)	68.7	(0.9)	F > G
Czech Republic	37.2	(1.1)	32.0	(1.4)	42.6	(1.7)	F > G
Denmark	25.5	(0.9)	24.6	(1.2)	26.4	(1.0)	
Finland	51.5	(0.9)	49.6	(1.2)	53.5	(1.1)	F > G
France	34.7	(0.9)	29.2	(1.4)	39.7	(1.2)	F > G
Germany	19.1	(0.9)	17.7	(1.3)	20.5	(1.0)	
Greece	64.5	(1.9)	58.5	(2.5)	70.1	(1.8)	F > G
Hungary	53.2	(1.4)	45.5	(1.8)	61.8	(1.8)	F > G
Iceland	36.1	(0.8)	30.7	(1.1)	41.8	(1.3)	F > G
Ireland	53.5	(1.1)	45.3	(1.6)	61.8	(1.4)	F > G
Italy	52.1	(1.2)	43.0	(1.7)	60.4	(1.6)	F > G
Japan	50.7	(1.3)	54.1	(2.1)	47.6	(2.2)	G > F
Korea	78.3	(1.0)	78.9	(2.0)	77.5	(2.0)	
Luxembourg	42.6	(0.6)	41.3	(1.0)	43.9	(1.1)	
Mexico	49.1	(1.5)	41.8	(1.7)	55.8	(1.6)	F > G
Netherlands	40.8	(1.5)	38.7	(2.0)	42.9	(1.6)	
New Zealand	38.8	(0.9)	38.2	(1.3)	39.5	(1.4)	
Norway	25.8	(0.9)	22.4	(1.0)	29.3	(1.2)	F > G
Poland	30.1	(1.0)	23.4	(1.1)	36.8	(1.2)	F > G
Portugal	52.2	(1.4)	43.7	(1.5)	59.9	(1.5)	F > G
Slovak Republic	43.0	(1.3)	37.9	(1.7)	48.3	(1.8)	F > G
Spain	48.4	(1.2)	40.7	(1.7)	55.7	(1.3)	F > G
Sweden	33.2	(1.1)	28.8	(1.2)	37.5	(1.4)	F > G
Switzerland	17.6	(1.4)	16.7	(1.6)	18.6	(1.4)	
Turkey	76.7	(1.8)	72.3	(2.4)	82.1	(1.9)	F > G
United States	64.4	(0.9)	61.2	(1.1)	67.6	(1.2)	F > G
Total OECD	**50.7**	**(0.3)**	**47.6**	**(0.5)**	**53.8**	**(0.5)**	**F > G**
Average OECD	**44.5**	**(0.2)**	**40.7**	**(0.3)**	**48.4**	**(0.3)**	**F > G**
United Kingdom[1]	31.5	(1.2)	27.0	(1.4)	35.4	(1.7)	F > G

1. Response rate insufficient to allow comparison.
S.E.: standard error.
Source: OECD PISA 2003 Database (OECD, 2007b).

Table 10.8. **Percentage of pupils expecting to exercise a highly qualified intellectual profession by the age of 30 years, by sex (2003)**

	Boys		Girls		Statistically significant difference
	%	S.E.	%	S.E.	
Australia	70.1	(1.1)	81.8	(0.7)	F > G
Austria	53.8	(2.2)	63.3	(2.0)	F > G
Belgium	60.5	(2.3)	75.1	(1.4)	F > G
Canada	m	m	m	m	m
Czech Republic	54.0	(1.8)	63.0	(1.8)	F > G
Denmark	m	m	m	m	m
Finland	m	m	m	m	m
France	67.7	(1.7)	71.5	(1.4)	F > G
Germany	52.6	(1.8)	69.8	(1.3)	F > G
Greece	72.0	(1.8)	81.8	(1.5)	F > G
Hungary	56.1	(2.3)	66.1	(1.8)	F > G
Iceland	65.3	(1.2)	75.7	(1.3)	F > G
Ireland	63.5	(1.7)	77.7	(1.3)	F > G
Italy	69.5	(1.9)	80.2	(1.4)	F > G
Japan	m	m	m	m	m
Korea	79.1	(1.1)	80.3	(1.4)	F > G
Luxembourg	m	m	m	m	m
Mexico	85.6	(1.0)	86.7	(0.9)	F > G
Netherlands	m	m	m	m	m
New Zealand	m	m	m	m	m
Norway	m	m	m	m	m
Poland	65.8	(1.3)	78.8	(1.2)	F > G
Portugal	79.8	(1.5)	88.3	(0.9)	F > G
Slovak Republic	55.5	(2.1)	64.0	(2.0)	F > G
Spain	m	m	m	m	m
Sweden	m	m	m	m	m
Switzerland	m	m	m	m	m
Turkey	m	m	m	m	m
United States	81.4	(0.9)	88.9	(0.8)	F > G
Total OECD	**68.2**	**(0.5)**	**74.8**	**(0.4)**	**F > G**
Average OECD	**59.0**	**(0.4)**	**66.5**	**(0.4)**	**F > G**
United Kingdom[1]	68.4	(1.7)	78.5	(1.4)	F > G

1. Response rate insufficient to allow comparison.
S.E.: standard error.
m: missing.
Source: *OECD PISA 2003 Database* (OECD, 2007b).

Changes in the provision of higher education

Another hypothesis to explain the rapid growth of female participation – and even the reversal of inequalities – relates to the supply of courses which accompanied the expansion of higher education. Some institutions or educational courses may have encouraged participation of women rather than men. For example, Long (2007) shows that the opening and spread of *community colleges* in the United States partly explains the elimination of the gap between men and women and perhaps its reversal. Older or part-time students are more likely to be women and study in a *community college*, among other things because they provide courses in traditionally "female" professions and have much lower fees than universities. In Japan, the rise in female participation is based partly on the opening of *junior colleges*. A similar process may have occurred in other OECD member countries, where some education remains predominantly female. It is, however, hard to demonstrate whether this new provision encouraged female demand or whether female demand encouraged the emergence of the new provision.

Feminisation of the teaching profession and discrimination against boys

In the line of gender-oriented socialising models mentioned above, it may be thought that the feminisation of the teaching profession motivates girls more than boys and explains in part the greater academic success and perseverance of girls. The empirical research on this subject gives mixed, not to say contradictory, results. It often relies, in fact, on databases which are too small. In the higher education sector in the United States, however, it seems to be an established fact that having a female teacher in certain subjects, in one's first course in a predominantly "male" subject encourages girls to persevere, and *vice versa* (Bettinger and Long, 2005). Dee (2004, 2005, 2007) shows from a national database that teachers view their students more positively if they are of the same sex and the same ethnic/minority background as them, especially if they come from the most disadvantaged backgrounds (or the South of the United States), and that students have better academic results when they have a teacher of the same sex and the same ethnic/minority background. Closely linked to racial issues, these results cannot necessarily be extrapolated outside the United States context. In Israel, a natural experiment comparing the marks of the same students in the same examination conditions by their teachers and external examiners who had no information about them showed systematic bias against boys in the nine subjects tested (and in arts, science and mathematics), irrespective of the teacher's sex (Lavy, 2004). Teachers could in fact favour girls, perhaps because of their better behaviour in school. In Sweden, where the superiority of girls' results over those of boys continues to rise, Holmlund and Sund (2007) show that the gap is wider in subjects mainly taught by women, without being able to attribute it to the fact of having a teacher of the same sex. The difference with regard to earlier studies might stem from the fact that the Swedish students in their sample were highly motivated and performing students, so that the positive effect of having a teacher of the same sex might not be valid for all types of students.

A final hypothesis: what if these differences were *biological?* Perhaps past discrimination prevented women from realising their full potential which is no longer the case today. In fact, neuro-scientific research has not as yet found any differences in the cognitive capacities of girls and boys (OECD, 2007c). Moreover, in terms of social policy, biological explanations can only be a last resort, because they tend to legitimise the *status quo*. After all, thirty years ago, the "biological" argument showed that men had superior cognitive capacities to women...

The above explanations are both partial and complementary. As in the past, several necessary reasons are often needed to understand facts or trends rather than a single sufficient reason. A systematic exploration of the various factors which might explain the reversal of educational gender inequalities in OECD member countries is therefore an important programme of research with which to inform public policies.

10.3. What is the future and importance of gender inequalities in higher education?

The reversal of gender inequalities seems to be a continuing trend in higher education (and one which will eventually emerge in the four OECD countries where it has not yet appeared). Indeed, all the explanatory factors mentioned above are very unlikely to change fundamentally or rapidly in coming decades. The gender balance in access to higher education and degree awards could be restored through a reversal of the trends that have contributed to the advance of women (*i.e.* a relative regression of women) or through the balancing of the factors which underlie the differences in the results achieved by men and women. Moreover, even were this to happen, it would take decades for such a trend to become visible in the rates of participation and obtaining of degrees by women and men. This is because, in the absence of highly dynamic lifelong learning, the replacement of generations is the major mechanism of change in education levels in OECD member countries and the pace is slow.

Will the reversal of inequalities last?

In terms of demographic factors, a reversal of the trend among women towards delaying getting married and starting a family until they have completed their studies and, more generally, towards control over fecundity, seems unlikely within the next two decades.

In terms of social change, the reduction in discrimination against women in the labour market and within the family is a social change found in all OECD member countries. Thanks to past and future struggles against inequalities to the detriment of women, the social and cultural barriers which stood in the way of female participation in higher education are likely to continue to disappear. Likewise, imitative socialising mechanisms point towards greater participation by women. The fact that a growing number of women are now graduating, and that more women than men are graduates in the younger generations, will continue to increase the participation of women, irrespective of their family environment, and favour females over males living in single-parent households (generally headed by women), if children are considered to be more influenced by their parent of the same sex. The impacts of peer groups would suggest the same conclusions. That will allow a catching up effect in countries and levels of studies where there is still a gap in favour of boys. In countries where almost two out of three students will be girls, there might even be a risk of new social stereotypes emerging and transforming higher education into a predominantly female activity, thereby further widening the gender gap. The impacts of peer groups are found to be even more pronounced on girls in respect of activities held to be "feminine". At the same time, the high level of subject segregation by gender reveals a far more complex picture.

From an economic standpoint, even if the return on degrees were similar for men and women in purely economic terms compared with secondary level education, it would probably still be higher for women once the return related to marriage is taken into account. Women are more likely to be poor because they are more likely to be the head of a single-parent household and to work part-time. Women graduates are more likely to avoid this situation, which can be enough to make the economic return on their degrees (in the broad sense) higher than for men, and thus, their incentives to study are stronger. However, the ageing of the population is likely to increase demand in the feminised service sectors, with two possible contradictory consequences: it might lead to a rise in demand among women for courses in subjects leading to those sectors or it might, on the contrary, lead to a decline in their rates of participation if the wages for jobs not requiring a higher qualification increased as a result of a shortage (which is unlikely, however).

Finally, and this is probably the major determining factor, the developments in educational factors have largely favoured women. Girls have always scored higher marks than boys at school, and the higher participation of boys in higher education could be attributed to their choice of subjects and their better results in mathematics and science. Over the past few decades, girls have maintained their advantage in terms of marks at school (which some regard as indicators of behaviour rather than aptitude), they have increased their advantage in languages and almost eliminated their disadvantage in science and mathematics, two subjects which have long been crucial to access to and success in higher education. Several countries continue to have public policies to encourage girls to study scientific subjects. Furthermore, the academic and professional aspirations of girls are higher than those of boys in almost all countries and have grown faster than those of boys in recent decades. Under these circumstances and in the absence of targeted policies, it is hard to see how boys would be able to catch up or even to prevent the gap from widening still further.

Certain economic factors might, however, offset these trends. Compulsory military service, war, rising unemployment or the absence of economic opportunities in "masculine" industries, for example, have in the past helped to fuel increases in boys' participation in higher education, thereby partly reflecting a strategy of avoidance. Other economic factors could have the same effects in the future. A decline in the number of boys leaving the educational system before the level required for entry into higher education or a stronger culture of lifelong learning or higher education for adults with a lower secondary school certificate might also offset this trend in the medium term (OECD, 2007d). However, as we have seen above, the gender gap is just as wide among older students, even though there are considerable differences between countries.

Do inequalities to the detriment of men matter?

Why should the new educational inequalities to the detriment of men matter to society? Research (or even speculation) on the subject is rare. If gender inequalities in higher education were merely the reflection of different preferences of boys and girls for education, perhaps they would be of little importance for society. It all depends on whether one considers gender equality in higher education desirable in itself or only as an instrument for gender equality in society. That said, the inequalities in the education sector may be both the effect and cause of inequalities in society. Modern democracies base their social hierarchy on a meritocracy in part founded on education, so that educational inequalities can amplify social inequalities, which would not be the case, for example, in societies based on a feudal system or a caste system where people's social position is determined from birth.

Insofar as the inequalities to the detriment of women in higher education reflected and prevented the reduction in social inequalities disadvantaging women, they were not necessarily symmetrical with inequalities to the detriment of men. It is possible to be in a dominant position without being numerically in the majority (Deleuze and Guattari, 1987). To the extent that men have not traditionally suffered from gender discrimination in OECD member countries, in the form of either legal barriers or belief in cultural stereotypes, the inequalities disadvantaging men in higher education may seem less important. Despite its impartiality in principle, the history of science and higher education has been strongly marked by discrimination against women (Le Doeuff, 2003). That would explain why policies and to a large extent the debates on gender inequalities in higher education focus mainly on the increasingly few cases where women are still at a disadvantage (Eurydice, 2007). Countries with educational policies in favour of boys are few in number.

The two social consequences of educational gender inequalities most often mentioned are related to demography and to gender inequalities in the labour market.

Could the reversal of gender inequalities have negative demographic consequences? Homogamy between higher education graduates is high and has increased over the past few decades (unmarried unions also follow the same trend) (Schwarzt and Mare, 2005; Qian and Preston, 1993). Furthermore, while men often married women less qualified than them, women tend to marry men more (or less) qualified than them (hypergamy). Were this trend to be maintained, the reversal of gender inequalities in higher education would lead to a risk of a reduction in fecundity in that the probability of women marrying and having children would diminish. This was in fact the case among higher education graduates at the turn of the century in the United States (Goldin, 2004) and what can currently be seen in Japan where the lower rate of marriage among women graduates apparently accounts for 20 to 33% of the overall decline in the marriage rate (Raymo and Iwasawa, 2005). The "privileges" of male graduates would increase because they could become more selective in the choice of a spouse with a higher education degree, the reverse being true of women with only a secondary school certificate. For many OECD countries, where the legislation on equality between men and women has made huge advances, this argument probably assumes too much rigidity in the behaviour of women. Moreover, it overlooks the possible effects of stratification within systems. In the United States, demographic research refutes the idea that better qualified women would remain celibate and childless, as was generally the case in the early twentieth century (Goldstein and Kenney, 2001). The trend among women to hypergamy declined markedly in the 1980s and 1990s, and even disappeared altogether according to some indicators. The remarkable trend in this area lies rather in the sharp fall of marriage rates of less educated men (Rose, 2006). More than a decline in fecundity, the maintenance of a high degree of homogamy among higher education graduates and the decline in the probability of marriage of less educated persons could, in fact, help to entrench the social inequalities related to education (by tying them more to socio-economic groups). In short, the demographic arguments which claim that the reversal of gender inequalities might lead to a decline in the number of marriages and which point to the already declining fecundity rates in many OECD countries do not seem very convincing.

A second demographic question relates to the gender inequality in life expectancy and mortality. In 2005, the life expectancy at birth of women was higher than that of men by an average of 5.7 years in OECD countries. Research on the links between health and education has revealed that there is a strong correlation between the level of higher education and life expectancy, between countries as well as within countries: studies have shown this for the United States, Canada, Israel, Western Europe, and Eastern Europe (Cutler and Lleras-Muney, 2006; Kunst and Mackenbach, 1994; Mackenbach *et al.*, 2007). The benefits of higher education in terms of extending life expectancy seem to have increased in Europe as well as in the United States (Mackenbach *et al.*, 2007; Pappas *et al.*, 1993; Preston and Elo, 1995). Several studies have shown that the increase in life expectancy in the past decade is concentrated in populations continuing on to higher education and that is has diminished in the groups having high school diplomas or less (Meara, Richards and Cutler, 2008; Goesling, 2007; Dobson, 2006).

One could then think that the reversal of gender inequalities in education could increase the gender gap of life expectancy in favour of women. In reality it is difficult to conclude, given the lack of comparative studies between the relative and absolute benefits of tertiary education to life expectancy for men and women (as well as on the composition effects of the gender gap in tertiary education participation and attainment). Many national studies show that there are more social inequalities linked with the level of education and mortality between men than there are between women (Mustard and Etches, 2003). The extension of life expectancy associated with higher education seems in this way larger for men than for women (compared with men and women with respectively lower levels of education) (Preston and Elo, 1995; Makenbach *et al.*, 2007; Meara, Richards and Cutler, 2008). These results do not contradict nor confirm the idea that the widening of the gender gap in tertiary education could accentuate the inequality in life expectancy between the sexes. The narrowing of the life expectancy gender gap in favour of women in industrialised countries in the past two decades also gives little response to this question: reasons for this trend are under debate, and we do not know what impact education has compared to other factors (Glei and Horiuchi, 2007).

Could the reversal of educational gender inequalities have negative social consequences? In particular, will it lead to a reversal of gender inequalities in the labour market, especially in terms of wages and access to the highest social positions in coming decades? An in-depth examination of this question lies outside the scope of this chapter and we shall limit ourselves to a few simple comments.

Combined with other factors, the rise in the level of education of women compared with men has contributed to the systematic decline in wage inequalities disadvantaging women in recent decades in all OECD member countries (OECD, 2002). Facilitating the increase in the level of education of women is also part of the arsenal of policy instruments used to reduce gender inequalities in the labour market, alongside other social policies, for example, relating to early childhood. However, the current reversal of gender inequalities in higher education and the continuation of this trend are probably not enough to achieve an evening-out of the conditions of men and women in the labour market in the medium term.

Indeed, the level of education of women is not enough in itself to explain the inequalities. The gender inequalities relating directly to the labour market may be more important than differences in education in explaining the differences in wages of young graduates of the two sexes, as is the case, for example, in the United States (Bobitt-Zeher, 2007). To understand this, it is simply worth recalling some of the factors which explain wage inequalities to the detriment of women. Women work on average fewer years than men (and thus earn less, even in the same sector), are more likely to work part-time, have greater difficulty in obtaining promotion to higher decision-making posts, often work in sectors or professions which pay less than those where men are in the majority, aspire on average less than men to work in the most lucrative sectors or professions (Chevalier, 2007; Correll, 2001), reduce their working time when they have children while men, conversely, increase it in under the same circumstances and, despite greater social egalitarianism, women continue to invest more than men in domestic activities and those related to children, whether by preference or in response to greater social pressure (Alwin, Braun and Scott, 1992). The reduction in gender wage inequalities was therefore attributed to the increase in women's education, and also the feminisation (or "integration") of traditionally male sectors or professions, the decline in wages of the least educated men, the emergence of more egalitarian social standards as a result of feminism, and social policies, both at the firm and government level, which allowed women and, to a lesser extent men, to reconcile family and working life better (OECD, 2007d). A recent OECD study offers a detailed international analysis of these questions (OECD, 2002), while Blau and Kahn (2000) and Reskin and Bielby (2005) present a summary of the results of economic and sociological research, pointing out the technical difficulties of measuring and understanding these inequalities.

Nevertheless, the rise in the level of education of women explains *in part* the decline in gender wage inequalities over the past few decades and the reversal of educational gender inequalities is likely to continue to contribute to this decline. The difference between men and women in their choice of fields of study explains to a greater extent the wage differences than differences in levels of education. Thus, studies shows that the reduction in wage inequalities is more likely to come about through the equalisation of choice of studies than through changes in the level of education (Bobbitt-Zeher, 2007; Christie and Shannon, 2001; Shannon and Kidd, 2001; Blau and Kahn, 2000). Despite the rise in the level of women's education in the younger generations (and the narrowing of the gap between men and women) it is not for all that certain that a generational rationale is sufficient to eliminate wage inequalities between men and women over the next thirty years (Chauvel, 2004), even if the retirement of the age groups in which such inequalities were the most pronounced will also automatically lead to a reduction in these inequalities (at the macro level).

Although it is likely that it will take more than two decades on average for wage inequalities to the detriment of women to disappear, the pattern of reversal of gender inequalities in higher education might well change. Average wages could in fact mask considerable differences in wage distribution by gender. Men might have a much more heterogeneous social condition than women, as their wage or social advantage is attributable to the very great success of a small proportion of men. In other words, as in the case of the boys' results in mathematics tests, it is not impossible that men, on average, may have wages higher than women but that the majority of men (or many of them) are less successful than women. One might find men over-represented in the higher or lower echelons of society, both in economic terms and social status. Were that to be the case, the configuration of social relations and stereotypes might change. Perhaps a not negligible proportion of men might become more dependent on women and more involved in domestic affairs. Perhaps a greater number of men might find themselves socially excluded. In fact, the political and social consequences of a new social division of work and distribution of power between the sexes remain to be determined. The difference in the destiny of men and women with no degree, as well as its evolution, also needs further study. It is not, however, impossible that the reversal of educational gender inequalities might have problematic social consequences.

10.4. Summary and conclusion

The reversal of gender inequalities now seems well established in OECD member countries. More women than men enter higher education, irrespective of age or type of higher education. It is only at the doctoral level that women have not yet caught up with men, although current trends suggest that this will happen within a few years. All fields of study have therefore become feminised, even though gender segregation along subject lines still remains very pronounced. Science is still the field that is becoming feminised more slowly and that is still very predominantly male, especially information technology and mathematics. This segregation matters to the extent that it explains the gender wage differences in the labour market. Male and female populations of working age now have the same level of education, but in younger generations women are better educated than men.

This reversal of the gender inequalities in higher education stems from various demographic, economic, sociological and educational factors. None of the factors which help to understand it appear likely to disappear or reverse in the next few decades. On the contrary, some of them point to more rapid growth in the level of women's education compared with men (which nevertheless continues to rise). Educational inequalities disadvantaging men are very likely to persist and increase. Generation replacement means that the female population will in any case continue to be better educated than the male population.

However, would lasting educational inequalities to the detriment of men lead to a social or demographic crisis or even to a reversal of gender wage inequalities in the labour market? It is hard to say. Would it therefore not be possible simply to ignore the educational inequalities disadvantaging men? This would, in fact, be neither prudent nor fair.

In democracies, combating inequalities is not just subordinate to equality in the labour market. It is a matter of principle. Equity consists of ensuring that everyone is given the right conditions in which to achieve his/her potential, but how can one be sure that the lesser academic achievements of boys do not reflect some form of discrimination against them? Furthermore, diversity (or in this case the mix) matters to the extent that it represents a social enrichment for all. For example, the elite American universities are starting to favour boys in their admission procedures because they think that the mix of their students is important for everyone. Lastly, educational inequalities in favour of women may also do them a disservice in the labour market if they are associated with greater gender segregation in terms of disciplines. Research shows that wage inequalities to the detriment of women are more associated with the percentage of girls studying a subject than the subject itself. While many countries encourage many girls to study science, to encourage a mix and promote gender wage equality, too few encourage men to improve their performance in languages and to work in feminised sectors. While girls must be encouraged to study disciplines dominated by boys, the new policies of equality between the sexes should pay more attention to boys and help them to improve their performance and participation in subjects dominated by girls (languages), and also those where the average performance of boys masks the weakness of the majority of boys and the excellence of a minority (mathematics and science). The trends in the academic performance and choice of studies by women over the past few decades show that these are not intangible factors. And such policies could be beneficial to men (from an educational point of view) and women (in terms of wages).

Another reason for concern about the reversal of inequalities has to do with the current ignorance of its possible social consequences. The permanent establishment of these new inequalities might, for example, give rise to undesirable social stereotypes, whereby higher studies would be the province of women. While they have little chance of becoming established in the most advantaged social milieus, they might be adopted in the most disadvantaged, where in several countries the inequalities to the detriment of boys are already the most pronounced, and strengthen social inequalities. Furthermore, it is not unusual for social stereotypes to bring about new social standards and latent discrimination (this time against boys). Lastly, to the extent that the demographic weighting means that it will take decades to restore greater educational equality between men and women if such inequalities continue to increase strongly, is it prudent to wait for their social consequences to emerge before trying to remedy them?

At the very least, there is a need now to review policies on educational equality between the sexes by taking note of the fact that it is not now women who are necessarily at a disadvantage, and also by paying attention to the achievement of boys.

Societies have accommodated themselves to inequalities to the detriment of women for centuries. They could no doubt just as easily accommodate themselves to inequalities to the detriment of men. Nevertheless, the ideal of equality remains preferable.

Notes

1. The analysis is based on data by age cohort from 5 years up to 39 years (15-19, 20-24, 25-29, etc.), and an aggregate age cohort of over 40 years. The data are also available by age alone.
2. Three types of higher education are distinguished in the International Standard Classification of Education: type A tertiary education (ISCED 5A) are tertiary programmes that are largely theoretically based and are intended to provide sufficient qualifications for gaining entry into advanced research programmes and professions with high skills requirements, such as medicine, dentistry or architecture. A minimum cumulative theoretical duration (at tertiary) of three years' full-time equivalent, although typically they are of 4 or more years. Type B tertiary education (ISCED 5B) is typically shorter than in 5A and focuses on occupationally specific skills geared for entry into the labour market, although some theoretical foundations may be covered in the respective programme. It has a minimum of two years' full-time equivalent duration. Advanced research qualification (ISCED 6) designates tertiary qualifications which are directly accredited by the award of degree in advanced research, a doctorate, for example.
3. This index of segregation, known as the Duncan index, is equal to $\frac{1}{2}\sum_{i=1}^{N}|m_i - f_i|$ where m_i is the proportion of male graduates obtaining a degree in subject i and f_i the proportion of all women graduates obtaining a degree in subject i, and N the number of subject categories.
4. The personal rate of return is estimated on the basis of the increase in professional income after tax depending on the level of education, after deducted the personal costs arising from those studies (income foregone and personal expenses, other than indirect personal costs such as accommodation, subsistence, clothing, leisure, etc.).
5. Secondary school certificate giving entitlement to admission to higher education.
6. Conducted by the IEA (International Association for the Evaluation for Educational Achievement), the FISS (First International Science Study), SISS (Second International Science Study) and TIMSS (Third International Mathematics and Science Study) studies test, respectively, students of 18, 23 and 42 countries (including 22 OECD countries) in mathematics and science and collect contextual data.

References

Akerlof, G.A. and R.E. Kranton (2002), "Identity and Schooling: Some Lessons for the Economics of Education", *Journal of Economic Literature,* Vol. 40(4), pp. 1167-1201.

Alwin, D.F., M. Braun and J. Scott (1992), "The Separation of Work and the Family: Attitudes towards Women's Labour-Force Participation in Germany, Great Britain, and the United States", *European Sociological Review*, Vol. 8(1), pp. 13-37.

Averett, S. and M.L. Burton (1996), "College Attendance and the College Wage Premium: Differences by Gender", *Economics of Education Review*, Vol. 15(1), pp. 37-49.

Bailey, M.J. (2006), "More Power to the Pill: The Impact of Contraceptive Freedom on Women's Life Cycle and Labor Supply", *Quarterly Journal of Economics*, Vol. 121(1), pp. 289-320.

Bailey, T. and V. Smith-Morest (ed.) (2006), *Defending the Community College Equity Agenda*, Johns Hopkins, Baltimore.

Bensusán, G. and I. Ahumada Lobo (2006), "Sistemas de jubilación en las instituciones públicas de educación superior y composición por edad del personal académico", ANUIES, *Revista de la Educación Superior*, Vol. XXXV(2), No. 138, pp. 7-35.

Bettinger, E.P. and B.T. Long (2005), "Do Faculty Serve as Role Models? The Impact of Instructor Gender on Female Students", *American Economic Review*, Vol. 95(2), pp. 152-157.

Blau, F.D. and L.M. Kahn (2000), "Gender Differences in Pay", *Journal of Economic Perspectives*, Vol. 14(4), pp. 75-99.

BMBF (Bundesministerium für Bildung und Forschung) (2005), *Frauen im Studium. Langzeitstudie 1983-2004*, Bonn, Berlin.

Bobbitt-Zeher, D. (2007), "The Gender Income Gap and the Role of Education", *Sociology of Education*, Vol. 80(1), pp. 1-22.

Brinbaum, Y. and A. Kieffer (2007), "Aspirations et parcours scolaires des jeunes issus de l'immigration: réussites et désillusions, transmissions et rupture entre générations ", Communication to the 3rd meeting of youth and societies in Europe and around the Mediterranean, Marseille.

Buchmann, C. and T.A. DiPrete (2006), "The Growing Female Advantage in College Completion: the Role of Family Background and Academic Achievement", *American Sociological Review*, Vol. 71, pp. 515-541.

Buchmann, C., T.A. DiPrete and A. McDaniel (2007), "Gender Inequalities in Education", manuscript to appear in the *Annual Review of Sociology*, Vol. 34.

Burgess, S., B. McConnell, C. Propper and D. Wilson (2004), "Girls Rock, Boys Roll: An Analysis of the Age 14-16 Gender Gap in English Schools", *Scottish Journal of Political Economy*, Vol. 51(2), pp. 209-229.

Card, D. and T. Lemieux (2001), "Going to College to Avoid the Draft: The Unintended Legacy of the Vietnam War", *American Economic Review*, Vol. 91(2), pp. 97-102.

Charles, K. and M.-C. Luoh (2003), "Gender Differences in Completed Schooling", *Review of Economics and Statistics*, Vol. 85(3), pp. 559-577.

Chauvel, L. (2004), "Vers l'égalité de genre: les tendances générationnelles sont-elles irréversibles?", *Revue de l'OFCE*, Vol. 90, pp. 69-84.

Chevalier, A. (2007), "Education, Occupation and Career Expectations: Determinants of the Gender Pay Gap for UK Graduates", *Oxford Bulletin of Economics and Statistics*, Vol. 69(6), pp. 819-842.

Cho, D. (2007), "The Role of High School Performance in Explaining Women's Rising College Enrolment", *Economics of Education Review*, Vol. 26, pp. 450-462.

Christie, P. and M. Shannon (2001), "Educational Attainment and the Gender Wage Gap: Evidence from the 1986 and 1991 Canadian Censuses", *Economics of Education Review*, Vol. 20, pp. 165-180.

Coleman, J.S. (1961), *The Adolescent Society: The Social Life of Teenagers and Its Impact on Education*, Free Press of Glencoe, New York.

Correll, S.J. (2001), "Gender and the Career Choice Process: The Role of Biased Self-Assessments", *American Journal of Sociology*, Vol. 106, pp. 1691-1730.

Cutler D.M. and A. Lleras-Muney (2006), "Education and Health: Evaluating Theories and Evidence", NBER Working Paper No. W12352.

Dee, T.S. (2004), "Teachers, Race and Student Achievement in a Randomized Experiment", *Review of Economics and Statistics*, Vol. 86(1), pp. 195-210.

Dee, T.S. (2005), "A Teacher Like Me: Does Race, Ethnicity and Gender Matter?", *American Economic Review*, Vol. 95(2), pp. 158-165.

Dee, T.S. (2007), "Teachers and the Gender Gaps in Student Achievement", *Journal of Human Resources*, Vol. 42(3), pp. 528-554.

Deleuze, G. and F. Guattari (1987), *A Thousand Plateaus*, University of Minnesota Press, Minneapolis (translation of *Mille Plateaux*, Éditions de Minuit, Paris, 1980).

DiPrete, T.A. and C. Buchmann (2006), "Gender-specific Trends in the Value of Education and the Emerging Gender Gap in College Completion", *Demography*, Vol. 43(1), pp. 1-24.

Dobson, R. (2006), "Health Gap between Educated and Less Educated Russians Widens", *British Medical Journal*, Vol. 332(7554), pp. 1350.

Dornbusch, S.M. (1989), "The Sociology of Adolescence", *Annual Review of Sociology*, Vol. 15, pp. 233-259.

Dougherty, C. (2005), "Why are the Returns to Schooling Higher for Women than for Men?", *Journal of Human Resources*, Vol. 40(4), pp. 969-988.

Dryler, H. (1998), "Parental Role Models, Gender and Educational Choice", *British Journal of Sociology*, Vol. 49(3), pp. 375-398.

Eccles, J.S., T.F. Adler and J.L. Meece (1984), "Sex Differences in Achievement: A Test of Alternate Theories", *Journal of Personality and Social Psychology*, Vol. 46(1), pp. 26-43.

Edwards, L.N. and M.P. Pasquale (2003), "Women's Higher Education in Japan: Family Background, Economic Factors and the Equal Employment Opportunity Law", *Journal of the Japanese and International Economies*, Vol. 17(1), pp. 1-32.

Eurydice (2007), "Gender Inequality in Performance and Attainment", Enquête n° 1592.

Frank, K.A., C. Muller, K. Schiller, C. Riegle-Crumb, A. Strassmann Mueller, R. Crosnoe and J. Pearson (forthcoming), "The Social Dynamics of Mathematics Course Taking in High School", *American Journal of Sociology*.

Gilligan, C. (1982), *In a Different Voice: Psychological Theory and Women's Development*, Cambridge, Harvard University Press, MA.

Givord, P. and D. Goux (2007), "France: Mass and Class – Persisting Inequalities in Postsecondary Education in France", in Y. Shavint, R. Arum and A. Gamoran (ed.), *Stratification in Higher Education*, Stanford University Press, Stanford, CA, United States.

Glei, D.A. and S. Horiuchi (2007), "The Narrowing Sex Differential in Life Expectancy in High-income Populations: Effects of Differences in the Age Pattern of Mortality", *Population Studies*, Vol. 61(2), pp. 141-159.

Goesling, B. (2007), "The Rising Significance of Education for Health?", *Social Forces*, Vol. 85(4), pp. 1621-1644.

Goldin, C. (2004), "The Long Road to the Fast Track: Career and Family", *The Annals of the American Academy of Political and Social Science*, Vol. 596, pp. 20-35.

Goldin, C. and L.F. Katz (2002), "The Power of the Pill: Oral Contraceptives and Women's Career and Marriage Decisions", *Journal of Political Economy*, Vol. 110(4), pp. 730-770.

Goldin, C., L. Katz and I. Kuziemko (2006), "The Homecoming of American College Women: The Reversal of the College Gender Gap", *Journal of Economic Perspectives*, Vol. 20(4), pp. 133-156.

Goldstein, J.R. and C.T. Kenney (2001), "Marriage Delayed or Marriage Forgone? New Cohort Forecasts of First Marriage for US Women", *American Sociological Review*, Vol. 66, pp. 506-519.

Gorard, S., G. Rees and J. Salisbury (2001), "Investigating the Patterns of Differential Attainment of Boys and Girls at School", *British Educational Research Journal*, Vol. 27(2), pp. 125-139.

Gradstein, M. and M. Kaganovich (2004), "Aging Population and Education Finance", *Journal of Public Economics*, Vol. 88, pp. 2469-2485.

Grob, U. and S. Wolter (2007), "Demographic Change and Public Education Spending: A Conflict between Young and Old?", *Education Economics*, Vol. 15(3), pp. 277-292.

Haberte, S. and M. Burton (1996), "College Attendance and the College Wage Premium: Differences by Gender", *Economics of Education Review*, Vol. 15(1), pp. 37-49.

Harris, A.R., W.N. Evans and R.M. Schwab (2001), "Education Spending in an Aging America", *Journal of Public Economics*, Vol. 81, pp. 449-472.

Holmlund, H. and K. Sund (2007), "Is the Gender Gap in School Performance Affected by the Sex of the Teacher?", *Labour Economics*.

Ishida, H. (2007), "Japan: Educational Expansion and Inequality in Access to Higher Education", in Y. Shavint, R. Arum and A. Gamoran (ed.), *Stratification in Higher Education*, Stanford University Press, Stanford, CA, United States.

Jacob, B. (2002), "Where the Boys Aren't: Non-cognitive Skills, Returns to School and the Gender Gap in Higher Education", *Economics of Education Review*, Vol. 21, pp. 589-598.

Kunst, A.E. and J.P. Mackenbach (1994), "The Size of Mortality Differences Associated with Educational Level in Nine Industrialized Countries", *American Journal of Public Health*, Vol. 84(6), pp. 932-1037.

Lavy, V. (2004), "Do Gender Stereotypes Reduce Girls' Human Capital Outcomes? Evidence from a Natural Experiment", NBER, Working Paper 10678.

Le Doeuff, M. (2003), *The Sex of Knowing*, Routledge, New York (translation of *Le sexe du savoir*, Aubier, Paris, 1998).

Long, B.T. (2007), "The Reversal of the College Gender Gap: the Role of Alternatives and College Supply", Harvard and NBER, unpublished manuscript.

Loury, L.D. (2004), "Siblings and Gender Differences in African-American College Attendance", *Economics of Education Review*, Vol. 23, pp. 213-219.

Machin, S. and S. McNally (2006), "Gender and Student Achievement in English Schools", Working Paper, Centre for the Economics of Education, LSE.

Mackenbach, J.P., I. Stirbu, A.-J. Roskam, M.M. Schaap, G. Menvielle, M. Leinsalu and A.E. Kunst (2007), "Socioeconomic Inequalities in Health in 22 European Countries", *New England Journal of Medicine*, Vol. 358(23), pp. 2468-2481.

Maurin, E. and T. Xenogiani (2007), "Demand for Education and Labor Market Outcomes. Lessons from the Abolition of Compulsory Conscription in France", *Journal of Human Resources*, Vol. 42(4), pp. 795-819.

McDaniel, A. (2007), "The Gender Gap in Educational Expectations, 1970-2003", Ohio State University, unpublished manuscript.

Meara, E.R., S. Richards and D.M. Cutler (2008), "The Gap Gets Bigger: Changes in Mortality and Life Expectancy, By Education, 1981-2000", *Health Affairs*, Vol. 27(2), pp. 350-361.

Murphy, K.M. and F. Welch (1992), "The Structure of Wages", *Quarterly Journal of Economics*, Vol. 107, pp. 215-236.

Mustard, C.A. and J. Etches (2003), "Gender Differences in Socioeconomic Inequality in Mortality", *Journal of Epidemiology and Community Health*, Vol. 57(12), pp. 974-980.

OECD (2002), "Women at Work: Who are They and How are they Faring?", in *OECD Employment Outlook 2002 – Surveying the Jobs Horizon*, OECD Publishing, Paris, *www.oecd.org/dataoecd/28/60/18982236.pdf*.

OECD (2007a), *PISA 2006: Science Competencies for Tomorrow's World*, OECD Publishing, Paris.

OECD (2007b), *Education at a Glance: OECD Indicators*, OECD Publishing, Paris.

OECD (2007c), *Understanding the Brain: The Birth of a Learning Science*, OECD Publishing, Paris.

OECD (2007d), "Policy Brief: Ten Steps to Equity in Education", *OECD Policy Briefs*, OECD Publishing, Paris.

OECD (2007e), *Babies and Bosses – Reconciling Work and Family Life: A Synthesis of Findings for OECD Countries*, OECD Publishing, Paris.

Ono, H. (2004), "Are Sons and Daughters Substitutable? Allocation of Family Resources in Contemporary Japan", *Journal of the Japanese and International Economics*, Vol. 18, pp. 143-160.

Pappas, G., S. Queen, W. Hadden and G. Fisher (1993), "The Increasing Disparity in Mortality Between Socioeconomic Groups in the United States, 1960 and 1986", *The New England Journal of Medicine*, Vol. 329, pp. 103-109.

Poterba, J.M. (1997), "Demographic Structure and the Political Economy of Public Education", *Journal of Policy Analysis and Management*, Vol. 16(1), pp. 48-66.

Poterba, J.M. (1998), "Demographic Change, Intergenerational Linkages, and Public Education", *American Economic Review*, Vol. 88(2), pp. 315-320.

Preston, S.H. and I.T. Elo (1995), "Are Educational Differentials in Adult Mortality Increasing in the United States", *Journal of Aging and Health*, Vol. 74, pp. 476-496.

Qian, Z. and S.H. Preston (1993), "Changes in American Marriage, 1972 to 1987: Availability and Forces of Attraction by Age and Education", *American Sociological Review*, Vol. 58, pp. 482-495.

Raymo, J.M. and M. Iwasawa (2005), "Marriage Market Mismatches in Japan: An Alternative View of the Relationship between Women's Education and Marriage", *American Sociological Review*, Vol. 70(5), pp. 801-822.

Reskin, B.F. and D.D. Bielby (2005), "A Sociological Perspective on Gender and Career Outcomes", *Journal of Economic Perspectives*, Vol. 19(1), pp. 71-86.

Ridgeway, C. and S. Correll (2004), "Unpacking the Gender System: A Theoretical Perspective on Gender Beliefs and Social Relations", *Gender and Society*, Vol. 18(4), pp. 510-531.

Rose, E. (2006), "Education, Hypergamy and the 'Success Gap'", University of Washington, unpublished manuscript.

Rosenwald, F. (2006), "Les filles et les garçons dans le système éducatif", Information note 06.06, *www.education.gouv.fr/stateval*.

Schwartz, C. and R.D. Mare (2005), "Trends in Educational Assortative Marriage from 1940 to 2003", *Demography*, Vol. 42(4), pp. 621-646.

Scott, J. (2006), "Family and Gender Roles: How Attitudes Are Changing", GeNet Working Paper No. 21.

Shannon, M. and M.P. Kidd (2001), "Projecting the Trend in the Canadian Gender Wage Gap 2001-2031: Will an Increase in Female Education Acquisition and Commitment Be Enough?", *Canadian Public Policy/Analyse de Politiques*, Vol. 27(4), pp. 447-467.

Shavit, Y., H. Ayalon, S. Chachasvili-Bolotin and G. Menahem (2007), "Israel: Diversification, Expansion, and Inequality in Higher Education", in Y. Shavit, R. Arum and A. Gamoran (ed.), *Stratification in Higher Education*, Stanford University Press, Stanford, CA, United States.

Tansel, A. (2002), "Determinants of School Attainment of Boys and Girls in Turkey: Individual, Household and Community Factors", *Economics of Education Review*, Vol. 21, pp. 455-470.

Tarde, G. (1890), *Les lois de l'imitation*, Editions Kimé, Paris.

Wissenschaftsrat (2006), *Empfehlungen zum arbeitsmarkt- und demographiegerechten Ausbau des Hochschulsystems*, Cologne.

Yonezawa, A. and T. Kim (2008), "The Future of Higher Education in a Context of a Shrinking Student Population: Policy Challenges for Japan and Korea", in S. Vincent-Lancrin (ed.), *Higher Education 2030. Volume 1: Demography*, OECD Publishing, Paris.

OECD PUBLISHING, 2, rue André-Pascal, 75775 PARIS CEDEX 16
PRINTED IN FRANCE
(96 2008 02 1 P) ISBN 978-92-64-04065-6 – No. 56445 2008

28th August 2013

143

147

128 Demand

120 Age [illegible] – Human Capital

3 E Learning – Can Also With (Capacity) → Student Recruitment
– Young
– Adult

* 88 Provisions (2008)

77 Academic Learning / Support (Develop)

14

234

232 * 119

Labour Quality / The Workforce

Regeneration Required

121